Powerful Command-Line Applications in Go

Build Fast and Maintainable Tools

Ricardo Gerardi

The Pragmatic Bookshelf

Raleigh, North Carolina

Many of the designations used by manufacturers and sellers to distinguish their products are claimed as trademarks. Where those designations appear in this book, and The Pragmatic Programmers, LLC was aware of a trademark claim, the designations have been printed in initial capital letters or in all capitals. The Pragmatic Starter Kit, The Pragmatic Programmer, Pragmatic Programming, Pragmatic Bookshelf, PragProg and the linking *g* device are trademarks of The Pragmatic Programmers, LLC.

Every precaution was taken in the preparation of this book. However, the publisher assumes no responsibility for errors or omissions, or for damages that may result from the use of information (including program listings) contained herein.

For our complete catalog of hands-on, practical, and Pragmatic content for software developers, please visit *https://pragprog.com*.

The team that produced this book includes:

CEO: Dave Rankin
COO: Janet Furlow
Managing Editor: Tammy Coron
Development Editor: Brian P. Hogan
Copy Editor: Corina Lebegioara
Indexing: Potomac Indexing, LLC
Layout: Gilson Graphics
Founders: Andy Hunt and Dave Thomas

For sales, volume licensing, and support, please contact *support@pragprog.com*.

For international rights, please contact *rights@pragprog.com*.

ISBN-13: 978-1-68050-696-9
Book version: P1.0—December 2021

To my beloved wife Kassia. My best friend, my greatest supporter. Sadly she passed away due to cancer before seeing this book completed.

To my four incredible daughters Gisele, Livia, Elena, and Alice. The reason for everything.

Contents

Foreword

In 2012 I began a journey of experimentation in investigating a new language, Go, which was born at Google and had just reached the 1.0 milestone. I learn best by building so I was looking for a project meaningful enough to actually learn Go. I was growing frustrated with the increasing cost and complexity of my WordPress-powered blog with entirely static content and decided that building a static site generator was the project for me to learn Go. I began writing my first Go project, Hugo[1].

Having previously designed several CMSs and command-line tools, I had a good sense of what I wanted to build. I opened up a terminal and began by typing commands for this not yet existing program to effectively sketch out how the user interface would be shaped. With this sketch in hand, I then began the process of building the application. As I was inexperienced with Go, I hoped to lean heavily on existing libraries, but as this was the dawn of the Go ecosystem, more often than not, the libraries I needed didn't exist.

Unable to find the right library to support the design pattern of [application] [command] [flag] [argument], I set out to write it myself. I also needed config file management as there was too much configurability to anticipate everything passed via the command line. As my goal was building Hugo, these were just Hugo packages initially, but I thought maybe someone else would benefit from this functionality too, and I pulled them out into standalone libraries and named them Cobra[2] and Viper[3], featured in Chapter 7, Using the Cobra CLI Framework, on page 213 of this book.

Through the experience of building Hugo, Cobra, and Viper, I had a revelation: while Go was initially targeted at large-scale server applications, the Go creators had developed a language perfectly suited for command-line tools. It had everything you needed and most of what you wanted:

---

1. https://gohugo.io
2. github.com/spf13/cobra
3. github.com/spf13/viper

- Static compilation, which created executables with no local dependencies: no runtimes or libraries needed. What could be easier to install than one file?

- Cross-compilation, eliminating the need for build farms.

- Lightning-fast builds so quick that it felt like a dynamic language.

- Native concurrency, enabling your applications to take full advantage of multicore machines.

Go had nearly all the advantages of a dynamic language during development and all the advantages of a compiled language during execution, plus additional unique advantages. In short, Go is uniquely perfect for both building and running command-line applications.

At the time, I was leading product, client engineering, customer engineering, and developer relations for MongoDB. I eralized that if we had written our CLI applications in Go, our support ticket volume would drop by more than half as the majority of issues users experienced were due to complications with runtime and library incompatibilities present in the Java and Python ecosystems we were then using, and the same would be true for .Net, Ruby, JavaScript, and other popular languages. Due to Go's focus on security and type safety, we would end up with far fewer issues to debug. We learned that in addition to these benefits, we also had happier, more productive developers writing Go.

Sometimes in life, the smallest things have a profound impact. This experiment I began in 2012 with this new language led to:

- MongoDB being one of Go's earliest adopters, which in part contributed to its massive success as one of the most valuable open source companies ever.

- My speaking at the first Gophercon, which led to several other speaking opportunities and established relationships that eventually led to me joining and co-leading the Go team at Google.

- Hugo growing to become the most popular static site generator in terms of number of public websites and in terms of GitHub stars with notable users such as Brave.com, LetsEncrypt.org, SmashingMagazine.com, and Digital.gov.

- Building CLIs in Go, which is the second most popular use for Go with 65% of Go developers writing CLIs.

- Cobra becoming the CLI framework for Go with virtually all major Go applications using it including Kubernetes, Docker and GitHub CLI.

Through this, I've also had the good fortune of getting to know Ricardo Gerardi, who has also been on a profound journey, which you will read about in the preface. Part of Ricardo's journey has been learning Go and discovering its power for creating CLI applications. Ricardo poured his experience into writing this excellent book on getting started with command-line applications in Go. It does a beautiful job of starting with basic concepts and slowly building on them with just the right balance of explanation so you can understand what is really happening. It takes the reader on a journey from building very small single-purpose tools to full-fledged command-line applications. Working through the book, I was able to relive the excitement I experienced a decade ago learning Go. This is a book that is best experienced alongside an editor and console.

I now invite you to start your own journey of experimentation. Along the way, you'll learn all you need to know about working with Go and designing command-line applications. You'll learn the basic techniques and libraries used to build applications like Go itself, Hugo, Docker, and Kubernetes. Most importantly, you'll discover the joy of programming. You'll be amazed at the new superpower you've developed—the ability to create applications that work exactly like you need them to. This book is your guide to unlocking your new superpowers. Enjoy the journey.

Steve Francia
Author of Cobra, Viper, and Hugo, and the Go Product Lead at Google

Acknowledgments

To start, I want to thank my late wife Kassia for her love and support during the 25 years we spent together. Kassia always believed in me, and she encouraged me to write this book. She kept pushing me to work on it even after she was diagnosed with incurable cancer. Kassia was an inspiring and brave woman who conquered cancer. Not because she was cured—sadly, she wasn't—but because she never let cancer change her, and she continued to inspire all those around her. Writing this book throughout her journey with cancer, and then throughout my own grief was a challenging task.

Thank you to my daughters Gisele, Livia, Elena, and Alice for your love, support, and courage.

Thank you, Brian Hogan, for editing this book and for helping me find its real soul. Thank you also for your patience and understanding with all the difficulties I faced while writing this book. You're a great mentor and a wonderful human being. I have learned a great deal from you.

Thank you, Andy Hunt and The Pragmatic Bookshelf, for publishing this book. You made a long-time dream come true.

Thank you, Tim Anema, Robert Bost, Ilija Eftimov, Mike Fridman, Philip Pearl, Petko Petkov, Renato Suero, and Will Langford, for reviewing the draft of this book, catching errors, and helping me improve it. This book wouldn't be what it is without your invaluable suggestions and constructive feedback.

Thank you, Marcelo Paternostro, for your insights, suggestions, and friendship.

This book is only possible because the Go programming language exists. Thank you, Robert Griesemer, Rob Pike, and Ken Thompson, for designing this incredible language. Thanks to all Go contributors for developing and maintaining it. Your continuous efforts make Go an amazing language to work with.

A special thanks to all beta readers who read this book while it was still being written. Thank you for your excellent feedback and for finding and reporting errors that would be otherwise hard to spot. I know this book took a long time to complete. Thank you for your patience, support, and kind messages while I dealt with personal issues and continued to work on the book.

While writing this book, I witnessed firsthand the challenges that someone living with cancer faces. For those out there in this situation, particularly women dealing with breast cancer, I acknowledge your challenges, your efforts, and your perseverance. For the caregivers, I understand the toll it takes on you, especially on your mental health. Take care of yourselves so you can take care of your loved ones. In honor of my wife's memory and out of respect for those impacted by cancer, I will donate part of the proceeds from this book to help those living with or caring for someone with cancer.

Preface

Whether you're a system administrator, a network engineer, a DevOps specialist, or any other modern IT professional, you use command-line applications to automate your environment and increase your productivity. These tools play an increasingly critical role in your infrastructure and therefore require the same level of governance as other software components. In this book, you'll use the Go programming language to develop command-line applications that are maintainable, cross-platform, fast, and reliable.

Go is a modern programming language that combines the reliability provided by the compilation process with the flexibility of dynamic typing. Go's ease of use and flexibility in prototyping new ideas make it a great choice for writing command-line tools. At the same time, Go allows the implementation of more complex scenarios by providing features like type safety, cross-compilation, testing, and benchmarks.

Many popular command-line tools you use are developed with Go. These include Docker, Podman, Kubectl, Openshift CLI, Hugo, and Terraform. If you've ever wondered how you can make your own tools like these, this book will show you how.

You'll apply your knowledge of Go's basic syntax and also employ more advanced concepts to develop several command-line applications. You can use these applications to automate tasks, analyze data, parse logs, talk to network services, or address other system requirements. You'll also employ different testing and benchmarking techniques to ensure your programs are fast and reliable.

What's in This Book

In Chapter 1, Your First Command-Line Program in Go, on page 1, you'll take a quick tour through the process of developing a command-line application with Go by building a word counter. You will start with the basic implementation, add some features, and explore testing. You'll also add command-line flags and build this application for different platforms.

In Chapter 2, Interacting with Your Users, on page 11, you'll design and write a command-line tool to manage lists of to-do items in accordance with common input/output standards by applying different techniques. You'll take input from the standard input (STDIN) stream, parse command-line parameters, and define flags for your tool using the flags package. You'll use environment variables to increase the flexibility of your tools. In addition, you'll display information and results back to the user through the standard output (STD-OUT) stream, and present errors using the standard error (STDERR) stream for proper error handling. Finally, you'll explore Go interfaces by applying the io.Reader interface in particular.

Next, in Chapter 3, Working with Files in Go, on page 45, you'll develop a tool to preview Markdown files using a web browser. You'll create and open files for reading and writing. You'll apply techniques to handle paths consistently across different operating systems. You'll use temporary files and apply the defer keyword to clean them up. You'll also make your tool flexible by using file templates. Finally, you'll use Go interfaces to make your code flexible, while writing and executing tests to ensure your code matches the requirements.

In Chapter 4, Navigating the File System, on page 77, you'll navigate through the file system and work with directories and file properties. You'll develop a CLI application to find, delete, and back up files according to different criteria. You'll perform common file system operations such as copying, compressing, and deleting files. You'll also log information to the screen or log files. Finally, you'll apply the concepts of table-driven testing and test helpers to write flexible and meaningful test cases for your application.

In Chapter 5, Improving the Performance of Your CLI Tools, on page 113, you'll develop a command-line tool that processes data from CSV files. Then you'll use Go's benchmarking, profiling, and tracing tools to analyze its performance, find bottlenecks, and redesign your CLI to improve its performance. You'll write and execute tests to ensure your application works reliably across the refactoring. You'll also apply Go's concurrency primitives such as goroutines and channels to ensure your application runs tasks concurrently in a safe way.

Chapter 6, Controlling Processes, on page 163, will allow you to expand your command-line applications' capabilities by executing external tools. You'll execute, control, and capture their output to develop a Continuous Integration tool for your Go programs. You'll explore different ways to execute external programs with various options such as timeouts that ensure your program doesn't run forever. You'll also handle operating system signals correctly to allow your tool to gracefully shut down.

Next, in Chapter 7, Using the Cobra CLI Framework, on page 213, you'll develop a network tool that executes a TCP port scan on remote machines by applying the Cobra CLI framework. Cobra is a popular framework that allows you to create flexible command-line tools that use subcommands compatible with the POSIX standard. You'll use Cobra to generate the boilerplate code for your application, allowing you to focus on its business logic.

In Chapter 8, Talking to REST APIs, on page 273, you'll improve your to-do application by making it available through a representational state transfer (REST) API. Then you'll develop a command-line client that interacts with this API using several HTTP methods. You'll parse JSON data and fine-tune specific parameters of your requests such as headers and timeouts. You'll also apply proper testing techniques that ensure your application works reliably without overloading web servers unnecessarily.

In Chapter 9, Developing Interactive Terminal Tools, on page 347, you'll build an interactive command-line application that uses terminal widgets to interact with the user. You'll use external packages to design and develop the interface. You'll also apply different Go concurrency techniques to manage this application asynchronously.

In Chapter 10, Persisting Data in a SQL Database, on page 395, you'll expand your interactive application by allowing users to save its data into a SQL database. You'll use Go's standard library and external packages to connect to standard databases by executing SQL operations. You'll query, insert, and delete data from databases and use a local *Sqlite3* database to persist data for your tool. You'll make this data available to the user by summarizing its content using the application interface.

And finally, in Chapter 11, Distributing Your Tool, on page 433, you'll explore several techniques to build your tool, including different build and cross-compilation options, allowing your tool to run in multiple operating systems. You'll apply build tags to change the behavior of your builds according to external conditions. You'll take a quick look at using CGO to embed C code in your Go applications. Then you'll apply techniques to package and distribute your application either as a Linux container or as source code via go get.

This book doesn't cover the basic syntax of the Go programming language. You should be familiar with declaring variables, types, custom types, flow control, and the general structure of a Go program. If you're starting with Go, take a look at these books and articles that do a great job explaining the language's syntax:

- *Learning Go [Jon21]*
- *Go in Action [KKS15]*
- A Tour of Go[1]
- Effective Go[2]

This book uses the Go standard library as much as possible. Go has a rich and diverse standard library that includes packages that address most of the requirements for creating command-line tools in general. By using the standard library, we benefit from Go's compatibility across different versions making the code accessible to a larger number of readers. cases, we'll use external packages when no equivalent functionality is available but we generally prefer to use the standard library even if an external package makes it easier to address a requirement. The notable exception to this rule is the Cobra CLI framework that you'll use in Chapter 7, Using the Cobra CLI Framework, on page 213, as this is a popular framework used by many developers and companies to extend Go's capabilities to manage command-line applications.

In each chapter, you'll typically develop a fully functional command-line tool. You'll start with the basic functionality, write some tests, and then add more features. At the end of each chapter, you'll find additional exercises to improve what you've learned in the chapter and practice your skills further. And you're encouraged to add more features on your own.

This book spends a fair amount of time on testing your code. In some cases, you'll see that the test examples are more intricate than the code examples. This is done for two significant reasons: as command-line tools become more critical to your infrastructure, it's essential that you ensure they work correctly; and Go provides out-of-the-box features to test and benchmark your code. You'll start by creating basic test functions. Then you'll develop more advanced concepts such as table-driven testing and dependency injection, culminating with mocking your own commands and artifacts for testing.

Finally, feel free to read this book in any order. If you have a particular interest or if one of the examples seems more appealing, feel free to jump around. Keep in mind that some chapters build on skills presented in previous chapters. A cross-reference usually points to where that concept was first discussed in the book so you can explore the topic in more detail.

---

1. tour.golang.org
2. golang.org/doc/effective_go.html

How to Use This Book

To best follow this book and test the code examples, you need Go 1.13 or higher installed on your machine. At the time of writing this book, the current version of Go is 1.16. You can find more information on installing Go in the official documentation.[3]

The code examples in the book use *Go modules* to manage package dependencies. For details, consult Go Modules, on page xxiii. By using Go modules, you're no longer required to code under the $GOPATH directory. Modules have been available since Go 1.11 and enabled by default since 1.13.

Make sure the Go binary go is in your $PATH variable so you can execute Go commands from anywhere without prefixing the absolute path. For example, to run tests, you type go test, and to build programs, you run go build. Some examples also execute the binary version of your tools. These are typically installed in the directory $HOME/go/bin. We expect that this directory exists and is included in your $PATH variable.

You'll also need a working Internet connection to download the source code and the external libraries required by some examples. Finally, you'll need a text editor to write your programs and access to a command shell to test and run them. We recommend using the Bash shell as most of the examples presented in the book use it.

For the most part, the example applications included in this book are compatible with any operating system supported by Go, such as Linux, macOS, and Windows. But when executing commands to interact with the operating system, for example, to create directories or list file contents, the book assumes you're running an operating system compatible with Linux or Unix standards. If you're using Windows, use the corresponding Windows commands to complete those tasks instead.

Typically, when the book instructs you to type commands, they'll look like this:

```
$ go test -v
```

The dollar sign ($) represents the shell prompt. You don't need to type it when typing the commands. Simply type the rest of the line after it.

---

3. golang.org/doc/install

Some examples present a series of commands and their output. In these cases, the lines starting with the dollar sign ($) represent the prompt and what you should type. The rest is the output from the commands:

```
$ ls
exceptionStep.go  main.go  main_test.go  step.go  testdata
$ go test -v
=== RUN    TestRun
=== RUN    TestRun/success
=== RUN    TestRun/fail
=== RUN    TestRun/failFormat
--- PASS: Test_Run (0.95s)
    --- PASS: TestRun/success (0.47s)
    --- PASS: TestRun/fail (0.03s)
    --- PASS: TestRun/failFormat (0.45s)
PASS
ok       pragprog.com/rggo/processes/goci       0.951s
```

In addition, throughout the book, you'll see that the examples are versioned from one section of the chapter to the next, by organizing the code into different directories, one for each version. This is necessary to make it easier to relate the examples with the source code shipped with the book. For example, in Chapter 5, Improving the Performance of Your CLI Tools, on page 113, the source code is split in the following directories:

```
$ find . -maxdepth 1 -mindepth 1 -type d | sort
./colStats
./colStats.v1
./colStats.v2
./colStats.v3
```

If you're developing the programs following the book, you don't need to create different directories for each version, unless you want to. In your case, it may be simpler to update the existing code according to the instructions in the book. You can also use a version control system, such as Git, to keep the different versions of your code available for reference.

If you've programmed with Go before, you'll notice that the code examples, as presented in the book, don't follow Go's formatting standards. In the book, the code is indented with spaces to ensure that the code fits the pages for printing. When copying the code from the book or downloading the examples, run gofmt to format the code automatically according to Go standards:

```
$ gofmt -w <source_file>.go
```

If your text editor is configured for automatic code reformatting, then save the file to update it according to the standards. Notice that there will be a difference between the code you see in the book's pages and the code you see in your text editor.

About the Example Code

The code provided in this book aims to illustrate concepts of the language that are useful when you're building your own programs and command-line tools.

This code isn't production-ready.

Even though each chapter shows a complete example you can use, the code may require additional features and checks to be used in real-life scenarios.

Go Modules

The code examples in this book rely on Go modules, the standard method to control and manage package dependencies for Go applications. By using Go modules, you can write your Go programs outside of the legacy $GOPATH required by older versions of Go prior to 1.11. Modules also enable reproducible builds as they record the specific version of Go and the external packages required to reliably build the application. You can find more information about Go modules in the official Go blog posts, *Using Go Modules*[4] and *New module changes in Go 1.16*.[5] To follow the examples, you need Go 1.13 or greater with modules enabled.

Modules provide a standard way to group related packages into a single unit that can be versioned together. They enable consistent dependency management for your Go applications. To use modules, create a directory for your code and use the go mod init command to initialize a new module, along with a unique module identifier. Typically, the unique module identifier is based on the version control path used to store the code. Since the code examples in the book aren't stored in a publicly accessible version control system, we'll use pragprog.com/rggo as the prefix for all example modules in the book. To better implement the book's examples, place your code in the $HOME/pragprog.com/rggo directory with sub-directories for each chapter. For example, initialize a new module like this:

```
$ mkdir -p $HOME/pragprog.com/rggo/firstProgram/wc
$ go mod init pragprog.com/rggo/firstProgram/wc
go: creating new go.mod: module pragprog.com/rggo/firstProgram/wc
```

---

4. blog.golang.org/using-go-modules
5. blog.golang.org/go116-module-changes

This directory is a suggestion. As long as you keep the same module path identifier when initializing the module, you can change the directory where you store the code, and you're still able to follow the examples as is.

Upon initializing a new module, Go creates a file go.mod in the root of your module directory and records the specific version of Go and the module path, like this:

```
$ cat go.mod
module pragprog.com/rggo/firstProgram/wc

go 1.16
```

If your code has external dependencies, you can record the specific version required in the go.mod file like this:

```
$ cat go.mod
module pragprog.com/rggo/workingFiles/mdp

go 1.16

require (
        github.com/microcosm-cc/bluemonday v1.0.2
        github.com/pmezard/go-difflib v1.0.0 // indirect
        github.com/russross/blackfriday/v2 v2.0.1
        github.com/shurcooL/sanitized_anchor_name v1.0.0 // indirect
)
```

For more details on how to use the external libraries with Go modules, consult their documentation.

Modules are fully integrated with the Go tooling. If you don't add the dependencies directly to your go.mod file, Go will automatically do that for you when you download it using go get. If you try to test or build your program using go test or go build, Go reports a missing dependency with a suggestion for how to obtain it. Go also creates a checksum file go.sum recording the specific checksum of each module used to build your program to ensure the next build uses the same version:

```
$ cat go.sum
github.com/microcosm-cc/bluemonday v1.0.2 h1:5lPfLTTAvAbtS0VqT+94yOtFnGfUWY...
github.com/microcosm-cc/bluemonday v1.0.2/go.mod h1:iVP4YcDBq+n/5fb23BhYFvI...
github.com/pmezard/go-difflib v1.0.0 h1:4DBwDE0NGyQoBHbLQYPwSUPoCMWR5BEzIk/...
github.com/pmezard/go-difflib v1.0.0/go.mod h1:iKH77koFhYxTK1pcRnkKkqfTogsb...
github.com/russross/blackfriday/v2 v2.0.1 h1:lPqVAte+HuHNfhJ/0LC98ESWRz8afy...
github.com/russross/blackfriday/v2 v2.0.1/go.mod h1:+Rmxgy9KzJVeS9/2gXHxylq...
github.com/shurcooL/sanitized_anchor_name v1.0.0 h1:PdmoCO6wvbs+7yrJyMORt4/...
github.com/shurcooL/sanitized_anchor_name v1.0.0/go.mod h1:1NzhyTcUVG4SuEtj...
golang.org/x/net v0.0.0-20181220203305-927f97764cc3 h1:eH6Eip3UpmR+yM/qI9Ij...
golang.org/x/net v0.0.0-20181220203305-927f97764cc3/go.mod h1:mL1N/T3taQHkD...
```

Notice that the output has been truncated to fit the book's page.

By using the files go.mod and go.sum, you ensure you're building the application with the same dependencies as the original developer. You can use these files provided with the book's source code to ensure your code will build exactly as shown in the book's examples.

Online Resources

The book's website[6] has links for downloading the source code and companion files.

If you're reading the electronic version of this book, you can click the box above the code excerpts to download that source code directly.

Now it's time to "go get" your feet wet. Let's start by developing a basic word counter command-line application that provides you with a working cross-platform tool. This also gives you an overview of the process for developing more complex applications.

---

6.   https://pragprog.com/titles/rggo/

## CHAPTER 1

Your First Command-Line Program in Go

Whether you're looking to automate a task, analyze data, parse logs, talk to network services, or address other requirements, writing your own command-line tool may be the fastest—and perhaps the most fun—way to achieve your goal. Go is a modern programming language that combines the reliability of compiled languages with the ease of use and speed of dynamically typed languages. It makes writing cross-platform command-line applications more approachable while providing the features required to ensure these tools are well designed and tested.

Before you dive into more complex programs that read and write files, parse data files, and communicate over networks, you'll create a word counter program that will give you an idea of how to build and test a command-line application using Go. You'll start with a basic implementation, add some features, and explore test-driven development along the way. When you're done, you'll have a functional word counter program and a better understanding of how to build more complex apps.

Throughout the book you'll develop other CLI applications to explore more advanced concepts.

Building the Basic Word Counter

Let's create a tool that counts the number of words or lines provided as input using the *standard input* (STDIN) connection. By default, this tool will count the number of words, unless it receives the -l flag, in which case it'll count the number of lines instead.

We'll start by creating the basic implementation. This version reads data from STDIN and displays the number of words. We'll eventually add more features, but this initial version will let you get comfortable with the code for a Go-based command-line application.

Before you dive into writing code for the word counter, let's set up a project directory. In your home directory, create the subdirectory pragprog.com/rggo/first-Program/wc and switch to it:

```
$ mkdir -p $HOME/pragprog.com/rggo/firstProgram/wc
$ cd $HOME/pragprog.com/rggo/firstProgram/wc
```

Go programs are composed of *packages*. A package consists of one or more Go source code files with code that can be combined into executable programs or libraries.

Starting with Go 1.11, you can combine one or more packages into Go modules. Modules are a new Go standard for grouping related packages into a single unit that can be versioned together. Modules enable consistent dependency management for your Go applications. For more information about Go modules, consult the official wiki page.[1]

Initialize a new Go module for your project:

```
$ go mod init pragprog.com/rggo/firstProgram/wc
go: creating new go.mod: module pragprog.com/rggo/firstProgram/wc
```

You create an executable program in Go by defining a package named main that contains a function called main(). This function takes no arguments and returns no values. It serves as the entry point for your program.

```
package main

func main() {
  «main contents»
}
```

Although not a requirement, by convention, the main package is usually defined in a file named main.go. You'll use this convention throughout this book.

Code Example File Path

 For brevity, the code example path omits the root directory $HOME/pragprog.com/rggo. For example, in the following code sample, the code path starts at firstProgram/wc.

Create the file main.go using your favorite text editor. Add the package main definition to the top of the file like this:

---

1. github.com/golang/go/wiki/Modules

firstProgram/wc/main.go
```go
package main
```

Next, add the import section to bring in the libraries you'll use to read data from STDIN and print results out.

firstProgram/wc/main.go
```go
import (
  "bufio"
  "fmt"
  "io"
  "os"
)
```

For this tool, you import the bufio package to read text, the fmt package to print formatted output, the io package which provides the io.Reader interface, and the os package so you can use operating system resources.

Your word counter will have two functions: main() and count(). The main() function is the starting point of the program. All Go programs that will be compiled into executable files require this function. Create this function by adding the following code into your main.go file. This function will call the count() function and print out that function's return value using the fmt.Println() function:

firstProgram/wc/main.go
```go
func main() {
  // Calling the count function to count the number of words
  // received from the Standard Input and printing it out
  fmt.Println(count(os.Stdin))
}
```

Next, define the count() function, which will perform the actual counting of the words. This function receives a single input argument: an io.Reader *interface*. You'll learn more about Go interfaces in Chapter 2, Interacting with Your Users, on page 11. For now, think of an io.Reader as any Go type from which you can read data. In this case, the function will receive the contents of the STDIN to process.

firstProgram/wc/main.go
```go
func count(r io.Reader) int {
  // A scanner is used to read text from a Reader (such as files)
  scanner := bufio.NewScanner(r)

  // Define the scanner split type to words (default is split by lines)
  scanner.Split(bufio.ScanWords)

  // Defining a counter
  wc := 0
```

```
  // For every word scanned, increment the counter
  for scanner.Scan() {
    wc++
  }

  // Return the total
  return wc
}
```

The count() function uses the NewScanner() function from the bufio package to create a new scanner. A scanner is a convenient way of reading data delimited by spaces or new lines. By default, a scanner reads lines of data, so we instruct the scanner to read words instead by setting the Split() function of the scanner to bufio.ScanWords(). We then define a variable, wc, to hold the word count and increment it by looping through each token using the scanner.Scan() function and adding 1 to the counter each time. We then return the word count.

In this example, for simplicity's sake, we are ignoring the error that may be generated during the scanning. In your code, always check for errors. You'll learn more about dealing with errors in the context of a command-line tool in Creating the Initial To-Do Command-Line Tool, on page 20.

You've completed the basic implementation of the word count tool. Save the file main.go with your changes. Next, you'll write tests to ensure this implementation works the way you expect it to.

Testing the Basic Word Counter

Go lets you test your code automatically without requiring external tools or frameworks. You'll learn more about how to test your command-line applications throughout the book. Right now, let's write a basic test for the word counter to ensure that it correctly counts the words in the given input.

Create a file called main_test.go in the same directory as your main.go file. Include the following content, which defines a testing function that tests the count() function you've already defined in the main program:

firstProgram/wc/main_test.go
```
package main

import (
  "bytes"
  "testing"
)

// TestCountWords tests the count function set to count words
func TestCountWords(t *testing.T) {
  b := bytes.NewBufferString("word1 word2 word3 word4\n")
```

```
  exp := 4
  res := count(b)
  if res != exp {
    t.Errorf("Expected %d, got %d instead.\n", exp, res)
  }
}
```

This test file contains a single test called TestCountWords(). In this test, we create a new buffer of bytes from a string containing four words and pass the buffer into the count() function. If this function returns anything other than 4, the test doesn't pass and we raise an error that shows what we expected and what we actually got instead.

To execute the test, use the go test tool like this:

```
$ ls
go.mod  main.go  main_test.go
$ go test -v
=== RUN    TestCountWords
--- PASS: TestCountWords (0.00s)
PASS
ok        pragprog.com/rggo/firstProgram/wc        0.002s
```

The test passes, so you can compile the program with go build. You'll learn more about the different options you can use to build Go programs in Chapter 11, Distributing Your Tool, on page 433. For now, build your command-line tool like this:

```
$ go build
```

This creates the wc executable in the current directory:

```
$ ls
go.mod  main.go  main_test.go  wc
```

Test the program out by passing it an input string:

```
$ echo "My first command line tool with Go" | ./wc
7
```

The program works as expected. Let's add the ability to count lines to this tool.

Adding Command-Line Flags

Good command-line tools provide flexibility through options. The current version of the word counter tool counts words. Let's add the ability to count lines as well by giving the user the option to decide when to switch this behavior through command-line flags.

Go provides the flag package, which you can use to create and manage command-line flags. You'll learn about it in more detail in Handling Multiple Command-Line Options, on page 27. For now, open the main.go file and add this package to your imports section:

```go
import (
    "bufio"
    "flag"
    "fmt"
    "io"
    "os"
)
```

Next, update the main() function by adding the definition for the new command-line flag:

```go
func main() {
    // Defining a boolean flag -l to count iines instead of words
    lines := flag.Bool("l", false, "Count lines")
    // Parsing the flags provided by the user
    flag.Parse()
```

This defines a new -l option that we'll use to indicate whether to count lines. The default value is false, which means that the normal behavior is to count words.

Complete the main() function by updating the call to the function count(), passing the value of the flag:

```go
    // Calling the count function to count the number of words (or lines)
    // received from the Standard Input and printing it out
    fmt.Println(count(os.Stdin, *lines))
}
```

Finally, update the count() function to accept this new Boolean argument and add a check to change the scanner.Split() function to bufio.ScanWords only if this parameter is false, since the default behavior of the scanner type is to count lines:

```go
func count(r io.Reader, countLines bool) int {
    // A scanner is used to read text from a Reader (such as files)
    scanner := bufio.NewScanner(r)

    // If the count lines flag is not set, we want to count words so we define
    // the scanner split type to words (default is split by lines)
    if !countLines {
        scanner.Split(bufio.ScanWords)
    }

    // Defining a counter
    wc := 0
```

```go
// For every word or line scanned, add 1 to the counter
for scanner.Scan() {
  wc++
}

// Return the total
return wc
}
```

Since you changed the count() function, it's a good idea to add another test to your test file to ensure the new feature works correctly. Do this by adding a new test function TestCountLines() to your main_test.go file:

```go
// TestCountLines tests the count function set to count lines
func TestCountLines(t *testing.T) {
  b := bytes.NewBufferString("word1 word2 word3\nline2\nline3 word1")

  exp := 3

  res := count(b, true)

  if res != exp {
    t.Errorf("Expected %d, got %d instead.\n", exp, res)
  }
}
```

This test uses a buffer to simulate an input with three lines by using the newline \n character. It then executes the updated count() function with this buffer and the parameter countLines set to true to count lines.

Before executing the tests, update the existing test function TestCountWords() by passing the value false as the new parameter to the count() function, or the test will fail.

```go
// TestCountWords tests the count function set to count words
func TestCountWords(t *testing.T) {
  b := bytes.NewBufferString("word1 word2 word3 word4\n")

  exp := 4

  res := count(b, false)

  if res != exp {
    t.Errorf("Expected %d, got %d instead.\n", exp, res)
  }
}
```

Now execute all the tests to verify the function works for both cases:

```
$ go test -v
=== RUN   TestCountWords
--- PASS: TestCountWords (0.00s)
=== RUN   TestCountLines
--- PASS: TestCountLines (0.00s)
```

```
PASS
  ok        pragprog.com/rggo/firstProgram/wc       0.003s
```

Build the program again:

```
$ go build
```

The wc tool now accepts the -l command-line flag to count lines instead of words. Use it to count the number of lines in the main.go command:

```
$ cat main.go | ./wc -l
43
```

By using command-line flags, you can extend the functionality of your tools without compromising any flexibility for your users. Next, we'll execute this tool on a different operating system.

Compiling Your Tool for Different Platforms

By default, the go build tool builds an executable binary for the current operating system and architecture. You can also use go build to build your command-line tool for a different platform even if you don't have access to that platform. For example, if you're using Linux, you can build a Windows or macOS binary that can be executed on those platforms without Go installed. This process is called *cross-compilation*. Let's build the word counter tool for the Windows platform by setting the GOOS environment variable to windows before running the build tool:

```
$ GOOS=windows go build
$ ls
go.mod   main.go   main_test.go   wc   wc.exe
```

Use the file command to get information about the new wc.exe file:

```
$ file wc.exe
wc.exe: PE32+ executable (console) x86-64 (stripped to external PDB),
  for MS Windows
```

As you can see, this creates a 64-bit executable file wc.exe for the Windows platform.

The documentation for go build contains a list[2] with all of the supported values for the GOOS environment variable.

Since this is a static binary, it doesn't require any runtime dependencies or anything else to run. Transfer this file directly to a Windows machine using your favorite file-sharing service or tool, and execute it.

---

2.   golang.org/src/go/build/syslist.go

```
C:\Temp>dir
Volume in drive C has no label.
Volume Serial Number is 741A-D791

Directory of C:\Temp

12/02/2018  07:00 PM    <DIR>          .
12/02/2018  07:00 PM    <DIR>          ..
06/02/2018  05:17 PM         2,083,840 wc.exe
   1 File(s)      2,083,840 bytes
   2 Dir(s)  31,320,055,808 bytes free

C:\Temp>echo "Testing wc command on Windows" | wc.exe
5
```

This command-line tool works as expected on a different platform and requires no additional components or runtimes to be installed.

Exercises

You can improve your understanding of the concepts discussed here by doing these exercises:

- Add another command-line flag, -b, to count the number of bytes in addition to words and lines.

- Then, update the count() function to accept another parameter, countBytes. When this input parameter is set to true, the function should count bytes. (Hint: check all the methods available for the type bufio.Scanner in the Go documentation.[3])

- Write tests to ensure the new feature works as intended.

Wrapping Up

In this chapter, you created your first command-line tool using Go. You tested it, built an executable file for two different operating systems, and executed it. This represents the basic workflow of writing command-line tools with Go.

Next, you'll dive into the concepts required to write more complex command-line tools, starting with getting input from your users and displaying information back to them.

---

3. golang.org/pkg/bufio

## CHAPTER 2

Interacting with Your Users

Unlike with a graphical program, the user of a CLI tool generally provides up front all the input and parameters required for the tool to work. The tool uses that input to do its job and provides results back to the user as text output on the screen. When an error occurs, a CLI tool usually provides details about it in a way that's easy and practical for the user to understand or potentially filter out.

In this chapter, you'll get comfortable working with input and output as you build a command-line tool for managing a list of "to-do" items. This tool will let you keep track of items left in a project or activity. The tool will save the list of items in a file using the JSON format.

To implement this tool, you'll accept input data from your users in a variety of ways. You'll get input from standard input (STDIN) and command-line parameters. You'll also use environment variables to modify how your program works. In addition, you'll display information back to the user through standard output (STDOUT) and output errors with the standard error (STDERR) stream for proper CLI error handling. Finally, you'll explore Go interfaces in general and the io.Reader interface in particular.

Let's start with a basic implementation of this tool and improve it along the way.

Organizing Your Code

Before you start developing command-line tools, let's talk a little about how to organize your code. Go is a relatively new programming language, so the community is still discussing different approaches for structuring Go programs. This section presents a common approach for developing command-line tools.

As you learned in Building the Basic Word Counter, on page 1, Go programs are composed of packages, which consist of one or more Go source code files that can be combined into executable programs or libraries. To create an executable program, you define a package named main which contains a function named main() that serves as the entry point for your executable program.

For this tool you'll use another common Go pattern to create a separate package containing the business logic, which in this case is the logic for working with to-do items. The command-line interface that works with this business logic is defined in a subdirectory named cmd.

By using this pattern, you separate the business logic from the command-line implementation and enable other developers to reuse the to-do code in their own programs.

This is the desired directory structure for this tool:

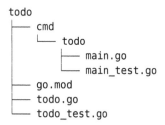

```
todo
├── cmd
│   └── todo
│       ├── main.go
│       └── main_test.go
├── go.mod
├── todo.go
└── todo_test.go
```

In this structure, the todo.go file represents the code for the todo package, which exposes a library to work with to-do items. The main.go file in the cmd/todo subdirectory contains the command-line interface implementation.

Let's implement the logic for dealing with to-do items.

Defining the To-Do API

To start your to-do tracking tool, you'll implement some business logic and an API to deal with to-do items.

In this version of the API, you'll implement two new custom types:

item: This type represents a single to-do item. You'll implement this type using a Go *struct*. A struct is a custom Go type composed of one or more named elements, or fields. Each field consists of a name and a type, each representing a property of the struct. You can find more information about Go structs in the official documentation.[1] This type won't be exported, so it can't be used by API users directly.

List: This type represents a list of to-do items. It's implemented by a slice of instances of the type item. This type is exported and visible outside the package.

---

1. golang.org/ref/spec#Struct_types

These custom types represent the data about the to-do items your application manages. To implement actions, like adding an item to the list or saving the list, you'll use *methods* associated with the List type. A method is a function that's associated with a specific type. This association allows the function to execute directly on the type's data. You can learn more about methods in the official documentation.[2]

Methods also allow types to implement interfaces, making your code more flexible and reusable. This will come in handy in Improving the List Output Format, on page 33.

For this application, you'll implement the following methods:

Complete: Marks a to-do item as completed.

Add: Creates a new to-do item and appends it to the list.

Delete: Deletes a to-do item from the list.

Save: Saves the list of items to a file using the JSON format.

Get: Obtains a list of items from a saved JSON file.

You'll add more methods when you need them.

Start by creating the directory structure for this project under your book's root directory:

```
$ mkdir -p $HOME/pragprog.com/rggo/interacting/todo
$ cd $HOME/pragprog.com/rggo/interacting/todo
$ mkdir -p cmd/todo
$ tree
.
└── cmd
    └── todo
  2 directories, 0 files
```

Then, initialize the Go module for this project. Ensure that you're in the top todo directory for this:

```
$ cd $HOME/pragprog.com/rggo/interacting/todo
$ go mod init pragprog.com/rggo/interacting/todo
go: creating new go.mod: module pragprog.com/rggo/interacting/todo
```

Create the todo.go file under the topmost todo directory in the program structure. Define the package name as todo and include the import section:

---

2. golang.org/ref/spec#Method_declarations

interacting/todo/todo.go
```go
package todo

import (
  "encoding/json"
  "errors"
  "fmt"
  "io/ioutil"
  "os"
  "time"
)
```

Next, create the two data structures that will be used in this package. The first is the item struct and its fields: Task of type string, Done of type bool, CreatedAt of type time.Time, and CompletedAt also of type time.Time. Since we don't want this type to be used outside this package, we don't export it. You do this by defining its name starting with a lowercase character:

interacting/todo/todo.go
```go
// item struct represents a ToDo item
type item struct {
  Task        string
  Done        bool
  CreatedAt   time.Time
  CompletedAt time.Time
}
```

Go Exported Types

 In Go, the visibility of a type or function is controlled by the case of the first character of its name. Names that start with an uppercase character are exported while lowercase names are considered private to the package.

The second data structure is the List type, which enables package users to manage the to-do items in the context of a list. Implement it as a slice of item instances ([]item). You could use the slice directly in your code, but by defining another type, you can attach methods to it and simplify the API. The List type must be visible outside the package so API users can use it. You define it as an exported type by specifying its name starting with an uppercase character:

interacting/todo/todo.go
```go
// List represents a list of ToDo items
type List []item
```

This approach leverages Go's statically typed nature to ensure, at compile time, that users of your API are using the appropriate type and methods to work with items in the context of a List. This avoids runtime errors that often happen in dynamic languages.

Now you'll attach the methods to the type List. Start with the Add() method to add an item to the list. To implement a method, define the function with an extra parameter, called a *receiver*, which is declared before the name of the function. The receiver works as a parameter declaration so it must have an identifier and a type. Unlike other languages, the identifier doesn't require any special name like this or that. You can use any valid Go identifier, but it's common to use the first letter of the type name as the identifier—in this case, l (lowercase L) for List.

The receiver type must be defined as the type you want to associate with the method or a pointer to this type. Generally speaking, you define the receiver as a pointer to the type when your method needs to modify the content of the receiver. Since the Add() method modifies the List by adding more items, we're using a pointer to the type *List as the receiver type. Otherwise, the method would change a copy of the list instead, and the change would be discarded when the method finishes. Declare the Add() method like this:

```
interacting/todo/todo.go
// Add creates a new todo item and appends it to the list
func (l *List) Add(task string) {
  t := item{
    Task:        task,
    Done:        false,
    CreatedAt:   time.Now(),
    CompletedAt: time.Time{},
  }

  *l = append(*l, t)
}
```

Note that you need to dereference the pointer to the List type with *l in the append call to access the underlying slice.

Next, create the Complete() method to mark an item as completed:

```
interacting/todo/todo.go
// Complete method marks a ToDo item as completed by
// setting Done = true and CompletedAt to the current time
func (l *List) Complete(i int) error {
  ls := *l
  if i <= 0 || i > len(ls) {
    return fmt.Errorf("Item %d does not exist", i)
  }
```

```
  // Adjusting index for 0 based index
  ls[i-1].Done = true
  ls[i-1].CompletedAt = time.Now()

  return nil
}
```

Strictly speaking, the Complete() method doesn't modify the list, so it doesn't require a pointer receiver. But it's a good practice to keep the entire method set of a single type with the same receiver type. In this case, we opted to declare the Complete() method with a pointer receiver as well.

Now, define the method Delete() to remove an item from the list:

interacting/todo/todo.go
```
// Delete method deletes a ToDo item from the list
func (l *List) Delete(i int) error {
  ls := *l
  if i <= 0 || i > len(ls) {
    return fmt.Errorf("Item %d does not exist", i)
  }

  // Adjusting index for 0 based index
  *l = append(ls[:i-1], ls[i:]...)

  return nil
}
```

The next two methods you'll implement are Save() and Get(), which save the list to a file and obtain the list from a file, respectively. This package uses the JSON format to save the list. Don't worry about the implementation right now. You'll learn about JSON in Chapter 8, Talking to REST APIs, on page 273, and about how to handle files in Chapter 3, Working with Files in Go, on page 45.

Add the Save() method, which converts the data to JSON and writes it to a file using the provided file name:

interacting/todo/todo.go
```
// Save method encodes the List as JSON and saves it
// using the provided file name
func (l *List) Save(filename string) error {
  js, err := json.Marshal(l)
  if err != nil {
    return err
  }

  return ioutil.WriteFile(filename, js, 0644)
}
```

io/ioutil Package in Go 1.16

Go 1.16 deprecated the package io/ioutil, and its functionality has been moved to other packages. This package will continue to work, and the book uses it to remain compatible with versions 1.13 and higher. If you're using Go 1.16, consider using the new functionality in accordance with the official release notes.[3]

Next, add the Get() method, which opens the file and decodes the JSON into the List data structure:

```
// Get method opens the provided file name, decodes
// the JSON data and parses it into a List
func (l *List) Get(filename string) error {
  file, err := ioutil.ReadFile(filename)
  if err != nil {
    if errors.Is(err, os.ErrNotExist) {
      return nil
    }
    return err
  }
  if len(file) == 0 {
    return nil
  }
  return json.Unmarshal(file, l)
}
```

This method also handles situations where the given file doesn't exist or is empty.

The code for the to-do API is complete. Let's write some tests to ensure it's working properly. Start by adding the package definition to a new file named todo_test.go:

interacting/todo/todo_test.go
```
package todo_test
```

In general, all files in the same directory must belong to the same Go package. An exception to this rule is when writing tests. You can define a different package for your tests to access only the exported types, variables, and functions from the package you're testing. This is a common practice when testing libraries because it ensures the tests only access the exposed API as a user would do. Define the package name as the original name followed by the "_test" suffix. In this case, we're using the name *todo_test*.

---

3. golang.org/doc/go1.16#ioutil

Now, add the import section with the required external libraries:

```
import (
  "io/ioutil"
  "os"
  "testing"

  "pragprog.com/rggo/interacting/todo"
)
```

For this test, you'll use the package ioutil to create temporary files, the package os to delete temporary files, and the testing package required for testing. Since you're defining the tests in a different package, you also need to import the todo package you're testing. Because we're using Go modules, we can use the module path pragprog.com/rggo/interacting/todo as the import path for this package.

Next, create the test cases. Start by creating a test to ensure we can add an item to the list:

```
// TestAdd tests the Add method of the List type
func TestAdd(t *testing.T) {
  l := todo.List{}

  taskName := "New Task"
  l.Add(taskName)

  if l[0].Task != taskName {
    t.Errorf("Expected %q, got %q instead.", taskName, l[0].Task)
  }

}
```

Then, add a test to verify the Complete() method:

```
// TestComplete tests the Complete method of the List type
func TestComplete(t *testing.T) {
  l := todo.List{}

  taskName := "New Task"
  l.Add(taskName)

  if l[0].Task != taskName {
    t.Errorf("Expected %q, got %q instead.", taskName, l[0].Task)
  }

  if l[0].Done {
    t.Errorf("New task should not be completed.")
  }

  l.Complete(1)

  if !l[0].Done {
    t.Errorf("New task should be completed.")
  }

}
```

Now, add a test to validate the Delete() method:

```go
// TestDelete tests the Delete method of the List type
func TestDelete(t *testing.T) {
  l := todo.List{}

  tasks := []string{
    "New Task 1",
    "New Task 2",
    "New Task 3",
  }

  for _, v := range tasks {
    l.Add(v)
  }

  if l[0].Task != tasks[0] {
    t.Errorf("Expected %q, got %q instead.", tasks[0], l[0].Task)
  }

  l.Delete(2)

  if len(l) != 2 {
    t.Errorf("Expected list length %d, got %d instead.", 2, len(l))
  }

  if l[1].Task != tasks[2] {
    t.Errorf("Expected %q, got %q instead.", tasks[2], l[1].Task)
  }
}
```

Finally, include a test that ensures we can save and load tests from a file:

```go
// TestSaveGet tests the Save and Get methods of the List type
func TestSaveGet(t *testing.T) {
  l1 := todo.List{}
  l2 := todo.List{}

  taskName := "New Task"
  l1.Add(taskName)

  if l1[0].Task != taskName {
    t.Errorf("Expected %q, got %q instead.", taskName, l1[0].Task)
  }

  tf, err := ioutil.TempFile("", "")

  if err != nil {
    t.Fatalf("Error creating temp file: %s", err)
  }
  defer os.Remove(tf.Name())

  if err := l1.Save(tf.Name()); err != nil {
    t.Fatalf("Error saving list to file: %s", err)
  }
```

```
if err := l2.Get(tf.Name()); err != nil {
  t.Fatalf("Error getting list from file: %s", err)
}

if l1[0].Task != l2[0].Task {
  t.Errorf("Task %q should match %q task.", l1[0].Task, l2[0].Task)
}
}
```

In this test case, you're creating two variables, l1 and l2, both of type todo.List. You're adding a task to l1 and saving it. Then you're loading it into l2 and comparing both values. The test fails if the values don't match, in which case you provide an error message showing the values you got.

Note that this test uses the TempFile() function from the ioutil package to create a temporary file. You then pass the temporary file's name to the Save() and Get() functions using the method tf.Name(). To ensure the temporary file is deleted at the end of the test, you defer the execution of the os.Remove() function.

Save the file and use the go test tool to execute the tests:

```
$ go test -v .
=== RUN   TestAdd
--- PASS: TestAdd (0.00s)
=== RUN   TestComplete
--- PASS: TestComplete (0.00s)
=== RUN   TestDelete
--- PASS: TestDelete (0.00s)
=== RUN   TestSaveGet
--- PASS: TestSaveGet (0.00s)
PASS
ok        pragprog.com/rggo/interacting/todo    0.002s
```

As you can see, all tests are passing so the API code is ready. Let's implement a command-line tool interface to use it.

Creating the Initial To-Do Command-Line Tool

You have a working to-do API, so now you can build a command-line interface on top of it. We'll start with an initial implementation that includes the following two features:

1. When executed without any arguments, the command will list the available to-do items.

2. When executed with one or more arguments, the command will concatenate the arguments as a new item and add it to the list.

Start by creating the file main.go in the cmd/todo directory as described in Organizing Your Code, on page 11.

```
$ cd $HOME/pragprog.com/rggo/interacting/todo/cmd/todo
```

Add the following code to the main.go file to define the package and imports you'll use:

interacting/todo/cmd/todo/main.go
```
package main

import (
  "fmt"
  "os"
  "strings"

  "pragprog.com/rggo/interacting/todo"
)
```

You'll use the Args variable from the os package to verify the arguments provided during your tool's execution. You'll use the fmt and strings packages to process input and output.

Similarly to what you've done in the todo_test.go file, you're importing your own todo package to use the to-do functionality.

Next, define a constant value for the file name. In this initial version you're effectively hard-coding the name of the file. This is fine for now. You'll change it later to something more flexible.

interacting/todo/cmd/todo/main.go
```
// Hardcoding the file name
const todoFileName = ".todo.json"
```

Now, create the main() function:

interacting/todo/cmd/todo/main.go
```
func main() {
```

Next, create a variable l (lowercase L) as a pointer to the type todo.List by using the address operator & to extract the address of an empty instance of todo.List. This variable represents the to-do items list you'll use throughout the code.

interacting/todo/cmd/todo/main.go
```
// Define an items list
l := &todo.List{}
```

Then, attempt to read existing items from the file by calling the method Get() of the List type. This method may return an error if it encounters any issues, so you can use it to check for potential errors. You can do this on the same line by using ; to separate the statements.

```
interacting/todo/cmd/todo/main.go
// Use the Get method to read to do items from file
if err := l.Get(todoFileName); err != nil {
  fmt.Fprintln(os.Stderr, err)
  os.Exit(1)
}
```

When developing command-line tools, it's a good practice to use the standard error (STDERR) output instead of the standard output (STDOUT) to display error messages as the user can easily filter them out if they desire.

Another good practice is to exit your program with a return code different than 0 (zero) when errors occur as this is a convention that clearly indicates that the program had an error or abnormal condition. This practice facilitates the use of your programs by other programs or scripts.

In this case, if the Get() method returns an error, print its value to the STDERR output by using the function Fprintln() of the fmt package and exit with code 1.

Next, use a switch statement to decide what the program should do based on the arguments it received. If the user only specifies the program's name, only one argument exists, so print out the items, one per line, by looping through the list using the function fmt.Println(item.Task):

```
interacting/todo/cmd/todo/main.go
// Decide what to do based on the number of arguments provided
switch {
// For no extra arguments, print the list
case len(os.Args) == 1:
  // List current to do items
  for _, item := range *l {
    fmt.Println(item.Task)
  }
```

Use a default case to check any other number of command-line arguments. To define the item that you add to the list, concatenate the arguments using the function strings.Join() and provide the slice os.Args[1:] as the first parameter, which excludes the program name and a space as the character used to join the strings:

```
interacting/todo/cmd/todo/main.go
// Concatenate all provided arguments with a space and
// add to the list as an item
default:
  // Concatenate all arguments with a space
  item := strings.Join(os.Args[1:], " ")
```

Then add the item to the list by calling the method Add() of the List type. Finally, try to save the file by using the method Save(). If any errors occur, use the same technique as before to print the error messages to the STDERR output, exiting with the status code 1.

```
// Add the task
l.Add(item)

// Save the new list
if err := l.Save(todoFileName); err != nil {
  fmt.Fprintln(os.Stderr, err)
  os.Exit(1)
}
}
}
```
interacting/todo/cmd/todo/main.go

The code is complete. Next, let's write some tests to ensure the code is working as intended.

Testing the Initial CLI Implementation

You can use different approaches to test your CLI tool. Since we already executed unit tests when developing the to-do API, we don't need to repeat them here. Our CLI implementation is a wrapper around the API. Let's leverage some of Go's features and write integration tests instead. This way we're testing the user interface of the tool instead of the business logic again.

One of the main benefits of Go is that it provides tools for automating the execution of tests out of the box; no additional frameworks or libraries are required. Since you write tests using Go itself, you can use any resources and features available with the language to write your test cases. In this case we will use the os/exec package, which lets us execute external commands. You'll learn more about this package in Chapter 6, Controlling Processes, on page 163.

For this test suite, we need to accomplish two main goals:

- Use the go build tool to compile the program into a binary file.
- Execute the binary file with different arguments and assert its correct behavior.

The recommended way for executing extra setup before your tests is by using the TestMain() function. This function helps you control the extra tasks required to set up or tear down the resources necessary for testing, keeping your test cases tidy and consistent.

Define the package name and import the required packages into a new file main_test.go in the same directory of your main.go. For these tests, we're using the following packages: fmt to print formatted output, os to use operating system types, os/exec to execute external commands, filepath to deal with directory paths, runtime to identify the running operating system, strings to compare strings, and testing to access testing tools.

interacting/todo/cmd/todo/main_test.go
```go
package main_test

import (
  "fmt"
  "os"
  "os/exec"
  "path/filepath"
  "runtime"
  "strings"
  "testing"
)
```

Then create two variables to hold the name of the binary file that we'll build during tests and the file name required to save the to-do list.

interacting/todo/cmd/todo/main_test.go
```go
var (
  binName  = "todo"
  fileName = ".todo.json"
)
```

Next, create the TestMain() function to call the go build tool that builds the executable binary for your tool, execute the tests using m.Run(), and clean up the produced files after the test is completed using the function os.Remove():

interacting/todo/cmd/todo/main_test.go
```go
func TestMain(m *testing.M) {
  fmt.Println("Building tool...")

  if runtime.GOOS == "windows" {
    binName += ".exe"
  }

  build := exec.Command("go", "build", "-o", binName)

  if err := build.Run(); err != nil {
    fmt.Fprintf(os.Stderr, "Cannot build tool %s: %s", binName, err)
    os.Exit(1)
  }

  fmt.Println("Running tests....")
  result := m.Run()

  fmt.Println("Cleaning up...")
  os.Remove(binName)
  os.Remove(fileName)

  os.Exit(result)
}
```

We're using the constant GOOS from the runtime package to check if the tests are running on the Windows operating system. In this case, we're appending the suffix .exe to the binary name so Go finds the executable during tests.

Finally, create the test cases by defining a function TestTodoCLI(). In this function, we use the subtests feature to execute tests that depend on each other by using the t.Run() method of the testing package.

Define the function and some variables required by the test such as the task name task, the current directory dir, and the cmdPath containing the path to the tool you compiled in the function TestMain():

interacting/todo/cmd/todo/main_test.go
```
func TestTodoCLI(t *testing.T) {
  task := "test task number 1"

  dir, err := os.Getwd()
  if err != nil {
    t.Fatal(err)
  }

  cmdPath := filepath.Join(dir, binName)
```

Then, create the first test which ensures the tool can add a new task by using the t.Run() method:

```
t.Run("AddNewTask", func(t *testing.T) {
  cmd := exec.Command(cmdPath, strings.Split(task, " ")...)

  if err := cmd.Run(); err != nil {
    t.Fatal(err)
  }
})
```

Notice that we're setting the name "AddNewTask" for this subtest as the first argument to t.Run() to make it easier to see the results. Also, we're executing the compiled binary with the expected argument by splitting the task variable. The test fails if an error occurs while adding the task.

Finally, include a test that ensures the tool can list the tasks:

```
t.Run("ListTasks", func(t *testing.T) {
  cmd := exec.Command(cmdPath)
  out, err := cmd.CombinedOutput()
  if err != nil {
    t.Fatal(err)
  }

  expected := task + "\n"
```

```
    if expected != string(out) {
      t.Errorf("Expected %q, got %q instead\n", expected, string(out))
    }
  })
}
```

For this subtest, we're setting the name to "ListTasks". Then we execute the tool with no arguments capturing its output in the variable out. The test fails immediately if an error occurs while executing the tool. If the execution succeeds, we compare the output with the task name, failing the test if they don't match.

Save the file main_test.go and execute the tests by calling the go test tool:

```
$ ls
main.go  main_test.go
$ go test -v
Building tool...
Running tests....
=== RUN    TestTodoCLI
=== RUN    TestTodoCLI/AddNewTask
=== RUN    TestTodoCLI/ListTasks
    --- PASS: TestTodoCLI (0.00s)
    --- PASS: TestTodoCLI/AddNewTask (0.00s)
    --- PASS: TestTodoCLI/ListTasks (0.00s)
PASS
Cleaning up...
ok         pragprog.com/rggo/interacting/todo   0.321s
$
```

Once all tests pass, you can try the tool by using go run:

```
$ ls
main.go main_test.go
$ go run main.go
```

Executing the tool with no arguments tries to list the content of the file, but since this is the first run, no file and results are presented. Run the code with any number of arguments to add a new item do the list:

```
$ go run main.go Add this to do item to the list
$ go run main.go
Add this to do item to the list
```

The second call to the tool with no arguments lists the existing items from the file. You can also check the file content:

```
$ ls -a
.   ..   main.go main_test.go .todo.json
$ cat .todo.json
[{"Task":"Add this to do item to the list","Done":false,"CreatedAt":"2018
-03-25T07:46:01.224119421-04:00","CompletedAt":"0001-01-01T00:00:00Z"}]$
$
```

Note that, when trying this version of the tool, you're constantly writing to the same file, .todo.json, since it's hardcoded in the program. We'll fix this shortly.

As you can see, the os.Args slice provides you with a quick way to access command-line arguments, but it's not very powerful. You can use it for simple programs, but if your tool requires many options, it can become complex quickly. For example, what if you wanted to add another option to this tool to complete items? You'd have to check every provided argument looking for the specific option. This approach isn't scalable and Go provides an easier way to deal with this.

Handling Multiple Command-Line Options

As you've seen while implementing the initial version of your command-line interface, using the os.Args variable isn't a flexible way of handling command-line arguments. Let's improve the tool by using the flag package to parse and handle multiple command-line options.

The flag package enables you to define command-line flags of specific types such as int or string so you don't need to convert them manually.

This version of the tool will accept three command-line arguments:

1. -list: A Boolean flag. When used, the tool will list all to-do items.

2. -task: A string flag. When used, the tool will include the string argument as a new to do item in the list.

3. -complete: An integer flag. When used, the tool will mark the item number as completed.

Example Code

 The complete example code for this section is under a subdirectory named todo.v1 to make it easy to find. In your case, it may be easier to simply update the existing code.

To use the flag package, include it in the import section of your program:

interacting/todo.v1/cmd/todo/main.go
```go
import (
    "flag"
    "fmt"
    "os"

    "pragprog.com/rggo/interacting/todo"
)
```

Also, ensure that the strings package isn't in the import list as it's no longer used in this version of the code.

To define a new flag using the flag package, call the function corresponding to the flag type you want to define. For example, to create a string flag, use flag.String(). These functions take three arguments: the flag name, the default value, and the help message.

Now, update the main() function by adding the three required flags to your program. Assign them to variables so that you can use their values in your program. After defining the flags, ensure that you call the function flag.Parse() from the flag package to parse them. If you forget it, the assigned variables will be empty which can lead to hard-to-find bugs.

interacting/todo.v1/cmd/todo/main.go
```go
func main() {
    // Parsing command line flags
    task := flag.String("task", "", "Task to be included in the ToDo list")
    list := flag.Bool("list", false, "List all tasks")
    complete := flag.Int("complete", 0, "Item to be completed")

    flag.Parse()
```

Keep in mind that the assigned variables are pointers so, to be used later, they have to be dereferenced using the operator *.

The next part of the main() function remains unchanged:

interacting/todo.v1/cmd/todo/main.go
```go
    // Define an items list
    l := &todo.List{}

    // Use the Get command to read to do items from file
    if err := l.Get(todoFileName); err != nil {
        fmt.Fprintln(os.Stderr, err)
        os.Exit(1)
    }
```

Update the switch statement to select the action based on the provided flag. In the first case statement, check if the -list flag was set. Use the * operator to get the value from the pointer variable list. Since the tool is now able to complete items, exclude the completed items from the output by checking the field item.Done before printing results:

interacting/todo.v1/cmd/todo/main.go
```go
// Decide what to do based on the provided flags
switch {
case *list:
  // List current to do items
  for _, item := range *l {
    if !item.Done {
      fmt.Println(item.Task)
    }
  }
}
```

In the next case statement, verify if the -complete flag was set with a value greater than zero (the default) and use a call to the method Complete() of the type List to complete the given item. Save the file afterward:

interacting/todo.v1/cmd/todo/main.go
```go
case *complete > 0:
  // Complete the given item
  if err := l.Complete(*complete); err != nil {
    fmt.Fprintln(os.Stderr, err)
    os.Exit(1)
  }

  // Save the new list
  if err := l.Save(todoFileName); err != nil {
    fmt.Fprintln(os.Stderr, err)
    os.Exit(1)
  }
```

In the final case, verify if the -task flag was set with a value different than the empty string and use its value as the new item in the call to the method Add(). Save the file afterward:

interacting/todo.v1/cmd/todo/main.go
```go
case *task != "":
  // Add the task
  l.Add(*task)

  // Save the new list
  if err := l.Save(todoFileName); err != nil {
    fmt.Fprintln(os.Stderr, err)
    os.Exit(1)
  }
```

To complete the tool, change the default case to print an error message to STDERR output in case an invalid option was provided:

interacting/todo.v1/cmd/todo/main.go
```go
    default:
      // Invalid flag provided
      fmt.Fprintln(os.Stderr, "Invalid option")
      os.Exit(1)
    }
}
```

Save the changes to main.go, and then update the test cases in your test suite to handle the new flags by changing these two lines in the main_test.go file:

interacting/todo.v1/cmd/todo/main_test.go
```go
func TestTodoCLI(t *testing.T) {
  task := "test task number 1"

  dir, err := os.Getwd()
  if err != nil {
    t.Fatal(err)
  }

  cmdPath := filepath.Join(dir, binName)

  t.Run("AddNewTask", func(t *testing.T) {
➤    cmd := exec.Command(cmdPath, "-task", task)

    if err := cmd.Run(); err != nil {
      t.Fatal(err)
    }
  })

  t.Run("ListTasks", func(t *testing.T) {
➤    cmd := exec.Command(cmdPath, "-list")
    out, err := cmd.CombinedOutput()
    if err != nil {
      t.Fatal(err)
    }

    expected := task + "\n"

    if expected != string(out) {
      t.Errorf("Expected %q, got %q instead\n", expected, string(out))
    }
  })
}
```

Also, delete the package strings from the import list as it's no longer used.

We won't write tests for the new options since they are very similar, but you should do so as an exercise.

Before running the tests, delete the file .todo.json if it exists from a previous test or the test execution will fail:

```
$ rm .todo.json
```

Now, run the tests to ensure the tool is still working as intended:

```
$ go test -v
Building tool...
Running tests....
=== RUN    TestTodoCLI
=== RUN    TestTodoCLI/AddNewTask
=== RUN    TestTodoCLI/ListTasks
    --- PASS: TestTodoCLI (0.00s)
    --- PASS: TestTodoCLI/AddNewTask (0.00s)
    --- PASS: TestTodoCLI/ListTasks (0.00s)
PASS
Cleaning up...
ok      pragprog.com/rggo/interacting/todo      0.299s
```

You can now try the improved tool:

```
$ go run main.go -list
$ go run main.go -task "One ToDo item"
$ go run main.go -task "Another ToDo item"
$ go run main.go -list
One ToDo item
Another ToDo item
$ go run main.go -complete 1
$ go run main.go -list
Another ToDo item
```

Notice that after completing an item, it's no longer displayed to the user. This is an improvement compared to the previous version.

> ## The Flag Package
>
> The flag package contains many other useful options, including managing command-line flags of different data types, automatic help generation, and the FlagSet type for managing subcommands. These options are beyond the scope of this chapter.
>
> Before moving on, you may want to check the documentation for the flag package[a] if you want to explore some of these additional options.
>
> _____
>
> a.   golang.org/pkg/flag/

Now let's present usage information to the user so they know how to use our tool.

Display Command-Line Tool Usage

Command-line tools should be helpful. Sometimes the user doesn't know how to use a tool or they don't remember all the options, so it's helpful if your tool displays usage information.

Another benefit of using the flag package is that it provides automatic usage information if the user gives an invalid option or specifically requests help. You don't have to do anything special to take advantage of this behavior either. Try it out by running your program with the -h option:

```
$ go build .
$ ./todo -h
Usage of ./todo:
  -complete int
        Item to be completed
  -list
        List all tasks
  -task string
        Task to be included in the ToDo list
```

You didn't have to include the -h flag in your code; the help feature and output are provided by the flag package by default. By default, the message includes the help text you included as the third parameter when defining each flag.

In addition, the flag package displays the usage information in case the tool receives an invalid flag:

```
$ ./todo -test
flag provided but not defined: -test
Usage of ./todo:
  -complete int
        Item to be completed
  -list
        List all tasks
  -task string
        Task to be included in the ToDo list
```

You can also call the usage information from your code at any time by using the function flag.Usage(). As a matter of fact, Usage is a variable that points to a function. You can change it to display a custom message. Inside your custom function, call the function PrintDefaults() to print the usage information for each flag. Test it by including the following code at the top of your main() function:

```
flag.Usage = func() {
  fmt.Fprintf(flag.CommandLine.Output(),
    "%s tool. Developed for The Pragmatic Bookshelf\n", os.Args[0])
  fmt.Fprintf(flag.CommandLine.Output(), "Copyright 2020\n")
  fmt.Fprintln(flag.CommandLine.Output(), "Usage information:")
  flag.PrintDefaults()
}
```

When you run the program again, you'll see the custom usage information presented:

```
$ ./todo -h
./todo tool. Developed for The Pragmatic Bookshelf
Copyright 2020
Usage information:
  -complete int
        Item to be completed
  -list
        List all tasks
  -task string
        Task to be included in the ToDo list
```

Now that the user can get proper usage information, let's improve this tool's output.

Improving the List Output Format

You've made good progress on your to-do list tool so far, but the list output is still not very informative. At this moment, this is what you see when executing the tool with the -list option:

```
$ ./todo -list
Another ToDo item
Improve usage
Improve output
```

Various ways exist for improving the output formatting. For instance, if you don't own the API code, your only alternative is to format the output in the command-line tool implementation. But you own the API, so we can leverage the powerful *Interfaces* feature of Go to implement the list output formatting in the todo.List type directly. With this approach, anyone using your API experiences a consistent output format.

An interface in Go implements a contract but, unlike other languages, Go interfaces define only behavior and not state. This means that an interface defines what a type should do and not what type of data it should hold.

So, to satisfy an interface, a type needs only to implement all the methods defined in the interface with the same signature. In addition, satisfying an interface doesn't require explicit declaration. Types will implicitly implement an interface by implementing all the defined methods.

This is a powerful concept that has a profound impact on how interfaces are used. By implicitly satisfying an interface, a given type can be used anywhere that interface is expected, enabling code decoupling and reuse.

You can get additional information about interfaces in the Go documentation.[4]

4.　golang.org/ref/spec#Interface_types

Now we'll implement the Stringer interface on the todo.List type. The Stringer interface is defined in the fmt package as follows:

```
type Stringer interface {
  String() string
}
```

Any types that implement the method String(), which returns a string, satisfy the Stringer interface. By satisfying this interface, you can provide the type to any formatting function that expects a string.

To implement the Stringer interface on the todo.List type, switch back to the topmost todo directory, and edit the todo.go file:

```
$ cd $HOME/pragprog.com/rggo/interacting/todo
```

Add the String() method like this:

interacting/todo.v2/todo.go
```
//String prints out a formatted list
//Implements the fmt.Stringer interface
func (l *List) String() string {
  formatted := ""

  for k, t := range *l {
    prefix := "  "
    if t.Done {
      prefix = "X "
    }

    // Adjust the item number k to print numbers starting from 1 instead of 0
    formatted += fmt.Sprintf("%s%d: %s\n", prefix, k+1, t.Task)
  }

  return formatted
}
```

This is a naive implementation that prints out all items, prefixed by an order number and an X if the item is completed. Save the file todo.go to complete the changes.

Now use this interface in the CLI implementation. Switch back to the cmd/todo subdirectory.

```
$ cd $HOME/pragprog.com/rggo/interacting/todo/cmd/todo
```

Open main.go in your editor and update the *list case in the switch statement like this:

```
interacting/todo.v2/cmd/todo/main.go
case *list:
  // List current to do items
  fmt.Print(l)
```

Notice that now you can call the fmt.Print() function, which requires no format specifier, as the format comes from the Stringer interface implemented by the variable l of type todo.List.

Now when you execute the test suite, the *List_tasks* test fails because the output has changed:

```
$ go test -v
Building tool...
Running tests....
=== RUN    TestTodoCLI
=== RUN    TestTodoCLI/AddNewTask
=== RUN    TestTodoCLI/ListTasks
--- FAIL: TestTodoCLI (0.01s)
    --- PASS: TestTodoCLI/AddNewTask (0.00s)
    --- FAIL: TestTodoCLI/ListTasks (0.00s)
        main_test.go:54: Expected "test task number 1\n",
            got " 1: test task number 1\n" instead
FAIL
Cleaning up...
exit status 1
FAIL    pragprog.com/rggo/interacting/todo/cmd/todo    0.426s
```

Fix this issue by updating the expected output in the corresponding test case, like this:

```
interacting/todo.v2/cmd/todo/main_test.go
t.Run("ListTasks", func(t *testing.T) {
  cmd := exec.Command(cmdPath, "-list")
  out, err := cmd.CombinedOutput()
  if err != nil {
    t.Fatal(err)
  }

  expected := fmt.Sprintf(" 1: %s\n", task)

  if expected != string(out) {
    t.Errorf("Expected %q, got %q instead\n", expected, string(out))
  }
})
```

Rerun the tests and ensure they pass:

```
$ go test -v
Building tool...
Running tests....
=== RUN    TestTodoCLI
=== RUN    TestTodoCLI/AddNewTask
=== RUN    TestTodoCLI/ListTasks
--- PASS: TestTodoCLI (0.01s)
    --- PASS: TestTodoCLI/AddNewTask (0.00s)
    --- PASS: TestTodoCLI/ListTasks (0.00s)
PASS
Cleaning up...
ok      pragprog.com/rggo/interacting/todo     0.299s
```

Now when you execute the tool using the -list option, you'll see something similar to the following output:

```
$ go run main.go -list
X 1: Add this to do item to the list
  2: Another ToDo item
  3: Improve usage
  4: Improve output
$ go run main.go -complete 3
$ go run main.go -list
X 1: Add this to do item to the list
  2: Another ToDo item
X 3: Improve usage
  4: Improve output
```

This output looks much more informative. Now let's implement an easier way to select the file we'll use to save the to-do list.

Increasing Flexibility with Environment Variables

With all the improvements you made to your to-do tool so far, you've provided your users with several useful features. But the user still can't select which file to save to the list of to-do items. You could use different approaches in this situation, such as adding another flag to allow the user to specify the file name, but another way to make your tool more flexible is by using environment variables.

Using environment variables allows your users to specify options once in their shell configuration, which means the user avoids typing that option for every command execution. It also lets the user have different configurations for different environments.

In Go, the os package provides functions to handle both the environment and environment variables. We'll use the function os.Getenv("TODO_FILENAME") to retrieve the value of the environment variable identified by the name TODO_FILENAME.

To add this feature to your to-do tool, make two changes to the main.go file. First, update the line where you define the todoFileName from a constant to a variable so it can be changed later in case the environment variable is defined. This line works as the default file name when the user doesn't set the environment variable:

interacting/todo.v3/cmd/todo/main.go
```
// Default file name
var todoFileName = ".todo.json"
```

Next, inside the function main(), include the following lines before you instantiate the todo.List type. The goal is to check if the environment variable TODO_FILENAME is set, assigning its value to the variable todoFileName. Otherwise, the variable will keep its default value.

interacting/todo.v3/cmd/todo/main.go
```
// Check if the user defined the ENV VAR for a custom file name
if os.Getenv("TODO_FILENAME") != "" {
  todoFileName = os.Getenv("TODO_FILENAME")
}
```

Execute the tool with the environment variable set to change the default file name:

```
$ ls
main.go main_test.go
$ export TODO_FILENAME=new-todo.json
$ go run main.go -task "Test env vars design"
$ ls
main.go  main_test.go new-todo.json
$ cat new-todo.json
[{"Task":"Test env vars design","Done":false,"CreatedAt":"2018-03
-25T23:08:39.780125489-04:00","CompletedAt":"0001-01-01T00:00:00Z"}]$
$ go run main.go -list
  1: Test env vars design
```

Making your tools more flexible enables more use cases, increasing the overall satisfaction of your users. Speaking of flexibility, let's provide another way to add new tasks.

Capturing Input from STDIN

Good command-line tools interact well with your users, but they also work well with other tools. A common way command-line programs interact with one another is by accepting input from the standard input (STDIN) stream.

Let's add one last feature to the program: the ability to add new tasks via STDIN, allowing your users to pipe new tasks from other command-line tools.

To start this update, add three new libraries to your main.go import list: bufio, io, and strings:

```
interacting/todo.v4/cmd/todo/main.go
import (
    "bufio"
    "flag"
    "fmt"

    "io"
    "os"

    "strings"

    "pragprog.com/rggo/interacting/todo"
)
```

You'll use the bufio package to read data from the STDIN input stream, the io package to use the io.Reader interface, and the function Join() from the strings package to join command-line arguments to compose a task name.

Next, you'll create a new helper function called getTask() that will determine where to get the input task from. This function leverages Go interfaces again by accepting the io.Reader interface as input. In Go, it's a good practice to take interfaces as function arguments instead of concrete types. This approach increases the flexibility of your functions by allowing different types to be used as input as long as they satisfy the given interface.

The io.Reader interface wraps up the Read() method. As interfaces are implicitly satisfied, it's common in Go to have simple interfaces composed of one or two methods. The io.Reader is an example of a simple interface that provides a lot of flexibility.

You can use this interface in your code whenever you expect to read data. Widely used types such as files, buffers, archives, HTTP requests, and others satisfy this interface. By using it, you decouple your implementation from specific types, allowing your code to work with any types that implement the io.Reader interface.

For example, in this version, you'll use the variable os.Stdin for STDIN input, but later on, you could change it to other types (such as files, buffers, or even network connections). For more information about this interface, check the io.Reader documentation.[5]

---

5. golang.org/pkg/io/#Reader

The getTask() function accepts as input the parameter r of type io.Reader interface and the parameter args, which consists of zero or more values of type string, represented by the ... operator preceding the parameter type. Go calls this function a *variadic* function.[6] The function getTask() returns a string and a potential error. This function verifies if any arguments were provided as the parameter args. If so, it returns all of them concatenated with a space, using the strings.Join() function. Otherwise, it uses the bufio.Scanner to scan for a single input line on the provided io.Reader interface. If an error occurs while reading the input or the input is blank, it returns an error. Define the function at the bottom of your main.go file, like this:

interacting/todo.v4/cmd/todo/main.go
```
// getTask function decides where to get the description for a new
// task from: arguments or STDIN
func getTask(r io.Reader, args ...string) (string, error) {
  if len(args) > 0 {
    return strings.Join(args, " "), nil
  }

  s := bufio.NewScanner(r)
  s.Scan()
  if err := s.Err(); err != nil {
    return "", err
  }

  if len(s.Text()) == 0 {
    return "", fmt.Errorf("Task cannot be blank")
  }

  return s.Text(), nil
}
```

Next, update the main() function to use the new getTask() function to obtain the task name. Since you're no longer getting the task directly from the flag, change the -task flag to -add with a boolean type instead of string. This new flag only indicates that something will be added, allowing you the flexibility to get the input from other sources.

interacting/todo.v4/cmd/todo/main.go
```
// Parsing command line flags
➤ add := flag.Bool("add", false, "Add task to the ToDo list")
list := flag.Bool("list", false, "List all tasks")
complete := flag.Int("complete", 0, "Item to be completed")
```

To complete the updates, change the case *task != "" block to case *add, calling the new getTask() function. Pass the variable os.Stdin, which represents the

---

6. golang.org/ref/spec#Function_types

standard input - STDIN, as the first input parameter, and pass flag.Args()... as the second parameter:

interacting/todo.v4/cmd/todo/main.go
```
case *add:
  // When any arguments (excluding flags) are provided, they will be
  // used as the new task
  t, err := getTask(os.Stdin, flag.Args()...)
  if err != nil {
    fmt.Fprintln(os.Stderr, err)
    os.Exit(1)
  }
  l.Add(t)

  // Save the new list
  if err := l.Save(todoFileName); err != nil {
    fmt.Fprintln(os.Stderr, err)
    os.Exit(1)
  }
```

You can use the os.Stdin variable as the first parameter for the getTask() function because its type *os.File implements the io.Reader interface. The flag.Args() function returns all the remaining non-flag arguments provided by the user as input when executing the tool. Notice that we are using the operator ... to expand the slice into a list of values as expected by the function. If the getTask() function returns an error, we're printing it out to STDERR and exiting with code 1.

Save the main.go file to complete the changes.

Now, update the test suite in the main_test.go file to include a test for this new case.

First, include the io package in the import list to use the function io.WriteString() to write a string to an io.Writer:

interacting/todo.v4/cmd/todo/main_test.go
```
import (
  "fmt"
  "path/filepath"
  "runtime"

  "io"
  "os"
  "os/exec"
  "testing"
)
```

Then, update the parameter to add a task from -task to -add in the existing *AddNewTask* test case. Include a new test case *AddNewTaskFromSTDIN* to test the new functionality you just added. In this test, use the method cmd.StdinPipe()

from the package os/exec to connect to the STDIN pipe of the command. Use the io.WriteString() function to write the contents of the variable task2 into the pipe. It's important to close the pipe by calling cmdStdIn.Close() to ensure the function Run() doesn't wait forever for input.

interacting/todo.v4/cmd/todo/main_test.go
```go
func TestTodoCLI(t *testing.T) {
  task := "test task number 1"

  dir, err := os.Getwd()
  if err != nil {
    t.Fatal(err)
  }

  cmdPath := filepath.Join(dir, binName)

  t.Run("AddNewTaskFromArguments", func(t *testing.T) {
    cmd := exec.Command(cmdPath, "-add", task)

    if err := cmd.Run(); err != nil {
      t.Fatal(err)
    }
  })

  task2 := "test task number 2"
  t.Run("AddNewTaskFromSTDIN", func(t *testing.T) {
    cmd := exec.Command(cmdPath, "-add")
    cmdStdIn, err := cmd.StdinPipe()
    if err != nil {
      t.Fatal(err)
    }
    io.WriteString(cmdStdIn, task2)
    cmdStdIn.Close()

    if err := cmd.Run(); err != nil {
      t.Fatal(err)
    }
  })

  t.Run("ListTasks", func(t *testing.T) {
    cmd := exec.Command(cmdPath, "-list")
    out, err := cmd.CombinedOutput()
    if err != nil {
      t.Fatal(err)
    }

    expected := fmt.Sprintf("  1: %s\n  2: %s\n", task, task2)

    if expected != string(out) {
      t.Errorf("Expected %q, got %q instead\n", expected, string(out))
    }
  })
}
```

Save the main_test.go file and ensure the TODO_FILENAME environment variable isn't set and the file .todo.json doesn't exist before you run the tests.

```
$ unset TODO_FILENAME
$ rm .todo.json
```

Execute the tests and assert the new test case pass:

```
$ go test -v
Building tool...
Running tests....
=== RUN    TestTodoCLI
=== RUN    TestTodoCLI/AddNewTaskFromArguments
=== RUN    TestTodoCLI/AddNewTaskFromSTDIN
=== RUN    TestTodoCLI/ListTasks
--- PASS: TestTodoCLI (0.01s)
    --- PASS: TestTodoCLI/AddNewTaskFromArguments (0.00s)
    --- PASS: TestTodoCLI/AddNewTaskFromSTDIN (0.00s)
    --- PASS: TestTodoCLI/ListTasks (0.00s)
PASS
Cleaning up...
ok      pragprog.com/rggo/interacting/todo      0.316s
```

Build and try this version of your tool:

```
$ ls
main.go main_test.go
$ go build
$ ./todo -add Including item from Args
$ ./todo -list
  1: Including item from Args
$ echo "This item comes from STDIN" | ./todo -add
$ ./todo -list
  1: Including item from Args
  2: This item comes from STDIN
```

You've completed your command-line tool for managing to-do lists.

Exercises

You can try the following exercises to expand your skills:

- Implement the flag -del to delete an item from the list. Use the Delete() method from the API to perform the action.

- Add another flag to enable verbose output, showing information like date/time.

- Add another flag to prevent displaying completed items.

- Update the custom usage function to include additional instructions on how to provide new tasks to the tool.

- Include test cases for the remaining options, such as -complete.

- Update the tests to use the TODO_FILENAME environment variable instead of hard-coding the test file name so that it doesn't cause conflicts with an existing file.

- Update the getTask() function allowing it to handle multiline input from STDIN. Each line should be a new task in the list.

Wrapping Up

In this chapter, you explored a few ways to get input from your users. You used command-line arguments, environment variables, and standard input. More importantly, you got more comfortable producing your own command-line tools by using common standards and practices.

In the next chapter, you'll build on these concepts by handling files, thus enabling you to create even more powerful and useful tools.

## CHAPTER 3

Working with Files in Go

Working with files is one of the most frequent tasks you have to perform when building your command-line tools. Your programs pull data from files and also save results in them. This is particularly important when working with Linux or Unix because system resources are represented as files.

To get comfortable working with files in CLI apps, you'll develop a tool to preview *Markdown* files locally, using a web browser.

Markdown is a lightweight markup language that uses plain text with special syntax to represent formatting compatible with HTML. It's used to write blog articles, comments, and *README* files for open source projects like those available in GitHub. Since it uses plain text, writing Markdown requires only a text editor, but it may be hard to visualize the end result.

The tool you'll write converts the Markdown source into HTML that can be viewed in a browser. To work with files in Go, you'll use the packages os and io from the standard library. You'll create and open files so that you can read data or save it to files using different methods. You'll handle paths consistently across multiple platforms to make your code more flexible, ensuring your tool works in cross-platform scenarios. You'll use the defer statement to effectively clean up used resources. In addition, you'll apply the io.Writer interface, which is a powerful concept of the language. Finally, you'll work with temporary files and templates.

Creating a Basic Markdown Preview Tool

Let's implement the initial version of the Markdown Preview tool. We'll call this tool mdp (for MarkDown Preview) and accept the file name of the Markdown file to be previewed as its argument. This tool will perform four main steps:

1. Read the contents of the input Markdown file.

2. Use some Go external libraries to parse Markdown and generate a valid HTML block.

3. Wrap the results with an HTML header and footer.

4. Save the buffer to an HTML file that you can view in a browser.

When writing Go programs, you can organize your code in many ways. For this tool, you'll keep all the code in a single package main since this functionality won't be used outside the CLI implementation. In Chapter 4, Navigating the File System, on page 77, you'll see how to organize your code as a single package with many files. For now, you'll keep the code in main.go.

You already know that to create executable files in Go, the program has to start from the main() function in the main package. But having all the code inside the main() function is inconvenient and makes it harder to automate testing. To address this issue, a common pattern is to break the main() function into smaller focused functions that can be tested independently. To coordinate the execution of these functions into a cohesive outcome, we use a coordinating function. In this case, we call this function run().

In addition to the main() and run() functions, you'll also implement parseContent(), to parse Markdown into HTML, and saveHTML(), to save the result into a file.

To transform Markdown into HTML, you'll use an external Go package called blackfriday. This package is open source and provides a flexible implementation that supports several formatting options. You can find more information on the project's GitHub page.[1]

While Blackfriday converts Markdown into HTML, according to its documentation, it doesn't sanitize the output to prevent malicious content. To ensure that your tool generates safe output, you'll sanitize the content using another external package called bluemonday. For more information, check this package's GitHub page.[2]

Using external packages helps you speed up development by reusing software that was developed by someone else, but it also adds a dependency to your project that you have to manage. Always think about the benefits versus the constraints when using external packages.

---

1. github.com/russross/blackfriday
2. github.com/microcosm-cc/bluemonday

To use these external packages in your program, you need to first install them in your local machine. Before doing this, let's set up the project directory. Create the directory for your new command-line tool in your book's root directory. Switch to the new directory afterward.

```
$ mkdir -p $HOME/pragprog.com/rggo/workingFiles/mdp
$ cd $HOME/pragprog.com/rggo/workingFiles/mdp
```

Then initialize the Go module for this project:

```
$ go mod init pragprog.com/rggo/workingFiles/mdp
go: creating new go.mod: module pragprog.com/rggo/workingFiles/mdp
```

Now, download the required external packages. In Go, you install external packages by using the go get tool. To install these two packages, run the following commands:

```
$ go get github.com/microcosm-cc/bluemonday
$ go get github.com/russross/blackfriday/v2
```

The command go get downloads the packages and adds them as a dependency in the go.mod file:

```
workingFiles/mdp/go.mod
module pragprog.com/rggo/workingFiles/mdp

go 1.16

require (
        github.com/microcosm-cc/bluemonday v1.0.15
        github.com/russross/blackfriday/v2 v2.1.0
)
```

Next, create the main.go file and open it in your editor.

Add the package and import sections. To use the external packages, you need to import them in the import section as you do with packages provided by the standard library, but specify them using the full module path, including the package path. For example, to import the package bluemonday, use github.com/microcosm-cc/bluemonday. If the module supports *semantic versioning* and you want to use a specific version, add the major version of the module as /vN at the end of the module path. For example, to use version 2.x of Blackfriday, use github.com/russross/blackfriday/v2. For more details, consult the package documentation and the Go Modules wiki.[3] Add this code to your main.go file:

---

3. github.com/golang/go/wiki/Modules#version-selection

workingFiles/mdp/main.go
```go
package main

import (
  "bytes"
  "flag"
  "fmt"
  "io/ioutil"
  "os"
  "path/filepath"

  "github.com/microcosm-cc/bluemonday"
  "github.com/russross/blackfriday/v2"
)
```

The blackfriday package generates the content based on the input Markdown, but it doesn't include the HTML header and footer required to view it in a browser. You'll add them to the file yourself and use them to wrap the results you get from Blackfriday. Define the constants header and footer to use later:

workingFiles/mdp/main.go
```go
const (
  header = `<!DOCTYPE html>
<html>
  <head>
    <meta http-equiv="content-type" content="text/html; charset=utf-8">
    <title>Markdown Preview Tool</title>
  </head>
  <body>
`
  footer = `
  </body>
</html>
`
)
```

Now create the main() function by adding code to parse the flag -file that specifies the input Markdown file. Check if the flag has been set and use it as input to the run() function. Otherwise, return the usage information to the user and terminate the program. Finally, check the error return value from the run() function, exiting with an error message in case it isn't nil.

workingFiles/mdp/main.go
```go
func main() {
  // Parse flags
  filename := flag.String("file", "", "Markdown file to preview")
  flag.Parse()

  // If user did not provide input file, show usage
  if *filename == "" {
    flag.Usage()
```

```
    os.Exit(1)
  }

  if err := run(*filename); err != nil {
    fmt.Fprintln(os.Stderr, err)
    os.Exit(1)
  }
}
```

Next, define the run() function to coordinate the execution of the remaining functions. This function receives one input, filename, representing the name of the Markdown file to preview, and returns a potential error. The function main() uses the return value to decide whether to exit the program with an error code.

```
workingFiles/mdp/main.go
func run(filename string) error {
  // Read all the data from the input file and check for errors
  input, err := ioutil.ReadFile(filename)
  if err != nil {
    return err
  }

  htmlData := parseContent(input)

  outName := fmt.Sprintf("%s.html", filepath.Base(filename))
  fmt.Println(outName)

  return saveHTML(outName, htmlData)
}
```

This function reads the content of the input Markdown file into a slice of bytes by using the convenience function ReadFile(path) from the ioutil package. We pass this content as input to the parseContent() function, responsible for converting Markdown to HTML. You'll implement this function shortly. Finally, we're using the htmlData returned from parseContent() as input to the saveHTML() function that saves the content to a file.

The saveHTML() function accepts another input parameter, outFname, which is the output HTML file name. For now, we're using the filepath package's Base() function to derive the outFname parameter from the file name of the path provided by the user. The filepath package provides this and other functions designed to work with paths compatible with the target operating system, which makes your tool ready to use in cross-platform scenarios. The saveHTML() function returns a potential error when writing the HTML file, which the function run() also returns as its error.

Now, let's implement the parseContent() function. This function receives a slice of bytes representing the content of the Markdown file and returns another slice of bytes with the converted content as HTML. Define it by adding the following code to the main.go file:

workingFiles/mdp/main.go
```
func parseContent(input []byte) []byte {
```

Blackfriday has various options and plugins you can use to customize the results; for a complete list of enabled extensions, take a look at the library's documentation.[4] For this tool, you'll use the Run([]byte) function that parses Markdown using the most common extensions, such as rendering tables and code blocks. This function requires a slice of bytes as input. Use the input parameter as input to Blackfriday and pass its returned content to Bluemonday, like this:

workingFiles/mdp/main.go
```
// Parse the markdown file through blackfriday and bluemonday
// to generate a valid and safe HTML
output := blackfriday.Run(input)
body := bluemonday.UGCPolicy().SanitizeBytes(output)
```

This block of code generated a valid block of HTML which constitutes the body of the page. Now combine this body with the header and footer defined as constants to generate the complete HTML content. Use a buffer of bytes bytes.Buffer from the bytes package to join all the HTML parts like this:

workingFiles/mdp/main.go
```
    // Create a buffer of bytes to write to file
    var buffer bytes.Buffer

    // Write html to bytes buffer
    buffer.WriteString(header)
    buffer.Write(body)
    buffer.WriteString(footer)

    return buffer.Bytes()
}
```

The function returns the content of the buffer as a slice of bytes by using the buffer.Bytes() method to extract the content of the buffer.

Finally, implement the saveHTML() function, which will receive the entire HTML content stored in the buffer and save it to a file specified by the parameter outFname. The ioutil package provides another convenient function to do this: ioutil.WriteFile(). Save the HTML content by adding this code to the main.go file:

---

4. godoc.org/gopkg.in/russross/blackfriday.v2#pkg-constants

```
workingFiles/mdp/main.go
func saveHTML(outFname string, data []byte) error {
  // Write the bytes to the file
  return ioutil.WriteFile(outFname, data, 0644)
}
```

The third parameter represents the file permissions. We're using 0644 for creating a file that's both readable and writable by the owner but only readable by anyone else. The function returns any errors from the WriteFile() call as output.

Now that the code is complete, let's write some tests to ensure it's working as designed.

Writing Tests for the Markdown Preview Tool

When you tested the todo tool in Testing the Initial CLI Implementation, on page 23, you wrote something similar to an integration test by compiling the tool and running it in the test cases. This was necessary as all the code was part of the main() function, which can't be tested. For this application, you'll take a different approach; you'll write individual unit tests for each function, and use an integration test to test the run() function. You can do this now because the run() function returns values that can be used in tests.

This means you're intentionally not testing some of the code that's still in the main() function, such as the block that parses the command-line flags. You don't have to write tests for that code because you can assume it's already been tested by the Go team. When using external libraries and packages, trust that they have been tested by the developers who provided them. If you don't trust the developers, don't use the library.

This also means you don't need to write unit tests for the saveHTML() function since it's essentially a wrapper around a function from Go's standard library. Its behavior is assured in the integration test you'll write.

You can use various techniques to test functions that require files. Later in Using Interfaces to Automate Tests, on page 58, you'll use the interfaces io.Reader or io.Writer to mock tests. For this case, you'll use a technique known as *golden files* where the expected results are saved into files that are loaded during the tests for validating the actual output. The benefit is that the results can be complex, such as an entire HTML file, and you can have many of them to test different cases.

For these tests, you'll create two files: the input Markdown file test1.md and the golden file test1.md.html. It's a good practice to put all files required by your tests in a subdirectory called testdata under your project's directory. The testdata directory has a special meaning in Go tooling that's ignored by the Go build tool when compiling your program to ensure that testing artifacts don't end up in your build.

```
$ cd $HOME/pragprog.com/rggo/workingFiles/mdp
$ mkdir testdata
$ cd testdata
```

Create the input Markdown file test1.md in the testdata directory using your favorite text editor.

Add the input Markdown code to test1.md:

workingFiles/mdp/testdata/test1.md
```
# Test Markdown File

Just a test

## Bullets:
* Links [Link1](https://example.com)

## Code Block
```
some code
```
```

Now create the golden file test1.md.html in the testdata directory, and add the expected HTML to it:

workingFiles/mdp/testdata/test1.md.html
```
<!DOCTYPE html>
<html>
  <head>
    <meta http-equiv="content-type" content="text/html; charset=utf-8">
    <title>Markdown Preview Tool</title>
  </head>
  <body>
<h1>Test Markdown File</h1>

<p>Just a test</p>

<h2>Bullets:</h2>

<ul>
<li>Links <a href="https://example.com" rel="nofollow">Link1</a></li>
</ul>

<h2>Code Block</h2>

<pre><code>some code
</code></pre>

  </body>
</html>
```

Then create the test file main_test.go in the same directory as your main.go file.

```
$ cd $HOME/pragprog.com/rggo/workingFiles/mdp
```

Edit the main_test.go file, adding the code for defining the package name, the import section, and some constants that are used throughout the tests:

workingFiles/mdp/main_test.go
```
package main

import (
  "bytes"
  "io/ioutil"
  "os"
  "testing"
)

const (
  inputFile  = "./testdata/test1.md"
  resultFile = "test1.md.html"
  goldenFile = "./testdata/test1.md.html"
)
```

You use the following packages: bytes to manipulate raw byte data, ioutil to read data from files, and os package to delete files. You also define three constants with the name of the files you'll use in the tests.

Write the first test case to test the ParseContent() function, by adding this code into main_test.go:

workingFiles/mdp/main_test.go
```
func TestParseContent(t *testing.T) {
  input, err := ioutil.ReadFile(inputFile)
  if err != nil {
    t.Fatal(err)
  }

  result := parseContent(input)

  expected, err := ioutil.ReadFile(goldenFile)
  if err != nil {
    t.Fatal(err)
  }

  if !bytes.Equal(expected, result) {
    t.Logf("golden:\n%s\n", expected)
    t.Logf("result:\n%s\n", result)
    t.Error("Result content does not match golden file")
  }
}
```

This test reads the content of the input test file, parses it with parseContent(), and compares it with the expected result in the golden file by using the function bytes.Equal(), which compares two slices of bytes.

Now write the integrated test case that tests the run() function by adding this code:

```
workingFiles/mdp/main_test.go
func TestRun(t *testing.T) {
  if err := run(inputFile); err != nil {
    t.Fatal(err)
  }

  result, err := ioutil.ReadFile(resultFile)
  if err != nil {
    t.Fatal(err)
  }

  expected, err := ioutil.ReadFile(goldenFile)
  if err != nil {
    t.Fatal(err)
  }

  if !bytes.Equal(expected, result) {
    t.Logf("golden:\n%s\n", expected)
    t.Logf("result:\n%s\n", result)
    t.Error("Result content does not match golden file")
  }

  os.Remove(resultFile)
}
```

In this test case, we execute the run() function that generates the result file. We then read both the results and golden files and compare them using the bytes.Equal() function again. At the end, we clean up the result file using os.Remove().

Save the main_test.go file and execute the tests using the go test tool:

```
$ ls
go.mod   main.go   main_test.go   testdata
$ go test -v
=== RUN    TestParseContent
--- PASS: TestParseContent (0.00s)
=== RUN    TestRun
test1.md.html
--- PASS: TestRun (0.00s)
PASS
ok        pragprog.com/rggo/workingFiles/mdp        0.011s
```

Once all the tests pass, we're ready to try the Markdown preview tool. Let's first create a Markdown file like this:

workingFiles/mdp/README.md
```
# Example Markdown File

This is an example Markdown file to test the preview tool

## Features:
* Support for links [PragProg](https://pragprog.com)
* Support for other features

## How to install:
```

go get github.com/user/program
```
```

Try your *mdp* tool providing this Markdown file as input:

```
$ ls
go.mod   go.sum   main.go   main_test.go   README.md   testdata
$ go run main.go -file README.md
README.md.html
$ ls
go.mod   go.sum   main.go   main_test.go   README.md   README.md.html   testdata
$
```

The *mdp* tool created a file README.md.html with the following contents:

workingFiles/mdp/README.md.html
```
<!DOCTYPE html>
<html>
  <head>
    <meta http-equiv="content-type" content="text/html; charset=utf-8">
    <title>Markdown Preview Tool</title>
  </head>
  <body>
<h1>Example Markdown File</h1>

<p>This is an example Markdown file to test the preview tool</p>

<h2>Features:</h2>

<ul>
<li>Support for links <a href="https://pragprog.com"
                       rel="nofollow">PragProg</a></li>
<li>Support for other features</li>
</ul>

<h2>How to install:</h2>

<pre><code>go get github.com/user/program
</code></pre>

  </body>
</html>
```

Open this file in a web browser to preview your Markdown file, as shown in Figure 1.

Figure 1—mdp Preview

The *mdp* tool works as designed, but if you use it many times, it will create these HTML files all over your system. This isn't ideal, so let's address it next.

Adding Temporary Files to the Markdown Preview Tool

In its current version, the *mdp* tool creates an HTML file with the same name as the Markdown file in the current directory. This isn't ideal as these files can accumulate on your system or could cause a clash if two or more users are previewing the same file simultaneously.

To address this issue, let's make a change to the *mdp* tool to create and use temporary files instead of local files. The ioutil package provides a function TempFile() to create temporary files with a random name. This allows it to run safely concurrently because the file names will never clash.

The ioutil.TempFile() function takes two arguments. The first is the directory where you create the file. If left blank, it uses the system-defined temporary directory. The second argument is a pattern that helps generate file names that are easier to find if desired. To add this functionality to your tool, let's change the run() function.

First, delete the package path/filepath from your import section since you're no longer using the function filepath.Base() to extract the current file name.

```
"path/filepath"
```

Then, use the function ioutil.TempFile() to create the temporary file using the pattern mdp*.html. The function TempFile() replaces the * character with a random number, generating a random name with the *mdp* prefix and an *.html* extension. Check and return any errors. After creating the temporary file, use the temp.Close() method to close it as we're not writing any data to it at this point. Finally, assign the temporary file name to the variable outName so it can be passed to saveHTML() later:

```
workingFiles/mdp.v1/main.go
func run(filename string) error {
  // Read all the data from the input file and check for errors
  input, err := ioutil.ReadFile(filename)
  if err != nil {
    return err
  }

  htmlData := parseContent(input)

  // Create temporary file and check for errors
  temp, err := ioutil.TempFile("", "mdp*.html")
  if err != nil {
    return err
  }
  if err := temp.Close(); err != nil {
    return err
  }

  outName := temp.Name()

  fmt.Println(outName)

  return saveHTML(outName, htmlData)
}
```

This completes the updates to the run() function. Save the file main.go.

Try to run the tests again and notice that a test fails because it expects a specific output file name:

```
$ go test -v
=== RUN   TestParseContent
--- PASS: TestParseContent (0.00s)
=== RUN   TestRun
/tmp/mdp842610791.html
--- FAIL: TestRun (0.00s)
    main_test.go:39: open test1.md.html: no such file or directory
FAIL
exit status 1
FAIL    pragprog.com/rggo/workingFiles/mdp      0.008s
```

The new version generates the file name dynamically, so we need to update the TestRun() test case to handle this condition.

Using Interfaces to Automate Tests

Sometimes you need a way to test output printed out to STDOUT. In this instance, when executing the integration tests, by testing the run() function, the name of the output file is created dynamically. The function prints this value to the screen so the user can use the file, but to automate tests, we need to capture this output from within the test case.

In Go, the idiomatic way to deal with this situation is by using interfaces, in this case io.Writer, to make your code more flexible. For this pattern, we update the function run() so that it takes the interface as an input parameter. We do this so we can call run() with different types that implement the interface depending on the situation: for the program, we use os.Stdout to print the output onscreen; for the tests, we use bytes.Buffer to capture the output in a buffer that we can use in the test.

To start, include the io package in the import section in order to use the io.Writer interface:

workingFiles/mdp.v2/main.go
```go
import (
  "bytes"
  "flag"
  "fmt"

  "io"
  "io/ioutil"
  "os"

  "github.com/microcosm-cc/bluemonday"
  "github.com/russross/blackfriday/v2"
)
```

Next, update the function run() like this:

workingFiles/mdp.v2/main.go
```go
func run(filename string, out io.Writer) error {
  // Read all the data from the input file and check for errors
  input, err := ioutil.ReadFile(filename)
  if err != nil {
    return err
  }

  htmlData := parseContent(input)

  // Create temporary file and check for errors
  temp, err := ioutil.TempFile("", "mdp*.html")
  if err != nil {
    return err
  }
```

```
  if err := temp.Close(); err != nil {
    return err
  }

  outName := temp.Name()

➤ fmt.Fprintln(out, outName)

  return saveHTML(outName, htmlData)
}
```

We're updating the function run() to take the interface as a second input parameter as well as replacing the function fmt.Println() with fmt.Fprintln(). This function takes an interface as the first argument and prints the remaining arguments to that interface.

Lastly, update the function main() to pass os.Stdout when calling run() so it prints the output onscreen:

workingFiles/mdp.v2/main.go
```
func main() {
  // Parse flags
  filename := flag.String("file", "", "Markdown file to preview")
  flag.Parse()

  // If user did not provide input file, show usage
  if *filename == "" {
    flag.Usage()
    os.Exit(1)
  }

➤ if err := run(*filename, os.Stdout); err != nil {
    fmt.Fprintln(os.Stderr, err)
    os.Exit(1)
  }
}
```

Once the function run() has been changed, we can update the tests to use the io.Writer interface. First, delete the line where we hard-coded the file name as it's no longer needed:

```
resultFile = "test1.md.html"
```

Next, update the test case function TestRun() to use the bytes.Buffer to capture the output file name, and use it as the resultFile, like this:

workingFiles/mdp.v2/main_test.go
```
func TestRun(t *testing.T) {
➤   var mockStdOut bytes.Buffer
➤
➤   if err := run(inputFile, &mockStdOut); err != nil {
    t.Fatal(err)
  }
```

```
    resultFile := strings.TrimSpace(mockStdOut.String())

    result, err := ioutil.ReadFile(resultFile)
    if err != nil {
      t.Fatal(err)
    }

    expected, err := ioutil.ReadFile(goldenFile)
    if err != nil {
      t.Fatal(err)
    }

    if !bytes.Equal(expected, result) {
      t.Logf("golden:\n%s\n", expected)
      t.Logf("result:\n%s\n", result)
      t.Error("Result content does not match golden file")
    }

    os.Remove(resultFile)
}
```

We're defining the variable mockStdOut of type bytes.Buffer. We then pass its address, using the address operator &, as input to the run() call. This is necessary as the type bytes.Buffer satisfies the io.Writer interface using the pointer receiver. We get the value out of the buffer by using its String() method and the function TrimSpace() from the strings package to remove the newline character at the end of it.

Remember to add the package strings to the import section before using it:

```
workingFiles/mdp.v2/main_test.go
import (
  "bytes"
  "io/ioutil"
  "os"

  "strings"
  "testing"
)
```

Let's execute the tests now:

```
$ go test -v
=== RUN   TestParseContent
--- PASS: TestParseContent (0.00s)
=== RUN   TestRun
--- PASS: TestRun (0.00s)
PASS
ok      pragprog.com/rggo/workingFiles/mdp      0.009s
```

This time, all the tests pass. Go ahead and try the tool out:

```
$ go run main.go -file README.md
/tmp/mdp807323568.html
```

The tool created the file mdp807323568.html in the standard temporary directory, in this case /tmp. Your results may be different depending on your operating system. Open this file in the browser to see the same preview as before.

Next, you'll increase the level of automation by providing a feature to auto-preview the resulting file in a browser.

Adding an Auto-Preview Feature

At this moment, your tool isn't automating the entire process. It converts the Markdown to HTML, but the user still has to open it in a browser to see the results. While this is a valid approach, it would be nice for the user to be able to run the tool and automatically see the results. We're assuming that most users want this feature, but it's nice to provide an option to disable it in case they prefer to open the file at a different time. As part of this implementation, we'll add another flag -s (skip-preview) to skip the auto-preview. This option also helps with executing the tests by avoiding automatically opening the files in the browser for every test.

To preview the file in a browser, let's add another function to this program called preview(). This function takes the temporary file name as input and returns an error in case it can't open the file. Create this function by adding this code at the end of your main.go file:

```
workingFiles/mdp.v3/main.go
func preview(fname string) error {
  cName := ""
  cParams := []string{}

  // Define executable based on OS
  switch runtime.GOOS {
  case "linux":
    cName = "xdg-open"
  case "windows":
    cName = "cmd.exe"
    cParams = []string{"/C", "start"}
  case "darwin":
    cName = "open"
  default:
    return fmt.Errorf("OS not supported")
  }

  // Append filename to parameters slice
  cParams = append(cParams, fname)

  // Locate executable in PATH
  cPath, err := exec.LookPath(cName)
```

```go
  if err != nil {
    return err
  }

  // Open the file using default program
  return exec.Command(cPath, cParams...).Run()
}
```

The preview() function uses the os/exec package to execute a separate process—in this case, a command that opens a default application based on the given file, such as xdg-open on Linux or open on macOS. You'll learn about the os/exec package in detail in Chapter 6, Controlling Processes, on page 163. The function also uses the runtime package's constant GOOS to determine the executable program and parameters based on the current operating system. You'll explore adding operating system–dependent data in Including OS-Specific Data, on page 436. The preview() function uses exec.LookPath() to locate the executable in the $PATH and executes it, passing the extra parameters and the temporary file name as arguments.

Import the required packages by adding them to the import section, like this:

workingFiles/mdp.v3/main.go
```go
import (
    "bytes"
    "flag"
    "fmt"
    "io"
    "io/ioutil"
    "os"

    "os/exec"
    "runtime"


    "github.com/microcosm-cc/bluemonday"
    "github.com/russross/blackfriday/v2"
)
```

Change the function run() signature to take an additional parameter skipPreview of type bool to decide whether to skip the auto-preview:

workingFiles/mdp.v3/main.go
```go
func run(filename string, out io.Writer, skipPreview bool) error {
```

Modify the line that calls the function saveHTML() to check for the error instead of directly returning it as the function now continues to preview the file. Next, include the code to check if skipPreview is true, returning nil without calling preview(). Otherwise, call preview() and return its error:

```
workingFiles/mdp.v3/main.go
func run(filename string, out io.Writer, skipPreview bool) error {
  // Read all the data from the input file and check for errors
  input, err := ioutil.ReadFile(filename)
  if err != nil {
    return err
  }

  htmlData := parseContent(input)

  // Create temporary file and check for errors
  temp, err := ioutil.TempFile("", "mdp*.html")
  if err != nil {
    return err
  }
  if err := temp.Close(); err != nil {
    return err
  }

  outName := temp.Name()

  fmt.Fprintln(out, outName)

  if err := saveHTML(outName, htmlData); err != nil {
    return err
  }

  if skipPreview {
    return nil
  }

  return preview(outName)
}
```

Finally, update the function main() by including the new flag and passing its value to the call to the run() function:

```
workingFiles/mdp.v3/main.go
func main() {
  // Parse flags
  filename := flag.String("file", "", "Markdown file to preview")
  skipPreview := flag.Bool("s", false, "Skip auto-preview")
  flag.Parse()

  // If user did not provide input file, show usage
  if *filename == "" {
    flag.Usage()
    os.Exit(1)
  }

  if err := run(*filename, os.Stdout, *skipPreview); err != nil {
    fmt.Fprintln(os.Stderr, err)
    os.Exit(1)
  }
}
```

This completes the changes to the program. Before running the tests, update the call to the run() function in the TestRun() test case to skip previewing the file. Do this by setting the skipPreview argument to true in the main_test.go file:

workingFiles/mdp.v3/main_test.go
```
if err := run(inputFile, &mockStdOut, true); err != nil {
```

Execute the tests and ensure they all pass:

```
$ go test -v
=== RUN   TestParseContent
--- PASS: TestParseContent (0.00s)
=== RUN   TestRun
--- PASS: TestRun (0.00s)
PASS
ok      pragprog.com/rggo/workingFiles/mdp      0.009s
$
```

Build and execute the new tool and notice the preview file opening automatically in the browser.

```
$ go build -o mdp
$ ./mdp -file README.md
/tmp/mdp575058439.html
$
```

This is an improvement compared to the previous version, but it's still not ideal as the files can accumulate in the temporary directory now. Let's address it next.

Cleaning Up Temporary Files

Currently, our program doesn't clean up the temporary files because the method we used to create them doesn't automatically clean them up. As you can see, running the tool multiple times creates different files:

```
$ go run main.go -file README.md
/tmp/mdp552496404.html
$ go run main.go -file README.md
/tmp/mdp016541878.html
$ ls -ltr /tmp/ | grep mdp
-rw------- 1 ricardo users   503 Apr 15 10:25 mdp807323568.html
-rw------- 1 ricardo users   503 Apr 15 10:27 mdp552496404.html
-rw------- 1 ricardo users   503 Apr 15 10:31 mdp016541878.html
```

This is expected as the program can't assume how and when the files will be used. It's your responsibility to delete the temporary files to keep the system clean. In your program, you can use the function os.Remove() to delete the files when they're no longer needed. In general, you defer the call to this function using the defer statement to ensure the file is deleted when the current function returns.

Update the run() function to delete the file like this:

workingFiles/mdp.v4/main.go

```go
func run(filename string, out io.Writer, skipPreview bool) error {
  // Read all the data from the input file and check for errors
  input, err := ioutil.ReadFile(filename)
  if err != nil {
    return err
  }

  htmlData := parseContent(input)

  // Create temporary file and check for errors
  temp, err := ioutil.TempFile("", "mdp*.html")
  if err != nil {
    return err
  }
  if err := temp.Close(); err != nil {
    return err
  }

  outName := temp.Name()

  fmt.Fprintln(out, outName)

  if err := saveHTML(outName, htmlData); err != nil {
    return err
  }

  if skipPreview {
    return nil
  }

➤ defer os.Remove(outName)

  return preview(outName)
}
```

This is another benefit of using the run() function; since it returns a value, instead of relying on os.Exit() to exit the program, you can safely use the defer statement to clean up the resources. Be cautious when using os.Exit() to exit the program as it exits immediately, not running any of the deferred function calls.

By deleting the file automatically, you introduce a small race condition in the program: the browser may not have time to open the file before it gets deleted. You can solve this in different ways, but to keep things simple, add a small delay to the preview() function before it returns, allowing the browser time to open the file. First, import the time package:

workingFiles/mdp.v4/main.go

```go
import (
  "bytes"
  "flag"
  "fmt"
  "io"
  "io/ioutil"
  "os"
  "os/exec"
  "runtime"

➤  "time"

  "github.com/microcosm-cc/bluemonday"
  "github.com/russross/blackfriday/v2"
)
```

Then, add a two-second delay to preview() like this:

workingFiles/mdp.v4/main.go

```go
func preview(fname string) error {
  cName := ""
  cParams := []string{}

  // Define executable based on OS
  switch runtime.GOOS {
  case "linux":
    cName = "xdg-open"
  case "windows":
    cName = "cmd.exe"
    cParams = []string{"/C", "start"}
  case "darwin":
    cName = "open"
  default:
    return fmt.Errorf("OS not supported")
  }

  // Append filename to parameters slice
  cParams = append(cParams, fname)

  // Locate executable in PATH
  cPath, err := exec.LookPath(cName)
  if err != nil {
    return err
  }

  // Open the file using default program
➤  err = exec.Command(cPath, cParams...).Run()
➤
➤  // Give the browser some time to open the file before deleting it
➤  time.Sleep(2 * time.Second)
➤  return err
  }
```

Keep in mind that adding a delay isn't a recommended long-term solution. This is a quick fix so you can focus on the cleanup functionality. Once you've explored Handling Signals, on page 204, you can update this function to clean up resources using a signal. Or, after you've explored Chapter 8, Talking to REST APIs, on page 273, you can create a small web server that serves the file directly to the browser.

Execute the tests ensuring they all pass:

```
$ go test -v
=== RUN    TestParseContent
--- PASS: TestParseContent (0.00s)
=== RUN    TestRun
--- PASS: TestRun (0.00s)
PASS
ok       pragprog.com/rggo/workingFiles/mdp   0.009s
```

Build and execute the new tool and notice the preview file opening automatically in the browser as before. In addition, the file is automatically deleted from the temporary directory.

```
$ go build
$ ./mdp -file README.md
/tmp/mdp335221060.html
$ ls -l /tmp/mdp335221060.html
ls: cannot access '/tmp/mdp335221060.html': No such file or directory
```

Once your tool creates and deletes temporary files appropriately, you can take advantage of the fact that this is a command-line tool to do some fancy stuff. For example, on Linux/Unix-like systems, create this script to preview your Markdown file every time you change it:

workingFiles/mdp.v4/autopreview.sh
```bash
#! /bin/bash

FHASH=`md5sum $1`
while true; do
  NHASH=`md5sum $1`
  if [ "$NHASH" != "$FHASH" ]; then
    ./mdp -file $1
    FHASH=$NHASH
  fi
  sleep 5
done
```

This script receives the name of the file you want to preview as an argument. It calculates the checksum of this file every five seconds. If the result is different from the previous one, the content of the file was changed, triggering the execution of the *mdp* tool to preview it.

Make the script executable:

```
$ chmod +x autopreview.sh
```

Now run the script, providing the name of the file you want to watch:

```
$ ./autopreview.sh README.md
```

With the script running, change the README.md file in a text editor, save it, and notice how the browser automatically shows the preview file. When you're done, use Ctrl+C to stop the script.

Next, let's use Go's templating features to remove the hard-coded header and footer from the code, improving the tool's maintainability.

Improving the Markdown Preview Tool with Templates

As the final improvement to the *mdp* tool, you'll update the way it writes the final HTML file. You currently have the HTML header and footer hard-coded in the program. It's a good start, but it makes the tool less flexible and harder to maintain. To address this issue, use the html/template package to create a data-driven template that allows you to inject code at predefined places at runtime.

Templates are perfect in situations where you need to write files with some fixed content and you want to inject dynamic data at runtime. Go provides another template package called text/template, but you should use the html/template when writing HTML content. Both packages share a similar interface, so understanding one makes it easier to use the other.

Let's build an implementation that provides a hardcoded default template but also allows the user to specify their own alternate version using a command-line flag -t. By doing this, we allow users to change the preview format and appearance without changing the application code, increasing its flexibility and maintainability.

Start by adding the package html/template to the import list as usual:

workingFiles/mdp.v5/main.go
```
import (
  "bytes"
  "flag"
  "fmt"
  "io"

  "html/template"
  "io/ioutil"
  "os"
  "os/exec"
```

```
    "runtime"
    "time"

    "github.com/microcosm-cc/bluemonday"
    "github.com/russross/blackfriday/v2"
)
```

Then replace the definition of the constants header and footer with a default template. This is the template that you'll use if the user doesn't specify an alternate template file with command-line options.

```
workingFiles/mdp.v5/main.go
const (
  defaultTemplate = `<!DOCTYPE html>
<html>
  <head>
    <meta http-equiv="content-type" content="text/html; charset=utf-8">
    <title>{{ .Title }}</title>
  </head>
  <body>
{{ .Body }}
  </body>
</html>
`
)
```

In this template the two special constructs {{ .Title }} and {{ .Body }} are the placeholders for injecting the dynamic data. Define these fields in a custom struct of type content that you'll use later in the code:

```
workingFiles/mdp.v5/main.go
// content type represents the HTML content tto add into the template
type content struct {
  Title string
  Body  template.HTML
}
```

This struct type defines two fields with the same names you defined in the template earlier: Title of type string and Body of type template.HTML. You can use this type for the body as it contains preformatted HTML provided by the blackfriday library and sanitized by bluemonday. Since this HTML has been sanitized, you can trust it to pass as is. Never use this type with HTML from untrusted sources, as it could present a security risk.

Now update the parseContent() function to parse and execute the template. First, update the function signature to include another input parameter tFname of type string. This parameter represents an alternate template file to load if the user provided one. Also, include an error return parameter. Since the html/template can return an error, we need to pass it back to the calling function:

workingFiles/mdp.v5/main.go

```
func parseContent(input []byte, tFname string) ([]byte, error) {
```

Then parse the input Markdown data through blackfriday and bluemonday to generate the HTML body exactly like before:

workingFiles/mdp.v5/main.go

```
// Parse the markdown file through blackfriday and bluemonday
// to generate a valid and safe HTML
output := blackfriday.Run(input)
body := bluemonday.UGCPolicy().SanitizeBytes(output)
```

Next, use the template.New() function from the package html/template to create a new Template instance and parse the contents of the defaultTemplate constant using the Parse() method from the Template type. Check and return any errors:

workingFiles/mdp.v5/main.go

```
// Parse the contents of the defaultTemplate const into a new Template
t, err := template.New("mdp").Parse(defaultTemplate)
if err != nil {
  return nil, err
}
```

Now verify if the variable tFname contains the name of an alternate template file provided by the user. If so, replace the Template instance t with the contents of the template file parsed using the function template.ParseFiles(). Check and return any errors:

workingFiles/mdp.v5/main.go

```
// If user provided alternate template file, replace template
if tFname != "" {
  t, err = template.ParseFiles(tFname)
  if err != nil {
    return nil, err
  }
}
```

By using this approach, you always have the default template ready to execute, but you can replace it with a user-provided template when necessary.

Next, instantiate a new variable of type content with the predefined title and body. Force a conversion of the body to type template.HTML:

workingFiles/mdp.v5/main.go

```
// Instantiate the content type, adding the title and body
c := content{
  Title: "Markdown Preview Tool",
  Body:  template.HTML(body),
}
```

Define a variable buffer of type bytes.Buffer to store the template execution's result:

workingFiles/mdp.v5/main.go
```go
// Create a buffer of bytes to write to file
var buffer bytes.Buffer
```

Remove the block where you write data to the buffer directly as it's no longer required. You'll write data to the buffer by executing the template:

```go
// Write html to bytes buffer
buffer.WriteString(header)
buffer.Write(body)
buffer.WriteString(footer)
```

Then, use the method t.Execute(&buffer, c) of your newly defined template t to execute the template. This method injects the data from the variable c into the template and writes the results to the buffer:

workingFiles/mdp.v5/main.go
```go
// Execute the template with the content type
if err := t.Execute(&buffer, c); err != nil {
  return nil, err
}
```

Update the return statement to include value nil as the error return parameter, indicating the function completed successfully:

workingFiles/mdp.v5/main.go
```go
  return buffer.Bytes(), nil
}
```

Here's the complete new version of this function:

workingFiles/mdp.v5/main.go
```go
func parseContent(input []byte, tFname string) ([]byte, error) {
  // Parse the markdown file through blackfriday and bluemonday
  // to generate a valid and safe HTML
  output := blackfriday.Run(input)
  body := bluemonday.UGCPolicy().SanitizeBytes(output)

  // Parse the contents of the defaultTemplate const into a new Template
  t, err := template.New("mdp").Parse(defaultTemplate)
  if err != nil {
    return nil, err
  }

  // If user provided alternate template file, replace template
  if tFname != "" {
    t, err = template.ParseFiles(tFname)
```

```
    if err != nil {
      return nil, err
    }
  }

  // Instantiate the content type, adding the title and body
  c := content{
    Title: "Markdown Preview Tool",
    Body:  template.HTML(body),
  }

  // Create a buffer of bytes to write to file
  var buffer bytes.Buffer

  // Execute the template with the content type
  if err := t.Execute(&buffer, c); err != nil {
    return nil, err
  }

  return buffer.Bytes(), nil
}
```

Update the definition of the run() function so it accepts another string input parameter called tFname that will represent the name of an alternate template file:

workingFiles/mdp.v5/main.go

```
func run(filename, tFname string, out io.Writer, skipPreview bool) error {
```

Since the parseContent() function now also returns an error, update the run() function to handle this condition when calling parseContent(), like this:

workingFiles/mdp.v5/main.go

```
func run(filename, tFname string, out io.Writer, skipPreview bool) error {
  // Read all the data from the input file and check for errors
  input, err := ioutil.ReadFile(filename)
  if err != nil {
    return err
  }

➤ htmlData, err := parseContent(input, tFname)
➤ if err != nil {
➤   return err
➤ }

  // Create temporary file and check for errors
  temp, err := ioutil.TempFile("", "mdp*.html")
  if err != nil {
    return err
  }
  if err := temp.Close(); err != nil {
    return err
  }
```

```
  outName := temp.Name()

  fmt.Fprintln(out, outName)

  if err := saveHTML(outName, htmlData); err != nil {
    return err
  }

  if skipPreview {
    return nil
  }

  defer os.Remove(outName)

  return preview(outName)
}
```

Finally, update the function main() to include a new command-line flag -t which allows the user to provide an alternate template file. Assign it to the variable tFname and pass it to the run() function:

workingFiles/mdp.v5/main.go
```
func main() {
  // Parse flags
  filename := flag.String("file", "", "Markdown file to preview")
  skipPreview := flag.Bool("s", false, "Skip auto-preview")
➤ tFname := flag.String("t", "", "Alternate template name")
  flag.Parse()

  // If user did not provide input file, show usage
  if *filename == "" {
    flag.Usage()
    os.Exit(1)
  }

➤ if err := run(*filename, *tFname, os.Stdout, *skipPreview); err != nil {
    fmt.Fprintln(os.Stderr, err)
    os.Exit(1)
  }
}
```

The application code is complete. Save the main.go file and edit the file main_test.go to update the tests. Start by updating the test case TestParseContent(), passing an empty string as the tFname parameter to parseContent(). Also, handle the potential error returned by parseContent(), like this:

workingFiles/mdp.v5/main_test.go
```
func TestParseContent(t *testing.T) {
  input, err := ioutil.ReadFile(inputFile)
  if err != nil {
    t.Fatal(err)
  }

➤ result, err := parseContent(input, "")
```

```
➤   if err != nil {
➤     t.Fatal(err)
➤   }

    expected, err := ioutil.ReadFile(goldenFile)
    if err != nil {
      t.Fatal(err)
    }

    if !bytes.Equal(expected, result) {
      t.Logf("golden:\n%s\n", expected)
      t.Logf("result:\n%s\n", result)
      t.Error("Result content does not match golden file")
    }
  }
```

Then update the TestRun() test case by passing an empty string as the tFname parameter to the run function:

workingFiles/mdp.v5/main_test.go
```
if err := run(inputFile, "", &mockStdOut, true); err != nil {
```

For brevity, we're not adding a test case to test an alternate template file, but you should do so as an additional exercise.

Save the main_test.go file and execute the tests to ensure that they pass and your code works as expected:

```
$ go test -v
=== RUN    TestParseContent
--- PASS: TestParseContent (0.00s)
=== RUN    TestRun
--- PASS: TestRun (0.00s)
PASS
  ok        pragprog.com/rggo/workingFiles/mdp          0.014s
```

Now when you execute the tool, the result will be similar to the previous versions, but the header and footer are coming from the template. Executing the tool with the sample README.md file produces this HTML:

workingFiles/mdp.v5/mdpPreview.html
```
<!DOCTYPE html>
<html>
  <head>
    <meta http-equiv="content-type" content="text/html; charset=utf-8">
    <title>Markdown Preview Tool</title>
  </head>
  <body>
    <h1>Example Markdown File</h1>

<p>This is an example Markdown file to test the preview tool</p>

<h2>Features:</h2>
```

```
<ul>
<li>Support for links
        <a href="https://pragprog.com" rel="nofollow">PragProg</a></li>
<li>Support for other features</li>
</ul>

<h2>How to install:</h2>

<pre><code>go get github.com/user/program
</code></pre>

  </body>
</html>
```

Notice that the placeholders for the title and body have been replaced with actual content according to the definitions in your tool.

Since your tool allows the user to specify an alternate template file, they can control the HTML formatting without changing the program. Create a new template file called template-fmt.html.tmpl with the same content as the default template, but add this CSS snippet to change the <h1> headings to blue instead of black:

workingFiles/mdp.v5/template-fmt.html.tmpl
```
<!DOCTYPE html>
<html>
  <head>
    <meta http-equiv="content-type" content="text/html; charset=utf-8">
    <title>{{ .Title }}</title>
    <style>
      h1 {
        color: blue
      }
    </style>
  </head>
  <body>
    {{ .Body }}
  </body>
</html>
```

Execute the tool and verify that the first heading is displayed in blue:

```
$ go run main.go -file README.md -t template-fmt.html.tmpl
```

You'll see the output shown in Figure 2 on page 76.

Templates are a great resource for increasing the flexibility of your tools. You can use them in a variety of situations, and they are well-suited to write dynamic configuration files, web pages, emails, and more.

Example Markdown File

This is an example Markdown file to test the preview tool

Features:

- Support for links <u>PragProg</u>
- Support for other features

How to install:

```
go get github.com/user/program
```

Figure 2—mdp Preview Using Template

Exercises

Try the following exercises to apply and improve the skills you've learned:

- Go back to the example in Chapter 1, Your First Command-Line Program in Go, on page 1, and update the *wc* tool to read data from files in addition to STDIN.

- Update the *wc* tool to process multiple files.

- Update the *mdp* tool template by adding another field that shows the name of the file being previewed.

- Update the *mdp* tool allowing the user to specify a default template using an environment variable.

- Update the *mdp* tool allowing the user to provide the input Markdown via STDIN.

Wrapping Up

In this chapter, you used several packages and functions to work with files. You opened files for reading and writing, used temporary files, worked with templates, and used the defer statement to ensure resources are cleaned up. These skills allow you to create powerful CLIs tools.

To complement these concepts, in the next chapter, you'll work with directories and file system objects.

## CHAPTER 4

Navigating the File System

When you're developing your own command-line tools, you'll often need to interact with the file system, navigate around the directory tree, or perform actions on files or directories. When you're building a tool that's supposed to work on multiple platforms, you have to pay special attention to how you manipulate paths and file names to ensure your tool works appropriately no matter where it's run.

For example, Windows uses a backslash \ as a path separator, such as C:\WINDOWS\SYSTEM, while most variations of UNIX use the forward slash / instead, as in /usr/lib. In these scenarios, hard-coding paths and file names into the program can lead to errors or unexpected results.

To avoid these complications, Go provides the filepath package to manipulate paths, ensuring compatibility across different operating systems. You'll use this package to develop a command-line tool called *walk*, which crawls into file system directories looking for specific files. When the tool finds the files it's looking for, it can list, archive, or delete them. By developing this tool, you'll apply the skills required to handle file system objects in your own programs, such as creating directories, copying and deleting files, and handling logs and compressed files. You'll also end up with a useful tool that helps you back up and clean up file systems. You can use this tool manually, or even better, you can schedule it to run automatically by using a background job scheduler such as *cron*.

Developing a File System Crawler

The *walk* tool has two main goals: descending into a directory tree to look for files that match a specified criteria and executing an action on these files. Let's start this tool by implementing the search and filter functionality. The only action we will implement now is listing the files. This enables us to try the tool and ensure it's finding the correct files. You'll implement other actions such as delete and archive later.

This initial version accepts four command-line parameters:

- -root: The root of the directory tree to start the search. The default is the current directory.

- -list: List files found by the tool. When specified, no other actions will be executed.

- -ext: File extension to search. When specified, the tool will only match files with this extension.

- -size: Minimum file size in bytes. When specified, the tool will only match files whose size is larger than this value.

Start by creating the directory fileSystem/walk for your new command-line tool in your book's project directory:

```
$ mkdir -p $HOME/pragprog.com/rggo/fileSystem/walk
$ cd $HOME/pragprog.com/rggo/fileSystem/walk
```

Then, initialize the Go module for this project:

```
$ go mod init pragprog.com/rggo/fileSystem/walk
go: creating new go.mod: module pragprog.com/rggo/fileSystem/walk
```

For this example, instead of adding all the code to a single file, let's break the code into different files. As the code base grows, splitting it into separate files makes it easier to maintain and check in your version control repository. Note that we are not creating a new package. All the code is still part of the package main.

You can split your code in as many files as you want with no limit. Do what makes sense in terms of management according to your requirements. For this project, we'll have two files: main.go, which contains the main() and run() functions as entry point to your program; and actions.go, which contains the function for file actions such as filter, list, and delete. Later, we'll also add the corresponding test files: main_test.go and actions_test.go.

Create the file main.go and add the package definition and the import section:

fileSystem/walk/main.go
```
package main

import (
    "flag"
    "fmt"
    "io"
```

```
  "os"
  "path/filepath"
)
```

For this tool, we're using the following packages: flag to handle command-line flags, fmt to print formatted output, io to use the io.Writer interface, os to communicate with the operating system, and path/filepath to handle file paths appropriately across different operating systems.

Before creating the main() function, define a new custom type config. To code this tool, you'll use the same pattern you used in Creating a Basic Markdown Preview Tool, on page 45, with the coordinating function run() to allow testing. But as the list of parameters to run() will be long, it's a common practice to provide some of these arguments packaged in a custom type. Functions with too many positional parameters become hard for humans to read and are error-prone.

Define the custom type config like this:

fileSystem/walk/main.go
```
type config struct {
  // extenstion to filter out
  ext string
  // min file size
  size int64
  // list files
  list bool
}
```

Now, add the function main() including the definition of the initial flags:

fileSystem/walk/main.go
```
func main() {
  // Parsing command line flags
  root := flag.String("root", ".", "Root directory to start")
  // Action options
  list := flag.Bool("list", false, "List files only")
  // Filter options
  ext := flag.String("ext", "", "File extension to filter out")
  size := flag.Int64("size", 0, "Minimum file size")
  flag.Parse()
```

Then, create an instance of the config struct, associating each of its fields with the flag values, so we can use them as input for run() later:

fileSystem/walk/main.go
```
c := config{
  ext:  *ext,
  size: *size,
  list: *list,
}
```

Then, call the function run(), check for errors, and print the errors out to STDERR if any occur. You'll define this function shortly.

fileSystem/walk/main.go
```go
  if err := run(*root, os.Stdout, c); err != nil {
    fmt.Fprintln(os.Stderr, err)
    os.Exit(1)
  }
}
```

Now create the run() function. Its input parameters are root (a string representing the root directory to start the search), out of type io.Writer interface (representing the output destination), and cfg of custom type config (for the remaining optional parameters). By using the io.Writer interface as the output destination, you can print results to the STDOUT in the program and to a bytes.Buffer when testing, which makes it easier to verify the output.

fileSystem/walk/main.go
```go
func run(root string, out io.Writer, cfg config) error {
```

In the run() function, define the logic to descend into the directory identified by the flag root and find all the files and sub-directories under it. The package filepath provides a function named Walk() that does exactly that.

The filepath.Walk(root string, walkFn WalkFunc) function finds all files and directories under root executing the function walkFn to each of them. The function walkFn is a function of type filepath.WalkFunc defined with the signature func(path string, info os.FileInfo, err error) error, where the arguments represent:

1. path: A string representing the path of the file or directory currently processed by Walk().

2. info: Of type os.FileInfo containing metadata about the file or directory named by path, such as name, size, permissions, and others.

3. err: Of type error containing the error in case Walk() has an issue walking to that specific file or directory.

In Go, functions are first-class citizens, which means you can pass them as arguments to other functions. In this case, you'll pass an anonymous function as the walkFn parameter of function filepath.Walk(). You can do this by defining the anonymous function with the same signature as the filepath.WalkFunc type. This anonymous function has two main responsibilities: it filters out files according to the parameters provided to the tool, and it executes the required action on the other files. Add the following code to call the filepath.Walk() function:

```
fileSystem/walk/main.go
  return filepath.Walk(root,
    func(path string, info os.FileInfo, err error) error {
      if err != nil {
        return err
      }

      if filterOut(path, cfg.ext, cfg.size, info) {
        return nil
      }

      // If list was explicitly set, don't do anything else
      if cfg.list {
        return listFile(path, out)
      }

      // List is the default option if nothing else was set
      return listFile(path, out)
    })
}
```

In this function, you're checking to see if the provided error is not nil, which means that Walk() was unable to walk to this file or directory. The error is exposed this way so you can handle it appropriately. In this case, you return the error to the calling function, which effectively stops processing any other files. Then you call a function named filterOut(), which you'll create shortly. It defines whether the current file or directory should be filtered out. If so, the function returns nil, which skips the rest of the function making Walk() process the next file or directory. Finally, you're executing the action which, for now, is to list the name of the file onscreen by calling the function listFile() that you'll create later.

Now, define the two additional functions called by the anonymous function: filter() and listFile() in the actions.go file. Save the file main.go and open actions.go. Include the package definition and the import list:

```
fileSystem/walk/actions.go
package main

import (
  "fmt"
  "io"
  "os"
  "path/filepath"
)
```

The filterOut() function checks if the given path has to be filtered out from the results according to the following conditions: the path points to a directory, the file size is less than the minimum size provided by the user, or the file extension doesn't match the extension provided by the user. This function returns a bool value indicating whether to filter out and ignore the current path. Implement this function by adding the following code to your actions.go file:

```
func filterOut(path, ext string, minSize int64, info os.FileInfo) bool {
  if info.IsDir() || info.Size() < minSize {
    return true
  }

  if ext != "" && filepath.Ext(path) != ext {
    return true
  }
  return false
}
```

In this function, you're using the argument info of type os.FileInfo to evaluate some metadata about the file or directory identified by path. The info.IsDir() function returns whether this is a directory while the info.Size() returns the file size in bytes, which you use to compare to the minimum size minSize provided as an argument to this function.

Finally, if the function received a value for the ext argument, you're using the filepath.Ext() function to extract the extension of the file and compare it to the ext argument.

The last piece for the initial version of this tool is the action that will be executed, in this case, listing the file path. Implement the listFile() function like this:

```
func listFile(path string, out io.Writer) error {
  _, err := fmt.Fprintln(out, path)
  return err
}
```

This function prints out the path of the current file to the specified io.Writer returning any potential error from that operation. Note that we're using the special *blank identifier* character _ to discard the first value returned from the fmt.Fprintln() function as we're not interested in the number of bytes written.

Save the file actions.go. Next, let's write some tests for this tool using the *table-driven testing* pattern.

Testing with Table-Driven Testing

When you're writing tests for your command-line tool, you often want to write test cases that cover different variations of the function or tool usage. By doing this, you ensure that the different parts of your code are working, increasing the reliability of your tests and tool. For example, to test the filterOut() function from the *walk* tool, it's a good idea to define test cases for the different conditions such as filtering with or without extension, matching or not, and minimum size.

One of the benefits of Go is that you can use Go itself to write test cases. You don't need a different language or external frameworks. By leveraging Go, you use all the language's features to help define your test cases. A common pattern for writing test cases that cover different variations of the function you're testing is known as *table-driven testing*. In this type of testing, you define your test cases as a slice of anonymous struct, containing the data required to run your tests and the expected results. You then iterate over this slice using loops to execute all test cases without repeating code. The Go testing package provides a convenient function Run() that runs a subtest with the specified name. Let's use this approach to test this version of the tool.

Create a new file called actions_test.go in the same directory as your actions.go file. Add the package definition and the import statement at the top of this file:

```
fileSystem/walk/actions_test.go
package main

import (
  "os"
  "testing"
)
```

You'll use the package os to handle file details; and the testing package that provides functions required to test your Go code.

Now, create a test function to test the filterOut() function.

```
fileSystem/walk/actions_test.go
func TestFilterOut(t *testing.T) {
```

Add the anonymous slice of struct with the definition of the test cases. The struct fields represent the values that we'll use for each test such as the test's name, file to read, extension to filter, minimum file size, and the expected test result:

```
fileSystem/walk/actions_test.go
testCases := []struct {
  name     string
  file     string
  ext      string
  minSize  int64
  expected bool
}{
```

```
{"FilterNoExtension", "testdata/dir.log", "", 0, false},
{"FilterExtensionMatch", "testdata/dir.log", ".log", 0, false},
{"FilterExtensionNoMatch", "testdata/dir.log", ".sh", 0, true},
{"FilterExtensionSizeMatch", "testdata/dir.log", ".log", 10, false},
{"FilterExtensionSizeNoMatch", "testdata/dir.log", ".log", 20, true},
}
```

Each element of the slice represents a test case. For example, the first test case's name is "FilterNoExtension". This uses the file testdata/dir.log, the extension to filter is blank, the minimum size is zero, and we expect this test to return the Boolean value false. This is similar for the remaining test cases, each with different values.

Once you have the test cases defined, add the for loop to iterate over each test case. For each case, call the t.Run() method, providing the test name as the first parameter and an anonymous function of type func(t *testing.T) as the second parameter. Inside the anonymous function run the tests using the test case attributes defined before:

fileSystem/walk/actions_test.go
```
for _, tc := range testCases {
  t.Run(tc.name, func(t *testing.T) {
    info, err := os.Stat(tc.file)
    if err != nil {
      t.Fatal(err)
    }

    f := filterOut(tc.file, tc.ext, tc.minSize, info)

    if f != tc.expected {
      t.Errorf("Expected '%t', got '%t' instead\n", tc.expected, f)
    }
  })
}
}
```

For these tests, you first retrieve the file's attributes using the function os.Stat(). Then execute the filterOut() function providing these attributes and the test case parameters. Finally, compare the result with the expected result from the test case, failing the test if they don't match.

Now, let's add the integration test cases. Save the file actions_test.go, create a file main_test.go, and edit it. Include the package definition and the import list:

fileSystem/walk/main_test.go
```
package main

import (
  "bytes"
  "testing"
)
```

You'll use the package bytes to manipulate slices of bytes (such as the output of the tool) and the testing package that provides functions required to test your Go code.

Follow the same approach to test variations of the integration tests. Start by defining the test cases using the anonymous struct, followed by the loop to test each case. The main difference is that you use the run() function defined in main.go instead of the function filterOut(). Write the integration tests:

```
fileSystem/walk/main_test.go
func TestRun(t *testing.T) {
  testCases := []struct {
    name      string
    root      string
    cfg       config
    expected string
  }{
    {name: "NoFilter", root: "testdata",
      cfg:       config{ext: "", size: 0, list: true},
      expected: "testdata/dir.log\ntestdata/dir2/script.sh\n"},
    {name: "FilterExtensionMatch", root: "testdata",
      cfg:       config{ext: ".log", size: 0, list: true},
      expected: "testdata/dir.log\n"},
    {name: "FilterExtensionSizeMatch", root: "testdata",
      cfg:       config{ext: ".log", size: 10, list: true},
      expected: "testdata/dir.log\n"},
    {name: "FilterExtensionSizeNoMatch", root: "testdata",
      cfg:       config{ext: ".log", size: 20, list: true},
      expected: ""},
    {name: "FilterExtensionNoMatch", root: "testdata",
      cfg:       config{ext: ".gz", size: 0, list: true},
      expected: ""},
  }

  for _, tc := range testCases {
    t.Run(tc.name, func(t *testing.T) {
      var buffer bytes.Buffer

      if err := run(tc.root, &buffer, tc.cfg); err != nil {
        t.Fatal(err)
      }

      res := buffer.String()

      if tc.expected != res {
        t.Errorf("Expected %q, got %q instead\n", tc.expected, res)
      }
    })
  }
}
```

Save the main_test.go file and use a terminal to create the files required for testing. We need to create the directory containing the files we defined in the test cases earlier. We will use Go's convention and name this directory testdata, similarly to what we did in Writing Tests for the Markdown Preview Tool, on page 51, so that the Go build tool ignores it when compiling the program.

```
$ mkdir -p testdata/dir2
$ echo "Just a test" > testdata/dir.log
$ touch testdata/dir2/script.sh
$ tree testdata
testdata
├── dir2
│   └── script.sh
└── dir.log

1 directory, 2 files
```

Execute the tests using the go test -v tool:

```
$ go test -v
=== RUN    TestFilterOut
=== RUN    TestFilterOut/FilterNoExtension
=== RUN    TestFilterOut/FilterExtensionMatch
=== RUN    TestFilterOut/FilterExtensionNoMatch
=== RUN    TestFilterOut/FilterExtensionSizeMatch
=== RUN    TestFilterOut/FilterExtensionSizeNoMatch
--- PASS: TestFilterOut (0.00s)
    --- PASS: TestFilterOut/FilterNoExtension (0.00s)
    --- PASS: TestFilterOut/FilterExtensionMatch (0.00s)
    --- PASS: TestFilterOut/FilterExtensionNoMatch (0.00s)
    --- PASS: TestFilterOut/FilterExtensionSizeMatch (0.00s)
    --- PASS: TestFilterOut/FilterExtensionSizeNoMatch (0.00s)
=== RUN    TestRun
=== RUN    TestRun/NoFilter
=== RUN    TestRun/FilterExtensionMatch
=== RUN    TestRun/FilterExtensionSizeMatch
=== RUN    TestRun/FilterExtensionSizeNoMatch
=== RUN    TestRun/FilterExtensionNoMatch
--- PASS: TestRun (0.00s)
    --- PASS: TestRun/NoFilter (0.00s)
    --- PASS: TestRun/FilterExtensionMatch (0.00s)
    --- PASS: TestRun/FilterExtensionSizeMatch (0.00s)
    --- PASS: TestRun/FilterExtensionSizeNoMatch (0.00s)
    --- PASS: TestRun/FilterExtensionNoMatch (0.00s)
PASS
ok      pragprog.com/rggo/fileSystem/walk        0.005s
```

Notice that Go executes all test cases for each test function, using the test name you configured to present the results. This makes it easier to reference each test and troubleshoot them in case a test doesn't pass.

Since the tool is passing all tests, let's try it out. First, create a small directory tree in the /tmp directory that you can explore with your program. This structure will contain some *.txt* files and some *.log* files:

```
$ mkdir -p /tmp/testdir/{text,logs}
$ touch /tmp/testdir/file1.txt
$ touch /tmp/testdir/text/{text1,text2,text3}.txt
$ touch /tmp/testdir/logs/{log1,log2,log3}.log
$ ls /tmp/testdir/
file1.txt  logs  text
```

Now try your command-line tool, providing the -root parameter set to the newly created /tmp/testdir:

```
$ go run . -root /tmp/testdir/
/tmp/testdir/file1.txt
/tmp/testdir/logs/log1.log
/tmp/testdir/logs/log2.log
/tmp/testdir/logs/log3.log
/tmp/testdir/text/text1.txt
/tmp/testdir/text/text2.txt
/tmp/testdir/text/text3.txt
```

All the files in the specified directory tree are listed. You can display only log files by providing the *.log* extension to the -ext parameter, like this:

```
$ go run . -root /tmp/testdir/ -ext .log
/tmp/testdir/logs/log1.log
/tmp/testdir/logs/log2.log
/tmp/testdir/logs/log3.log
$
```

You can also filter results based on the file size, but I'll leave that as an exercise for you to do later.

This initial version of the tool lists all the files in a directory tree, but listing the names isn't useful. So we'll add another action to make this tool more useful.

Deleting Matched Files

Let's make the *walk* tool a little more useful by adding the ability to delete the files it finds. To do this, you'll add another action to the tool and a new flag del of type bool, allowing the user to enable file deletion.

Learning how to write code that deletes files is an important aspect of creating tools that work with files and perform system administration tasks, but it comes with the risk that you might accidentally delete files you didn't intend to delete. Make sure that your code is correct to prevent the accidental deletion of files on your computer. Never run this code as a privileged user, as it could cause loss of data or damage to your operating system's files.

Let's add another action function called delFile() to the file actions.go. This function receives one argument: the file path to be deleted. It returns a potential error that can occur when deleting the file. In the function's body, call the Remove() function from the os package to delete the file. Return the potential error from os.Remove() directly as the return value of your function. If os.Remove() fails to delete the file, its error will bubble up, stopping the tool's execution and showing the error message to the user. Define the function delFile() like this:

```
fileSystem/walk.v1/actions.go
func delFile(path string) error {
  return os.Remove(path)
}
```

Save the file actions.go and open the file main.go to use the delFile() function. Start by including the new flag. Add the following line into your main() function:

```
fileSystem/walk.v1/main.go
// Parsing command line flags
root := flag.String("root", ".", "Root directory to start")
// Action options
list := flag.Bool("list", false, "List files only")
➤ del := flag.Bool("del", false, "Delete files")
// Filter options
ext := flag.String("ext", "", "File extension to filter out")
```

Then, update the config struct to include a new field for the delete option:

```
fileSystem/walk.v1/main.go
type config struct {
  // extenstion to filter out
  ext string
  // min file size
  size int64
  // list files
  list bool
➤ // delete files
➤ del bool
}
```

Now, update the config instance c, mapping the field del to the flag value so that it's passed to run():

```
fileSystem/walk.v1/main.go
c := config{
  ext:  *ext,
  size: *size,
  list: *list,
```

➤   del: *del,
    }

Now, in the anonymous walkFn() function call, check if the variable cfg.del is set, and, if so, call the delFile() function to delete the file.

fileSystem/walk.v1/main.go
```
// If list was explicitly set, don't do anything else
if cfg.list {
  return listFile(path, out)
}
```
➤ `// Delete files`
➤ `if cfg.del {`
➤ `  return delFile(path)`
➤ `}`
```
// List is the default option if nothing else was set
```

Save the file to complete the updates. Let's update the test file to test the new functionality.

Testing with the Help of Test Helpers

When you wrote the integration tests for the list functionality, you used the testdata directory and a set of files to support your test cases. This procedure works well when the directory structure doesn't change. But if you want to test file deletion, this may not be the best option because the files will be deleted after the first test, and you would have to keep creating them for every test run.

Instead, automate the creation and cleanup of the test directory and files for every test. In Go, you accomplish this by writing a test helper function and calling this function from within each test. A test helper function is similar to other functions, but you explicitly mark it as a test helper by calling the method t.Helper() from the package testing. For example, when printing line and file information, if the helper function fails with t.Fatal(), Go prints the line in the test function that called the helper function, instead of within the helper function. This helps with troubleshooting test errors, particularly if the helper function is called many times by different tests.

It's also important to clean up after your tests. Cleaning up prevents wasting system resources and ensures that previous tests artifacts don't impact future tests. To clean up after these tests, your test helper function will return a cleanup function that the caller can defer executing until after the tests finish. If you're using Go 1.14 or later, you can also use the method t.Cleanup() to register a cleanup function instead of returning one. For more information consult Go's testing documentation.[1]

Let's add a helper function to the main_test.go file to create the directory structure to test file deletion. Before writing the function, add some more packages to the import list so that you can use them when writing the helper function. You'll use fmt to format strings, ioutil to create files, os to interface with the operating system, and path/filepath to process path definition in a multiplatform fashion. Open the main_test.go file and add these packages to the import list:

fileSystem/walk.v1/main_test.go
```
import (
    "bytes"
➤   "fmt"
➤   "io/ioutil"
➤   "os"
➤   "path/filepath"
➤
    "testing"
)
```

Add the helper function definition at the end of the file. This function takes two parameters: a pointer of type testing.T for calling testing-related functions and files of type map[string]int for defining the number of files this function will create for each extension. The function returns two values: the directory name of the created directory, so you can use it during testing, and the cleanup function cleanup of type func().

fileSystem/walk.v1/main_test.go
```
func createTempDir(t *testing.T,
    files map[string]int) (dirname string, cleanup func()) {
```

Mark this function as a test helper by calling the t.Helper() method:

fileSystem/walk.v1/main_test.go
```
t.Helper()
```

Next, create the temporary directory using the ioutil.TempDir() function, with the prefix walktest:

fileSystem/walk.v1/main_test.go
```
tempDir, err := ioutil.TempDir("", "walktest")
if err != nil {
    t.Fatal(err)
}
```

---

1. pkg.go.dev/testing#T.Cleanup

Iterate over the files map, creating the specified number of dummy files for each provided extension:

fileSystem/walk.v1/main_test.go
```
for k, n := range files {
  for j := 1; j <= n; j++ {
    fname := fmt.Sprintf("file%d%s", j, k)
    fpath := filepath.Join(tempDir, fname)
    if err := ioutil.WriteFile(fpath, []byte("dummy"), 0644); err != nil {
      t.Fatal(err)
    }
  }
}
```

Notice that we're using the filepath.Join() function to join the temporary directory name with the file name in order to have the full path in accordance with the target operating system's rules. We use this path to create the dummy file using the ioutil.WriteFile() function.

Finally, complete this function by returning the temporary directory name tempDir and an anonymous function which, when called, executes os.RemoveAll() to completely remove the temporary directory.

fileSystem/walk.v1/main_test.go
```
  return tempDir, func() { os.RemoveAll(tempDir) }
}
```

With the helper in place, add the test to ensure the deletion feature works. This function will be similar to the one you wrote to test the list feature. You could even update the original TestRun() function to include additional cases, but since this is a different functionality, you'll create a separate function with the specific deletion test cases. This keeps the test logic less complex, making it easier to manage the tests.

In the main_test.go file, add the definition for the new test function TestRunDelExtension() and the anonymous struct with the test cases:

fileSystem/walk.v1/main_test.go
```
func TestRunDelExtension(t *testing.T) {
  testCases := []struct {
    name        string
    cfg         config
    extNoDelete string
    nDelete     int
    nNoDelete   int
    expected    string
  }{
    {name: "DeleteExtensionNoMatch",
      cfg:       config{ext: ".log", del: true},
```

```
      extNoDelete: ".gz", nDelete: 0, nNoDelete: 10,
      expected: ""},
    {name: "DeleteExtensionMatch",
      cfg:           config{ext: ".log", del: true},
      extNoDelete: "", nDelete: 10, nNoDelete: 0,
      expected: ""},
    {name: "DeleteExtensionMixed",
      cfg:           config{ext: ".log", del: true},
      extNoDelete: ".gz", nDelete: 5, nNoDelete: 5,
      expected: ""},
  }
```

Next, iterate over each test case as before, executing the tests with t.Run(). The main difference is that in this case, we will call the helper function to create the temporary directory and files:

fileSystem/walk.v1/main_test.go
```go
// Execute RunDel test cases
for _, tc := range testCases {
  t.Run(tc.name, func(t *testing.T) {
    var buffer bytes.Buffer

    tempDir, cleanup := createTempDir(t, map[string]int{
      tc.cfg.ext:       tc.nDelete,
      tc.extNoDelete: tc.nNoDelete,
    })
    defer cleanup()
```

Notice that we're also deferring the call to cleanup(), which is the function returned from the helper's call. This ensures that it gets executed at the end of the test, cleaning up the temporary directory.

Then, call the run() function by passing the temporary directory path tempDir as input, and check the output, failing the test if it doesn't match the expected value:

fileSystem/walk.v1/main_test.go
```go
if err := run(tempDir, &buffer, tc.cfg); err != nil {
  t.Fatal(err)
}

res := buffer.String()

if tc.expected != res {
  t.Errorf("Expected %q, got %q instead\n", tc.expected, res)
}
```

Finally, read the files that were left in the directory after the delete operation by using the ioutil.ReadDir() function on the temporary test directory. Compare the number of files left with the expected number, failing the test if they don't match.

```
fileSystem/walk.v1/main_test.go
      filesLeft, err := ioutil.ReadDir(tempDir)
      if err != nil {
        t.Error(err)
      }

      if len(filesLeft) != tc.nNoDelete {
        t.Errorf("Expected %d files left, got %d instead\n",
          tc.nNoDelete, len(filesLeft))
      }
    })
  }
}
```

Save the file and execute the tests:

```
$ go test -v
=== RUN    TestFilterOut
=== RUN    TestFilterOut/FilterNoExtension
=== RUN    TestFilterOut/FilterExtensionMatch
=== RUN    TestFilterOut/FilterExtensionNoMatch
=== RUN    TestFilterOut/FilterExtensionSizeMatch
=== RUN    TestFilterOut/FilterExtensionSizeNoMatch
--- PASS: TestFilterOut (0.00s)
    --- PASS: TestFilterOut/FilterNoExtension (0.00s)
    --- PASS: TestFilterOut/FilterExtensionMatch (0.00s)
    --- PASS: TestFilterOut/FilterExtensionNoMatch (0.00s)
    --- PASS: TestFilterOut/FilterExtensionSizeMatch (0.00s)
    --- PASS: TestFilterOut/FilterExtensionSizeNoMatch (0.00s)
=== RUN    TestRun
=== RUN    TestRun/NoFilter
=== RUN    TestRun/FilterExtensionMatch
=== RUN    TestRun/FilterExtensionSizeMatch
=== RUN    TestRun/FilterExtensionSizeNoMatch
=== RUN    TestRun/FilterExtensionNoMatch
--- PASS: TestRun (0.00s)
    --- PASS: TestRun/NoFilter (0.00s)
    --- PASS: TestRun/FilterExtensionMatch (0.00s)
    --- PASS: TestRun/FilterExtensionSizeMatch (0.00s)
    --- PASS: TestRun/FilterExtensionSizeNoMatch (0.00s)
    --- PASS: TestRun/FilterExtensionNoMatch (0.00s)
=== RUN    TestRunDelExtension
=== RUN    TestRunDelExtension/DeleteExtensionNoMatch
=== RUN    TestRunDelExtension/DeleteExtensionMatch
=== RUN    TestRunDelExtension/DeleteExtensionMixed
--- PASS: TestRunDelExtension (0.00s)
    --- PASS: TestRunDelExtension/DeleteExtensionNoMatch (0.00s)
    --- PASS: TestRunDelExtension/DeleteExtensionMatch (0.00s)
    --- PASS: TestRunDelExtension/DeleteExtensionMixed (0.00s)
PASS
ok      pragprog.com/rggo/fileSystem/walk        0.006s
```

Once all tests are passing, you can try this version of the tool.

Be Careful When Deleting Files

 Be careful when trying this tool on your system. The files will be deleted without any prompt or user confirmation.

Never run this tool as a privileged user such as *root* or *Administrator* because it can cause irreversible damage to your system.

Let's try this new functionality in the same /tmp/testdir directory tree you created in Developing a File System Crawler, on page 77. Suppose you want to delete all the log files under that directory. First, run the tool with the list flag and ext set to .log to list all log files:

```
$ go run . -root /tmp/testdir/ -ext .log -list
/tmp/testdir/logs/log1.log
/tmp/testdir/logs/log2.log
/tmp/testdir/logs/log3.log
```

This directory tree has three log files. Delete them using the del flag:

```
$ go run . -root /tmp/testdir/ -ext .log -del
```

The tool doesn't display anything while deleting the files. You can confirm that the log files have been deleted by running the tool again and listing all files under that directory:

```
$ go run . -root /tmp/testdir/ -list
/tmp/testdir/file1.txt
/tmp/testdir/text/text1.txt
/tmp/testdir/text/text2.txt
/tmp/testdir/text/text3.txt
```

With command-line tools, it's a good idea to provide constant feedback to the user so they know that the tool is working. Let's do that next.

Logging Deleted Files

Command-line tools can be executed interactively by a user, but they are often used as part of a larger script that coordinates several other tasks to automate a process. In both cases, it's a good idea to provide constant feedback so the user or script knows that the tool is doing some work and it hasn't hung unexpectedly.

In general, you use STDOUT to provide feedback to the user onscreen. For scripts or tools that are executed in the background, such as a batch job, it's useful to provide feedback in log files so the user can verify them later.

Go's standard library provides the log package to facilitate logging information. By default, it will log information to STDERR, but you can configure it to log to a file instead. In addition to writing out the message, the logger automatically adds the date and time to each log entry. You can also configure it to add a prefix string to each entry which helps improve searchability.

Let's update the *walk* tool to log deleted files using this package.

Begin by updating the imports section in the file actions.go, adding the log package:

fileSystem/walk.v2/actions.go
```go
import (
    "fmt"
    "io"

    "log"
    "os"
    "path/filepath"
)
```

Next, update the delFile() function so it accepts an additional argument called delLogger, which is a pointer to log.Logger. Use this logger in the body of the function to log information about the deleted file if the delete operation completed without errors:

fileSystem/walk.v2/actions.go
```go
func delFile(path string, delLogger *log.Logger) error {
    if err := os.Remove(path); err != nil {
        return err
    }

    delLogger.Println(path)
    return nil
}
```

Now, save the actions.go file and open main.go. Add the log package to its import list as well:

fileSystem/walk.v2/main.go
```go
import (
    "flag"
    "fmt"
    "io"

    "log"
    "os"
    "path/filepath"
)
```

Then, add another field wLog of type io.Writer to the config struct. This field represents the log destination. By using the io.Writer interface here, we make our code flexible, accepting a file in the main program or a buffer that we can use while testing the tool.

fileSystem/walk.v2/main.go
```go
type config struct {
  // extenstion to filter out
  ext string
  // min file size
  size int64
  // list files
  list bool
  // delete files
  del bool
➤ // log destination writer
➤ wLog io.Writer
}
```

Next, update the main() function. First, add a new command-line flag to the tool, allowing the user to specify a log file name, like this:

fileSystem/walk.v2/main.go
```go
// Parsing command line flags
root := flag.String("root", ".", "Root directory to start")
➤ logFile := flag.String("log", "", "Log deletes to this file")
// Action options
list := flag.Bool("list", false, "List files only")
del := flag.Bool("del", false, "Delete files")
```

The default value for this flag is an empty string so if the user doesn't provide a name, the program will send output to STDOUT.

Then, check whether the user provided a value for this flag. If so, open the file for writing by using these parameters with the os.OpenFile() function:

- *logFile: The name of the log file as provided by the user. Remember to dereference it using the operator * as flags are pointers.

- os.O_APPEND: Enables data to be appended to the end of the file in case it already exists.

- os.O_CREATE: Creates the file in case it doesn't exist.

- os.O_RDWR: Opens the file for reading and writing.

- 0644: Permissions for the file in case it's created.

```
fileSystem/walk.v2/main.go
var (
  f   = os.Stdout
  err error
)

if *logFile != "" {
  f, err = os.OpenFile(*logFile, os.O_APPEND|os.O_CREATE|os.O_RDWR, 0644)
  if err != nil {
    fmt.Fprintln(os.Stderr, err)
    os.Exit(1)
  }
  defer f.Close()
}
```

The os.OpenFile() function returns a value f of type os.File that implements the io.Writer interface, which means you can use it as the value for the wLog field in the config struct.

Notice that by adding this block of code in the function main() we aren't able to test it. But it allows us to have the run() function receive an io.Writer interface which makes it easier to test the logging functionality. This is a good trade-off since this block of code is opening a file using the standard library functionality which has already been tested by the Go team. If you require this block to be tested, you can follow other testing approaches as previously presented.

Now, complete the updates to the function main() by mapping the variable f to the field wLog in the config instance c that's passed to run():

```
fileSystem/walk.v2/main.go
c := config{
  ext:  *ext,
  size: *size,
  list: *list,
  del:  *del,
➤ wLog: f,
}
```

Next, update the run() function. Create a new instance of log.Logger by using the function log.New() from the log package:

```
fileSystem/walk.v2/main.go
func run(root string, out io.Writer, cfg config) error {
➤  delLogger := log.New(cfg.wLog, "DELETED FILE: ", log.LstdFlags)

   return filepath.Walk(root,
```

In this call, we're creating the log.Logger instance to log deleted files to the provided io.Writer interface instance cfg.wLog. We're also adding the prefix *DELETED FILE:* to every log line allowing users to use other tools—such as *grep*—to search for them. Finally, we're specifying the constant log.LstdFlags as the third parameter to create the log.Logger instance using default log flags, such as date and time.

Finally, pass the delLogger instance as the second parameter to the new delFile() function:

fileSystem/walk.v2/main.go
```
if cfg.list {
  return listFile(path, out)
}

// Delete files
if cfg.del {
  return delFile(path, delLogger)
}

// List is the default option if nothing else was set
```

You're done with the code updates. Save the main.go file. Let's update the test cases now to include tests for the logging functionality.

Open the file main_test.go, and update the test function TestRunDelExtension() to verify that logging works.

In the body of the subtest execution function t.Run(), define a new variable called logBuffer of type bytes.Buffer that you'll use to capture the log as it implements the interface io.Writer:

fileSystem/walk.v2/main_test.go
```
var (
  buffer    bytes.Buffer
  logBuffer bytes.Buffer
)
```

Assign the address of the logBuffer variable to the wLog field of the test case config instance tc.cfg.wLog. This is the config instance that you'll pass as input to run().

fileSystem/walk.v2/main_test.go
```
tc.cfg.wLog = &logBuffer
```

Finally, at the end of the function, add the code to verify the log output. Since the program adds a log line for each deleted file, we can count the number of lines in the log output and compare it to the number of deleted files plus one for the final new line added to the end. If they don't match, the test fails. To count the lines, use the bytes.Split() function passing the newline character

\n as an argument. This function outputs a slice so you can use the built-in len() function to obtain its length.

fileSystem/walk.v2/main_test.go

```go
    expLogLines := tc.nDelete + 1
    lines := bytes.Split(logBuffer.Bytes(), []byte("\n"))
    if len(lines) != expLogLines {
      t.Errorf("Expected %d log lines, got %d instead\n",
        expLogLines, len(lines))
    }
  })
 }
}
```

Save the file and run the tests to ensure the code is working properly:

```
$ go test -v
=== RUN    TestFilterOut
=== RUN    TestFilterOut/FilterNoExtension
=== RUN    TestFilterOut/FilterExtensionMatch
=== RUN    TestFilterOut/FilterExtensionNoMatch
=== RUN    TestFilterOut/FilterExtensionSizeMatch
=== RUN    TestFilterOut/FilterExtensionSizeNoMatch
--- PASS: TestFilterOut (0.00s)
    --- PASS: TestFilterOut/FilterNoExtension (0.00s)
    --- PASS: TestFilterOut/FilterExtensionMatch (0.00s)
    --- PASS: TestFilterOut/FilterExtensionNoMatch (0.00s)
    --- PASS: TestFilterOut/FilterExtensionSizeMatch (0.00s)
    --- PASS: TestFilterOut/FilterExtensionSizeNoMatch (0.00s)
=== RUN    TestRun
=== RUN    TestRun/NoFilter
=== RUN    TestRun/FilterExtensionMatch
=== RUN    TestRun/FilterExtensionSizeMatch
=== RUN    TestRun/FilterExtensionSizeNoMatch
=== RUN    TestRun/FilterExtensionNoMatch
--- PASS: TestRun (0.00s)
    --- PASS: TestRun/NoFilter (0.00s)
    --- PASS: TestRun/FilterExtensionMatch (0.00s)
    --- PASS: TestRun/FilterExtensionSizeMatch (0.00s)
    --- PASS: TestRun/FilterExtensionSizeNoMatch (0.00s)
    --- PASS: TestRun/FilterExtensionNoMatch (0.00s)
=== RUN    TestRunDelExtension
=== RUN    TestRunDelExtension/DeleteExtensionNoMatch
=== RUN    TestRunDelExtension/DeleteExtensionMatch
=== RUN    TestRunDelExtension/DeleteExtensionMixed
--- PASS: TestRunDelExtension (0.00s)
    --- PASS: TestRunDelExtension/DeleteExtensionNoMatch (0.00s)
    --- PASS: TestRunDelExtension/DeleteExtensionMatch (0.00s)
    --- PASS: TestRunDelExtension/DeleteExtensionMixed (0.00s)
PASS
ok      pragprog.com/rggo/fileSystem/walk      0.009s
```

Try out the new logging option using the same testing directory /tmp/testdir you created before. First, list all files in that directory:

```
$ go run . -root /tmp/testdir/ -list
/tmp/testdir/file1.txt
/tmp/testdir/text/text1.txt
/tmp/testdir/text/text2.txt
/tmp/testdir/text/text3.txt
```

Now remove all the *.txt* files, logging the information to a file named deleted_files.log:

```
$ go run . -root /tmp/testdir/ -ext .txt -log deleted_files.log -del
$
```

You still don't see anything onscreen because the information was logged to the specified file. Check the contents of the deleted_files.log to see which files were deleted by the tool:

```
$ cat deleted_files.log
DELETED FILE: 2018/05/19 09:13:34 /tmp/testdir/file1.txt
DELETED FILE: 2018/05/19 09:13:34 /tmp/testdir/text/text1.txt
DELETED FILE: 2018/05/19 09:13:34 /tmp/testdir/text/text2.txt
DELETED FILE: 2018/05/19 09:13:34 /tmp/testdir/text/text3.txt
$
```

Notice that all lines in this log file were prefixed by the string *DELETED FILE*. If there were additional entries in the file, you could use this string to search for all deleted files.

Once you add the ability to log the information to a log file you enable more complex and useful scenarios, like scheduling a directory cleanup every day with *cron*. To do this, first build and install the binary version of *walk*:

```
$ go install
$ type walk
walk is /home/ricardo/go/bin/walk
```

With the *walk* tool built and installed in your $GOPATH/bin directory, you can now schedule an automatic cleanup of all log files from an application directory where the size is above 10MB. To run this task with *cron*, execute the following command:

```
$ crontab -e
```

Your visual editor opens. Add the following line to the file to schedule the task to run every day at 10 a.m.:

```
00 10 * * * $GOPATH/bin/walk -root /myapp -ext .log -size 10485760
  -log /tmp/myapp_deleted_files.log -del
```

Enter this as a single line. It's only broken on multiple lines here because a single line is too long to fit on the page.

During a successful execution, this tool adds the deleted file information to the log file so you can check which files were deleted. After the tool runs, you'll see results like these in its log file:

```
$ cat /tmp/myapp_deleted_files.log
DELETED FILE: 2018/05/17 10:00:01 /myapp/logs/access.log
DELETED FILE: 2018/05/18 10:00:03 /myapp/logs/error.log
DELETED FILE: 2018/05/19 10:00:01 /myapp/logs/access.log
$
```

The *walk* tool now has the ability to log deleted files. To complete this tool, let's add one more feature: compressing and archiving files before deleting them.

Archiving Files

Before deleting files that are consuming too much space, you might want to back them up in a compressed form so you can keep them around in case you need them later. Let's add an archiving feature to the *walk* tool to enable this feature.

To add this new feature, you'll use the standard library package compress/gzip to compress data using the *gzip* format, and io, which provides functions to help with Input/Output operations such as copying data. The package io is already included in the import list. Add the compress/gzip package to the import list in the file actions.go:

```
fileSystem/walk.v3/actions.go
import (
    "compress/gzip"

    "fmt"
    "io"
    "log"
    "os"
    "path/filepath"
)
```

Define the new action function archiveFile(destDir, root, path string) to archive the files. This function has two main responsibilities: to preserve the relative directory tree so the files are archived in the same directories relative to the source root and to compress the data. This function accepts the following arguments, all of type string:

1. destDir: The destination directory where the files will be archived.

2. root: The root directory where the search was started. You'll use this value to determine the relative path of the files to archive so you can create a similar directory tree in the destination directory.

3. path: The path of the file to be archived.

The function returns a potential error, so the calling function can check its value and interrupt processing when issues occur. Start with the function definition:

fileSystem/walk.v3/actions.go
```go
func archiveFile(destDir, root, path string) error {
```

First, check if the argument destDir is a directory. Do this by calling the os.Stat() function and then the info.IsDir() method of the os.FileInfo type, like this:

fileSystem/walk.v3/actions.go
```go
info, err := os.Stat(destDir)
if err != nil {
  return err
}

if !info.IsDir() {
  return fmt.Errorf("%s is not a directory", destDir)
}
```

If the argument isn't a directory, you return a new error using the fmt.Errorf() function with the appropriate error message.

Then determine the relative directory of the file to be archived in relation to its source root path using the function Rel() from the package filepath:

fileSystem/walk.v3/actions.go
```go
relDir, err := filepath.Rel(root, filepath.Dir(path))
if err != nil {
  return err
}
```

Create the new file name by adding the *.gz* suffix to the original file name which you obtain by calling the filepath.Base() function. Define the target path by joining all three pieces together: the destination directory, the relative directory, and the file name, using the filepath.Join() function:

fileSystem/walk.v3/actions.go
```go
dest := fmt.Sprintf("%s.gz", filepath.Base(path))
targetPath := filepath.Join(destDir, relDir, dest)
```

By using the functions from the package filepath, you ensure the paths are built in accordance with the operating system where the program is running, making it cross-platform. With the target path defined, create the target directory tree using os.MkdirAll():

fileSystem/walk.v3/actions.go

```
if err := os.MkdirAll(filepath.Dir(targetPath), 0755); err != nil {
  return err
}
```

The os.MkdirAll() function creates all the required directories at once but will do nothing if the directories already exist, which means you don't have to write any additional checks.

This completes the first goal of this function. Once you have the target path, you can create the compressed archive. To do this, you'll use the io.Copy() function to copy data from the source file to the destination file. But instead of using the destination file directly as an argument, you'll use the type gzip.Writer.

The gzip.Writer type implements the io.Writer interface, which allows it to be used as an argument to any functions that expect that interface as input, such as io.Copy(), but it writes the data in compressed form. To create an instance of this type, call the gzip.NewWriter() function, passing a pointer to the destination os.File type as input. This is the implementation:

fileSystem/walk.v3/actions.go

```
  out, err := os.OpenFile(targetPath, os.O_RDWR|os.O_CREATE, 0644)
  if err != nil {
    return err
  }
  defer out.Close()

  in, err := os.Open(path)
  if err != nil {
    return err
  }
  defer in.Close()

  zw := gzip.NewWriter(out)

  zw.Name = filepath.Base(path)

  if _, err = io.Copy(zw, in); err != nil {
    return err
  }

  if err := zw.Close(); err != nil {
    return err
  }

  return out.Close()
}
```

The gzip.Writer type accepts metadata about the compressed file. In this example, you're using the zw.Name field to store the source file name in the compressed file. Notice also that we're not deferring the call to zw.Close() as we want to ensure we return any potential errors because, if the compressing fails, the calling function will get an error and decide how to proceed. At the end, we're returning the error from closing the output file as well, to avoid any potential data loss.

This completes the changes to actions.go. Save the file and open main.go to update the main program.

Start by adding a new field called archive to the config struct to represent the target archive directory.

```
fileSystem/walk.v3/main.go
type config struct {
  // extenstion to filter out
  ext string
  // min file size
  size int64
  // list files
  list bool
  // delete files
  del bool
  // log destination writer
  wLog io.Writer
  // archive directory
  archive string
}
```

Now update the main() function. To make it configurable, first add a flag called archive which allows the user to specify the directory in which to archive files. If this option is specified, we'll assume the user wants to archive the files. If it's not, the archiving will be skipped.

```
fileSystem/walk.v3/main.go
// Parsing command line flags
root := flag.String("root", ".", "Root directory to start")
logFile := flag.String("log", "", "Log deletes to this file")
// Action options
list := flag.Bool("list", false, "List files only")
archive := flag.String("archive", "", "Archive directory")
del := flag.Bool("del", false, "Delete files")
```

Next, map the archive flag value to the corresponding field in the config struct instance c so it will be passed to run():

```
fileSystem/walk.v3/main.go
c := config{
  ext:  *ext,
  size: *size,
  list: *list,
  del:  *del,
  wLog: f,
➤ archive: *archive,
}
```

Finally, update the run() function to include a call to the archiveFile() function if required:

```
fileSystem/walk.v3/main.go
// If list was explicitly set, don't do anything else
if cfg.list {
  return listFile(path, out)
}

➤ // Archive files and continue if successful
➤ if cfg.archive != "" {
➤   if err := archiveFile(cfg.archive, root, path); err != nil {
➤     return err
➤   }
➤ }

// Delete files
if cfg.del {
```

Notice that when using the archiving option, the function should only return if there is an error, allowing the next action function delFile() to execute if the user requested it.

Save the file main.go. Let's include tests for the archiving feature next. Open the file main_test.go and add the package strings to the import list. You'll use it to execute operations on strings such as joining or removing spaces:

```
fileSystem/walk.v3/main_test.go
import (
  "bytes"
  "fmt"
  "io/ioutil"
  "os"
  "path/filepath"

➤ "strings"
  "testing"
)
```

Then, at the end of the file, add another test function called TestRunArchive() to test the archiving functionality:

fileSystem/walk.v3/main_test.go
```
func TestRunArchive(t *testing.T) {
```

Start by defining three test cases using the table-driven testing concepts that you used in Testing with Table-Driven Testing, on page 82: one where no match occurs, one where all files match the filter, and one where some files match the filter:

fileSystem/walk.v3/main_test.go
```
// Archiving test cases
testCases := []struct {
  name         string
  cfg          config
  extNoArchive string
  nArchive     int
  nNoArchive   int
}{
  {name: "ArchiveExtensionNoMatch",
    cfg:           config{ext: ".log"},
    extNoArchive: ".gz", nArchive: 0, nNoArchive: 10},
  {name: "ArchiveExtensionMatch",
    cfg:           config{ext: ".log"},
    extNoArchive: "", nArchive: 10, nNoArchive: 0},
  {name: "ArchiveExtensionMixed",
    cfg:           config{ext: ".log"},
    extNoArchive: ".gz", nArchive: 5, nNoArchive: 5},
}
```

Then, loop through the test cases and execute them using the t.Run() subtest function:

fileSystem/walk.v3/main_test.go
```
// Execute RunArchive test cases
for _, tc := range testCases {
  t.Run(tc.name, func(t *testing.T) {
```

To start executing the test cases, define a buffer variable to capture the output of the tool:

fileSystem/walk.v3/main_test.go
```
// Buffer for RunArchive output
var buffer bytes.Buffer
```

For this test, you'll use the same test helper function you used to develop tests for the delete functionality in Testing with the Help of Test Helpers, on page 89, but in this case, you'll use createTempDir() to create both the origin directory and the archiving directory.

```
fileSystem/walk.v3/main_test.go
// Create temp dirs for RunArchive test
tempDir, cleanup := createTempDir(t, map[string]int{
  tc.cfg.ext:       tc.nArchive,
  tc.extNoArchive: tc.nNoArchive,
})
defer cleanup()

archiveDir, cleanupArchive := createTempDir(t, nil)
defer cleanupArchive()
```

To create the temporary archive directory using the helper function, we provide a value of nil as the file map input since we don't need any files in this directory.

Assign the archiveDir variable containing the name of the archive directory to the field tc.cfg.archive to be used as input for the function run(). Then, execute the function run() providing the temporary directory, the address to the buffer, and the config instance tc.cfg as input:

```
fileSystem/walk.v3/main_test.go
tc.cfg.archive = archiveDir

if err := run(tempDir, &buffer, tc.cfg); err != nil {
  t.Fatal(err)
}
```

If the run() function returns an error, we fail the test using the method t.Fatal() from the testing type. Assuming the function completes successfully, we validate the output content and the number of files archived.

Start by validating the tool's output. The archiving feature outputs the name of each archived file, so you'll need a list of files that you expect to be archived to compare with the actual results. Since the test creates the directory and files dynamically for each test, you don't have the name of the files beforehand. Create this list dynamically by reading the data from the temporary directory. Use the Glob() function from the filepath package to find all file names from the temporary directory tempDir that match the archiving extension. Use the function Join() from the filepath package to concatenate the pattern with the temporary directory path:

```
fileSystem/walk.v3/main_test.go
pattern := filepath.Join(tempDir, fmt.Sprintf("*%s", tc.cfg.ext))
expFiles, err := filepath.Glob(pattern)
if err != nil {
  t.Fatal(err)
}
```

To create the final list as a string to compare with the output, use the strings.Join() function from the strings package to join each file path in the expFiles slice with the newline character:

```
fileSystem/walk.v3/main_test.go
expOut := strings.Join(expFiles, "\n")
```

Before comparing the two values, remove the last new line from the output by using the strings.TrimSpace() function on the output variable buffer.

```
fileSystem/walk.v3/main_test.go
res := strings.TrimSpace(buffer.String())
```

We use the String() method from the bytes.Buffer type to extract the content of the buffer as a string.

Now compare the expected output expOut with the actual output res, failing the test if they don't match:

```
fileSystem/walk.v3/main_test.go
if expOut != res {
  t.Errorf("Expected %q, got %q instead\n", expOut, res)
}
```

Next, validate the number of files archived. Start by reading the content of the temporary archive directory archiveDir, using the ReadDir() function again. Store the results into the slice filesArchived:

```
fileSystem/walk.v3/main_test.go
filesArchived, err := ioutil.ReadDir(archiveDir)
if err != nil {
  t.Fatal(err)
}
```

Then, compare the number of files archived with the expected number of files that should be archived, tc.nArchive, failing the test if they don't match. Use the built-in function len() to obtain the number of files in the filesArchived slice:

```
fileSystem/walk.v3/main_test.go
      if len(filesArchived) != tc.nArchive {
        t.Errorf("Expected %d files archived, got %d instead\n",
          tc.nArchive, len(filesArchived))
      }
    })
  }
}
```

The test function for archiving is complete. Save the file and execute the tests:

```
$ go test -v
=== RUN    TestFilterOut
=== RUN    TestFilterOut/FilterNoExtension
=== RUN    TestFilterOut/FilterExtensionMatch
=== RUN    TestFilterOut/FilterExtensionNoMatch
=== RUN    TestFilterOut/FilterExtensionSizeMatch
=== RUN    TestFilterOut/FilterExtensionSizeNoMatch
--- PASS: TestFilterOut (0.00s)
    --- PASS: TestFilterOut/FilterNoExtension (0.00s)
    --- PASS: TestFilterOut/FilterExtensionMatch (0.00s)
    --- PASS: TestFilterOut/FilterExtensionNoMatch (0.00s)
    --- PASS: TestFilterOut/FilterExtensionSizeMatch (0.00s)
    --- PASS: TestFilterOut/FilterExtensionSizeNoMatch (0.00s)
=== RUN    TestRun
=== RUN    TestRun/NoFilter
=== RUN    TestRun/FilterExtensionMatch
=== RUN    TestRun/FilterExtensionSizeMatch
=== RUN    TestRun/FilterExtensionSizeNoMatch
=== RUN    TestRun/FilterExtensionNoMatch
--- PASS: TestRun (0.00s)
    --- PASS: TestRun/NoFilter (0.00s)
    --- PASS: TestRun/FilterExtensionMatch (0.00s)
    --- PASS: TestRun/FilterExtensionSizeMatch (0.00s)
    --- PASS: TestRun/FilterExtensionSizeNoMatch (0.00s)
    --- PASS: TestRun/FilterExtensionNoMatch (0.00s)
=== RUN    TestRunDelExtension
=== RUN    TestRunDelExtension/DeleteExtensionNoMatch
=== RUN    TestRunDelExtension/DeleteExtensionMatch
=== RUN    TestRunDelExtension/DeleteExtensionMixed
--- PASS: TestRunDelExtension (0.00s)
    --- PASS: TestRunDelExtension/DeleteExtensionNoMatch (0.00s)
    --- PASS: TestRunDelExtension/DeleteExtensionMatch (0.00s)
    --- PASS: TestRunDelExtension/DeleteExtensionMixed (0.00s)
=== RUN    TestRunArchive
=== RUN    TestRunArchive/ArchiveExtensionNoMatch
=== RUN    TestRunArchive/ArchiveExtensionMatch
=== RUN    TestRunArchive/ArchiveExtensionMixed
--- PASS: TestRunArchive (0.01s)
    --- PASS: TestRunArchive/ArchiveExtensionNoMatch (0.00s)
    --- PASS: TestRunArchive/ArchiveExtensionMatch (0.01s)
    --- PASS: TestRunArchive/ArchiveExtensionMixed (0.00s)
PASS
ok      pragprog.com/rggo/fileSystem/walk      0.016s
```

The new version of the *walk* tool is ready to try, but to do that, you need some files to archive. Your Go installation comes with a copy of its source code which contains several .go files. Let's use the subdirectory misc to try the new tool. Since you may want to delete some files to check the functionality, first copy it to a temporary directory. You can find where the Go installation files are located on your system by running go env GOROOT, like this:

```
$ go env GOROOT
/usr/lib/go
```

Create a local temporary directory and copy the Go misc tree to this local directory for testing:

```
$ mkdir /tmp/gomisc
$ cd /tmp/gomisc
$ cp -r /usr/lib/go/misc/ .
$ ls
misc
$ cd -
```

Use the *walk* tool to list all .go files under the gomisc directory:

```
$ go run . -root /tmp/gomisc/ -ext .go -list
/tmp/gomisc/misc/android/go_android_exec.go
/tmp/gomisc/misc/cgo/errors/badsym_test.go
/tmp/gomisc/misc/cgo/errors/errors_test.go
...
/tmp/gomisc/misc/swig/callback/callback_test.go
/tmp/gomisc/misc/swig/stdio/file.go
/tmp/gomisc/misc/swig/stdio/file_test.go
$
```

Create a directory to archive the files and run the tool using the archive option to archive files into this directory:

```
$ mkdir /tmp/gomisc_bkp
$ go run . -root /tmp/gomisc/ -ext .go -archive /tmp/gomisc_bkp
/tmp/gomisc/misc/android/go_android_exec.go
/tmp/gomisc/misc/cgo/errors/badsym_test.go
/tmp/gomisc/misc/cgo/errors/errors_test.go
...
/tmp/gomisc/misc/swig/callback/callback_test.go
/tmp/gomisc/misc/swig/stdio/file.go
/tmp/gomisc/misc/swig/stdio/file_test.go
```

Check the contents of the /tmp/gomisc_bkp directory to see the go files compressed:

```
$ cd /tmp/gomisc_bkp/misc/
$ ls
android  cgo  ios  linkcheck  reboot  swig
$ cd reboot
$ ls
experiment_toolid_test.go.gz  overlaydir_test.go.gz  reboot_test.go.gz
```

```
$ gzip -l *
compressed        uncompressed  ratio uncompressed_name
      1230                3048  61.1% experiment_toolid_test.go
       920                1892  53.3% overlaydir_test.go
       641                1236  50.8% reboot_test.go
      2791                6176  55.3% (totals)
```

The command gzip -l shows details about the compressed files including the original name obtained from the metadata you added to the compressed file.

If you want, use the del and log options to try the entire functionality of your *walk* tool. This will archive, delete, and log all files:

```
$ rm -r /tmp/gomisc_bkp/misc/
$ go run . -root /tmp/gomisc -ext .go -archive /tmp/gomisc_bkp/ \
> -del -log deleted_gomisc.log
$ cat deleted_gomisc.log
DELETED FILE: 2021/07/24 20:33:51 /tmp/gomisc/misc/android/go_android_exec.go
DELETED FILE: 2021/07/24 20:33:51 /tmp/gomisc/misc/cgo/errors/badsym_test.go
...
DELETED FILE: 2021/07/24 20:33:51 /tmp/gomisc/misc/swig/stdio/file.go
DELETED FILE: 2021/07/24 20:33:51 /tmp/gomisc/misc/swig/stdio/file_test.go
$
```

This version of the tool is useful as it can archive and delete files to save space, but it may need some additional adjustments before you use it in a production scenario; you might want to check for symbolic links or special files. That's something you can explore on your own later.

Exercises

You can try the following exercises to improve the skills you learned:

- Update the *walk* tool so that it allows the user to provide more than one file extension.

- Improve the *walk* tool by adding more filtering options, such as files modified after a certain date or files with long file names.

- Create a companion tool for *walk* that restores the archived files in case they are needed again. Recreate the original directory by using the same approach you used to create the destination directory in the archiveFile() function. Then use the gzip.Reader type from the compress/gzip package to uncompress the archive files.

Wrapping Up

In this chapter, you used several standard library packages to navigate the file system and deal with files and directories consistently across different operating systems. You performed common operations, such as copying and deleting files, and created entire directory structures. Finally, you used common packages to create log files and compressed archives.

In the next chapter, you'll improve the performance of your command-line tools by using an iterative approach guided by Go benchmarks and profiling results. By leveraging tests appropriately, you'll ensure that the code continues to do what it's required to do, allowing for safer and quicker code refactoring.

## CHAPTER 5

Improving the Performance
of Your CLI Tools

Ensuring that your command-line tools perform well is an important requirement, especially when designing tools that process a large amount of information, like data analysis tools. But designing tools that perform well isn't an easy task. Performance is often a subjective concept; it varies from person to person and also according to the context. In this book, we'll define performance as the speed of execution, or how fast our program can handle its workload.

Go provides tools that help you measure and analyze a program's performance. It has integrated tools for testing, benchmarking, profiling, and tracing.

To explore those tools, you'll build a CLI application that executes statistical operations on a *CSV* file. The CSV format consists of tabular data separated by commas. This format is commonly used to store numeric data for statistical and data analysis.

Here is an example of a CSV file:

```
IP Address,Timestamp,Response Time,Bytes
192.168.0.199,1520698621,236,3475
192.168.0.88,1520698776,220,3200
192.168.0.199,1520699033,226,3200
192.168.0.100,1520699142,218,3475
192.168.0.199,1520699379,238,3822
```

You'll build an initial version of this tool, test it to ensure it works correctly, and measure its performance by executing benchmarks. Then you'll analyze its performance by executing profiling and tracing, and you'll use an iterative approach to improve it. You'll use different strategies to improve the program, including applying Go's concurrency primitives to build a version of the tool that executes concurrently.

Let's get started.

Developing the Initial Version of colStats

Let's build the *colStats* tool and make sure it works before looking for ways to optimize it. The program will receive two optional input parameters each with a default value:

1. -col: The column on which to execute the operation. It defaults to 1.
2. -op: The operation to execute on the selected column. Initially, this tool will support two operations: sum, which calculates the sum of all values in the column, and avg, which determines the average value of the column. You can add more operations later if you want.

In addition to the two optional flags, this tool accepts any number of file names to process. If the user provides more than one file name, the tool combines the results for the same column in all files.

Create the directory performance/colStats under your book project's directory:

```
$ mkdir -p $HOME/pragprog.com/rggo/performance/colStats
$ cd $HOME/pragprog.com/rggo/performance/colStats
```

Then initialize the Go module for this project:

```
$ go mod init pragprog.com/rggo/performance/colStats
go: creating new go.mod: module pragprog.com/rggo/performance/colStats
```

For this tool, you'll organize the code into multiple files again, similar to what you've done in Developing a File System Crawler, on page 77. You'll create three files: errors.go (which contains error definitions), csv.go (which contains the functions to process CSV data), and main.go (which contains the main() and run() functions). You'll also add the corresponding test files later.

You'll learn more about error handling in Handling Errors, on page 167. For now, start by creating the file errors.go to define some error values to use throughout the package. By defining error values, you can use them during error handling instead of defining only error strings. You can also wrap them with an additional message to provide more information for the user while keeping the original error available for inspection, using the function errors.Is() from the errors package. You'll use this during tests.

Create the file and add the package definition and the import section. For this file, you'll use the errors package to create new error values:

performance/colStats/errors.go
```
package main

import "errors"
```

Then define the error values as variables. By convention, these variables are exported and their names start with Err:

performance/colStats/errors.go
```
var (
    ErrNotNumber        = errors.New("Data is not numeric")
    ErrInvalidColumn    = errors.New("Invalid column number")
    ErrNoFiles          = errors.New("No input files")
    ErrInvalidOperation = errors.New("Invalid operation")
)
```

Save and close this file and create the file csv.go to define the function to process data from CSV files. Open it in your text editor, and add the package definition:

performance/colStats/csv.go
```
package main
```

To develop these functions, you'll use some standard library packages:

- encoding/csv: To read data from CSV files.
- fmt: To print formatted results out.
- io: To provide the io.Reader interface.
- strconv: To convert string data into numeric data.

The encoding/csv package provides methods that read data as string. To perform calculations you need to convert the data into a numeric type, such as float64.

Add the import section to include these packages in your program:

performance/colStats/csv.go
```
import (
    "encoding/csv"
    "fmt"
    "io"
    "strconv"
)
```

Then create the functions to perform calculations on the data, starting with sum() and avg(). You can add more functions later if you need them.

performance/colStats/csv.go
```
func sum(data []float64) float64 {
    sum := 0.0

    for _, v := range data {
        sum += v
    }
```

```
    return sum
}

func avg(data []float64) float64 {
  return sum(data) / float64(len(data))
}
```

Notice that both functions have the same signature; they take as input a slice of float64 numbers and return a float64 value: func(data []float64) float64. Let's create an auxiliary type statsFunc using the same signature to make it easier to use these functions later. This new type represents a class of functions with this signature, which means that any function that matches the signature qualifies as this type. Add the new type definition like this:

performance/colStats/csv.go
```
// statsFunc defines a generic statistical function
type statsFunc func(data []float64) float64
```

You can use this new type as the input parameter whenever you need a new calculation function. This makes the code more concise and easier to test.

The last function you'll implement in this file is the function csv2float(), to parse the contents of the CSV file into a slice of floating point numbers that you can use to perform the calculations. This function accepts two input parameters: an io.Reader interface representing the source of CSV data and an int representing the column to extract data from. It returns a slice of float64 numbers and a potential error:

performance/colStats/csv.go
```
func csv2float(r io.Reader, column int) ([]float64, error) {
```

This uses a similar pattern to what you've done previously; you're providing the io.Reader interface as the input parameter for the function. This makes testing easier because you can call the function passing a buffer that contains test data instead of a file.

To read CSV data, you'll use the csv.Reader type from the csv package. This type provides the methods ReadAll() and Read() to read in CSV data. This package handles some corner cases such as alternative separators, spacing, quotation marks, or multiline fields, which you may encounter when processing CSV data. By using the package you don't need to handle these cases yourself.

Use the function csv.NewReader() to create a csv.Reader type from the provided input io.Reader:

performance/colStats/csv.go
```
// Create the CSV Reader used to read in data from CSV files
cr := csv.NewReader(r)
```

The program assumes the user will input the column starting from one (1) as it's more natural for users to understand. Let's adjust for a zero (0)-based slice index by subtracting one from the column variable:

performance/colStats/csv.go
```
// Adjusting for 0 based index
column--
```

Next, use the method cr.ReadAll() of your csv.Reader type to read in the entire CSV data into a variable allData. If a data-reading error occurs, return a new error using the function fmt.Errorf() with the verb %w to wrap the original error. This allows you to decorate the error with additional information for the users while keeping the original error available for inspections:

performance/colStats/csv.go
```
// Read in all CSV data
allData, err := cr.ReadAll()
if err != nil {
    return nil, fmt.Errorf("Cannot read data from file: %w", err)
}
```

The method ReadAll() reads in all records (lines) from the CSV file as a slice of fields (columns), where each field is itself a slice of strings. Go represents this data structure as [][]string. Since this method reads data as strings, you need to convert it to a float64 number to perform calculations. Create a variable data of type slice of float64 to hold the results of this conversion:

performance/colStats/csv.go
```
var data []float64
```

Now, loop through all the records by using the range operator on the variable allData. Inside the loop, first check if this is the first line (i == 0) and skip this iteration by using the continue keyword to discard the title line:

performance/colStats/csv.go
```
// Looping through all records
for i, row := range allData {
    if i == 0 {
        continue
    }
```

Then compare the length of the variable row, which represents a single record, with the column number provided by the user. If the column is too large, return an error wrapping your error value ErrInvalidColumn so you can check for it during tests:

performance/colStats/csv.go
```
// Checking number of columns in CSV file
if len(row) <= column {
```

```
  // File does not have that many columns
  return nil,
    fmt.Errorf("%w: File has only %d columns", ErrInvalidColumn, len(row))
}
```

Finally, try to convert the value of the given column to a float64 by using the function ParseFloat() of the strconv package. If the conversion fails, return an error wrapping ErrNotNumber. Otherwise, append the value to the data slice.

performance/colStats/csv.go
```
  // Try to convert data read into a float number
  v, err := strconv.ParseFloat(row[column], 64)
  if err != nil {
    return nil, fmt.Errorf("%w: %s", ErrNotNumber, err)
  }

  data = append(data, v)
}
```

When the loop finishes iterating over the entire slice, return the variable data and the value nil for the error:

performance/colStats/csv.go
```
  // Return the slice of float64 and nil error
  return data, nil
}
```

Save the file csv.go and create the file main.go to define the main() function. Open the file and add the package and import sections. You'll need the flag package to parse command-line options, the fmt package to print formatted output and create new errors, the io package so you can use the io.Writer interface, and the os package to interact with the operating system:

performance/colStats/main.go
```
package main

import (
  "flag"
  "fmt"
  "io"
  "os"
)
```

Next, create the function main() to parse the command-line arguments and call the function run(), which is responsible for the main logic of the tool.

performance/colStats/main.go
```
func main() {
  // Verify and parse arguments
  op := flag.String("op", "sum", "Operation to be executed")
  column := flag.Int("col", 1, "CSV column on which to execute operation")
```

```
  flag.Parse()
  if err := run(flag.Args(), *op, *column, os.Stdout); err != nil {
    fmt.Fprintln(os.Stderr, err)
    os.Exit(1)
  }
}
```

If the run() function returns any errors, print them out to STDERR and exit the program with the exit code 1.

Next, define the run() function.

performance/colStats/main.go
```
func run(filenames []string, op string, column int, out io.Writer) error {
```

This function accepts four input parameters:

1. filenames of type []string: A slice of strings representing the file names to process.

2. op of type string: A string representing the operation to execute, such as sum or average.

3. column of type int: An integer representing the column on which to execute the operation.

4. out of type io.Writer: An io.Writer interface to print out the results. By using the interface, you can print to STDOUT in the program while allowing tests to capture results using a buffer.

The run() function returns a potential error, which is useful in the main program to print out information to the user or in tests to validate if the function is executed correctly.

In the run() function, start by creating an empty variable opFunc of type statsFunc. Later, this variable will store the calculation function corresponding to the desired operation according to the parameter the user provided.

performance/colStats/main.go
```
var opFunc statsFunc
```

Next, validate the user-provided parameters. Command-line tools are user interfaces, and it's important to provide a good experience to users. Validating the user input allows the user to receive quick feedback if they make a mistake and prevents the program from running into a known error condition. For this scenario, let's add the validations as part of the run() function. For more complex validations you may want to write specific validation functions.

Check to see if the length of the filenames parameter equals zero. If it does, return the error ErrNoFiles indicating that the user didn't provide any files to process.

performance/colStats/main.go
```
if len(filenames) == 0 {
  return ErrNoFiles
}
```

Then, check the column parameter. By using the flag.Int() function from the flag package to capture the input, Go ensures the input is an integer number, so you don't need to check that. But you still need to validate the column number, which is a number greater than one. Add the validation like this:

performance/colStats/main.go
```
if column < 1 {
  return fmt.Errorf("%w: %d", ErrInvalidColumn, column)
}
```

Use a switch statement to validate the user-provided operation, assigning the corresponding statsFunc function to the opFunc variable:

performance/colStats/main.go
```
// Validate the operation and define the opFunc accordingly
switch op {
case "sum":
  opFunc = sum
case "avg":
  opFunc = avg
default:
  return fmt.Errorf("%w: %s", ErrInvalidOperation, op)
}
```

The default clause returns a new error wrapping the ErrInvalidOperation error, indicating the user provided an invalid operation.

Now add the logic to process the CSV files. Create a variable called consolidate of type []float64 (slice of float64) to consolidate the data that you'll extract from the given column on each input file.

performance/colStats/main.go
```
consolidate := make([]float64, 0)
```

Loop through each input file, opening the file for reading using the os.Open() function. Parse the given column into a slice of float64 numbers using the csv2float() function you created earlier, and then close the file to release system resources immediately. Finally, append the parsed data into the consolidate variable.

```
performance/colStats/main.go
// Loop through all files adding their data to consolidate
for _, fname := range filenames {
  // Open the file for reading
  f, err := os.Open(fname)
  if err != nil {
    return fmt.Errorf("Cannot open file: %w", err)
  }

  // Parse the CSV into a slice of float64 numbers
  data, err := csv2float(f, column)
  if err != nil {
    return err
  }

  if err := f.Close(); err != nil {
    return err
  }

  // Append the data to consolidate
  consolidate = append(consolidate, data...)
}
```

Once you finish the loop and have the data consolidated for all input files, execute the specified operation by using the variable opFunc which stores the calculation function, print out the results, and return any potential errors:

```
performance/colStats/main.go
  _, err := fmt.Fprintln(out, opFunc(consolidate))
  return err
}
```

This prints the results to STDOUT via the out io.Writer interface. Later, when testing this function, you'll set out to a buffer to capture and validate the print operation. This is the same pattern you used in Using Interfaces to Automate Tests, on page 58.

This is all the code for the *colStats* tool. Let's write some tests to ensure it's working properly.

Writing Tests for colStats

You're going to make a lot of changes to this code base to improve its performance. Before doing that, let's write tests to make sure the program works correctly. Then you can use those tests to ensure the program still works as you change the underlying code.

For these tests, you'll follow the same approach used to define tests in Writing Tests for the Markdown Preview Tool, on page 51. You'll create unit tests for the avg() and sum() statistics functions as well as for the csv2float() function. For the integration tests, you'll test the function run(). You'll also apply table-driven testing as you did for Testing with Table-Driven Testing, on page 82.

Let's start by writing unit tests for the statistics operations. In the same directory as the csv.go file, create the tests file csv_test.go. Open it in your text editor and add the package section:

performance/colStats/csv_test.go
```
package main
```

Add the import section. For these tests, you'll use the bytes package to create buffers to capture the output, the errors package to validate errors, the io package to use the io.Reader interface, the testing package which is required to execute tests, and the iotest package to assist in executing tests that fail to read data.

performance/colStats/csv_test.go
```
import (
  "bytes"
  "errors"
  "fmt"
  "io"
  "testing"
  "testing/iotest"
)
```

Add the definition for the first test function TestOperations(). You'll use a single test function to test all operation functions by applying the statsFunc type you defined to abstract the operations functions:

performance/colStats/csv_test.go
```
func TestOperations(t *testing.T) {
```

Create a data variable to hold the input data for the tests as a slice of slices of floating point numbers:

performance/colStats/csv_test.go
```
data := [][]float64{
  {10, 20, 15, 30, 45, 50, 100, 30},
  {5.5, 8, 2.2, 9.75, 8.45, 3, 2.5, 10.25, 4.75, 6.1, 7.67, 12.287, 5.47},
  {-10, -20},
  {102, 37, 44, 57, 67, 129},
}
```

Next, define the test cases by using the table-driven testing concept. Each test case has a name, the operation function to execute, and the expected results:

performance/colStats/csv_test.go
```go
// Test cases for Operations Test
testCases := []struct {
  name string
  op   statsFunc
  exp  []float64
}{
  {"Sum", sum, []float64{300, 85.927, -30, 436}},
  {"Avg", avg, []float64{37.5, 6.609769230769231, -15, 72.666666666666666}},
}
```

Finally, loop through all the test cases using the range operator. For each test case, iterate over all data/results to execute multiple tests with different data points. Execute each test as a subtest using the method Run() from the testing.T type. Execute the test by applying the given operation stored in the variable tc.op with the corresponding input data, storing the result in the variable res. Then compare the result with the expected value exp, failing the test if they don't match:

performance/colStats/csv_test.go
```go
  // Operations Tests execution
  for _, tc := range testCases {
    for k, exp := range tc.exp {
      name := fmt.Sprintf("%sData%d", tc.name, k)
      t.Run(name, func(t *testing.T) {
        res := tc.op(data[k])

        if res != exp {
          t.Errorf("Expected %g, got %g instead", exp, res)
        }
      })
    }
  }
}
```

Comparing Floating Point Numbers

Comparing two floating point numbers like we're doing in these tests can be tricky because floating point numbers are inherently imprecise. To work around this, you generally introduce a small tolerance for comparison, but this is beyond the scope of this book. For brevity, these tests execute a direct comparison, but for production code, you should write a specific compare function.

Take a look at Go's source code for the math package[1] for an example of how the standard library handles these kinds of tests.

---

1.   golang.org/src/math/all_test.go

Now let's write the tests for the csv2float() function. Add the test function definition to your csv_test.go file:

performance/colStats/csv_test.go

```
func TestCSV2Float(t *testing.T) {
```

Create the variable csvData of type string to hold the input data for the tests. Use the raw string literal operator ` (a backtick) to create a multiline string. You'll use this variable for all subtests, so you don't need to define data for each test case:

performance/colStats/csv_test.go

```
  csvData := `IP Address,Requests,Response Time
192.168.0.199,2056,236
192.168.0.88,899,220
192.168.0.199,3054,226
192.168.0.100,4133,218
192.168.0.199,950,238
`
```

Next, define the use cases using table-driven tests again. For this test, each case contains the name, the column col, the expected result exp, the expected error expErr, and the input io.Reader r:

performance/colStats/csv_test.go

```
// Test cases for CSV2Float Test
testCases := []struct {
  name    string
  col     int
  exp     []float64
  expErr  error
  r       io.Reader
}{
  {name: "Column2", col: 2,
    exp:    []float64{2056, 899, 3054, 4133, 950},
    expErr: nil,
    r:      bytes.NewBufferString(csvData),
  },
  {name: "Column3", col: 3,
    exp:    []float64{236, 220, 226, 218, 238},
    expErr: nil,
    r:      bytes.NewBufferString(csvData),
  },
  {name: "FailRead", col: 1,
    exp:    nil,
    expErr: iotest.ErrTimeout,
    r:      iotest.TimeoutReader(bytes.NewReader([]byte{0})),
  },
  {name: "FailedNotNumber", col: 1,
    exp:    nil,
```

```
      expErr: ErrNotNumber,
      r:      bytes.NewBufferString(csvData),
    },
    {name: "FailedInvalidColumn", col: 4,
      exp:    nil,
      expErr: ErrInvalidColumn,
      r:      bytes.NewBufferString(csvData),
    },
}
```

Notice that for the first two test cases, you're defining a bytes.Buffer pointing to the csvData as the input variable r. You can do this because the bytes.Buffer type implements the io.Reader interface. But for the third test case, you're using the function iotest.TimeoutReader() to simulate a reading failure. This function returns an io.Reader that returns a timeout error when it tries to read the data from it.

Add this code to execute the tests by looping through the test cases the same way you did for the previous test function. For each case, execute the csv2float() function providing the io.Reader and column from the test case:

performance/colStats/csv_test.go
```
// CSV2Float Tests execution
for _, tc := range testCases {
  t.Run(tc.name, func(t *testing.T) {
    res, err := csv2float(tc.r, tc.col)
```

Since the csv2float() function returns a potential error, for this test, first handle the cases where you expect an error when the variable tc.expErr isn't nil. Validate that the err isn't nil and use the function errors.Is() to inspect the error. This function returns true if the err variable matches the expected error value or err wraps the expected error. This is useful because you can apply this function to validate expected errors even if you wrapped the original error to add more information for the user.

performance/colStats/csv_test.go
```
// Check for errors if expErr is not nil
if tc.expErr != nil {
  if err == nil {
    t.Errorf("Expected error. Got nil instead")
  }

  if ! errors.Is(err, tc.expErr) {
    t.Errorf("Expected error %q, got %q instead", tc.expErr, err)
  }

  return
}
```

Notice that you're using the return statement to finish the subtest and prevent the execution of the remaining checks.

Using error values instead of comparing error strings makes your tests more resilient and more maintainable, preventing failures when the underlying message changes. But it's still only a basic approach for error handling that is useful for small applications. For more complex scenarios, you may want to use another approach such as custom error types. You'll learn more about error handling using custom types in Handling Errors, on page 167.

Now let's handle the case where you don't expect any errors. Ensure the err is nil, and fail the test otherwise. Then verify the result variable res. Since it's a slice of float64, use a loop to check each element of the slice:

performance/colStats/csv_test.go
```go
        // Check results if errors are not expected
        if err != nil {
          t.Errorf("Unexpected error: %q", err)
        }

        for i, exp := range tc.exp {
          if res[i] != exp {
            t.Errorf("Expected %g, got %g instead", exp, res[i])
          }
        }
      })
    }
}
```

Comparing Complex Data Structures

As an alternative method to compare more complex data structures, such as slices or maps, you can write your own comparing function or test helper. You may use the reflect package that provides functions that introspect Go objects. For more information about this package, consult its documentation.[2]

You can also use external packages to compare complex data structures. Several packages are available for this purpose with different features, but this is the scope of this book.

That completes the tests for the csv2float() function. Let's add the integration tests now by using the same table-driven testing approach. Save the csv_test.go file and create the main_test.go file.

---

2.   golang.org/pkg/reflect/

In the main_test.go file, add the package definition and the import section. For these tests, you'll use the bytes package to create buffers to capture the output, the errors package to verify errors, the os package to validate operating system errors, and the testing package, which is required to execute tests.

performance/colStats/main_test.go

```
package main

import (
  "bytes"
  "errors"

  "os"
  "testing"
)
```

For the integration tests, test the function run() that coordinates the entire program's execution. Add the test function:

performance/colStats/main_test.go

```
func TestRun(t *testing.T) {
```

Inside the function block, define the test cases. For these tests, each case contains the name, the column col, the operation op, the expected result exp, a slice of strings with the name of the input files files, and the expected error expErr:

performance/colStats/main_test.go

```
// Test cases for Run Tests
testCases := []struct {
  name    string
  col     int
  op      string
  exp     string
  files   []string
  expErr  error
}{
  {name: "RunAvg1File", col: 3, op: "avg", exp: "227.6\n",
    files: []string{"./testdata/example.csv"},
    expErr: nil,
  },
  {name: "RunAvgMultiFiles", col: 3, op: "avg", exp: "233.84\n",
    files: []string{"./testdata/example.csv", "./testdata/example2.csv"},
    expErr: nil,
  },
  {name: "RunFailRead", col: 2, op: "avg", exp: "",
    files: []string{"./testdata/example.csv", "./testdata/fakefile.csv"},
    expErr: os.ErrNotExist,
  },
```

```
{name: "RunFailColumn", col: 0, op: "avg", exp: "",
    files:  []string{"./testdata/example.csv"},
    expErr: ErrInvalidColumn,
},
{name: "RunFailNoFiles", col: 2, op: "avg", exp: "",
    files:  []string{},
    expErr: ErrNoFiles,
},
{name: "RunFailOperation", col: 2, op: "invalid", exp: "",
    files:  []string{"./testdata/example.csv"},
    expErr: ErrInvalidOperation,
},
}
```

These test cases include executing tests that provide a single file or multiple files. They also include several failure cases such as providing no files or an invalid column number. Since you're using files as input for these tests, you'll create them in the testdata directory shortly.

Add this code to execute the tests, looping through the test cases and using the table-driven testing pattern:

performance/colStats/main_test.go
```go
// Run tests execution
for _, tc := range testCases {
    t.Run(tc.name, func(t *testing.T) {
        var res bytes.Buffer
        err := run(tc.files, tc.op, tc.col, &res)

        if tc.expErr != nil {
            if err == nil {
                t.Errorf("Expected error. Got nil instead")
            }

            if ! errors.Is(err, tc.expErr) {
                t.Errorf("Expected error %q, got %q instead", tc.expErr, err)
            }

            return
        }

        if err != nil {
            t.Errorf("Unexpected error: %q", err)
        }

        if res.String() != tc.exp {
            t.Errorf("Expected %q, got %q instead", tc.exp, &res)
        }
    })
}
}
```

This loop is almost the same as the previous one you wrote for the csv2float() tests, including the error checking. The main difference is defining a bytes.Buffer to capture the output and executing the run() function instead.

Finally, to complete the tests you need to create the input CSV files for the integration tests. You'll create them under the testdata subdirectory in the project directory. This is the recommended practice for adding files required by the tests as this directory is ignored by the Go build tools. In your project directory, create the subdirectory:

```
$ mkdir testdata
```

Then create the two files example.csv and example2.csv under the testdata directory:

```
$ cat << 'EOF' > testdata/example.csv
> IP Address,Timestamp,Response Time,Bytes
> 192.168.0.199,1520698621,236,3475
> 192.168.0.88,1520698776,220,3200
> 192.168.0.199,1520699033,226,3200
> 192.168.0.100,1520699142,218,3475
> 192.168.0.199,1520699379,238,3822
> EOF

$ cat << 'EOF' > testdata/example2.csv
> IP Address,Timestamp,Response Time,Bytes
> 192.168.0.199,1520698621,236,3475
> 192.168.0.88,1520698776,220,3200
> 192.168.0.199,1520699033,226,3200
> 192.168.0.100,1520699142,218,3475
> 192.168.0.199,1520699379,238,3822
> 192.168.0.199,1520699379,238,3822
> 192.168.0.199,1520699379,238,3822
> 192.168.0.199,1520699379,238,3822
> 192.168.0.199,1520699379,238,3822
> 192.168.0.199,1520699379,238,3822
> 192.168.0.199,1520699379,238,3822
> 192.168.0.199,1520699379,238,3822
> 192.168.0.199,1520699379,238,3822
> 192.168.0.199,1520699379,238,3822
> 192.168.0.199,1520699379,238,3822
> 192.168.0.199,1520699379,238,3822
> 192.168.0.199,1520699379,238,3822
> 192.168.0.199,1520699379,238,3822
> 192.168.0.199,1520699379,238,3822
> EOF
```

Verify that the files are there with the tree command:

```
$ tree
.
├── csv.go
├── csv_test.go
├── errors.go
├── go.mod
├── main.go
├── main_test.go
└── testdata
    ├── example2.csv
    └── example.csv

1 directory, 8 files
```

You're ready to test your tool. Execute all the tests in verbose mode, using go test -v to see detailed output for all the tests:

```
$ go test -v
=== RUN    TestOperations
=== RUN    TestOperations/SumData0
=== RUN    TestOperations/SumData1
=== RUN    TestOperations/SumData2
=== RUN    TestOperations/SumData3
=== RUN    TestOperations/AvgData0
=== RUN    TestOperations/AvgData1
=== RUN    TestOperations/AvgData2
=== RUN    TestOperations/AvgData3
--- PASS: TestOperations (0.00s)
    --- PASS: TestOperations/SumData0 (0.00s)
    --- PASS: TestOperations/SumData1 (0.00s)
    --- PASS: TestOperations/SumData2 (0.00s)
    --- PASS: TestOperations/SumData3 (0.00s)
    --- PASS: TestOperations/AvgData0 (0.00s)
    --- PASS: TestOperations/AvgData1 (0.00s)
    --- PASS: TestOperations/AvgData2 (0.00s)
    --- PASS: TestOperations/AvgData3 (0.00s)
=== RUN    TestCSV2Float
=== RUN    TestCSV2Float/Column2
=== RUN    TestCSV2Float/Column3
=== RUN    TestCSV2Float/FailRead
=== RUN    TestCSV2Float/FailedNotNumber
=== RUN    TestCSV2Float/FailedInvalidColumn
--- PASS: TestCSV2Float (0.00s)
    --- PASS: TestCSV2Float/Column2 (0.00s)
    --- PASS: TestCSV2Float/Column3 (0.00s)
    --- PASS: TestCSV2Float/FailRead (0.00s)
    --- PASS: TestCSV2Float/FailedNotNumber (0.00s)
    --- PASS: TestCSV2Float/FailedInvalidColumn (0.00s)
```

```
=== RUN    TestRun
=== RUN    TestRun/RunAvg1File
=== RUN    TestRun/RunAvgMultiFiles
=== RUN    TestRun/RunFailRead
=== RUN    TestRun/RunFailColumn
=== RUN    TestRun/RunFailNoFiles
=== RUN    TestRun/RunFailOperation
--- PASS: TestRun (0.00s)
    --- PASS: TestRun/RunAvg1File (0.00s)
    --- PASS: TestRun/RunAvgMultiFiles (0.00s)
    --- PASS: TestRun/RunFailRead (0.00s)
    --- PASS: TestRun/RunFailColumn (0.00s)
    --- PASS: TestRun/RunFailNoFiles (0.00s)
    --- PASS: TestRun/RunFailOperation (0.00s)
PASS
ok      pragprog.com/rggo/performance/colStats   0.004s
```

You can also build the program and try it out. Let's use it to find the average value of the third column on the file testdata/example.csv:

```
$ go build
$ ./colStats -op avg -col 3 testdata/example.csv
227.6
```

The tool also works on multiple input files:

```
$ ./colStats -op avg -col 3 testdata/example.csv testdata/example2.csv
233.84
```

With your tests in place, you can quickly validate that the tool continues working as designed while you refactor it. Now let's benchmark the tool to assess whether its performance is acceptable.

Benchmarking Your Tool

Before you start thinking about improving the performance of your tools or programs, you first need to determine what the current status is and define a baseline for comparison. For this exercise, we'll state that performance means how fast the tool takes to process its workload. Perhaps it's currently good enough, but we may not know. To determine the current state, we need to measure it.

In the Linux/Unix world the quickest way to determine how fast your applications works is by using the time command. The time command executes the application and prints out how long it took to run. For example, to measure how long your tool takes to process data from the two test files in the testdata directory, run this command:

```
$ time ./colStats -op avg -col 3 testdata/example.csv testdata/example2.csv
233.84

real    0m0.008s
user    0m0.001s
sys     0m0.008s
```

In this example, it took 0.008 seconds to process those two files. The output line starting with real shows the total elapsed time.

This value doesn't look bad. In fact, if all you're planning to do with this tool is to process a few small files, then this is good enough and you don't need to do anything more. But let's assume that this tool will be used to process performance data coming from hundreds or thousands of files.

When you're benchmarking your tools or programs, it's important to know your workload. Programs behave differently depending on the type of load they're submitted to. Let's change our example to process a thousand files at once. The code included with this book has a tarball file containing one thousand CSV files. Copy the file colStatsBenchmarkData.tar.gz to your project's root directory and extract the contents of this file into the testdata directory:

```
$ tar -xzvf colStatsBenchmarkData.tar.gz -C testdata/
benchmark/
benchmark/file307.csv
benchmark/file932.csv
«... skipping long output...»
benchmark/file268.csv
benchmark/file316.csv
benchmark/file328.csv
$
$ ls testdata/
benchmark  example2.csv  example.csv
```

This command created the directory benchmark under testdata containing a thousand files. These files are simple CSV files with two columns: the first containing text and the second containing a random number. Take a look at one of the files using the head command:

```
$ head -5 testdata/benchmark/file1.csv
Col1,Col2
Data0,60707
Data1,25641
Data2,79731
Data3,18485
```

Each file has 2501 lines where the first is the title row. The total number of data lines for this set is 2.5 million:

```
$ wc -l testdata/benchmark/file1.csv
2501 testdata/benchmark/file1.csv
$ wc -l testdata/benchmark/*.csv
    2501 testdata/benchmark/file0.csv
    2501 testdata/benchmark/file100.csv
    «... skipping long output...»
    2501 testdata/benchmark/file99.csv
    2501 testdata/benchmark/file9.csv
 2501000 total
```

Execute the tool again to calculate the average of the second column in all these files:

```
$ time ./colStats -op avg -col 2 testdata/benchmark/*.csv
50006.0653788

real    0m1.217s
user    0m1.174s
sys     0m0.083s
$
```

As you can see, the time has increased to 1.2 seconds. This is still a small amount of time, but it's orders of magnitude larger than the first one of 0.008 seconds. If you follow this trend, you can extrapolate this to an even larger number if you keep increasing the number of files to process.

Go provides a much richer benchmark feature included with the testing package. Running Go benchmarks is similar to executing tests. First, you write the benchmark functions in the test file using the testing.B type included in the testing package. Then you run the benchmarks using the go test tool with the -bench parameter. You can find more information about the benchmark tool in the documentation.[3]

Let's write a benchmark function to benchmark the tool. Open the file main_test.go in your editor and add two new packages to the import section: ioutil, which provides Input/Output utilities, and filepath, which provides multiplatform functions to interact with the file system:

performance/colStats/main_test.go
```
"io/ioutil"
"path/filepath"
```

Then add the benchmark function definition at the bottom of the file, after all the tests:

performance/colStats/main_test.go
```
func BenchmarkRun(b *testing.B) {
```

---

3.   golang.org/pkg/testing/#hdr-Benchmarks

The benchmark function takes a single input parameter: a pointer to a testing.B type. This type provides the methods and fields you can use to control your benchmark, such as the benchmark time or the number of iterations to perform.

Inside the function's body, define a new variable called filenames which contains all the files you'll use for the benchmark. You want to benchmark the tool according to the main use case: processing hundreds of files. Use the Glob() function from the filepath module to create a slice containing the names of all files in the testdata/benchmark directory:

performance/colStats/main_test.go
```go
filenames, err := filepath.Glob("./testdata/benchmark/*.csv")
if err != nil {
  b.Fatal(err)
}
```

Then, before you run the main benchmark loop, use the ResetTimer() function from the B type to reset the benchmark clock. This is important as it will ignore any time used in preparing for the benchmark's execution.

performance/colStats/main_test.go
```go
b.ResetTimer()
```

Execute the benchmark using a loop where the upper limit is defined by b.N, where b.N is adjusted by the benchmark function according to the program's speed to last roughly one second. For each iteration of the loop, execute the run() function to benchmark the entire tool:

performance/colStats/main_test.go
```go
  for i := 0; i < b.N; i++ {
    if err := run(filenames, "avg", 2, ioutil.Discard); err != nil {
      b.Error(err)
    }
  }
}
```

For this execution of run(), you're providing the variable ioutil.Discard as the output destination. This variable implements the io.Writer interface but discards anything written to it. Since the output itself is irrelevant for the benchmark, you can safely discard it.

Save the file so you can execute the benchmark. To run the benchmarks, use the go test tool with the -bench regexp parameter. The regexp parameter is a regular expression that matches the benchmarks you want to execute. In this case, you can use the . (dot) to execute all the benchmarks. In addition, provide the argument -run ^$ to skip running any of the tests in the test file while executing the benchmark to prevent impacting the results.

```
$ go test -bench . -run ^$
goos: linux
goarch: amd64
pkg: pragprog.com/rggo/performance/colStats
Benchmark_Run-4                    1        1181570105 ns/op
PASS
ok      pragprog.com/rggo/performance/colStats    1.193s
$
```

The benchmark only executed one time. This is because it processed a thou-sand files and it took more than one second to complete. The benchmark tool also prints the average time per operation in nanoseconds. In this case, each operation is taking 1,181,570,105 ns which is roughly 1.2 seconds.

Because you're processing many files, the benchmark doesn't have time to execute more than once. You can force additional executions by using the -benchtime parameter. This parameter accepts a duration in time for the benchmark or a fixed number of executions. For example, let's set it for ten executions:

```
$ go test -bench . -benchtime=10x -run ^$
goos: linux
goarch: amd64
pkg: pragprog.com/rggo/performance/colStats
Benchmark_Run-4                   10        1024746971 ns/op
PASS
ok      pragprog.com/rggo/performance/colStats    11.414s
```

By executing the benchmark more times, we get rid of potential noise that can skew the results. In this case, you can see that the tool is taking an average of about one second to process all the files.

Save this output to a file so you can compare it with future executions later and see if it's improving. You can use the tee command on a Linux/Unix system to output the results of the benchmark to STDOUT and to a file at the same time. This way you save the results for later while quickly reviewing the results onscreen.

```
$ go test -bench . -benchtime=10x -run ^$ | tee benchresults00.txt
goos: linux
goarch: amd64
pkg: pragprog.com/rggo/performance/colStats
Benchmark_Run-4                   10        1020311416 ns/op
PASS
ok      pragprog.com/rggo/performance/colStats    11.508s
$ ls
benchresults00.txt  colStats  main.go  main_test.go  testdata
```

This result represents our baseline for comparison. Next, let's profile the tool's execution and look for improvement areas.

Profiling Your Tool

Go provides several tools to help you analyze your programs for performance-related issues. You've already seen the *benchmarking* feature and how you can use it to accurately determine how fast your programs execute. In addition to benchmarks, Go provides two analytical tools to help you find contentions or bottlenecks in your programs: the *profiling* and *tracing* tools.

You'll explore the *tracing* tool in Tracing Your Tool, on page 145. For now, let's dive into the *profiling* tool.

The Go profiler shows you a breakdown of where your program spends its execution time. By running the profiler, you can determine which functions consume most of the program's execution time and target them for optimization.

You have two ways to enable profiling on your programs: by adding code directly to your program or by running the profiler integrated with the testing and benchmarking tools. The first approach requires that you maintain additional code in your application and control the profiling execution yourself. The second approach tends to be easier since it's already integrated with the benchmark tool, so you don't need to add any more code to your program. You'll use this approach in this example since you already have a benchmark available.

Run the benchmarks again, but this time, enable the CPU profiler:

```
$ go test -bench . -benchtime=10x -run ^$ -cpuprofile cpu00.pprof
goos: linux
goarch: amd64
pkg: pragprog.com/rggo/performance/colStats
Benchmark_Run-4                10        1012377660 ns/op
PASS
ok      pragprog.com/rggo/performance/colStats   11.438s
$ ls
benchresults00.txt  colStats  colStats.test  cpu00.pprof
main.go  main_test.go  testdata
```

When you execute the profiler this way, it creates two files: the profile cpu00.pprof as specified in the command-line; and the compiled binary colStats.test. If you're using a Go version older than 1.10, you need to pass this binary file when using the go tool pprof later to analyze the profile. This isn't required for newer versions of Go.

Analyze the profiling results by using the go tool pprof command, providing the profile name that you created previously:

```
$ go tool pprof cpu00.pprof
File: colStats.test
Type: cpu
Time: Apr 9, 2019 at 11:21pm (EDT)
Duration: 11.31s, Total samples = 12.04s (106.42%)
Entering interactive mode (type "help" for commands, "o" for options)
(pprof)
```

When the profiler is enabled, it stops the program execution every 10 milliseconds and takes a sample of the function stack. This sample contains all functions that are executing or waiting to execute at that time. The more often a function appears in these samples, the more time your program is spending on that function. Use the top command on the *pprof* prompt to see where your program is spending most of its time:

```
(pprof) top
Showing nodes accounting for 7770ms, 64.53% of 12040ms total
Dropped 132 nodes (cum <= 60.20ms)
Showing top 10 nodes out of 78
      flat  flat%   sum%        cum   cum%
    1810ms 15.03% 15.03%     1920ms 15.95%  runtime.heapBitsSetType
    1200ms  9.97% 25.00%     6980ms 57.97%  encoding/csv.(*Reader).readRecord
     870ms  7.23% 32.23%     4450ms 36.96%  runtime.mallocgc
     770ms  6.40% 38.62%      770ms  6.40%  runtime.memmove
     770ms  6.40% 45.02%      770ms  6.40%  strconv.readFloat
     690ms  5.73% 50.75%      690ms  5.73%  indexbytebody
     640ms  5.32% 56.06%      640ms  5.32%  runtime.memclrNoHeapPointers
     410ms  3.41% 59.47%      930ms  7.72%  bufio.(*Reader).ReadSlice
     340ms  2.82% 62.29%      340ms  2.82%  runtime.nextFreeFast
     270ms  2.24% 64.53%     8350ms 69.35%  encoding/csv.(*Reader).ReadAll
(pprof)
```

By default, the top subcommand sorts the function based on *flat* time, which means the time the function spends executing on the CPU. In this example, the program spent about 15% of its CPU time executing the function runtime.heap-BitsSetType(). But it's difficult to understand the context from this view alone. You can sort based on the *cumulative* time by using the option -cum with the top command:

```
(pprof) top -cum
Showing nodes accounting for 4.42s, 36.71% of 12.04s total
Dropped 132 nodes (cum <= 0.06s)
```

```
Showing top 10 nodes out of 78
      flat   flat%   sum%      cum   cum%
         0     0%     0%    10.75s 89.29%  pragprog.com/.../colStats.Benchmark_Run
         0     0%     0%    10.75s 89.29%  pragprog.com/.../colStats.run
         0     0%     0%    10.75s 89.29%  testing.(*B).runN
     0.19s  1.58%  1.58%    10.24s 85.05%  pragprog.com/.../colStats.csv2float
         0     0%  1.58%     9.70s 80.56%  testing.(*B).launch
     0.27s  2.24%  3.82%     8.35s 69.35%  encoding/csv.(*Reader).ReadAll
     1.20s  9.97% 13.79%     6.98s 57.97%  encoding/csv.(*Reader).readRecord
     0.87s  7.23% 21.01%     4.45s 36.96%  runtime.mallocgc
     0.08s  0.66% 21.68%     2.68s 22.26%  runtime.makeslice
     1.81s 15.03% 36.71%     1.92s 15.95%  runtime.heapBitsSetType
(pprof)
```

The cumulative time accounts for the time the function was executing or waiting for a called function to return. In our example, the program spends most of its time on functions related to the benchmark functionality, which are irrelevant to us. You can see from this output that your program is spending over 85% of its time on the csv2float() function. This is important since this is a function that you wrote.

You can take a deeper look at how this function is spending its time by using the list subcommand. This subcommand displays the source code of the function annotated with the time spent to run each line of code. This subcommand takes a regular expression parameter. It shows the source code for any functions matching the regular expression. Use it to list the contents of the csv2float() function:

```
(pprof) list csv2float
Total: 12.04s
«... skipping long output...»
         .          .     91:    column--
         .          .     92:
         .          .     93:    // Read in all CSV data
         .      8.35s     94:    allData, err := cr.ReadAll()
         .          .     95:    if err != nil {
«... skipping long output...»
(pprof)
```

This output shows that the program is spending 8.35s of the total 12.04s that the benchmark took to complete the ReadAll() function. That's a long time. You need to dig into that function to see how it's spending its time. You could continue to use the list subcommand to do this, but you have an easier, more visual way to find the relationship between the functions.

Run the subcommand web to generate a relationship graph. The web subcommand requires the *graphviz*[4] libraries to work. You can install the required libraries using your Linux package manager. For other operating systems, check the Graphviz download page.[5] The resulting graph opens automatically in your default browser:

```
(pprof) web
```

Take a look at the generated graph shown in Figure 3 on page 140.

The graph shows the hot path, or the path where the program spends most of its time, in red. Based on this graph, the program spends close to 37% of the total time in runtime.mallocgc(), which you can trace back to ReadAll() from three different points. The runtime.mallocgc() function allocates memory and runs the garbage collector. This means that we're spending a lot of time in garbage collection due to memory allocation.

Quit the profile visualization tool by typing quit at the interactive prompt:

```
(pprof) quit
```

You can see how much memory the program is allocating by executing a memory profile. The procedure is similar to creating a CPU profile, but you use the -memprofile option instead. Run the benchmark again with this option to create a memory profile:

```
$ go test -bench . -benchtime=10x -run ^$ -memprofile mem00.pprof
goos: linux
goarch: amd64
pkg: pragprog.com/rggo/performance/colStats
Benchmark_Run-4              10         1030229000 ns/op
PASS
ok      pragprog.com/rggo/performance/colStats   11.762s
```

This command saved the memory profile to the mem00.pprof file. You can view the results using the go tool pprof again, passing the option -alloc_space to see the allocated memory:

```
$ go tool pprof -alloc_space mem00.pprof
File: colStats.test
Type: alloc_space
Time: Apr 11, 2019 at 12:07am (EDT)
Entering interactive mode (type "help" for commands, "o" for options)
(pprof)
```

---

4. www.graphviz.org

5. www.graphviz.org/download/

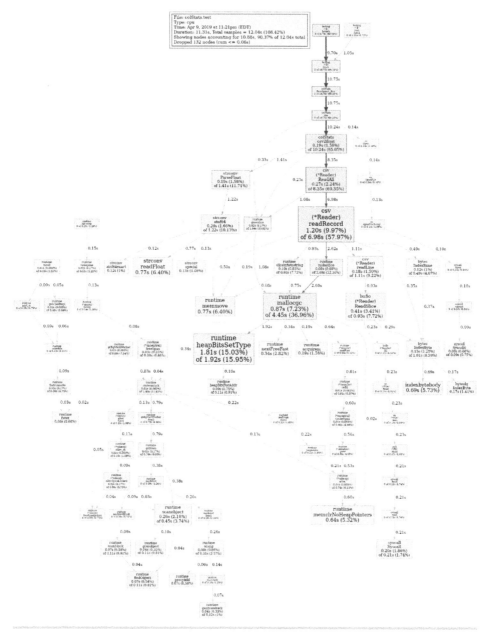

Figure 3—CPU Profiler Graph

Similarly to the CPU profiler, use the subcommand top -cum to see the cumulative allocated memory:

```
(pprof) top -cum
Showing nodes accounting for 5.81GB, 100% of 5.82GB total
Dropped 10 nodes (cum <= 0.03GB)
Showing top 10 nodes out of 11
    flat  flat%   sum%       cum    cum%
       0     0%     0%    5.81GB    100%  pragprog.com/.../colStats.Benchmark_Run
  1.05GB 18.03% 18.03%    5.81GB    100%  pragprog.com/...ormance/colStats.run
       0     0% 18.03%    5.81GB    100%  testing.(*B).runN
       0     0% 18.03%    5.27GB 90.55%  testing.(*B).launch
  0.80GB 13.84% 31.87%    4.76GB 81.93%  pragprog.com/.../colStats.csv2float
  2.66GB 45.78% 77.65%    3.92GB 67.38%  encoding/csv.(*Reader).ReadAll
  1.26GB 21.60% 99.26%    1.26GB 21.60%  encoding/csv.(*Reader).readRecord
       0     0% 99.26%    0.55GB  9.44%  testing.(*B).run1.func1
       0     0% 99.26%    0.04GB  0.71%  bufio.NewReader
  0.04GB  0.71%   100%    0.04GB  0.71%  bufio.NewReaderSize
(pprof)
```

As we suspected, the ReadAll() function from the encoding/csv package is responsible for the allocation of almost 4GB of memory, which corresponds to 67% of all the memory allocation for this program. The more memory we allocate, the more garbage collection has to run, increasing the time it takes to run the program.

We need to find a way to reduce the memory allocation, but before we try that, run the benchmark one more time, using the parameter -benchmem to display the total memory allocation. You can use this value later to compare and see if our modifications are improving it. Save the result to the file benchresults00m.txt piping it to the tee command:

```
$ go test -bench . -benchtime=10x -run ^$ -benchmem | tee benchresults00m.txt
goos: linux
goarch: amd64
pkg: pragprog.com/rggo/performance/colStats
  Benchmark_Run-4            10       1042029902 ns/op \
                                      564385222 B/op    5043008 allocs/op
PASS
ok      pragprog.com/rggo/performance/colStats    11.627s
```

Now you're ready to address the memory allocation issue.

Reducing Memory Allocation

You now know that the tool spends a lot of time with the garbage collector because it's allocating too much memory. You also know that the bulk of the memory allocation comes from the ReadAll() function of the encoding/csv package, which you're calling from the csv2float() function.

If you follow the program's logic, it's reading all the records from each CSV file into memory and then processing them one at a time with a loop, storing the result in another slice. It's not doing anything that requires the entire content of the file to be in memory, so you can replace the calls to ReadAll() with the function Read() from the encoding/csv package. This function reads one record at a time, so you can execute it directly inside the loop, preventing the whole file from being read at once.

Start by removing the call to ReadAll() and the associated error check. Remove these lines from the csv2float() function in the csv.go file:

```
// Read in all CSV data
allData, err := cr.ReadAll()
if err != nil {
  return nil, fmt.Errorf("Cannot read data from file: %w", err)
}
```

Next, replace the loop header. Instead of using the range operator on allData, use an infinite loop since you don't know beforehand how many records it needs to read:

performance/colStats.v1/csv.go
```
for i := 0; ; i++ {
```

Inside the loop, use the Read() function to read a record from the file:

performance/colStats.v1/csv.go
```
row, err := cr.Read()
```

Since you're using an infinite loop, you need to determine when you reach the end of the file and break out of the loop to ensure the program doesn't run forever. Do this by checking if the call to Read() returns an error of type io.EOF and then break out of the loop. Also, check and return any unexpected errors:

performance/colStats.v1/csv.go
```
if err == io.EOF {
  break
}

if err != nil {
  return nil, fmt.Errorf("Cannot read data from file: %w", err)
}
```

Finally, now that you're using the Read() method to read in each record, you can enable its ReuseRecord option to reuse the same slice for each read operation, reducing the memory allocation even more. Set this option to the variable cr of type csv.Reader right after you define it at the beginning of the function:

performance/colStats.v1/csv.go

```go
// Create the CSV Reader used to read in data from CSV files
cr := csv.NewReader(r)
cr.ReuseRecord = true
```

Your complete csv2float() function now looks like this:

performance/colStats.v1/csv.go

```go
func csv2float(r io.Reader, column int) ([]float64, error) {
  // Create the CSV Reader used to read in data from CSV files
  cr := csv.NewReader(r)
  cr.ReuseRecord = true

  // Adjusting for 0 based index
  column--

  var data []float64

  // Looping through all records
  for i := 0; ; i++ {
    row, err := cr.Read()
    if err == io.EOF {
      break
    }

    if err != nil {
      return nil, fmt.Errorf("Cannot read data from file: %w", err)
    }

    if i == 0 {
      continue
    }

    // Checking number of columns in CSV file
    if len(row) <= column {
      // File does not have that many columns
      return nil,
        fmt.Errorf("%w: File has only %d columns", ErrInvalidColumn, len(row))
    }

    // Try to convert data read into a float number
    v, err := strconv.ParseFloat(row[column], 64)
    if err != nil {
      return nil, fmt.Errorf("%w: %s", ErrNotNumber, err)
    }

    data = append(data, v)
  }

  // Return the slice of float64 and nil error
  return data, nil
}
```

Once you're done refactoring the code, execute the tests again to ensure it still works as designed:

```
$ go test
PASS
ok      pragprog.com/rggo/performance/colStats      0.006s
```

All the tests passed, so execute the benchmark again to see if the updates improved the program. Run the benchmark and save the results to the file benchresults01m.txt to compare with the previous results:

```
$ go test -bench . -benchtime=10x -run ^$ -benchmem | tee benchresults01m.txt
goos: linux
goarch: amd64
pkg: pragprog.com/rggo/performance/colStats
Benchmark_Run-4           10          618936266 ns/op \
                                      230447420 B/op    2527988 allocs/op
PASS
ok      pragprog.com/rggo/performance/colStats      6.981s
```

You can see right away that the benchmark executed faster, in almost 7 seconds, compared to the previous 12 seconds. That's a good improvement. You can determine how much faster this new version is by comparing both benchmark results with a tool called *benchcmp*. Install it on your system by running this command:

```
$ go get -u -v golang.org/x/tools/cmd/benchcmp
```

Now, run benchcmp providing the previous and current benchmarks results files:

```
$ benchcmp benchresults00m.txt benchresults01m.txt
benchmark            old ns/op       new ns/op       delta
Benchmark_Run-4      1018451552      618936266       -39.23%

benchmark            old allocs      new allocs      delta
Benchmark_Run-4      5043009         2527988         -49.87%

benchmark            old bytes       new bytes       delta
Benchmark_Run-4      564385358       230447420       -59.17%
```

As you can see, the changes improved the program's execution time by close to 40% while reducing memory allocation by half. Less allocation, less garbage collection.

Run the profiler again to see what the CPU utilization looks like now:

```
$ go test -bench . -benchtime=10x -run ^$ -cpuprofile cpu01.pprof
goos: linux
goarch: amd64
pkg: pragprog.com/rggo/performance/colStats
```

```
Benchmark_Run-4                    10        617226982 ns/op
PASS
ok       pragprog.com/rggo/performance/colStats        7.129s
```

Use the go tool pprof on the new file to view the results. List the top 10 functions by cumulative time.

```
$ go tool pprof cpu01.pprof
File: colStats.v1.test
Type: cpu
Time: Apr 11, 2019 at 12:40am (EDT)
Duration: 7.11s, Total samples = 7.31s (102.83%)
Entering interactive mode (type "help" for commands, "o" for options)
(pprof) top -cum
Showing nodes accounting for 2160ms, 29.55% of 7310ms total
Dropped 84 nodes (cum <= 36.55ms)
Showing top 10 nodes out of 77
   flat   flat%   sum%        cum   cum%
      0      0%      0%     6690ms 91.52%  pragprog.com/...lStats%2ev1.Benchmark_Run
      0      0%      0%     6690ms 91.52%  pragprog.com/.../colStats%2ev1.run
      0      0%      0%     6690ms 91.52%  testing.(*B).runN
  200ms   2.74%   2.74%     6280ms 85.91%  pragprog.com/.../colStats%2ev1.csv2float
      0      0%   2.74%     6020ms 82.35%  testing.(*B).launch
  200ms   2.74%   5.47%     4710ms 64.43%  encoding/csv.(*Reader).Read
 1250ms  17.10%  22.57%     4510ms 61.70%  encoding/csv.(*Reader).readRecord
  110ms   1.50%  24.08%     1220ms 16.69%  strconv.ParseFloat
  220ms   3.01%  27.09%     1110ms 15.18%  strconv.atof64
  180ms   2.46%  29.55%     1090ms 14.91%  runtime.slicebytetostring
(pprof)
```

The profiling has changed slightly. The top part is still the same, as the same functions are responsible for executing the program. The csv2float() function is still there, which also makes sense. But in the bottom part of the output, the functions related to memory allocation and garbage collection are no longer in the top 10. This is the result of the changes you've made to the code.

You can continue to explore the profiler and look for other areas for improvement. When you're done, type quit to close the *pprof* tool. For our example, let's assume that we are satisfied with the current results.

Next, let's run the tracer on the program to see if we can find other areas for improvement, outside the CPU execution time.

Tracing Your Tool

The Go profiler is a great tool to help you understand how your program is spending CPU time. However, sometimes a program is spending time waiting for resources to be available. For example, it could be spending time waiting for a network connection or a file to be read. To help you understand those cases, Go provides another tool: the *Tracer*.

Similarly to the profiler, the tracer is also integrated with the testing and benchmarking features through the go test tool. Run the benchmarks again with the -trace option to create a trace:

```
$ go test -bench . -benchtime=10x -run ^$ -trace trace01.out
goos: linux
goarch: amd64
pkg: pragprog.com/rggo/performance/colStats
Benchmark_Run-4                   10          685356800 ns/op
PASS
ok      pragprog.com/rggo/performance/colStats          7.712s
```

Once the trace is created, view the results with the go tool trace command:

```
$ go tool trace trace01.out
2019/04/14 14:55:26 Parsing trace...
2019/04/14 14:55:27 Splitting trace...
2019/04/14 14:55:28 Opening browser. Trace viewer is listening on
  http://127.0.0.1:45561
```

The go tool trace command parses the contents of the trace file and makes the results available on a web server running on a random port on localhost. You can see the URL in the output. It will also try to open this URL in your default browser automatically. Switch to your browser to see the index page as shown in Figure 4:

View trace
Goroutine analysis
Network blocking profile (⬇)
Synchronization blocking profile (⬇)
Syscall blocking profile (⬇)
Scheduler latency profile (⬇)
User-defined tasks
User-defined regions
Minimum mutator utilization

Figure 4—Go Tracer Results Index

The Go tracer captures several types of events related to your program execution, such as details about Goroutines, syscalls, network calls, heap size, garbage collector activity, and more. The index page gives you an idea of resources you can check. Start viewing the trace by clicking the *View trace* link as shown in Figure 5:

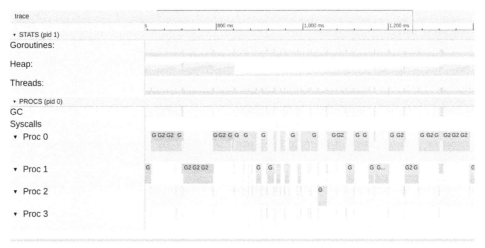

Figure 5—Go Tracer Viewer

This opens the *Trace Viewer* interactive web tool. This tool only works on Chrome or Chromium browsers. This tool shows details about the program execution. You can zoom in or move around to see more granular detail. Zoom in by using the toolbar or by pressing 3 and moving the mouse to control the zoom amount as seen in Figure 6:

Figure 6—Go Tracer Viewer - Zoom

On the top screen, labeled *STATS*, you'll see an overview of the distribution of Goroutines, memory allocation, and number of threads. In the middle of the screen, labeled *PROCS* you can see how the Goroutines are distributed across all the CPUs/cores on the executing machine. It also includes garbage collection and syscalls execution. The bottom part of the screen is reserved to present details about events. You can see details by clicking any area of the previous two screens. For example, click the Goroutines line to see details about running Goroutines at that specific time as shown in Figure 7:

3 items selected.	Counter Samples (3)		
Counter	**Series**	**Time**	**Value**
Goroutines	GCWaiting	1217.1232360000001	0
Goroutines	Runnable	1217.1232360000001	0
Goroutines	Running	1217.1232360000001	1

Figure 7—Go Tracer Viewer - Details

One thing that you'll notice by looking at the tracer is that the program isn't using all four available CPUs effectively. Only one Goroutine is running at a time. Since we're processing several files, it would be more efficient to use more CPUs. Let's address this issue next.

Improving the colStats Tool to Process Files Concurrently

As you noticed from the tracer output, the tool is processing files sequentially. This isn't efficient since several files have to be processed. By changing the program to process files concurrently, you can benefit from multiprocessor machines and use more CPUs, generally making the program run faster. The program will spend less time waiting for resources and more time processing files.

One of the main benefits of Go is its concurrency model. Go includes concurrency primitives that allow you to add concurrency to your programs in a more intuitive way. By using goroutines and channels. you can modify the current *colStats* tool to process several files concurrently by making changes to the run() function only. The other functions remain unchanged.

First, add the sync package to the imports section, which provides synchronization types such as the WaitGroup:

```
performance/colStats.v2/main.go
import (
  "flag"
  "fmt"
  "io"
  "os"
  "sync"
)
```

You'll update the run() function to process files concurrently by creating a new goroutine for each file you need to process. But first you'll need to create some channels to communicate between the goroutines. You'll use three channels: resCh of type chan []float64 to communicate results of processing each file, errCh of type chan error to communicate potential errors, and doneCh of type chan struct{} to communicate when all files have been processed. Define these channels after defining the consolidate variable:

performance/colStats.v2/main.go
```
// Create the channel to receive results or errors of operations
resCh := make(chan []float64)
errCh := make(chan error)
doneCh := make(chan struct{})
```

Notice that you're using an empty struct as the type for the doneCh channel. This is a common pattern since this channel doesn't need to send any data. It only sends a signal indicating the processing is done. By using the empty struct, the program doesn't allocate any memory for this channel.

Next, define a variable wg of type sync.WaitGroup. The WaitGroup provides a mechanism to coordinate the goroutines execution. For each goroutine you create, add 1 to the WaitGroup. When a goroutine is done, subtract 1 from the WaitGroup. Later in the code use the method Wait() to wait until all the goroutines are done before continuing with the execution.

performance/colStats.v2/main.go
```
wg := sync.WaitGroup{}
```

Then, update the main loop. Instead of processing each file directly, wrap them in an anonymous function that you'll call as a goroutine by prefixing it with the go keyword. Inside the loop, first add 1 to the WaitGroup:

performance/colStats.v2/main.go
```
// Loop through all files and create a goroutine to process
// each one concurrently
for _, fname := range filenames {
  wg.Add(1)
```

Next, define the anonymous function that takes the file name fname as an input parameter. You must redeclare or pass the variable fname as an argument to the anonymous function to prevent it from *closing* on the outside variable and effectively run all goroutines using the last known value of that variable. For more details on this, see the related Go FAQ article.[6]

performance/colStats.v2/main.go
```
go func(fname string) {
```

Note that you're calling this function with the go keyword to create a new goroutine.

---

6. golang.org/doc/faq#closures_and_goroutines

Inside the new function, defer a call to the method wg.Done() to subtract 1 from the WaitGroup when the function finishes.

performance/colStats.v2/main.go
```
defer wg.Done()
```

Then execute the file processing as before, but this time you handle errors differently since this is a goroutine executing asynchronously. In this case, send any potential errors to the error channel ErrCh:

performance/colStats.v2/main.go
```
// Open the file for reading
f, err := os.Open(fname)
if err != nil {
  errCh <- fmt.Errorf("Cannot open file: %w", err)
  return
}

// Parse the CSV into a slice of float64 numbers
data, err := csv2float(f, column)
if err != nil {
  errCh <- err
}

if err := f.Close(); err != nil {
  errCh <- err
}
```

If the csv2float() function returns the data with no errors, then send the result variable data into the result channel resCh. Later, another goroutine will consolidate this data to run the final operations.

performance/colStats.v2/main.go
```
resCh <- data
```

Data Race Condition

You might be wondering why we're not using the consolidate variable to append the results directly in the goroutine. Since multiple goroutines can be running simultaneously and accessing the same variable, it would lead to a data race condition and cause unpredictable results or data loss.

To prevent this, you could protect the variable with a sync.Mutex. In Go, it's more idiomatic to use a channel to communicate the values between goroutines instead. By doing this, you can run the consolidation on another goroutine that has exclusive access to the consolidate variable, preventing the race condition.

Complete the anonymous function, ensuring that you also execute it and pass the variable fname as input:

performance/colStats.v2/main.go

```
  }(fname)
}
```

Next, create another goroutine using an anonymous function to wait until all files have been processed. Use the function Wait() from the WaitGroup type you created before to block the current goroutine from proceeding until all the other goroutines finish their work. When this happens, it unblocks the current goroutine allowing it to execute the next line which closes the channel doneCh signaling that the process is complete.

performance/colStats.v2/main.go

```
go func() {
  wg.Wait()
  close(doneCh)
}()
```

Finally, back in the main goroutine (the default one that starts when you run the program), consolidate the results coming from the resCh channel into the consolidate variable. Then check for errors coming from the error channel errCh and decide when to stop processing. Then print the results. Do this by running an infinite loop with a select statement. The select statement works similarly to a switch statement where you evaluate multiple conditions. But for the select statement, the conditions are communication operations through a channel.

Create a select block with three conditions. For the first conditions, if you receive an error from the error channel errCh, return this error, terminating the function. In this program, returning the error effectively terminates the program, which cleans up any outstanding goroutines. This approach works for short-lived command-line tools like this. If you're developing a long-running program like an API or web server, you may need to add code to clean up goroutines properly avoiding leaks.

Continuing with the second condition of the select block, if you receive data from the result channel resCh, consolidate the data into the consolidate slice using the built-in append() function.,

In the final condition of the select block, if you receive the signal on the done channel doneCh, you know that you're done processing files, so you run the desired operation, print the results, and return the potential error from fmt.Fprintln(), completing the function.

performance/colStats.v2/main.go
```go
  for {
    select {
    case err := <-errCh:
      return err
    case data := <-resCh:
      consolidate = append(consolidate, data...)
    case <-doneCh:
      _, err := fmt.Fprintln(out, opFunc(consolidate))
      return err
    }
  }
}
```

The select statement works in this case because it blocks the execution of the program until any of the channels is ready to communicate. It effectively selects on multiple channel operations. It's a powerful concept in Go.

The complete refactored run() function looks like this:

performance/colStats.v2/main.go
```go
func run(filenames []string, op string, column int, out io.Writer) error {
  var opFunc statsFunc

  if len(filenames) == 0 {
    return ErrNoFiles
  }

  if column < 1 {
    return fmt.Errorf("%w: %d", ErrInvalidColumn, column)
  }

  // Validate the operation and define the opFunc accordingly
  switch op {
  case "sum":
    opFunc = sum
  case "avg":
    opFunc = avg
  default:
    return fmt.Errorf("%w: %s", ErrInvalidOperation, op)
  }

  consolidate := make([]float64, 0)

  // Create the channel to receive results or errors of operations
  resCh := make(chan []float64)
  errCh := make(chan error)
  doneCh := make(chan struct{})

  wg := sync.WaitGroup{}
```

```go
// Loop through all files and create a goroutine to process
// each one concurrently
for _, fname := range filenames {
  wg.Add(1)
  go func(fname string) {

    defer wg.Done()

    // Open the file for reading
    f, err := os.Open(fname)
    if err != nil {
      errCh <- fmt.Errorf("Cannot open file: %w", err)
      return
    }

    // Parse the CSV into a slice of float64 numbers
    data, err := csv2float(f, column)
    if err != nil {
      errCh <- err
    }

    if err := f.Close(); err != nil {
      errCh <- err
    }

    resCh <- data
  }(fname)
}

go func() {
  wg.Wait()
  close(doneCh)
}()

for {
  select {
  case err := <-errCh:
    return err
  case data := <-resCh:
    consolidate = append(consolidate, data...)
  case <-doneCh:
    _, err := fmt.Fprintln(out, opFunc(consolidate))
    return err
  }
}
}
```

The code is complete. Save your file with the changes and execute the tests to ensure it works properly:

```
$ go test
PASS
ok      pragprog.com/rggo/performance/colStats       0.006s
```

The tests passed. Execute the benchmark again to see if it improved the execution speed. Save the results into a file to compare:

```
$ go test -bench . -benchtime=10x -run ^$ -benchmem | tee benchresults02m.txt
goos: linux
goarch: amd64
pkg: pragprog.com/rggo/performance/colStats
  Benchmark_Run-4                  10          345375068 ns/op \
                                               230537908 B/op    2529105 allocs/op
PASS
ok      pragprog.com/rggo/performance/colStats       3.913s
```

Now compare with the previous results:

```
$ benchcmp benchresults01m.txt benchresults02m.txt
benchmark           old ns/op      new ns/op      delta
Benchmark_Run-4     618936266      345375068      -44.20%

benchmark           old allocs     new allocs      delta
Benchmark_Run-4     2527988        2529105         +0.04%

benchmark           old bytes      new bytes      delta
Benchmark_Run-4     230447420      230537908      +0.04%
```

This is another great improvement; it's almost twice as fast as the previous version. Run the tracer again to see how it looks now:

```
$ go test -bench . -benchtime=10x -run ^$ -trace trace02.out
goos: linux
goarch: amd64
pkg: pragprog.com/rggo/performance/colStats
Benchmark_Run-4                  10          365519710 ns/op
PASS
ok      pragprog.com/rggo/performance/colStats       4.140s
```

Open the results using the go tool trace:

```
$ go tool trace trace02.out
2019/04/14 21:51:29 Parsing trace...
2019/04/14 21:51:30 Splitting trace...
2019/04/14 21:51:32 Opening browser. Trace viewer is listening on
  http://127.0.0.1:41997
```

Switch to the browser and click the *View Trace* link to open the tracer viewer shown in Figure 8:

Figure 8—Go Tracer Viewer - Concurrent

As you can see, the program used all four CPUs, improving the speed of the tool. You can also see at the top of the screen the *Goroutines* showing spikes, which corresponds to the new logic where we create one goroutine per file. Click one of those spikes to see the details, as shown in Figure 9:

3 items selected.	Counter Samples (3)		
Counter	**Series**	**Time**	**Value**
Goroutines	GCWaiting	1309.885514	0
Goroutines	Runnable	1309.885514	882
Goroutines	Running	1309.885514	4

Figure 9—Go Tracer Viewer - Concurrent Details

In this example, a large number of goroutines are in the *Runnable* state, but only four are actually running. This could be an indication that we are creating too many goroutines, which can increase the time the scheduler spends scheduling them. Let's see if that's the case. Go back to the index page and click the *Goroutine Analysis* link to open the Goroutines details as seen in Figure 10 on page 156.

The Goroutine Analysis shows that the program created over eleven thousand goroutines for run.func1(), which corresponds to the anonymous function you're

Goroutines:

github.com/rgerardi/rggo/performance/colStats%2ev2.run.func1 N=11005

runtime.gcBgMarkWorker N=18

testing.(*B).launch N=1

runtime.bgsweep N=1

testing.(*B).run1.func1 N=1

runtime/trace.Start.func1 N=1

testing.tRunner N=16

runtime.main N=1

github.com/rgerardi/rggo/performance/colStats%2ev2.run.func2 N=14

testing.runTests.func1.1 N=1

N=2

Figure 10—Go Tracer - Goroutine Analysis

using to process each file. Click this link to open the details about these goroutines. Double-click the *Scheduler wait* column to sort based on this column as seen in Figure 11:

Goroutine Name: github.com/rgerardi/rggo/performance/colStats%2ev2.run.func1
Number of Goroutines: 11005
Execution Time: 89.17% of total program execution time
Network Wait Time: graph(download)
Sync Block Time: graph(download)
Blocking Syscall Time: graph(download)
Scheduler Wait Time: graph(download)

Goroutine	Total	Execution	Network wait	Sync block	Blocking syscall	Scheduler wait	GC sweeping	GC pause
8484	342ms	1821µs	0ns	24ms	2774ns	316ms	0ns (0.0%)	67ms (19.6%)
2829	337ms	1738µs	0ns	22ms	0ns	312ms	34µs (0.0%)	59ms (17.5%)
2658	337ms	1091µs	0ns	24ms	0ns	312ms	0ns (0.0%)	59ms (17.5%)
2099	339ms	1928µs	0ns	24ms	0ns	312ms	0ns (0.0%)	59ms (17.4%)
2796	337ms	1466µs	0ns	23ms	0ns	312ms	0ns (0.0%)	59ms (17.5%)
8544	342ms	1086µs	0ns	29ms	1875ns	312ms	0ns (0.0%)	67ms (19.6%)
2869	337ms	995µs	0ns	24ms	0ns	312ms	32µs (0.0%)	59ms (17.5%)
8542	342ms	1158µs	0ns	29ms	0ns	311ms	0ns (0.0%)	67ms (19.6%)
8543	342ms	1107µs	0ns	30ms	0ns	311ms	0ns (0.0%)	67ms (19.6%)

Figure 11—Go Tracer - Goroutine Details

The results show that many of these goroutines are waiting too long to be scheduled. This confirms the scheduling contention you saw in the tracer viewer. Let's reduce it.

Reduce Scheduling Contention

Goroutines are relatively cheap, and in some cases it makes sense to create many of them. For example, if the goroutines wait a long time on IO or network response, then the scheduler can execute other goroutines while these are waiting, increasing the efficiency of the program. In our case, the goroutines are mostly CPU-bound, so creating many of them doesn't improve the efficiency. Instead, creating too many causes scheduling contention. Let's address this issue by modifying our program to use *worker queues*. Instead of creating one goroutine per file, you'll create one goroutine per available CPU. These will be our workers. Another goroutine sends the jobs to be executed by the workers. When no more jobs exist, the workers are done and the program finishes.

Start by adding another package to the import list. The package runtime contains several functions that deal with the Go runtime. You'll use this package to determine the number of available CPUs:

performance/colStats.v3/main.go
```go
import (
  "flag"
  "fmt"
  "io"
  "os"
  "runtime"
  "sync"
)
```

Next, edit the function run(). Add another channel called filesCh of type chan string. This is the queue; you'll add files to be processed to this channel, and the worker goroutines will take them from this channel and process them.

performance/colStats.v3/main.go
```go
filesCh := make(chan string)
```

Now create a goroutine to iterate through all the files, sending each file to the filesCh channel. At the end, close the channel, indicating no more work is left to do:

performance/colStats.v3/main.go
```go
// Loop through all files sending them through the channel
// so each one will be processed when a worker is available
go func() {
  defer close(filesCh)
  for _, fname := range filenames {
    filesCh <- fname
  }
}()
```

Then update the main loop. Instead of ranging through all the files, use a regular loop with a counter i. The upper limit of the loop is the total number of CPUs available on the executing machine, which you obtain by calling the function runtime.NumCPU() from the runtime package:

performance/colStats.v3/main.go
```go
for i := 0; i < runtime.NumCPU(); i++ {
```

Inside the loop, you still add 1 to the WaitGroup to indicate a running goroutine, and you use the same logic for the rest of the program. Then, define the anonymous function to execute as the goroutine. This time you don't need the input parameter because the function will get the file names via the channel:

performance/colStats.v3/main.go
```
wg.Add(1)
go func() {
```

In the anonymous function's body, use defer to ensure the function wg.Done() executes at the end. Then define a loop using the range operator to range over the filesCh channel. When you range over a channel, the loop gets values from the channel until it's closed. Because you close this channel when it's done sending files, you ensure this loop terminates, causing the goroutine to finish.

performance/colStats.v3/main.go
```
  defer wg.Done()
  for fname := range filesCh {
    // Open the file for reading
    f, err := os.Open(fname)
    if err != nil {
      errCh <- fmt.Errorf("Cannot open file: %w", err)
      return
    }

    // Parse the CSV into a slice of float64 numbers
    data, err := csv2float(f, column)
    if err != nil {
      errCh <- err
    }

    if err := f.Close(); err != nil {
      errCh <- err
    }

    resCh <- data
  }
}()
```

The rest of the body is the same as before. Open the file, process it, and send the data to the result channel. If errors occur, send it to the error channel.

This is the new version of the run() function:

performance/colStats.v3/main.go
```
func run(filenames []string, op string, column int, out io.Writer) error {
  var opFunc statsFunc

  if len(filenames) == 0 {
    return ErrNoFiles
  }
```

```go
if column < 1 {
  return fmt.Errorf("%w: %d", ErrInvalidColumn, column)
}

// Validate the operation and define the opFunc accordingly
switch op {
case "sum":
  opFunc = sum
case "avg":
  opFunc = avg
default:
  return fmt.Errorf("%w: %s", ErrInvalidOperation, op)
}

consolidate := make([]float64, 0)

// Create the channel to receive results or errors of operations
resCh := make(chan []float64)
errCh := make(chan error)
doneCh := make(chan struct{})
filesCh := make(chan string)

wg := sync.WaitGroup{}

// Loop through all files sending them through the channel
// so each one will be processed when a worker is available
go func() {
  defer close(filesCh)
  for _, fname := range filenames {
    filesCh <- fname
  }
}()

for i := 0; i < runtime.NumCPU(); i++ {
  wg.Add(1)
  go func() {
    defer wg.Done()
    for fname := range filesCh {
      // Open the file for reading
      f, err := os.Open(fname)
      if err != nil {
        errCh <- fmt.Errorf("Cannot open file: %w", err)
        return
      }

      // Parse the CSV into a slice of float64 numbers
      data, err := csv2float(f, column)
      if err != nil {
        errCh <- err
      }

      if err := f.Close(); err != nil {
        errCh <- err
      }
```

```
        resCh <- data
      }
    }()
  }

  go func() {
    wg.Wait()
    close(doneCh)
  }()

  for {
    select {
    case err := <-errCh:
      return err
    case data := <-resCh:
      consolidate = append(consolidate, data...)
    case <-doneCh:
      _, err := fmt.Fprintln(out, opFunc(consolidate))
      return err
    }
  }
}
```

Save the file and run the tests to ensure the program is still working:

```
$ go test
PASS
ok      pragprog.com/rggo/performance/colStats      0.004s
```

Once all tests pass, run the benchmark to see if this update improved the performance. Save the results to a file to compare with the previous results:

```
$ go test -bench . -benchtime=10x -run ^$ -benchmem | tee benchresults03m.txt
goos: linux
goarch: amd64
pkg: pragprog.com/rggo/performance/colStats
  Benchmark_Run-4                  10          308737148 ns/op \
                                              230444710 B/op    2527944 allocs/op
PASS
ok      pragprog.com/rggo/performance/colStats      3.602s
```

Compare with the previous results to assess improvements:

```
$ benchcmp benchresults02m.txt benchresults03m.txt
benchmark              old ns/op       new ns/op       delta
Benchmark_Run-4        345375068       308737148       -10.61%

benchmark              old allocs      new allocs      delta
Benchmark_Run-4        2529105         2527944         -0.05%

benchmark              old bytes       new bytes       delta
Benchmark_Run-4        230537908       230444710       -0.04%
```

As you can see, this version runs over 10% faster than the previous version. Compare this benchmark result with the original version to see how much you've improved the performance in total:

```
$ benchcmp benchresults00m.txt benchresults03m.txt
benchmark              old ns/op        new ns/op       delta
Benchmark_Run-4        1042029902       308737148       -70.37%

benchmark              old allocs       new allocs      delta
Benchmark_Run-4        5043008          2527944         -49.87%

benchmark              old bytes        new bytes       delta
Benchmark_Run-4        564385222        230444710       -59.17%
```

According to the benchmarks, this version of the tool is over three times faster than the original. It also allocates 60% less memory than the original.

To finish up, compile your tool and run it using the time command to compare with the original:

```
$ go build
$ time ./colStats -op avg -col 2 testdata/benchmark/*.csv
50006.0653788

real    0m0.381s
user    0m1.057s
sys     0m0.104s
```

This time, the program processed all one thousand files in 0.38 seconds, compared to the original 1.2 seconds. This is around three times faster, which is similar to the results of our benchmarks.

Exercises

Before you move on, you may want to expand the skills and techniques you've explored in this chapter. Here are some suggestions:

- Execute the tracer on the last version of the tool. Look for the new goroutine pattern. Is there a difference between this version and the previous version? Have you addressed the scheduling contention?

- Improve the *colStats* tool by adding more functions such as Min and Max, which return the lowest and the largest values in a given column. Write tests for these functions.

- Write benchmarks for the new functions Min and Max.

- Profile the functions Min and Max, looking for improvement areas.

Wrapping Up

In this chapter, you used several tools provided by Go to measure and analyze the performance of your programs. You started by developing a tool that processes content from CSV files. You used benchmarks to measure its speed. Then you used the profiler to look for bottlenecks. You iteratively improved the tool by using the results of the profiler and tracer tools. You developed a new version of the tool that processes files concurrently. Finally, you used the same techniques to analyze this version and made improvements to run the code more efficiently across the available CPUs.

In the next chapter, you'll design tools that execute external commands and capture their output. You'll interact with system processes. You'll use some of the concurrency techniques you've learned here to handle system signals and exit appropriately. You'll also use contexts to time out of long-running external commands.

## CHAPTER 6

Controlling Processes

So far, you've developed several command-line tools with Go by executing tasks with your own algorithms. In some situations, it's easier to delegate some of these tasks to more specialized programs that are already available on your system. For example, you may want to use git to execute version control commands against a Git repository or launch Firefox to display a web page on a browser, as you did in Adding an Auto-Preview Feature, on page 61, when you built the Markdown Preview tool.

In some cases, these specialized programs have an API available that you can call directly from your program. When this isn't available, you have to use their functionality by executing external commands from your Go program.

Go provides some lower-level libraries, such as syscall, but, unless you have specific requirements, it's best to use the higher-level interface provided by the os/exec package.

In this chapter, you'll apply the os/exec package to develop a simple, but useful, implementation of a Continuous Integration (CI) tool for your Go programs. A typical CI pipeline consists of several automated steps that continuously ensure a code base or an application is ready to be merged with some other developer's code, usually in a shared version control repository.

For this example, the CI pipeline consists of:

- Building the program using go build to verify if the program structure is valid.

- Executing tests using go test to ensure the program does what it's intended to do.

- Executing gofmt to ensure the program's format conforms to the standards.

- Executing git push to push the code to the remote shared Git repository that hosts the program code.

We'll call this tool *goci*. As usual, you'll start with a primitive implementation that will grow as you move along.

Executing External Programs

In this initial version of the *goci* tool, you'll define the main structure of your program and then execute the first step of the CI pipeline: building the program. Start by creating a directory called processes/goci for this tool under your book project's root directory:

```
$ mkdir -p $HOME/pragprog.com/rggo/processes/goci
$ cd $HOME/pragprog.com/rggo/processes/goci
```

Initialize a new Go module for this project called goci:

```
$ go mod init pragprog.com/rggo/processes/goci
go: creating new go.mod: module pragprog.com/rggo/processes/goci
```

For this tool, you'll use the *run* function pattern that you saw in Creating a Basic Markdown Preview Tool, on page 45. The run() function contains the main logic of the program, while the function main() contains only the code that parses the command-line flags and calls the run() function. This approach allows the execution of integration tests by executing the run() function during tests.

Create the file main.go in the goci directory and open it in your editor. Define the package name and add the import section. Import the flag package to parse command-line options, the fmt package to handle output, the io package that provides the io.Writer interface, the os package to interact with the operating system, and the os/exec package to execute external programs:

processes/goci/main.go
```go
package main

import (
    "flag"
    "fmt"
    "io"
    "os"
    "os/exec"
)
```

Now, define the run() function, which contains the main logic of your program. This function takes two input parameters. The first parameter, proj of type string, represents the Go project directory on which to execute the CI pipeline steps. The second parameter, out is an io.Writer interface that you use for out-putting the status of your tool. The function returns an error if something fails:

processes/goci/main.go
```
func run(proj string, out io.Writer) error {
```

In the run() function's body, first check if the project directory was provided and return an error if it was not:

processes/goci/main.go
```
if proj == "" {
  return fmt.Errorf("Project directory is required")
}
```

Add code to execute the first step in the pipeline, go build. To execute external commands in Go, you'll use the Cmd type from the os/exec package. The exec.Cmd type provides parameters and methods to execute commands with a variety of options. To create a new instance of the exec.Cmd type, you use the function exec.Command(). It takes the name of the executable program as the first argu-ment and zero or more arguments that will be passed to the executable during execution.

The executable program is go. Since you'll build the target project in this first step, define the list of arguments for the Go tool as a slice of strings where the first argument is build. The next argument is the current directory represented by a . (dot). The goal of executing go build as part of the pipeline is to validate the program's correctness, rather than creating an executable file. To execute go build without creating an executable file, you'll take advantage of the fact that go build doesn't create a file when building multiple packages at the same time. So, for the last argument, use the name of a package from Go's standard library, for example, the errors package. Define the arguments list like this:

processes/goci/main.go
```
args := []string{"build", ".", "errors"}
```

By using this approach you avoid creating a file that you would have to clean up after.

Now, create an instance of the exec.Cmd type by using the function exec.Command() like this:

processes/goci/main.go
```
cmd := exec.Command("go", args...)
```

Notice that the exec.Command() function expects a variable list of strings as the arguments for the command, so we're using the ... operator on the args slice to expand it into a list of strings.

Then, before executing the command, set the working directory for the external command execution to the target project directory by setting the cmd.Dir field from the exec.Cmd type:

```
processes/goci/main.go
cmd.Dir = proj
```

Now execute the command by calling its Run() method. Check for errors and return a new error if the command execution failed:

```
processes/goci/main.go
if err := cmd.Run(); err != nil {
  return fmt.Errorf("'go build' failed: %s", err)
}
```

Complete the run() function by printing out a success message to the user using the out interface, and return its error status:

```
processes/goci/main.go
  _, err := fmt.Fprintln(out, "Go Build: SUCCESS")

  return err
}
```

Once the run() function is complete, define the function main(). This function parses the command-line flags and then calls the function run(). As we add more features to this tool later, we'll modify the run() function, but the main() function won't change. The *goci* tool accepts only one flag -p of type string, which represents the Go project directory on which to execute the CI pipeline steps.

```
processes/goci/main.go
func main() {
  proj := flag.String("p", "", "Project directory")
  flag.Parse()

  if err := run(*proj, os.Stdout); err != nil {
    fmt.Fprintln(os.Stderr, err)
    os.Exit(1)
  }
}
```

We're using the os.Stdout type as the value for the out parameter in the run() function call to output results to the user's screen. Later when testing, you'll provide a bytes.Buffer to capture the output and verify its value.

The initial version of the code is completed, but we're not handling errors effectively. Let's address that next.

Handling Errors

At this point your application handles errors by defining error strings, using the function fmt.Errorf() from package fmt. This is a valid approach for small applications, but it's harder to maintain as your application grows in complexity. For instance, relying only on comparing the error message isn't a resilient method as the error message may change.

As an alternative, in Developing the Initial Version of colStats, on page 114, you handled errors by defining error values as exported variables. You can use this approach here to handle simple errors, such as validating input parameters. Add a file errors.go to your project and edit it. Add the package definition and the import section. For this file, you're using the package errors to define error values, and the package fmt to format messages:

```
processes/goci.v1/errors.go
package main

import (
  "errors"
  "fmt"
)
```

Now add the error value variable ErrValidation representing a validation error:

```
processes/goci.v1/errors.go
var (
  ErrValidation = errors.New("Validation failed")
)
```

Save and close this file and edit the file main.go. Update the line that returns the project directory validation error. Use the verb %w from fmt.Errorf to wrap your custom error value ErrValidation into the message:

```
processes/goci.v1/main.go
if proj == "" {
  return fmt.Errorf("Project directory is required: %w", ErrValidation)
}
```

As discussed in Developing the Initial Version of colStats, on page 114, by wrapping an error you add context and information that are useful for the user as output but keep the error available for inspection regardless of whether it's required by the business logic or tests.

The package errors includes a function errors.Is() that allows you to inspect errors. It returns true if a given error matches a target error, whether the error directly matches it or the target error is wrapped in the error at any level of the error chain. You'll use this function to inspect errors in your tests.

Using error values works well for some types of errors, especially if you're only interested in handling a particular category without checking specific conditions. You can extend these errors a bit using the wrapping technique but to handle specific cases, you have to either define a new error value or dig into the error message.

The main goal of this application is defining different CI steps to perform different tasks. To handle errors for each step in a particular way you'd have to create different error values, which isn't ideal. Instead, for handling these errors you can define your own custom error types.

In Go, the built-in type error is an interface that defines a single method with the signature Error() string. You can use any types that implement this method as an error. Open the file errors.go again and define a new custom type stepErr representing a class of errors associated with the CI steps, with three fields: step to record the step name in an error; a message msg that describes the condition; and a cause to store the underlying error that caused this step error:

processes/goci.v1/errors.go
```go
type stepErr struct {
  step   string
  msg    string
  cause error
}
```

Then, attach the method Error() to implement the error interface on this new type. Use fmt.Sprintf() to return an error message that contains the step name, the message, and the underlying cause:

processes/goci.v1/errors.go
```go
func (s *stepErr) Error() string {
  return fmt.Sprintf("Step: %q: %s: Cause: %v", s.step, s.msg, s.cause)
}
```

processes/goci.v1/errors.go
```go
func (s *stepErr) Is(target error) bool {
  t, ok := target.(*stepErr)
  if !ok {
    return false
  }

  return t.step == s.step
}
```

Finally, function errors.Is() may also try to unwrap the error to see if an underlying error matches the target, by calling a method Unwrap() if the custom error implements it. Define this method returning the error stored in the cause field:

```
processes/goci.v1/errors.go
func (s *stepErr) Unwrap() error {
  return s.cause
}
```

Now, let's use this new type to define a custom error for the application. Close and save this file and edit the main.go file. Replace the line that returns the error for the command execution by instantiating and returning a new stepErr defining the step name, message, and the underlying cause as the error obtained from executing the command:

```
processes/goci.v1/main.go
if err := cmd.Run(); err != nil {
  return &stepErr{step: "go build", msg: "go build failed", cause: err}
}
```

You can find more information about handling errors in Go by consulting the errors package documentation[1] or by reading this blog post[2] on the official Go blog.

The initial version of the code is complete. Let's write some tests to ensure it's working as intended.

Writing Tests for Goci

The *goci* tool executes tasks on a Go project. To write tests for it, we need to create a few small Go programs. Let's start with two test cases, one for a successful build and one for a failed build so we can test the error handling. Create a directory testdata under your project directory to hold the files required for the testing. When building *goci* any files under this directory are ignored. In addition, create two subdirectories under testdata to hold the code for each case: tool and toolErr:

```
$ mkdir -p $HOME/pragprog.com/rggo/processes/goci/testdata/{tool,toolErr}
```

Switch to the newly created testdata/tool directory and initialize a new dummy module for this project:

```
$ cd $HOME/pragprog.com/rggo/processes/goci/testdata/tool
$ go mod init testdata/tool
go: creating new go.mod: module testdata/tool
```

Now, create a basic Go library to serve as test subject. Add a file add.go under testdata/tool with the following content:

---

1. pkg.go.dev/errors
2. blog.golang.org/go1.13-errors

processes/goci.v1/testdata/tool/add.go
```
package add

func add(a, b int) int {
  return a + b
}
```

Verify that you can build testdata/tool/add.go without any errors:

```
$ go build
```

Then switch to the testdata/toolErr directory and copy both files from the tool directory:

```
$ cd $HOME/pragprog.com/rggo/processes/goci/testdata/toolErr
$ cp ../tool/{add.go,go.mod} .
```

Edit the file add.go under testdata/toolErr, and introduce an invalid variable c in the return call of the add() function to force a build error:

processes/goci.v1/testdata/toolErr/add.go
```
package add

func add(a, b int) int {
  return c + b
}
```

Then, verify that building testdata/toolErr/add.go causes an error since the variable c is undefined:

```
$ go build
# testdata/tool
./add.go:4:9: undefined: c
```

Switch back to the root directory of your project to create the test file:

```
$ cd $HOME/pragprog.com/rggo/processes/goci
```

Now create the file main_test.go in the root of your goci directory. Edit the file and add the package definition and import sections. For this test file, import the packages bytes to create a buffer to capture the output, the errors package to check errors, and the testing package which provides the testing functions:

processes/goci.v1/main_test.go
```
package main

import (
  "bytes"
  "errors"
  "testing"
)
```

Add the function TestRun() to test the run() function of your program. This works as an integration test:

processes/goci.v1/main_test.go
```
func TestRun(t *testing.T) {
```

You only need one test function for now since you'll use the concept of Table Driven Testing that you used in Testing with Table-Driven Testing, on page 82. Using this approach, you can add more tests cases quickly when you add new features to the program. Define the test cases. You'll have two tests at this time, matching the test data that you created before: a success test and a fail test:

processes/goci.v1/main_test.go
```
var testCases = []struct {
  name    string
  proj    string
  out     string
  expErr error
}{
  {name: "success", proj: "./testdata/tool/",
    out:    "Go Build: SUCCESS\n",
    expErr: nil},
  {name: "fail", proj: "./testdata/toolErr",
    out:    "",
    expErr: &stepErr{step: "go build"}},
}
```

For each test case, you're defining a name, the target project directory, the expected output message, and the expected error, if any. For the *fail* test, define the expected error using your custom error type stepErr with the expected step &stepErr{step: "go build"}.

Next, loop through and execute each test case using the method t.Run(), providing the test name tc.name as input:

processes/goci.v1/main_test.go
```
for _, tc := range testCases {
  t.Run(tc.name, func(t *testing.T) {
```

In the body of the anonymous testing function, define an out variable of type bytes.Buffer to capture the output. The type bytes.Buffer implements the io.Writer interface and can be used as the out parameter for the function run(). Execute the function run(), providing the project directory name tc.proj and the buffer as parameters:

processes/goci.v1/main_test.go
```
var out bytes.Buffer
err := run(tc.proj, &out)
```

Then verify the results. First, ensure the error handling works. When the test expects an error, verify that it received an error. Then use the function errors.Is() to validate that the received error matches the expected error. Since your custom error type stepErr implements the method Is(), function errors.Is() calls it automatically to verify the received and expected errors are equivalent. Fail the test if they aren't:

processes/goci.v1/main_test.go
```
if tc.expErr != nil {
  if err == nil {
    t.Errorf("Expected error: %q. Got 'nil' instead.", tc.expErr)
    return
  }

  if !errors.Is(err, tc.expErr) {
    t.Errorf("Expected error: %q. Got %q.", tc.expErr, err)
  }
  return
}
```

When the test doesn't expect an error, verify that no error was generated and that the output matches the expected output message. Fail the test otherwise:

processes/goci.v1/main_test.go
```
      if err != nil {
        t.Errorf("Unexpected error: %q", err)
      }

      if out.String() != tc.out {
        t.Errorf("Expected output: %q. Got %q", tc.out, out.String())
      }
    })
  }
}
```

Save the main_test.go file and execute the tests with go test -v:

```
$ go test -v
=== RUN   TestRun
=== RUN   TestRun/success
=== RUN   TestRun/fail
--- PASS: TestRun (0.18s)
    --- PASS: TestRun/success (0.09s)
    --- PASS: TestRun/fail (0.09s)
PASS
ok      pragprog.com/rggo/processes/goci        0.178s
```

All the tests passed. You can also execute the tool manually to see it working:

```
$ go run . -p testdata/tool
Go Build: SUCCESS
```

Now you can execute an external program, but the steps are hard-coded into the program. Let's make some changes to the structure to make it more reusable.

Defining a Pipeline

At this point, your tool executes the first step in the CI pipeline: Go Build. In its current state, the information to execute this step is hard-coded into the run() function. While this is a valid approach, adding more steps to this tool using the same approach would cause extensive code repetition. We want a tool that's maintainable and easy to extend, so let's make a change to the program's structure to make the code more reusable.

To do that, you'll refactor the part of the run() function that executes the external program into its own function. To make it easier to configure, let's add a custom type step that represents a pipeline step and associate the method execute() to it. You'll also add a constructor function called newStep() to create a new step. By doing this, when you want to add a new step to the pipeline, you instantiate the step type with the appropriate values.

Before you do that, break the code into different files so it will be easier to maintain, as you did in Developing a File System Crawler, on page 77.

Create a file called step.go in the goci directory and open it in your editor. Include the package definition and the import sections. Use the os/exec package to execute external programs:

```
processes/goci.v2/step.go
package main

import (
  "os/exec"
)
```

Next, add the definition of the new type step. This custom type has five fields: name of type string representing the step name, exe also string representing the executable name of the external tool we want to execute, args of type slice of strings which contains the arguments for the executable, message of type string which is the output message in case of success, and proj of type string representing the target project on which to execute the task:

```
processes/goci.v2/step.go
type step struct {
  name     string
  exe      string
  args     []string
  message  string
  proj     string
}
```

Then, create the constructor function newStep() that instantiates and returns a new step. This function accepts as input parameters values equivalent to the fields in the step type. Go doesn't have formal constructors like other object-oriented languages, but this is a good practice to ensure callers instantiate types correctly:

```
processes/goci.v2/step.go
func newStep(name, exe, message, proj string, args []string) step {
  return step{
    name:    name,
    exe:     exe,
    message: message,
    args:    args,
    proj:    proj,
  }
}
```

Finally, define the method execute() on the type step. This method takes no input parameters and returns a string and an error:

```
processes/goci.v2/step.go
func (s step) execute() (string, error) {
```

Notice that to define a function as a method on the type step you're adding the receiver (s step) parameter in the function definition. This makes all fields of the step instance available in the body of the function through the variable s.

The function contains the same code you used previously to execute the external program in the function run(), except that it uses the step instance fields instead of hardcoded values. Define the body of the function like this:

```
processes/goci.v2/step.go
cmd := exec.Command(s.exe, s.args...)
cmd.Dir = s.proj

if err := cmd.Run(); err != nil {
  return "", &stepErr{
    step:  s.name,
    msg:   "failed to execute",
    cause: err,
  }
}
```

If the execution is successful execution, return the successful message s.message and a nil value as the error:

processes/goci.v2/step.go
```
   return s.message, nil
}
```

This completes the definition of the step type and its execute() method. Save and quit the step.go file. Let's change the run() function in the main.go file to use this type now. Open main.go to edit.

First, remove all the code you used to execute the external Go tool directly from the run() function:

```
args := []string{"build", ".", "errors"}

cmd := exec.Command("go", args...)

cmd.Dir = proj

if err := cmd.Run(); err != nil {
  return &stepErr{step: "go build", msg: "go build failed", cause: err}
}

_, err := fmt.Fprintln(out, "Go Build: SUCCESS")
```

Remove also the package os/exec from the import list:

```
"os/exec"
```

Then, add the definition of the new pipeline. Define the variable pipeline as a slice of step []step:

processes/goci.v2/main.go
```
pipeline := make([]step, 1)
```

For now, the pipeline contains only one element but you'll add more later. Define the first element of the pipeline using the constructor function newStep() with the field values required to run the Go build step:

processes/goci.v2/main.go
```
pipeline[0] = newStep(
  "go build",
  "go",
  "Go Build: SUCCESS",
  proj,
  []string{"build", ".", "errors"},
)
```

Next, since you now have a slice of steps, loop through them executing each one:

```
processes/goci.v2/main.go
for _, s := range pipeline {
  msg, err := s.execute()
  if err != nil {
    return err
  }

  _, err = fmt.Fprintln(out, msg)
  if err != nil {
    return err
  }
}
```

If the execution of any step returns an error, return it and exit the run() function.

Finally, return the value nil as the error when the loop completes successfully.

```
processes/goci.v2/main.go
  return nil
}
```

This completes the updates. Save the main.go file and execute the tests to ensure the code still works as before:

```
$ go test -v
=== RUN    TestRun
=== RUN    TestRun/success
=== RUN    TestRun/fail
--- PASS: TestRun (0.16s)
    --- PASS: TestRun/success (0.08s)
    --- PASS: TestRun/fail (0.08s)
PASS
ok      pragprog.com/rggo/processes/goci        0.163s
```

The program works the same way as before, but now you've structured the code so you can add more steps with less effort. So let's add another step to the process.

Adding Another Step to the Pipeline

You've structured your code so you can add more steps to the pipeline by instantiating a new step and adding it to the pipeline slice. According to the initial plan, the next step in the pipeline is the execution of tests using the go test command. But before you add that step, add a test file with a single test case to the add package you're using for testing.

Switch to the subdirectory testdata/tool, where you have the file add.go:

```
$ cd testdata/tool
```

In this subdirectory, create the test file add_test.go, and add a single test case to test the add() function:

```
processes/goci.v3/testdata/tool/add_test.go
package add

import (
  "testing"
)

func TestAdd(t *testing.T) {
  a := 2
  b := 3

  exp := 5

  res := add(a, b)

  if exp != res {
    t.Errorf("Expected %d, got %d.", exp, res)
  }
}
```

Save the file and execute the test to ensure it works:

```
$ go test -v
=== RUN   TestAdd
--- PASS: TestAdd (0.00s)
PASS
ok      testdata/tool   0.003s
```

Copy the test file to the subdirectory testdata/toolErr where you have the test code that fails to build. Even though the pipeline stops in the first step due to the build failure, it's a good idea to have the test file there in case you want to use it in the future:

```
$ cp add_test.go ../toolErr
```

Switch back to the root of your project:

```
$ cd ../..
```

Next, add the new step to the run() function. Edit the file main.go and update the definition of the variable pipeline increasing its length to two:

```
processes/goci.v3/main.go
pipeline := make([]step, 2)
```

Then, add the definition of the new step, which is similar to the previous one. Use go test as the step name, go as the executable, []string{"test", "-v"} as arguments for the Go executable to execute tests, and "Go Test: SUCCESS" as the output message:

```
processes/goci.v3/main.go
pipeline[1] = newStep(
  "go test",
  "go",
  "Go Test: SUCCESS",
  proj,
  []string{"test", "-v"},
)
```

Since the loop was already defined to iterate over all steps, you don't need to make any more changes. Save the file to complete the updates.

Finally, update the success test case to include the new message as part of the expected output. Edit the file main_test.go and update the test case:

```
processes/goci.v3/main_test.go
out:     "Go Build: SUCCESS\nGo Test: SUCCESS\n",
```

You don't need to update the fail test case since it'll still fail at the build step. Save the file to complete the updates and execute the tests:

```
$ go test -v
=== RUN   TestRun
=== RUN   TestRun/success
=== RUN   TestRun/fail
--- PASS: TestRun (0.50s)
    --- PASS: TestRun/success (0.43s)
    --- PASS: TestRun/fail (0.07s)
PASS
ok      pragprog.com/rggo/processes/goci        0.500s
```

All the tests pass, which means that the tool is executing both the build and test steps successfully. Try it for yourself. First, build the tool:

```
$ go build
```

Then execute the tool, using the -p option to pass a directory containing a Go project. Use the testdata/tool directory:

```
$ ./goci -p testdata/tool
Go Build: SUCCESS
Go Test: SUCCESS
```

Next, you'll include a pipeline step that requires you to parse the external program's output to determine whether it succeeded or failed.

Handling Output from External Programs

The two external programs you've executed are well-behaved; if something goes wrong, they return an error that you can capture and use to make decisions. Unfortunately, not all programs work like that.

In some cases, the program exits with a successful return code even when something goes wrong. In these cases a message in STDOUT or STDERR generally provides details about the error condition. In other cases, a program completes successfully as designed but something on its output tells you that the condition represents an error.

When executing external programs in Go you can handle both of these scenarios by capturing the program's output and parsing it to make decisions.

The next step in the pipeline is the execution of the gofmt tool to validate whether the target project conforms to the Go code formatting standards or not. The gofmt tool doesn't return an error. Its default behavior is to print the properly formatted version of the Go program to STDOUT. Typically, users run gofmt with the -w option to overwrite the original file with the correctly formatted version. But in this case, you only want to verify the program and validate the formatting as part of the CI pipeline. You can use the -l option which returns the name of the file if the file doesn't match the correct formatting. You can find more information about the gofmt tool in the official documentation.[3]

In your next pipeline step, you'll execute gofmt -l, examine its output, and verify if it's different than an empty string, in which case you'll return an error. The current version of the execute() method of the step type doesn't handle the program output. Instead of adding more complexity to the current method to handle this condition, you'll create another type called exceptionStep that extends the step type, and implements another version of the execute() method designed specifically for this purpose. This approach results in less complex functions that are easier to maintain.

You'll also introduce a new interface called executer that expects a single execute() method that returns a string and an error. You'll use this interface in the pipeline definition, allowing any types that implement this interface to be added to the pipeline.

Start by adding the new type. Create the file exceptionStep.go in the same goci directory where main.go exists and open it in your editor. Add the package definition

---

3.   golang.org/cmd/gofmt/

and the import section. For this file, we'll import packages fmt and os/exec again, and the package bytes to define a buffer to capture the program's output:

processes/goci.v4/exceptionStep.go
```
package main

import (
  "bytes"
  "fmt"
  "os/exec"
)
```

Next, define the new type exceptionStep by extending the step type. Do this by embedding the step type into the new type, like this:

processes/goci.v4/exceptionStep.go
```
type exceptionStep struct {
  step
}
```

You're not adding any new fields to the new type. You'll use the same fields as the step type, as you're only implementing a new version of the execute() method.

Now, define a new constructor for this type. Since you're not adding new fields, you can call the constructor function for the embedded step type:

processes/goci.v4/exceptionStep.go
```
func newExceptionStep(name, exe, message, proj string,
  args []string) exceptionStep {

  s := exceptionStep{}

  s.step = newStep(name, exe, message, proj, args)

  return s
}
```

By embedding one type into another, you make all the fields and methods of the embedded type available to the embedding type. This is a common re-usability pattern in Go.

Then define the new version of the execute() method. Use the same signature as the version defined in the type step to ensure this new type implements the executer interface, making it available to use in the pipeline.

processes/goci.v4/exceptionStep.go
```
func (s exceptionStep) execute() (string, error) {
```

Define the variable cmd of type *exec.Cmd you'll use to execute the command.

processes/goci.v4/exceptionStep.go
```
cmd := exec.Command(s.exe, s.args...)
```

Before executing the command, add a new bytes.Buffer variable out and attach it to the Stdout field of the instance cmd. Later when you execute the command its output will be copied to the buffer and available for inspection.

processes/goci.v4/exceptionStep.go
```
var out bytes.Buffer
cmd.Stdout = &out
```

Also, ensure the program executes in the target project directory by defining the field cmd.Dir as the project path represented by the field s.proj from the step type you embedded into exceptionStep:

processes/goci.v4/exceptionStep.go
```
cmd.Dir = s.proj
```

Now execute the command using its Run() method. Check for potential errors and return them if needed. Even though the command itself doesn't return an error, you could have other errors while trying to execute it, for example, permission errors. Always check and handle errors.

processes/goci.v4/exceptionStep.go
```
if err := cmd.Run(); err != nil {
  return "", &stepErr{
    step:  s.name,
    msg:   "failed to execute",
    cause: err,
  }
}
```

Once the command finishes executing with no errors, verify the size of the output buffer by using the method Len() of the bytes.Buffer type. If it contains anything, the size will be greater than zero which indicates that at least one file in the project doesn't match the format. In this case, return a new stepErr error including the captured output in the message, indicating which files failed the check. Define the cause of this error as nil as it doesn't have an underlying cause:

processes/goci.v4/exceptionStep.go
```
if out.Len() > 0 {
  return "", &stepErr{
    step:  s.name,
    msg:   fmt.Sprintf("invalid format: %s", out.String()),
    cause: nil,
  }
}
```

Finally, in case it worked, return the success message and nil as the error, completing the function.

processes/goci.v4/exceptionStep.go
```
  return s.message, nil
}
```

The code for the new type is complete. Save and close the file. Let's use this new type in the pipeline now. Open the file main.go and add the definition of the executer interface after the import section:

processes/goci.v4/main.go
```
type executer interface {
  execute() (string, error)
}
```

Then, in the body of the function run(), update the definition of the variable pipeline slice. It should now be a slice of the interface executer instead of type step. This lets you use any types that implement the executer interface as elements of this slice. Also, increase its size to three to include the new step:

processes/goci.v4/main.go
```
pipeline := make([]executer, 3)
```

You don't need to make any changes to any of the existing elements since they use the step type which implements the executer interface. This is the flexibility we get by using Go's interfaces. Add the definition of the third element using the constructor function newExceptionStep() to instantiate a new exceptionStep. Include the parameters required to run the gofmt -l tool:

processes/goci.v4/main.go
```
pipeline[2] = newExceptionStep(
  "go fmt",
  "gofmt",
  "Gofmt: SUCCESS",
  proj,
  []string{"-l", "."},
)
```

Save and close the main.go file. Let's update the test to include a case to test the format fail. Before we do it, we need to add another project in the testdata directory with code that doesn't conform to the formatting standard. Copy the testdata/tool subdirectory into a new subdirectory testdata/toolFmtErr:

```
$ cp -r testdata/tool testdata/toolFmtErr
```

Then, execute this command to replace the contents of file testdata/toolFmtErr/add.go with content that doesn't match Go's format standards:

```
$ cat << 'EOF' > testdata/toolFmtErr/add.go
> package add
> func add(a, b int) int {
> return a + b
> }
> EOF
```

The new file looks like this:

processes/goci.v4/testdata/toolFmtErr/add.go
```
package add
func add(a, b int) int {
return a + b
}
```

This code is still functional, it compiles and runs, but it doesn't match the Go format standard. Verify it by running gofmt -l:

```
$ gofmt -l testdata/toolFmtErr/*.go
testdata/toolFmtErr/add.go
```

Also, to ensure that the tests pass, make sure the .go files in the other two test directories match the standard format. Run the command gofmt -w to update them if necessary:

```
$ gofmt -w testdata/tool/*.go
$ gofmt -w testdata/toolErr/*.go
```

Next, open the file main_test.go and update the success case to include the new success message:

processes/goci.v4/main_test.go
```
{name: "success", proj: "./testdata/tool/",
  out:     "Go Build: SUCCESS\nGo Test: SUCCESS\nGofmt: SUCCESS\n",
```

Add another test case to the testCases struct to test the formatting fail condition. Use the directory testdata/toolFmtErr as the project and an instance of stepErr with step set to go fmt as the expected error:

processes/goci.v4/main_test.go
```
{name: "failFormat", proj: "./testdata/toolFmtErr",
  out:     "",
  expErr: &stepErr{step: "go fmt"}},
```

Save and close the file. Execute the tests to ensure the program is working:

```
$ go test -v
=== RUN    TestRun
=== RUN    TestRun/success
=== RUN    TestRun/fail
```

```
=== RUN    TestRun/failFormat
--- PASS: TestRun (0.91s)
    --- PASS: TestRun/success (0.41s)
    --- PASS: TestRun/fail (0.08s)
    --- PASS: TestRun/failFormat (0.42s)
PASS
ok      pragprog.com/rggo/processes/goci        0.910s
```

All tests passed. You can now execute the program to see it working. Use the directory testdata/toolFmtErr/ as the target project to see the formatting error message:

```
$ go run . -p testdata/toolFmtErr/
Go Build: SUCCESS
Go Test: SUCCESS
Step: "go fmt": invalid format: add.go
: Cause: <nil>
exit status 1
```

The execution fails in the Go formatting check step, as expected, and it displays the name of the file that failed the check. Next, you'll add the final step to the pipeline: pushing the changes to a remote Git repository.

Running Commands with Contexts

The final step your Go CI has to perform is pushing code changes to the remote Git repository. For this step, you'll use some concepts from the Git Version Control System, such as, commits, local and remote repositories, branches, and pushing commits to remote repositories. If you need more information about these concepts, take a look at Git's official documentation.[4] If you want to try this tool locally, you'll also need Git installed on your machine.

To push code you'll add another step to your pipeline to execute the command git with the appropriate options. For now, let's simplify it and assume that we're pushing code to the remote repo identified by origin using the branch master. The complete command is git push origin master.

You could implement this feature by adding another step using the existing step type with the necessary options. But in this case, this command will try to push the code to a remote repository over the network - and potentially over the Internet. If there's a network issue, it could cause the command to hang which would cause the *goci* tool to hang. If you're executing the *goci* tool manually it's not too bad as you can cancel its execution after a while,

---

4. git-scm.com/docs

but if you're running it as part of an automation process or script, this is an undesirable situation.

As a rule of thumb, when running external commands that can potentially take a long time to complete, it is a good idea to set a timeout which, upon expiration, stops the command execution. In Go, you accomplish this by using the context package. You'll put this into practice by extending the step type into a new type named timeoutStep. This new type shares the same fields with the original step, but it includes the timeout field of type time.Duration representing the timeout value for this step. Then, you'll override the execute() method to use the timeout field, stopping the command execution when the timeout expires, returning a timeout error.

Create a new file named timeoutStep.go to hold the new type. Add the package definition and the import section to the file. For this type, you'll use the context package to create a context to carry the timeout, the os/exec package to execute external commands, and the time package to define time values.

processes/goci.v5/timeoutStep.go
```
package main

import (
  "context"
  "os/exec"
  "time"
)
```

Then define the new type timeoutStep as an extension of the existing step type by embedding the step type into the definition. Include the new timeout field of type time.Duration:

processes/goci.v5/timeoutStep.go
```
type timeoutStep struct {
  step
  timeout time.Duration
}
```

Next, define the constructor function newTimeoutStep() you'll use to instantiate this new type. This is similar to the constructor function for the step and exceptionStep you defined before, but it also accepts the timeout parameter.

processes/goci.v5/timeoutStep.go
```
func newTimeoutStep(name, exe, message, proj string,
  args []string, timeout time.Duration) timeoutStep {
  s := timeoutStep{}

  s.step = newStep(name, exe, message, proj, args)
```

```
  s.timeout = timeout
  if s.timeout == 0 {
    s.timeout = 30 * time.Second
  }

  return s
}
```

Notice that this defines the value of the timeout field to use the value provided as input to the constructor function, but if no timeout was provided, it sets the value to a default of 30 seconds by multiplying 30 by the constant time.Second from the time package.

Now implement the execute() method to execute the command. Add the function definition keeping the same inputs and outputs as the previous versions so it can implement the executer interface, allowing you to use it in the pipeline:

processes/goci.v5/timeoutStep.go
```
func (s timeoutStep) execute() (string, error) {
```

Then, define a context called ctx to carry the timeout value and use the context.WithTimeout() function from the context package. This function accepts two input parameters: a parent context and the timeout value. For the parent context, since this is the first, and only, context you're defining, use the context.Background() function from the context package to add a new empty context. For the timeout value, use the s.timeout property from the current timeoutStep instance:

processes/goci.v5/timeoutStep.go
```
ctx, cancel := context.WithTimeout(context.Background(), s.timeout)
```

The function context.WithTimeout() returns two values: the context which you store in the variable ctx, and a cancellation function that you store in the variable cancel. You have to execute the cancellation function when the context is no longer required to free up its resources. Use a defer statement to run the cancellation function when the execute() method returns:

processes/goci.v5/timeoutStep.go
```
defer cancel()
```

Once you have the context including the timeout, you can use it to create an instance of type exec.Cmd to execute the command. Instead of using the function exec.Command() that you used in the previous versions, use the function exec.CommandContext() to create a command that includes a context. The created command uses the context to kill the executing process in case the context becomes done before the command completes. In our case, it will kill the running process if the timeout defined in the context expires before the command completes:

processes/goci.v5/timeoutStep.go
```go
cmd := exec.CommandContext(ctx, s.exe, s.args...)
```

Ensure the command's working directory is set to the target project directory:

processes/goci.v5/timeoutStep.go
```go
cmd.Dir = s.proj
```

Now execute the command with the Run() method and check for errors. Add a condition to verify if the context ctx returned the error context.DeadlineExceeded which means the context timeout expired. In this case, return a new error that includes the message failed time out, indicating to the user that the command timed out before completing its execution. If there's another error condition, return it instead.

processes/goci.v5/timeoutStep.go
```go
if err := cmd.Run(); err != nil {
  if ctx.Err() == context.DeadlineExceeded {
    return "", &stepErr{
      step:  s.name,
      msg:   "failed time out",
      cause: context.DeadlineExceeded,
    }
  }

  return "", &stepErr{
    step:  s.name,
    msg:   "failed to execute",
    cause: err,
  }
}
```

If the command completed successfully with no errors or timeouts, return the success message and nil as the error:

processes/goci.v5/timeoutStep.go
```go
  return s.message, nil
}
```

The timeoutStep type is complete. Save the file and open the main.go file to add another step to the pipeline.

In the main.go file, add the time package to the import list. You'll use it to define the timeout value when adding the new step later:

```
processes/goci.v5/main.go
import (
  "flag"
  "fmt"
  "io"
  "os"

  "time"
)
```

Then, in the body of the run() function, update the pipeline variable definition increasing its length from 3 to 4 making room for another step.

```
processes/goci.v5/main.go
pipeline := make([]executer, 4)
```

Finally, add the definition of the fourth element in the pipeline slice using the constructor function newTimeoutStep() to instantiate a new timeoutStep. Include the parameters required to run the git push command, define the success message as Git Push: SUCCESS, and define the timeout value as ten seconds:

```
processes/goci.v5/main.go
pipeline[3] = newTimeoutStep(
  "git push",
  "git",
  "Git Push: SUCCESS",
  proj,
  []string{"push", "origin", "master"},
  10*time.Second,
)
```

No other changes are required since the type timeoutStep implements the executer interface. The code will loop through all the steps, including this new one, executing each one of them in order. Save the main.go to complete the updates.

Lastly, update the success test case to include the expected success message from the Git push step. Edit the file main_test.go and update the test case message:

```
processes/goci.v5/main_test.go
out: "Go Build: SUCCESS\nGo Test: SUCCESS\nGofmt: SUCCESS\nGit Push: SUCCESS\n",
```

You'll add more test cases later but for now this is the only change required. Save the file to finish the changes.

Don't Execute Tests if Using a Git Repository

If you're writing your code in a directory that's part of a Git repository associated with a remote repository, don't execute this test right away as it will try to push changes directly to your remote Master branch. The example in the book assumes the code isn't part of a Git repository yet.

Execute the tests. For this example, you're running these tests in a project directory that's not part of a Git repository and expecting this test to fail. First, ensure that this directory isn't part of a Git repository:

```
$ git status
fatal: not a git repository (or any parent up to mount point /)
Stopping at filesystem boundary (GIT_DISCOVERY_ACROSS_FILESYSTEM not set).
```

Next, switch to the directory testdata/tool and verify it's also not a Git repository:

```
$ cd testdata/tool
$ git status
fatal: not a git repository (or any parent up to mount point /)
Stopping at filesystem boundary (GIT_DISCOVERY_ACROSS_FILESYSTEM not set).
```

Then, switch back to your project directory where the file main_test.go resides and execute the tests:

```
$ cd ../..
$ go test -v
=== RUN    TestRun
=== RUN    TestRun/success
main_test.go:44: Unexpected error: "Step: \"git push\": failed to execute:
Cause: exit status 128"
main_test.go:48: Expected output: "Go Build: SUCCESS\nGo Test: SUCCESS\n
Gofmt: SUCCESS\nGit Push: SUCESS\n". Got "Go Build: SUCCESS\nGo Test: SUCCESS\n
Gofmt: SUCCESS\n"
=== RUN    TestRun/fail
=== RUN    TestRun/failFormat
--- FAIL: TestRun (0.83s)
    --- FAIL: TestRun/success (0.42s)
    --- PASS: TestRun/fail (0.07s)
    --- PASS: TestRun/failFormat (0.33s)
FAIL
exit status 1
FAIL    pragprog.com/rggo/processes/goci        0.832s
```

Note that the output is different from the original to fit the book page. Your results will be slightly different.

The test failed as expected since there's no Git repository to push the changes to. This is one challenge when testing external commands that depend on other services or that make irreversible changes to an external resource. There are essentially two ways to deal with this situation: instantiate the required service or resource to run an integration test; or use a mock service/resource to simulate it. Let's try the first approach next.

Integration Tests with a Local Git Server

When you're writing tests for your application, you need to ensure that the tests run on a reproducible environment, to guarantee that the results match the expected values. This is a challenge when executing external commands that modify the state of an external resource, as the test conditions will be different the second time you execute the tests. The first strategy you'll apply to handle this issue involves instantiating a local Git server by using a test helper function, similarly to what you did in Testing with the Help of Test Helpers, on page 89.

The test helper function setupGit() uses the git command to create a *Bare* Git repository that works like an external Git service such as GitLab or GitHub. A bare Git repository is a repository that contains only the git data but no working directory so it cannot be used to make local modifications to the code. This characteristic makes it well suited to serve as a remote repository. For more information about it, consult the official Git book.[5]

At a high level, the helper function will perform the following steps:

1. Create a temporary directory.

2. Create a Bare Git repository on this temporary directory.

3. Initialize a Git repository on the target project directory.

4. Add the Bare Git repository as a remote repository in the empty Git repository in the target project directory.

5. Stage a file to commit.

6. Commit the changes to the Git repository.

These steps prepare a reproducible environment to test the *goci* tool allowing it to perform the Git Push step, pushing the committed changes to the Bare Git repository on the temporary directory. The helper function returns a

---

cleanup function that deletes everything at the end of the test, ensuring the test can be repeated again.

Start the changes by opening the file main_test.go for edit. Include the new packages in the import list. For this new version, in addition to packages bytes, errors, and testing, include the fmt package to print formatted output, the ioutil package to create the temporary directory, the os package to interact with the operating system, the os/exec package to execute external programs, and the path/filepath package to handle path operations consistently.

processes/goci.v6/main_test.go
```go
import (
  "bytes"
  "errors"
  "fmt"
  "io/ioutil"
  "os"
  "os/exec"
  "path/filepath"
  "testing"
)
```

Next, at the end of the file, add the definition for the helper function setupGit(). This function takes two input parameters: an instance t of type *testing.T and the target project path proj of type string. It returns the cleanup function type func():

processes/goci.v6/main_test.go
```go
func setupGit(t *testing.T, proj string) func() {
```

Mark this function as a test helper function by using the method t.Helper() of the type testing.T. This ensures that error messages generated during the execution of the helper function point to the line where this function was called during the test execution, facilitating troubleshooting. For more information, consult Testing with the Help of Test Helpers, on page 89:

processes/goci.v6/main_test.go
```go
t.Helper()
```

Then use the function LookPath() from the os/exec package to verify whether the command git is available or not. Since git is required to execute the setup steps, we cannot proceed without it. This is a good way to fail fast in case a required external command isn't available on the system:

processes/goci.v6/main_test.go
```go
gitExec, err := exec.LookPath("git")
if err != nil {
  t.Fatal(err)
}
```

Next, use the function ioutil.TempDir() to create a temporary directory for the simulated remote Git repository. Prefix the temporary directory name with gocitest:

```
processes/goci.v6/main_test.go
tempDir, err := ioutil.TempDir("", "gocitest")
if err != nil {
  t.Fatal(err)
}
```

Now, define two variables that you'll use during the setup: projPath which contains the full path of the target project directory; and remoteURI which stores the URI of the simulated remote Git repository. First, define projPath by using the function filepath.Abs() to obtain the absolute path of the target project directory proj:

```
processes/goci.v6/main_test.go
projPath, err := filepath.Abs(proj)
if err != nil {
  t.Fatal(err)
}
```

Then, define the remoteURI by using the function fmt.Sprintf() to print a formatted string into a variable. Since you're simulating the remote repository locally, you can use the protocol file:// for the URI. The URI path points to the temporary directory tempDir:

```
processes/goci.v6/main_test.go
remoteURI := fmt.Sprintf("file://%s", tempDir)
```

According to the initial outline, the helper function has to execute a series of five git commands to set up the test environment. Instead of adding the code to execute each step, you will use a loop. First, create a slice of structs that contains the data for the loop. This anonymous struct contains the fields args with the arguments for the git command, dir with the directory on which to execute the command, and env with a list of environment variables to use during the execution:

```
processes/goci.v6/main_test.go
var gitCmdList = []struct {
  args []string
  dir  string
  env  []string
}{
  {[]string{"init", "--bare"}, tempDir, nil},
  {[]string{"init"}, projPath, nil},
  {[]string{"remote", "add", "origin", remoteURI}, projPath, nil},
  {[]string{"add", "."}, projPath, nil},
```

```
    {[]string{"commit", "-m", "test"}, projPath,
      []string{
        "GIT_COMMITTER_NAME=test",
        "GIT_COMMITTER_EMAIL=test@example.com",
        "GIT_AUTHOR_NAME=test",
        "GIT_AUTHOR_EMAIL=test@example.com",
      }},
  }
```

Use a for loop with the range operator to iterate over the command list, executing each one in sequence, by using the os/exec package, similarly to what you do in the goci tool:

processes/goci.v6/main_test.go
```
for _, g := range gitCmdList {
  gitCmd := exec.Command(gitExec, g.args...)
  gitCmd.Dir = g.dir

  if g.env != nil {
    gitCmd.Env = append(os.Environ(), g.env...)
  }

  if err := gitCmd.Run(); err != nil {
    t.Fatal(err)
  }
}
```

Notice that this uses the Env field from the type exec.Cmd to inject environment variables into the external command environment. The Env field contains a slice of strings where each represents an environment variable in the format key=value. You're adding more environment variables by appending them to the existing environment with the built in append() function.

When the loop completes, return the cleanup function that deletes both the temporary directory and the local .git subdirectory from the target project directory:

processes/goci.v6/main_test.go
```
  return func() {
    os.RemoveAll(tempDir)
    os.RemoveAll(filepath.Join(projPath, ".git"))
  }
}
```

The setupGit() helper function is complete. Update the test function TestRun() to use the helper function. First, since the command git is required to execute this test, skip the test by using the function t.Skip() if git isn't available:

processes/goci.v6/main_test.go
```
func TestRun(t *testing.T) {
  _, err := exec.LookPath("git")
```

```
if err != nil {
  t.Skip("Git not installed. Skipping test.")
}
```

Next, update the test cases by including a new parameter setupGit of type bool. This parameter indicates whether or not the test needs to call the helper function to setup the Git environment. Update the first test case with setupGit: true as this test case requires the Git environment. The remaining test cases fail before getting to the Git step, therefore setting up the environment isn't required. Set setupGit: false for them to avoid spending time with an unnecessary setup:

processes/goci.v6/main_test.go
```
var testCases = []struct {
  name    string
  proj    string
  out     string
  expErr  error
  setupGit bool
}{
  {name: "success", proj: "./testdata/tool/",
    out: "Go Build: SUCCESS\n" +
         "Go Test: SUCCESS\n" +
         "Gofmt: SUCCESS\n" +
         "Git Push: SUCCESS\n",
    expErr: nil,
    setupGit: true},
  {name: "fail", proj: "./testdata/toolErr",
    out:      "",
    expErr:   &stepErr{step: "go build"},
    setupGit: false},
  {name: "failFormat", proj: "./testdata/toolFmtErr",
    out:      "",
    expErr:   &stepErr{step: "go fmt"},
    setupGit: false},
}
```

Finally, in the test case execution function t.Run(), check if the parameter tc.setupGit is set, execute the helper function and defer the execution of the cleanup function to ensure the resources are deleted at the end:

processes/goci.v6/main_test.go
```
for _, tc := range testCases {
  t.Run(tc.name, func(t *testing.T) {
    if tc.setupGit {
      cleanup := setupGit(t, tc.proj)
      defer cleanup()
    }
```

No other changes are required as the test executes all the CI steps using the Git environment setup by the helper function. Save the file main_test.go and execute the tests:

```
$ go test -v
=== RUN    TestRun
=== RUN    TestRun/success
=== RUN    TestRun/fail
=== RUN    TestRun/failFormat
--- PASS: TestRun (0.94s)
    --- PASS: TestRun/success (0.44s)
    --- PASS: TestRun/fail (0.11s)
    --- PASS: TestRun/failFormat (0.39s)
PASS
ok       pragprog.com/rggo/processes/goci        0.942s
```

Troubleshooting the Helper Function

If you need to troubleshoot the helper function, you can comment out the defer cleanup() line to prevent the cleanup function from deleting the resources. Remember to clean up the resources manually after you're done.

You've successfully tested an external command execution by setting up a local Git repository. Next, you'll apply a strategy to execute tests when the external command isn't available.

Testing Commands with Mock Resources

So far, you've been testing the external commands by executing them directly. This is a perfectly valid approach. But sometimes it's not desirable or possible to execute a command directly on the machine where you're testing the code. For these cases, you'll mock the external commands by using Go function during tests. This approach also allows you to use Go code to simulate abnormal conditions, such as timeouts, which are harder to simulate using external services. Go's standard library applies this approach to test the function from the os/exec package. For more information check the source code for the exec_test.go file from the standard library.[6]

To use this approach you'll write a test function that replaces the function exec.CommandContext() from the exec package that you use to create the exec.Cmd type, during tests. First, edit the file timeoutStep.go and add a package variable command assigning the original function exec.CommandContext():

---

6.   golang.org/src/os/exec/exec_test.go

processes/goci.v7/timeoutStep.go
```
    return s
}
```
➤ `var command = exec.CommandContext`
➤
```
func (s timeoutStep) execute() (string, error) {
  return s.message, nil
}
```

Since functions are first class types in Go, you can assign them to variables and pass them as arguments. In this case, you created a variable of type func (context.Context, string, ...string) *exec.Cmd and assigned the original exec.CommandContext() value as its initial value. Later, when testing, you'll use this variable to override the original function with the mock function.

Then, use the function stored in the variable to create the exec.Cmd instance in the execute() method, instead of the original exec.CommandContext() function:

processes/goci.v7/timeoutStep.go
```
func (s timeoutStep) execute() (string, error) {
  ctx, cancel := context.WithTimeout(context.Background(), s.timeout)
  defer cancel()

➤ cmd := command(ctx, s.exe, s.args...)
  cmd.Dir = s.proj

  if err := cmd.Run(); err != nil {
    if ctx.Err() == context.DeadlineExceeded {
      return "", &stepErr{
        step:  s.name,
        msg:   "failed time out",
        cause: context.DeadlineExceeded,
      }
    }

    return "", &stepErr{
      step:  s.name,
      msg:   "failed to execute",
      cause: err,
    }
  }

  return s.message, nil
}
```

Note that this usage of a package variable is acceptable since you're only overriding it during tests. It also lets you explore the concept without working through a more complicated example. For a more robust approach, you can pass the function you want to override as a parameter or use an interface.

The preparation step is complete. Save the file timeoutStep.go and edit the file main_test.go to update the tests.

Add two packages to the import list: context to define command contexts, and package time to simulate a timeout.

```
processes/goci.v7/main_test.go
import (
    "bytes"
➤   "context"
    "errors"
    "fmt"
    "io/ioutil"
    "os"
    "os/exec"
    "path/filepath"
    "testing"

➤   "time"
)
```

To mock an executable command during tests, you'll use a feature of Go testing. When you run go test to execute a test, Go actually compiles an executable program and runs it, passing any flags and parameters you set. You can see this if you list running processes while running go test:

```
$ ps -eo args | grep go
go test -v
/tmp/go-build498058748/b001/goci.test -test.v=true -test.timeout=10m0s
```

Because Go is running a command, it stores the name of the executable in the os.Args[0] variable, and all additional arguments passed to it in the remaining slice elements os.Args[1:]. Our mock command creates a new command that executes the same test binary passing the flag -test.run to execute a specific test function. Following the standard library convention, you'll name this function TestHelperProcess(). It is this function that simulates the command behavior you want to test, in this case, the command git.

Since this is a regular test function func Test... Go will try to execute it directly as part of the tests. You'll use an environment variable called GO_WANT_HELPER_PROCESS to skip the test unless it was called as part of the mock test. You'll add this environment variable to the simulated command environment so when Go runs the function TestHelperProcess() as part of the simulation, it will not be skipped.

Create the function mockCmdContext() to mock the exec.CommandContext() function. It has the same signature as the original func (context.Context, string, ...string) *exec.Cmd:

```
processes/goci.v7/main_test.go
func mockCmdContext(ctx context.Context, exe string,
  args ...string) *exec.Cmd {
```

Create the arguments list that will be passed to the command. First the -test.run:

```
processes/goci.v7/main_test.go
cs := []string{"-test.run=TestHelperProcess"}
```

Then, append the command and arguments that would be passed to the real command to execute your external command:

```
processes/goci.v7/main_test.go
cs = append(cs, exe)
cs = append(cs, args...)
```

Now, create an instance of the type exec.Cmd by calling the function exec.CommandContext(). Use the variable os.Args[0] to run the test binary, and the arguments slice cs you defined earlier:

```
processes/goci.v7/main_test.go
cmd := exec.CommandContext(ctx, os.Args[0], cs...)
```

Add the environment variable GO_WANT_HELPER_PROCESS=1 to the cmd environment to ensure the test isn't skipped, and return the newly created command cmd to complete the function:

```
processes/goci.v7/main_test.go
  cmd.Env = []string{"GO_WANT_HELPER_PROCESS=1"}
  return cmd
}
```

Next, add another mock function to simulate a command that times out. Execute the mockCmdContext() function to create a command and append the environment variable GO_HELPER_TIMEOUT=1 to its environment. You'll use this environment variable in the TestHelperProcess() function to indicate it should simulate a long-running process.

```
processes/goci.v7/main_test.go
func mockCmdTimeout(ctx context.Context, exe string,
  args ...string) *exec.Cmd {

  cmd := mockCmdContext(ctx, exe, args...)
  cmd.Env = append(cmd.Env, "GO_HELPER_TIMEOUT=1")
  return cmd
}
```

Add the TestHelperProcess() function that simulates the command. This is a regular test function so it takes an instance t of type *testing.T and doesn't return any values:

```
processes/goci.v7/main_test.go
func TestHelperProcess(t *testing.T) {
```

Check if the environment variable GO_WANT_HELPER_PROCESS is different than one (1) and return immediately. This prevents the execution if it was not called from the mock command:

```
processes/goci.v7/main_test.go
if os.Getenv("GO_WANT_HELPER_PROCESS") != "1" {
  return
}
```

Check if the environment variable GO_HELPER_TIMEOUT is set to one (1) and simulate a long=running process by using the time.Sleep() function:

```
processes/goci.v7/main_test.go
if os.Getenv("GO_HELPER_TIMEOUT") == "1" {
  time.Sleep(15 * time.Second)
}
```

Next, check if the name of the executable provided to the mock function matches git. This is the command that would be executed by the real function. You want to ensure it matches the expected value. For completeness, you could also check the arguments provided, but for this test, the executable name is enough. If the executable name matches git return the expected output message and exit with a return code zero (0) indicating the command completed successfully. If any other executables are provided, exit with code one (1) indicating an error:

```
processes/goci.v7/main_test.go
  if os.Args[2] == "git" {
    fmt.Fprintln(os.Stdout, "Everything up-to-date")
    os.Exit(0)
  }
  os.Exit(1)
}
```

Now, all the functions required to mock the external command are ready. Let's update the TestRun() test to use them. First, remove the lines that skip the test if git isn't installed, since you can now execute the test via mock commands. You'll run this check later when running the test cases.

```
_, err := exec.LookPath("git")
if err != nil {
  t.Skip("Git not installed. Skipping test.")
}
```

Next, add a new field mockCmd to the test cases. This variable contains the function used to mock a command if required. Update the existing test cases setting this variable to nil. Include two new test cases using the mock commands: for successMock set the mockCmd field to mockCmdContext(); for failTimeout use mockCmdTimeout():

processes/goci.v7/main_test.go

```go
var testCases = []struct {
  name    string
  proj    string
  out     string
  expErr  error
  setupGit bool
  mockCmd  func(ctx context.Context, name string, arg ...string) *exec.Cmd
}{
  {name: "success", proj: "./testdata/tool/",
    out: "Go Build: SUCCESS\n"+
         "Go Test: SUCCESS\n"+
         "Gofmt: SUCCESS\n"+
         "Git Push: SUCCESS\n",
    expErr: nil,
    setupGit: true,
    mockCmd:  nil},
  {name: "successMock", proj: "./testdata/tool/",
    out: "Go Build: SUCCESS\n"+
         "Go Test: SUCCESS\n"+
         "Gofmt: SUCCESS\n"+
         "Git Push: SUCCESS\n",
    expErr:  nil,
    setupGit: false,
    mockCmd:  mockCmdContext},
  {name: "fail", proj: "./testdata/toolErr",
    out:     "",
    expErr:  &stepErr{step: "go build"},
    setupGit: false,
    mockCmd:  nil},
  {name: "failFormat", proj: "./testdata/toolFmtErr",
    out:     "",
    expErr:  &stepErr{step: "go fmt"},
    setupGit: false,
    mockCmd:  nil},
  {name: "failTimeout", proj: "./testdata/tool",
    out:     "",
    expErr:  context.DeadlineExceeded,
    setupGit: false,
    mockCmd:  mockCmdTimeout},
}
```

Then, read the git check during the test cases execution if setting up Git is required:

processes/goci.v7/main_test.go

```
for _, tc := range testCases {
  t.Run(tc.name, func(t *testing.T) {
    if tc.setupGit {
➤      _, err := exec.LookPath("git")
➤      if err != nil {
➤        t.Skip("Git not installed. Skipping test.")
➤      }

      cleanup := setupGit(t, tc.proj)
      defer cleanup()
    }
```

Finally, check if the tc.mockCmd is defined for the test case and override the package variable command with the given mock function:

processes/goci.v7/main_test.go

```
    defer cleanup()
  }

➤ if tc.mockCmd != nil {
➤   command = tc.mockCmd
➤ }

  var out bytes.Buffer
```

These are all the changes required. This is the complete new version of the TestRun() function:

processes/goci.v7/main_test.go

```
func TestRun(t *testing.T) {
  var testCases = []struct {
    name     string
    proj     string
    out      string
    expErr   error
    setupGit bool
    mockCmd  func(ctx context.Context, name string, arg ...string) *exec.Cmd
  }{
    {name: "success", proj: "./testdata/tool/",
      out: "Go Build: SUCCESS\n"+
          "Go Test: SUCCESS\n"+
          "Gofmt: SUCCESS\n"+
          "Git Push: SUCCESS\n",
      expErr: nil,
      setupGit: true,
      mockCmd:  nil},
```

```
        {name: "successMock", proj: "./testdata/tool/",
          out: "Go Build: SUCCESS\n"+
               "Go Test: SUCCESS\n"+
               "Gofmt: SUCCESS\n"+
               "Git Push: SUCCESS\n",
          expErr:  nil,
          setupGit: false,
          mockCmd:  mockCmdContext},
        {name: "fail", proj: "./testdata/toolErr",
          out:     "",
          expErr:  &stepErr{step: "go build"},
          setupGit: false,
          mockCmd:  nil},
        {name: "failFormat", proj: "./testdata/toolFmtErr",
          out:     "",
          expErr:  &stepErr{step: "go fmt"},
          setupGit: false,
          mockCmd:  nil},
        {name: "failTimeout", proj: "./testdata/tool",
          out:     "",
          expErr:  context.DeadlineExceeded,
          setupGit: false,
          mockCmd:  mockCmdTimeout},
    }

    for _, tc := range testCases {
      t.Run(tc.name, func(t *testing.T) {
        if tc.setupGit {
➤         _, err := exec.LookPath("git")
➤         if err != nil {
➤           t.Skip("Git not installed. Skipping test.")
➤         }

          cleanup := setupGit(t, tc.proj)
          defer cleanup()
        }

➤       if tc.mockCmd != nil {
➤         command = tc.mockCmd
➤       }

        var out bytes.Buffer
        err := run(tc.proj, &out)

        if tc.expErr != nil {
          if err == nil {
            t.Errorf("Expected error: %q. Got 'nil' instead.", tc.expErr)
            return
          }
```

```
      if !errors.Is(err, tc.expErr) {
        t.Errorf("Expected error: %q. Got %q.", tc.expErr, err)
      }
      return
    }

    if err != nil {
      t.Errorf("Unexpected error: %q", err)
    }

    if out.String() != tc.out {
      t.Errorf("Expected output: %q. Got %q", tc.out, out.String())
    }
  })
  }
}
```

Save the file main_test.go and execute the tests:

```
$ go test -v
=== RUN    TestHelperProcess
--- PASS: TestHelperProcess (0.00s)
=== RUN    TestRun
=== RUN    TestRun/success
=== RUN    TestRun/successMock
=== RUN    TestRun/fail
=== RUN    TestRun/failFormat
=== RUN    TestRun/failTimeout
--- PASS: TestRun (11.69s)
    --- PASS: TestRun/success (0.44s)
    --- PASS: TestRun/successMock (0.40s)
    --- PASS: TestRun/fail (0.08s)
    --- PASS: TestRun/failFormat (0.39s)
    --- PASS: TestRun/failTimeout (10.38s)
PASS
ok        pragprog.com/rggo/processes/goci          11.694s
```

While executing the tests, you can see the mock command executing by listing the running processes:

```
$ ps -eo args | grep go
go test -v
/tmp/go-build498058748/b001/goci.test -test.v=true -test.timeout=10m0s
/tmp/go-build498058748/b001/goci.test -test.run=TestHelperProcess git push
origin master
```

As expected, the mock test runs the test binary, passing the argument -test.run= TestHelperProcess followed by the original git command line git push origin master.

Now you can test the external command execution, using two different strategies. Next, let's update goci to handle operating system signals.

Handling Signals

The last feature you'll add to goci is the ability to handle operating system signals. Signals are commonly used on Unix/Linux operating systems to communicate events among running processes. Typically, signals are used to terminate programs that aren't responding or are running for a long time. For example, pressing Ctrl+C on the keyboard sends the 8nterrupt signal (SIGINT) to a running program, which interrupts its execution.

In Go, you handle signals by using the os/signal package. For more information consult its documentation.[7]

By default, when a program receives an interrupt signal, it stops executing immediately. This can lead to data loss and other consequences. It's important to handle signals appropriately so the program has a chance to clean up used resources, save data, and exit cleanly. This is even more relevant for an automation tool such as goci as it can receive a signal from other parts of the automation process.

For goci specifically, no cleanup is needed. When handling signals, the tool will exit cleanly but provide an appropriate error status and message, which makes downstream applications aware that goci didn't finish properly, allowing them to decide which actions to take. Since this error occurs outside a CI step, handle it using another error value instead of your custom error type that was designed to handle step errors. Edit the file errors.go and add another error value ErrSignal representing an error when receiving a signal:

processes/goci.v8/errors.go
```
var (
  ErrValidation = errors.New("Validation failed")
  ErrSignal = errors.New("Received signal")
)
```

Save and quit this file. To handle signals you'll apply some of the concurrency concepts you used in Reduce Scheduling Contention, on page 156. such as channels and goroutines. Edit the file main.go and include two new packages to the import list: os/signal to handle signals and syscall to use the signal definitions:

processes/goci.v8/main.go
```
import (
  "flag"
  "fmt"
  "io"
```

---

7.   golang.org/pkg/os/signal/

```
    "os"
➤   "os/signal"
➤   "syscall"
➤
    "time"
)
```

Go relays signals using a channel of type os.Signal. Add the signal definition right after defining all elements in the pipeline slice:

processes/goci.v8/main.go
```
sig := make(chan os.Signal, 1)
```

You're creating a buffered channel of size one (1) which allows the application to handle at least one signal correctly in case it receives many signals.

You'll update this function to run the CI pipeline steps in a goroutine, concurrently with the signal notification. That's why you add two more channels to communicate the status back to the main goroutine: an error channel to communicate potential errors, and the done channel of type struct{} to communicate the loop conclusion.

processes/goci.v8/main.go
```
errCh := make(chan error)
done := make(chan struct{})
```

Now use the function signal.Notify() from the os/signal package to relay signals to the channel sig. You're only interested in two termination signals: SIGINT and SIGTERM, so pass them as parameters to the function call. All other signals will be ignored and not relayed to this channel:

processes/goci.v8/main.go
```
signal.Notify(sig, syscall.SIGINT, syscall.SIGTERM)
```

Then, wrap the main loop in an anonymous goroutine, allowing its concurrent execution with the signal.Notify() function. When the loop finishes, close the done channel to notify the loop completion:

processes/goci.v8/main.go
```
go func() {
  for _, s := range pipeline {
    msg, err := s.execute()
    if err != nil {
      errCh <- err
      return
    }

    _, err = fmt.Fprintln(out, msg)
    if err != nil {
      errCh <- err
```

```
        return
      }
   }
 }
 close(done)
}()
```

Notice that in case of errors during the loop execution, you're no longer returning them directly. You're communicating to them using the errCh channel and then returning to exit the goroutine, ensuring no other steps run after an error.

Next, add an infinite loop with the select statement to decide what to do based on communication received in one of the three channels:

processes/goci.v8/main.go
```
for {
  select {
```

In the first case, handle the signal. In case the application receives any of the monitored signals, they'll be relayed to the sig channel. To handle it, use the function signal.Stop() from the os/signal package to stop receiving more signals on the sig channel. Then return a new error that includes the name of the received signal and wraps the error value ErrSignal, which allows you to inspect it during tests. This effectively finishes the run() function and exits the program with the error message and error code:

processes/goci.v8/main.go
```
case rec := <-sig:
  signal.Stop(sig)
  return fmt.Errorf("%s: Exiting: %w", rec, ErrSignal)
```

Finally, handle the communications on the remaining channels errCh or done returning, respectively, the error message or the value nil, completing the function run():

processes/goci.v8/main.go
```
    case err := <-errCh:
      return err
    case <-done:
      return nil
    }
  }
}
```

Save the file main.go and open the file main_test.go to include a test for the signal-handling feature. Add the packages os/signal and syscall to the import list:

```
processes/goci.v8/main_test.go
import (
  "bytes"
  "context"
  "errors"
  "fmt"
  "io/ioutil"
  "os"
  "os/exec"

➤  "os/signal"
  "path/filepath"

➤  "syscall"
  "testing"
  "time"
)
```

Add another test function TestRunKill() to test the signal handling:

```
processes/goci.v8/main_test.go
func TestRunKill(t *testing.T) {
```

Define three test cases: one for each of the relevant signals you handle in the application and another one to ensure the application doesn't handle a different signal:

```
processes/goci.v8/main_test.go
// RunKill Test Cases
var testCases = []struct {
  name   string
  proj   string
  sig    syscall.Signal
  expErr error
}{
  {"SIGINT", "./testdata/tool", syscall.SIGINT, ErrSignal},
  {"SIGTERM", "./testdata/tool", syscall.SIGTERM, ErrSignal},
  {"SIGQUIT", "./testdata/tool", syscall.SIGQUIT, nil},
}
```

Then, execute each test case in a loop. To give the application some time to pass signals, override the package variable command with the function mockCmd-Timeout() you created in Testing Commands with Mock Resources, on page 195:

```
processes/goci.v8/main_test.go
// RunKill Test Execution
for _, tc := range testCases {
  t.Run(tc.name, func(t *testing.T) {
    command = mockCmdTimeout
```

Since you're still handling signals, the test will run the functions concurrently. Create three channels to deal with the communication from the goroutines: an error channel, an os.Signal channel to trap expected signals, and another os.signal channel to trap the remaining signal SIGQUIT which should be ignored. By trapping this signal here, the test can ensure the application doesn't handle it because it's not one of the signals that the application should handle:

```
processes/goci.v8/main_test.go
errCh := make(chan error)
ignSigCh := make(chan os.Signal, 1)
expSigCh := make(chan os.Signal, 1)
```

Use the signal.Notify() function here to relay the SIGQUIT to the newly created ignSigCh channel, and defer the execution of the signal.Stop() function to stop handling signals and cleanup after each test:

```
processes/goci.v8/main_test.go
signal.Notify(ignSigCh, syscall.SIGQUIT)
defer signal.Stop(ignSigCh)
```

Use another call to signal.Notify() to handle the expected signals and ensure the correct signal was processed. Defer calling signal.Stop() again to clean up:

```
processes/goci.v8/main_test.go
signal.Notify(expSigCh, tc.sig)
defer signal.Stop(expSigCh)
```

Now execute two goroutines. The first executes the run() function sending the error to the error channel. The other sends the desired signal to the test executable by using the functions syscall.Kill() to send the signal and syscall.Getpid() to obtain the process ID of the running program:

```
processes/goci.v8/main_test.go
go func() {
  errCh <- run(tc.proj, ioutil.Discard)
}()
go func() {
  time.Sleep(2 * time.Second)
  syscall.Kill(syscall.Getpid(), tc.sig)
}()
```

Then, use a select statement to determine what to do based on the channel communication. For the first two test cases, the test expects an error message on channel errCh that matches ErrSignal specified as the expErr in the test case. Fail the test if no error is received or if the error type doesn't match the expected type:

processes/goci.v8/main_test.go

```go
// select error
select {
case err := <-errCh:
  if err == nil {
    t.Errorf("Expected error. Got 'nil' instead.")
    return
  }

  if !errors.Is(err, tc.expErr) {
    t.Errorf("Expected error: %q. Got %q", tc.expErr, err)
  }
```

Nest another select statement to verify if the correct signal was sent to the expSigCh channel. Fail the test if the signals don't match. Use a default case to fail the test in case it received no signals:

processes/goci.v8/main_test.go

```go
// select signal
select {
case rec := <-expSigCh:
  if rec != tc.sig {
    t.Errorf("Expected signal %q, got %q", tc.sig, rec)
  }
default:
  t.Errorf("Signal not received")
}
```

The third test case expects the signal to be received on the ignSigCh channel:

processes/goci.v8/main_test.go

```go
      case <-ignSigCh:
      }
    })
  }
}
```

Save the file main_test.go and execute the tests to ensure the application works as expected:

```
$ go test -v
=== RUN   TestHelperProcess
--- PASS: TestHelperProcess (0.00s)
=== RUN   TestRun
=== RUN   TestRun/success
=== RUN   TestRun/successMock
=== RUN   TestRun/fail
=== RUN   TestRun/failFormat
=== RUN   TestRun/failTimeout
```

```
--- PASS: TestRun (11.84s)
    --- PASS: TestRun/success (0.51s)
    --- PASS: TestRun/successMock (0.41s)
    --- PASS: TestRun/fail (0.08s)
    --- PASS: TestRun/failFormat (0.44s)
    --- PASS: TestRun/failTimeout (10.40s)
=== RUN   TestRunKill
=== RUN   TestRunKill/SIGINT
=== RUN   TestRunKill/SIGTERM
=== RUN   TestRunKill/SIGQUIT
--- PASS: TestRunKill (6.00s)
    --- PASS: TestRunKill/SIGINT (2.00s)
    --- PASS: TestRunKill/SIGTERM (2.00s)
    --- PASS: TestRunKill/SIGQUIT (2.00s)
PASS
ok      pragprog.com/rggo/processes/goci         17.845s
```

This completes the goci tool. You have an application that automates the process of building and testing your Go projects while handling signals appropriately if required.

Exercises

Try these exercises to improve the skills you learned:

- Add another step to the pipeline: code linting using golangci-lint. For more information consult its home page.[8]

- Add gocyclo to the pipeline. Capture its output and return an error if gocyclo returns any functions with a complexity score of 10 or greater. For more information about this tool, consult its GitHub page.[9]

- Add environment variables to handle Git authentication with remote repositories that require it.

- Add another command-line flag to your tool asking for the Git branch to push. Update the Git step to accept a configurable branch instead of master.

- Get the Pipeline configuration from a file instead of hard-coding it in the run() function.

---

8. golangci-lint.run/
9. github.com/fzipp/gocyclo

Wrapping Up

In this chapter, you designed and built a flexible tool that uses other tools and commands to execute specialized tasks in an automated way. You executed external commands, managed their error conditions, captured their output, and handled long-running processes appropriately. You tested your application using two different strategies: using a test helper to build a temporary local infrastructure, and mocking the external command. Finally, you ensured your application handles the operating system signal in a clean way to correctly communicate status to downstream applications and to prevent data loss.

In the next chapter, you'll use the Cobra CLI framework to help you develop a command-line network port scanner by generating the boilerplate code for the application and handling flags and configuration in a more comprehensive way.

## CHAPTER 7

Using the Cobra CLI Framework

Up to this point, you've had to write all of the code to define the command-line interface for your programs. You've had to handle flags, environment variables, and the execution logic. Cobra[1] is a popular framework for designing CLI applications, and in this chapter, you'll use it to handle the user interface of your program. If you work with Go and CLI tools, then it's likely that you'll encounter Cobra. Many modern tools are built with Cobra, including Kubernetes, Openshift, Podman, Hugo, and Docker.

Cobra provides a library that allows you to design CLI applications supporting *POSIX*[2]-compliant flags, subcommands, suggestions, autocompletion, and automatic help creation. It integrates with Viper[3] to provide management of configuration and environment variables for your applications. Cobra also provides a generator program that creates boilerplate code for you, allowing you to focus on your tool's business logic.

In this chapter, you'll use Cobra to develop *pScan*, a CLI tool that uses subcommands, similar to Git or Kubernetes. This tool executes a TCP port scan on a list of hosts similarly to the Nmap[4] command. It allows you to add, list, and delete hosts from the list using the subcommand hosts. It executes the scan on selected ports using the subcommand scan. Users can specify the ports using a command-line flag. It also features command completion using the subcommand completion and manual page generation with the subcommand docs. Cobra helps you define the subcommand structure by associating these subcommands in a tree data structure. When done, your application will have this subcommand layout:

---

1.   github.com/spf13/cobra
2.   en.wikipedia.org/wiki/POSIX
3.   github.com/spf13/viper
4.   nmap.org/

```
pScan
├── completion
├── docs
├── help
├── hosts
│   ├── add
│   ├── delete
│   └── list
└── scan
```

The purpose of this application is to demonstrate how to use Cobra to help you create command-line applications and use Go to create networking applications. You can use this application to monitor your system, but remember to never port scan systems you don't own.

Let's install Cobra and use it to initialize this application.

Starting Your Cobra Application

Start this project by creating a directory structure for your *pScan* application under the book's root directory, and switch to the new directory:

```
$ mkdir -p $HOME/pragprog.com/rggo/cobra/pScan
$ cd $HOME/pragprog.com/rggo/cobra/pScan
```

Next, initialize the Go module for this application:

```
$ go mod init pragprog.com/rggo/cobra/pScan
go: creating new go.mod: module pragprog.com/rggo/cobra/pScan
```

The Cobra CLI framework works as a library to write CLI applications, and as a code generator to generate boilerplate code for a new CLI tool. You need to install the cobra executable command to generate code. Use go get to download and install Cobra:

```
$ go get -u github.com/spf13/cobra/cobra@v1.1.3
```

This command downloads Cobra v1.1.3, which is what the book uses, including all its dependencies. If you want, you can use a later version, but you need to make a few minor adjustments to the code. This command also installs the cobra tool in the $GOBIN or $GOPATH/bin directories. Ensure the correct directory is included in the $PATH so you can execute cobra directly:

```
$ export PATH=$(go env GOPATH)/bin:$PATH
```

To ensure you installed Cobra correctly and you're able to run it, check the Cobra help:

```
$ cobra --help
Cobra is a CLI library for Go that empowers applications.
This application is a tool to generate the needed files
to quickly create a Cobra application.

Usage:
  cobra [command]

Available Commands:
  add         Add a command to a Cobra Application
  help        Help about any command
  init        Initialize a Cobra Application

Flags:
  -a, --author string     author name for copyright attribution
                            (default "YOUR NAME")
      --config string     config file (default is $HOME/.cobra.yaml)
  -h, --help              help for cobra
  -l, --license string    name of license for the project
      --viper             use Viper for configuration (default true)

Use "cobra [command] --help" for more information about a command.
```

This help shows the subcommands you can use when running the Cobra code generator. Shortly, you'll use the init subcommand to initialize a new application.

When Cobra generates code, it automatically includes copyright information, such as author's name and license, in the generated code. By default, it uses YOUR NAME for the author and the Apache v2 license. You can change these options by specifying the flags -a for the author and -l for the license, every time you run the Cobra command. Since adding these two flags for every execution is tedious and error-prone, create a configuration file .cobra.yaml in your home directory to record your options. Cobra uses the values from this file automatically.

```
author: The Pragmatic Programmers, LLC
license:
  header: |
    Copyrights apply to this source code.
    Check LICENSE for details.
  text: |
    {{ .copyright }}

    Copyrights apply to this source code. You may use the source code in your
    own projects, however the source code may not be used to create training
    material, courses, books, articles, and the like.
    We make no guarantees that this source code is fit for any purpose.
```

In this example, we're defining a custom license by specifying its content in the header and text fields. Before proceeding, adapt this configuration to your requirements, starting with updating the author field with your own name. Optionally, update the content of the header and text fields with your own license terms.

Alternatively, you can specify common open source licenses such as GPLv2, GPLv3, or MIT. To do this, remove the header and text fields and specify the license you want to use as the value for the license field. For example, you would use the MIT license by defining the configuration like this:

```
author: The Pragmatic Programmers, LLC
license: MIT
```

Next, initialize your Cobra application using the init subcommand. You need to specify the package name you used when initializing the module for your application using the --pkg-name flag, like this:

```
$ cobra init --pkg-name pragprog.com/rggo/cobra/pScan
Using config file: /home/ricardo/.cobra.yaml
Your Cobra application is ready at
/home/ricardo/pragprog.com/rggo/cobra/pScan
```

The Cobra generator created several files for your application, including a LICENSE file with the license content as per the configuration file:

```
$ tree
.
├── cmd
│   └── root.go
├── go.mod
├── go.sum
├── LICENSE
└── main.go

1 directory, 5 files
```

Verify the LICENSE content:

cobra/pScan/LICENSE
```
Copyright © 2020 The Pragmatic Programmers, LLC

Copyrights apply to this source code. You may use the source code in your
own projects, however the source code may not be used to create training
material, courses, books, articles, and the like.
We make no guarantees that this source code is fit for any purpose.
```

You now have a working application. It doesn't do anything useful yet, but you can execute it to ensure it works. Before executing it, run the command go get to download any missing dependencies, and then run the application:

```
$ go get
$ go run main.go
A longer description that spans multiple lines and likely contains
examples and usage of using your application. For example:

Cobra is a CLI library for Go that empowers applications.
This application is a tool to generate the needed files
to quickly create a Cobra application.
```

The first time you execute the application, it looks for some of Cobra's dependencies and adds them to the go.mod file. After that, it will only print the help information.

You created the general structure and initialized your Cobra application. Next, let's start adding functionality to this tool.

Navigating Your New Cobra Application

Cobra structures your application by creating a simple main.go file that only imports the package cmd and executes the application. The main.go file looks like this:

cobra/pScan/main.go
```
/*
Copyright © 2020 The Pragmatic Programmers, LLC
Copyrights apply to this source code.
Check LICENSE for details.

*/
package main

import "pragprog.com/rggo/cobra/pScan/cmd"

func main() {
  cmd.Execute()
}
```

The core functionality of your application resides in the cmd package. When you run the command, the main() function calls cmd.Execute() to execute the root command of your application. You can find this function and the general structure of the program in the cmd/root.go file. The Execute() function executes the rootCmd.Execute() method on an instance of the cobra.Command type:

cobra/pScan/cmd/root.go
```
func Execute() {
  if err := rootCmd.Execute(); err != nil {
    fmt.Println(err)
    os.Exit(1)
  }
}
```

The cobra.Command type is the main type in the Cobra library. It represents a command or subcommand that your tool executes. You can combine commands in a parent-child relationship to form a tree structure of subcommands. When Cobra initializes the application, it starts this structure by defining a variable called rootCmd as an instance of the type cobra.Command in the cmd/root.go file. This type has several properties that you'll use later to build your application. The general properties required to create a cobra.Command are: Use, which represents the command usage, and a Short or Long description. Here's the default definition of the root command:

```
cobra/pScan/cmd/root.go
var rootCmd = &cobra.Command{
  Use:   "pScan",
  Short: "A brief description of your application",
  Long: `A longer description that spans multiple lines and likely contains
examples and usage of using your application. For example:

Cobra is a CLI library for Go that empowers applications.
This application is a tool to generate the needed files
to quickly create a Cobra application.`,
  // Uncomment the following line if your bare application
  // has an action associated with it:
  //   Run: func(cmd *cobra.Command, args []string) { },
}
```

By default, the root command doesn't execute any action, serving only as the parent for other subcommands. For that reason, the property Run is commented out. If you want the root command to execute actions, you can uncomment this property and implement its function. For this application, the root command doesn't execute any actions, so we'll leave it as is.

Notice that the long description matches the message you got when executing the tool for the first time. Update the description to provide your users with an overview of your program's functionality, like this:

```
cobra/pScan.v1/cmd/root.go
  Short: "Fast TCP port scanner",
  Long: `pScan - short for Port Scanner - executes TCP port scan
on a list of hosts.

pScan allows you to add, list, and delete hosts from the list.

pScan executes a port scan on specified TCP ports. You can customize the
target ports using a command line flag.`,
```

Run the tool again to see your updated description:

```
$ go run main.go
pScan - short for Port Scanner - executes TCP port scan
on a list of hosts.
```

pScan allows you to add, list, and delete hosts from the list.

pScan executes a port scan on specified TCP ports. You can customize the target ports using a command-line flag.

You can also have Cobra automatically print your application's version. Add the property Version to the rootCmd command and save the file:

cobra/pScan.v1/cmd/root.go
```
Version: "0.1",
```

When you add this property, Cobra includes the command-line flag -v and --version in your application. Running the application with one of those flags prints the version information:

```
$ go run main.go -v
pScan version 0.1
$ go run main.go --version
pScan version 0.1
```

Cobra defines two additional functions for you in the cmd/root.go file: init() and initConfig(). The init() function runs before main(). Use it to include additional functionality in your command that can't be defined as properties, such as adding command-line flags. For the root command, Cobra uses the cobra.OnInitialize() function to run the initConfig() function when the application runs. The function initConfig() uses the package viper to include configuration management for your application. You'll use this package later in Using Viper for Configuration Management, on page 262.

For example, use the method rootCmd.SetVersionTemplate() within the init() function to update the version template so it prints the short description of your application with the version information:

cobra/pScan.v1/cmd/root.go
```
func init() {
  cobra.OnInitialize(initConfig)

  // Here you will define your flags and configuration settings.
  // Cobra supports persistent flags, which, if defined here,
  // will be global for your application.

  rootCmd.PersistentFlags().StringVar(&cfgFile, "config", "",
    "config file (default is $HOME/.pScan.yaml)")

  // Cobra also supports local flags, which will only run
  // when this action is called directly.
  rootCmd.Flags().BoolP("toggle", "t", false, "Help message for toggle")

  versionTemplate := `{{printf "%s: %s - version %s\n" .Name .Short .Version}}`
  rootCmd.SetVersionTemplate(versionTemplate)
}
```

Save the file and run the application using the -v flag to see the new version information:

```
$ go run main.go -v
pScan: Fast TCP port scanner - version 0.1
```

Now that you understand the general structure of a Cobra application, let's add the first subcommand to it.

Adding the First Subcommand to Your Application

After initializing the application, use the Cobra generator to add subcommands to it. The generator includes a file in the cmd directory for each subcommand. Each file includes boilerplate code for the subcommand. It also adds the subcommand to its parent, forming the tree-like structure.

Add a new subcommand called hosts to your application to manage hosts in the hosts list. By default, Cobra adds this subcommand to the root command:

```
$ cobra add hosts
Using config file: /home/ricardo/.cobra.yaml
hosts created at /home/ricardo/pragprog.com/rggo/cobra/pScan
```

At this point, your application directory looks like this:

```
$ tree
.
├── cmd
│   ├── hosts.go
│   └── root.go
├── go.mod
├── go.sum
├── LICENSE
└── main.go

1 directory, 6 files
```

Edit the cmd/hosts.go file and change the command's short description to provide a one-line summary of the command's purpose. Edit the long description to provide additional information on how to use the command and its suboptions:

```
cobra/pScan.v2/cmd/hosts.go
/*
Copyright © 2020 The Pragmatic Programmers, LLC
Copyrights apply to this source code.
Check LICENSE for details.
*/
package cmd
```

```
import (
  "fmt"

  "github.com/spf13/cobra"
)

// hostsCmd represents the hosts command
var hostsCmd = &cobra.Command{
  Use: "hosts",
➤   Short: "Manage the hosts list",
➤   Long: `Manages the hosts lists for pScan
➤
➤ Add hosts with the add command
➤ Delete hosts with the delete command
➤ List hosts with the list command.`,
    Run: func(cmd *cobra.Command, args []string) {
      fmt.Println("hosts called")
    },
}

func init() {
  rootCmd.AddCommand(hostsCmd)

  // Here you will define your flags and configuration settings.

  // Cobra supports Persistent Flags which will work for this command
  // and all subcommands, e.g.:
  // hostsCmd.PersistentFlags().String("foo", "", "A help for foo")

  // Cobra supports local flags which will only run when this command
  // is called directly, e.g.:
  // hostsCmd.Flags().BoolP("toggle", "t", false, "Help message for toggle")
}
```

The init() function uses the AddCommand() method of the root command instance
rootCmd to attach the hostsCmd command to the root. Save the file and run the
tool again to see if the output changes to include possible subcommands:

```
$ go run main.go
pScan - short for Port Scanner - executes TCP port scan
on a list of hosts.

pScan allows you to add, list, and delete hosts from the list.

pScan executes a port scan on specified TCP ports. You can customize the
target ports using a command-line flag.

Usage:
  pScan [command]

Available Commands:
  help       Help about any command
  hosts      Manage the hosts list
```

```
Flags:
      --config string   config file (default is $HOME/.pScan.yaml)
  -h, --help            help for pScan
  -t, --toggle          Help message for toggle
  -v, --version         version for pScan
```

Use "*pScan [command] --help*" **for** more information about a command.

Cobra also creates a help message for the new command. You can see it by running the help subcommand or using the flag -h with the hosts subcommand:

```
$ go run main.go help hosts
Manages the hosts lists for pScan

Add hosts with the add command
Delete hosts with the delete command
List hosts with the list command.

Usage:
  pScan hosts [flags]

Flags:
  -h, --help   help for hosts

Global Flags:
      --config string   config file (default is $HOME/.pScan.yaml)
```

The new command has a dummy implementation. Execute it to see the message hosts called:

```
$ go run main.go hosts
hosts called
```

Finally, Cobra also implements autosuggestions in case the users misspell a command. For example, if you type host instead of hosts, you see this suggestion:

```
$ go run main.go host
Error: unknown command "host" for "pScan"

Did you mean this?
        hosts

Run 'pScan --help' for usage.
unknown command "host" for "pScan"

Did you mean this?
        hosts

exit status 1
```

If you don't want this behavior, you can disable it by setting the property DisableSuggestions to true in your instance of the root command. We'll leave this enabled for now.

Your application is starting to look more polished from applying some of Cobra's features. Next, you'll add the functionality of managing hosts for the application.

Starting the Scan Package

You have the skeleton of your application ready, so let's add the port scanning functionality, starting with the hosts list management. For this tool, you'll create a separate package scan to develop the business logic, similar to the approach you used in Chapter 2, Interacting with Your Users, on page 11.

In your application's root directory, create a new directory named scan and switch to it:

```
$ cd $HOME/pragprog.com/rggo/cobra/pScan
$ mkdir scan
$ cd scan
```

Now, create and edit the file hostsList.go. Start by defining the package name scan and the import list. For this package you'll use the fOllowing packages: bufio to read data from files, errors to define error values, fmt to print formatted output, io/ioutil to write data to files, os for operating system-related functions, and sort to sort the hosts list content:

cobra/pScan.v3/scan/hostsList.go
```go
// Package scan provides types and functions to perform TCP port
// scans on a list of hosts
package scan

import (
  "bufio"
  "errors"
  "fmt"
  "io/ioutil"
  "os"
  "sort"
)
```

Define two error variables using the function errors.New() from the errors package. The first error indicates that a host is already in the list, and the second error indicates that a host isn't in the list. You'll use these errors during tests and to help manage the host list:

cobra/pScan.v3/scan/hostsList.go
```go
var (
  ErrExists = errors.New("Host already in the list")
  ErrNotExists = errors.New("Host not in the list")
)
```

Next, define a new struct type HostsList that represents a list of hosts on which you can execute a port scan. This type wraps a slice of strings so we can add methods to it:

```
cobra/pScan.v3/scan/hostsList.go
// HostsList represents a list of hosts to run port scan
type HostsList struct {
  Hosts []string
}
```

Then define the methods for this new type. The first method is a private method search() that searches for a host in the list. Other methods, such as the Add() method, will use this method to ensure that no duplicate entries are present in the list:

```
cobra/pScan.v3/scan/hostsList.go
// search searches for hosts in the list
func (hl *HostsList) search(host string) (bool, int) {
  sort.Strings(hl.Hosts)

  i := sort.SearchStrings(hl.Hosts, host)
  if i < len(hl.Hosts) && hl.Hosts[i] == host {
    return true, i
  }

  return false, -1
}
```

This method uses the function sort.Strings() from the sort package to sort the HostsList alphabetically and then uses the function sort.SearchStrings() also from the sort package to search for the host in the list. It returns true and the element index if it finds the host or false and the integer -1 if the host isn't in the list.

Next, define the Add() method to include new hosts in the list:

```
cobra/pScan.v3/scan/hostsList.go
// Add adds a host to the list
func (hl *HostsList) Add(host string) error {
  if found, _ := hl.search(host); found {
    return fmt.Errorf("%w: %s", ErrExists, host)
  }

  hl.Hosts = append(hl.Hosts, host)
  return nil
}
```

This method uses the search() method to search for the given host in the list and adds it to the list if it's not there. If the element already exists, it returns an error that wraps the error ErrExists you defined before.

Next, create the Remove() method to delete a given host from the list. The name *Delete* isn't a good choice because it can cause confusion with Go's delete keyword:

cobra/pScan.v3/scan/hostsList.go
```go
// Remove deletes a host from the list
func (hl *HostsList) Remove(host string) error {
  if found, i := hl.search(host); found {
    hl.Hosts = append(hl.Hosts[:i], hl.Hosts[i+1:]...)
    return nil
  }

  return fmt.Errorf("%w: %s", ErrNotExists, host)
}
```

This method is similar to the Add() method but in reverse. It searches for the given host in the list, deleting it if found. It returns an error wrapping ErrNotExist if the host isn't in the list.

Finally, define methods to load and save the HostsList. First define the Load() method, which tries to load hosts from a given hostsFile. This method does nothing if the file doesn't exist but it returns an error if it can't open the file:

cobra/pScan.v3/scan/hostsList.go
```go
// Load obtains hosts from a hosts file
func (hl *HostsList) Load(hostsFile string) error {
  f, err := os.Open(hostsFile)
  if err != nil {
    if errors.Is(err, os.ErrNotExist) {
      return nil
    }
    return err
  }
  defer f.Close()

  scanner := bufio.NewScanner(f)

  for scanner.Scan() {
    hl.Hosts = append(hl.Hosts, scanner.Text())
  }
  return nil
}
```

Finally, create the Save() method that attempts to save the list into the given hostsFile, returning an error if it can't complete the operation:

cobra/pScan.v3/scan/hostsList.go
```go
// Save saves hosts to a hosts file
func (hl *HostsList) Save(hostsFile string) error {
  output := ""
```

```
  for _, h := range hl.Hosts {
    output += fmt.Sprintln(h)
  }

  return ioutil.WriteFile(hostsFile, []byte(output), 0644)
}
```

Now, let's write some tests for this package. Save the file hostsList.go and create and edit a new test file hostsList_test.go.

Then add the package definition. For these tests, you'll use the same approach you used in Defining the To-Do API, on page 12 to test the exposed API, but here you'll define the package name scan_test. Also, you'll add the import list. You'll use the errors package to perform error verification, the ioutil package to create temporary files, the os package to delete the temporary files, the testing package for the test functionality, and the scan package that you're testing:

cobra/pScan.v3/scan/hostsList_test.go
```
package scan_test

import (
  "errors"
  "io/ioutil"
  "os"
  "testing"

  "pragprog.com/rggo/cobra/pScan/scan"
)
```

Next, include a function to test the method Add(). This test function uses the table-driven testing technique that you first used in Testing with Table-Driven Testing, on page 82. Define two test cases, one to add a new host and another to add an existing host which should return an error.

cobra/pScan.v3/scan/hostsList_test.go
```
func TestAdd(t *testing.T) {
  testCases := []struct {
    name      string
    host      string
    expectLen int
    expectErr error
  }{
    {"AddNew", "host2", 2, nil},
    {"AddExisting", "host1", 1, scan.ErrExists},
  }

  for _, tc := range testCases {
    t.Run(tc.name, func(t *testing.T) {
      hl := &scan.HostsList{}
```

```
    // Initialize list
    if err := hl.Add("host1"); err != nil {
      t.Fatal(err)
    }

    err := hl.Add(tc.host)

    if tc.expectErr != nil {
      if err == nil {
        t.Fatalf("Expected error, got nil instead\n")
      }

      if ! errors.Is(err, tc.expectErr) {
        t.Errorf("Expected error %q, got %q instead\n",
          tc.expectErr, err)
      }

      return
    }

    if err != nil {
      t.Fatalf("Expected no error, got %q instead\n", err)
    }

    if len(hl.Hosts) != tc.expectLen {
      t.Errorf("Expected list length %d, got %d instead\n",
        tc.expectLen, len(hl.Hosts))
    }

    if hl.Hosts[1] != tc.host {
      t.Errorf("Expected host name %q as index 1, got %q instead\n",
        tc.host, hl.Hosts[1])
    }
  })
 }
}
```

The test loop initializes a HostsList instance and then executes the Add() method
on it with each test case parameter. Then it compares the expected values
with the results, returning errors if they don't match.

Now, define a test function to test the method Remove(). This function also
uses the table-driven testing technique with two test cases. This is similar to
the TestAdd() function, but it executes the Remove() method instead:

```
cobra/pScan.v3/scan/hostsList_test.go
func TestRemove(t *testing.T) {
  testCases := []struct {
    name       string
    host       string
    expectLen  int
    expectErr  error
  }{
```

```
    {"RemoveExisting", "host1", 1, nil},
    {"RemoveNotFound", "host3", 1, scan.ErrNotExists},
  }

  for _, tc := range testCases {
    t.Run(tc.name, func(t *testing.T) {
      hl := &scan.HostsList{}

      // Initialize list
      for _, h := range []string{"host1", "host2"} {
        if err := hl.Add(h); err != nil {
          t.Fatal(err)
        }
      }

      err := hl.Remove(tc.host)

      if tc.expectErr != nil {
        if err == nil {
          t.Fatalf("Expected error, got nil instead\n")
        }

        if ! errors.Is(err, tc.expectErr) {
          t.Errorf("Expected error %q, got %q instead\n",
            tc.expectErr, err)
        }

        return
      }

      if err != nil {
        t.Fatalf("Expected no error, got %q instead\n", err)
      }

      if len(hl.Hosts) != tc.expectLen {
        t.Errorf("Expected list length %d, got %d instead\n",
          tc.expectLen, len(hl.Hosts))
      }

      if hl.Hosts[0] == tc.host {
        t.Errorf("Host name %q should not be in the list\n", tc.host)
      }
    })
  }
}
```

Next, create a test function to test the Save() and Load() methods. This function creates two HostsList instances, initializes the first list, and uses the Save() method to save it to a temporary file. Then, it uses the Load() method to load the contents of the temporary file into the second list and compares both of them. The test fails if the contents of the lists don't match.

cobra/pScan.v3/scan/hostsList_test.go
```
func TestSaveLoad(t *testing.T) {
```

```
hl1 := scan.HostsList{}
hl2 := scan.HostsList{}

hostName := "host1"
hl1.Add(hostName)

tf, err := ioutil.TempFile("", "")

if err != nil {
  t.Fatalf("Error creating temp file: %s", err)

}
defer os.Remove(tf.Name())

if err := hl1.Save(tf.Name()); err != nil {
  t.Fatalf("Error saving list to file: %s", err)

}

if err := hl2.Load(tf.Name()); err != nil {
  t.Fatalf("Error getting list from file: %s", err)

}

if hl1.Hosts[0] != hl2.Hosts[0] {
  t.Errorf("Host %q should match %q host.", hl1.Hosts[0], hl2.Hosts[0])
  }
}
```

Finally, define a test case for a specific scenario where the Load() method attempts to load a file that doesn't exist.

cobra/pScan.v3/scan/hostsList_test.go
```
func TestLoadNoFile(t *testing.T) {
  tf, err := ioutil.TempFile("", "")

  if err != nil {
    t.Fatalf("Error creating temp file: %s", err)
  }

  if err := os.Remove(tf.Name()); err != nil {
    t.Fatalf("Error deleting temp file: %s", err)
  }

  hl := &scan.HostsList{}

  if err := hl.Load(tf.Name()); err != nil {
    t.Errorf("Expected no error, got %q instead\n", err)
  }
}
```

To ensure this test works reliably even when executed multiple times, it creates a temporary file and then deletes it. By creating the temporary file, it ensures it's using a file name that doesn't conflict with any existing file. By deleting the temporary file, the test ensures that the file doesn't exist, which is the test goal.

This completes the test cases. Save the file and execute the tests to confirm the package works as desired:

```
$ go test -v
=== RUN    TestAdd
=== RUN    TestAdd/AddNew
=== RUN    TestAdd/AddExisting
--- PASS: TestAdd (0.00s)
    --- PASS: TestAdd/AddNew (0.00s)
    --- PASS: TestAdd/AddExisting (0.00s)
=== RUN    TestRemove
=== RUN    TestRemove/RemoveExisting
=== RUN    TestRemove/RemoveNotFound
--- PASS: TestRemove (0.00s)
    --- PASS: TestRemove/RemoveExisting (0.00s)
    --- PASS: TestRemove/RemoveNotFound (0.00s)
=== RUN    TestSaveLoad
--- PASS: TestSaveLoad (0.00s)
=== RUN    TestLoadNoFile
--- PASS: TestLoadNoFile (0.00s)
PASS
ok       pragprog.com/rggo/cobra/pScan/scan       0.003s
```

The business logic for the hosts list is complete. Let's implement the subcommands to manage the hosts list.

Creating the Subcommands to Manage Hosts

The business logic for the hosts list is ready, so let's write the code to manage the hosts list under the hosts subcommand. These commands are: add to add a new host to the list, delete to delete a host from the list, and list to print all hosts in the list.

These subcommands all require a file to save and load the hosts to. Before including these commands, make a change to the root command to add a persistent flag --hosts-file, allowing the user to specify the name of the file they want to use to save the hosts to. A persistent flag makes it available to the command and all subcommands under that command. By adding this flag to the root command, we make it global which makes sense in this case because all the subcommands under hosts and later the scan subcommand require it.

To add the persistent flag, edit the file cmd/root.go and then add the following line to the init() function:

cobra/pScan.v3/cmd/root.go
```
func init() {
  cobra.OnInitialize(initConfig)
```

```
// Here you will define your flags and configuration settings.
// Cobra supports persistent flags, which, if defined here,
// will be global for your application.

rootCmd.PersistentFlags().StringVar(&cfgFile, "config", "",
  "config file (default is $HOME/.pScan.yaml)")

rootCmd.PersistentFlags().StringP("hosts-file", "f", "pScan.hosts",
  "pScan hosts file")

versionTemplate := `{{printf "%s: %s - version %s\n" .Name .Short .Version}}`
rootCmd.SetVersionTemplate(versionTemplate)
}
```

This adds a flag using the method StringP() of the flag.FlagSet type obtained by using the rootCmd.PersistentFlags() method of the rootCmd instance. The flag package is an alias to the package pflag, which is a replacement for Go's standard flag package that includes support for POSIX flags. Cobra automatically imports the pflag package for you so you don't have to do it explicitly. For more information about the pflag package, consult its GitHub page.[5]

The StringP() method lets you specify a shorthand option for your flag. In this case, users can specify this flag as either --hosts-file or -f. If the user doesn't specify this flag when running the command, it defaults to value pScan.hosts.

Since you're editing the root.go file, remove the lines that define a dummy example flag that your application doesn't require:

```
// Cobra also supports local flags, which will only run
// when this action is called directly.
rootCmd.Flags().BoolP("toggle", "t", false, "Help message for toggle")
```

In addition, we don't want the hosts subcommand to execute any actions when called without a subcommand. This should work as a group for the remaining hosts management subcommands. To disable the action, edit the file cmd/hosts.go and delete the property Run from the hostsCmd instance:

```
Run: func(cmd *cobra.Command, args []string) {
  fmt.Println("hosts called")
},
```

The hostsCmd instance definition now looks like this:

cobra/pScan.v3/cmd/hosts.go
```
var hostsCmd = &cobra.Command{
  Use:   "hosts",
  Short: "Manage the hosts list",
  Long: `Manages the hosts lists for pScan
```

_____

5. github.com/spf13/pflag

```
Add hosts with the add command
Delete hosts with the delete command
List hosts with the list command.`,
}
```

Now use the cobra add command again to generate the boilerplate code for the list subcommand and add it under the hosts command. Use the -p flag and the instance name hostsCmd to assign this command as the parent command instead of the root command:

```
$ cobra add list -p hostsCmd
Using config file: /home/ricardo/.cobra.yaml
list created at /home/ricardo/pragprog.com/rggo/cobra/pScan
```

Even though the command name is hosts, you need to use the instance variable hostsCmd as the value for the parent command so Cobra makes the correct association. If you provide the value hosts, Cobra will try to associate this command with an instance variable that doesn't exist, causing a build error.

Now that the list command is in place, do the same for the add and delete subcommands:

```
$ cobra add add -p hostsCmd
Using config file: /home/ricardo/.cobra.yaml
add created at /home/ricardo/pragprog.com/rggo/cobra/pScan
```

```
$ cobra add delete -p hostsCmd
Using config file: /home/ricardo/.cobra.yaml
delete created at /home/ricardo/pragprog.com/rggo/cobra/pScan
```

At this point, Cobra added three additional files in the cmd directory, one for each of the new commands. Your directory structure looks like this now:

```
$ tree
.
├── cmd
│   ├── add.go
│   ├── delete.go
│   ├── hosts.go
│   ├── list.go
│   └── root.go
├── go.mod
├── go.sum
├── LICENSE
├── main.go
└── scan
    ├── hostsList.go
    └── hostsList_test.go

2 directories, 11 files
```

To add the subcommand under the hostsCmd command, Cobra uses the method hostsCmd.AddCommand() in the init() function for each subcommand. For example, the init() function in the cmd/list.go file is this:

```
cobra/pScan.v3/cmd/list.go
func init() {
  hostsCmd.AddCommand(listCmd)

  // Here you will define your flags and configuration settings.

  // Cobra supports Persistent Flags which will work for this command
  // and all subcommands, e.g.:
  // listCmd.PersistentFlags().String("foo", "", "A help for foo")

  // Cobra supports local flags which will only run when this command
  // is called directly, e.g.:
  // listCmd.Flags().BoolP("toggle", "t", false, "Help message for toggle")
}
```

These files currently contain only boilerplate code. Let's modify them according to the application requirements. Start with the list command. Edit the file cmd/list.go and update the import section to include the io package to use the io.Writer interface, the os package to use os.Stdout for output, and your pragprog.com/rggo/cobra/pScan/scan package to use the application business logic you developed earlier:

```
cobra/pScan.v3/cmd/list.go
import (
  "fmt"
➤ "io"
➤ "os"
➤

  "github.com/spf13/cobra"
➤ "pragprog.com/rggo/cobra/pScan/scan"
)
```

Next, update the listCmd instance definition. Add the property Aliases to identify an alias to this subcommand so users can call it by using list or l:

```
Aliases: []string{"l"},
```

Update the short description to List hosts in hosts list and delete the property Long to remove the long description for this command:

```
Short:   "List hosts in hosts list",
```

Now, you need to configure the command to execute an action. By default, Cobra adds the property Run to the boilerplate code. This property specifies a function that Cobra executes when running this command, but it doesn't return an error. You'll replace it with the property RunE, which returns an error that's displayed to the user if needed.

For general functionality, you can implement this function directly. But since it's implemented as a property of the command instance, it's hard to test. To overcome this, you'll define an external function called listAction() that you can test independently. Then the function defined by the RunE property only has to parse command-line flags that depend on the command instance and use them as parameters to call the external action function. Define this property like this:

```
RunE: func(cmd *cobra.Command, args []string) error {
  hostsFile, err := cmd.Flags().GetString("hosts-file")
  if err != nil {
    return err
  }

  return listAction(os.Stdout, hostsFile, args)
},
```

Cobra automatically makes all command-line flags available to the current command using the method cmd.Flags(). This code gets the value for the hosts-file flag defined before using its name hosts-file as a parameter to the method GetString() since this is a string type flag.

The complete definition for the listCmd instance looks like this:

```
cobra/pScan.v3/cmd/list.go
var listCmd = &cobra.Command{
  Use:     "list",
  Aliases: []string{"l"},
  Short:   "List hosts in hosts list",
  RunE: func(cmd *cobra.Command, args []string) error {
    hostsFile, err := cmd.Flags().GetString("hosts-file")
    if err != nil {
      return err
    }

    return listAction(os.Stdout, hostsFile, args)
  },
}
```

Now, define the listAction() function. It accepts an io.Writer interface representing where to print output to, the string hostsFile that contains the name of the file to load the hosts list from, and a slice of string args that has any other arguments passed by the user. It returns a potential error. Even though this function doesn't use the args parameter, we'll leave it there so it's similar to other actions we'll add later:

```
cobra/pScan.v3/cmd/list.go
func listAction(out io.Writer, hostsFile string, args []string) error {
  hl := &scan.HostsList{}
```

```
  if err := hl.Load(hostsFile); err != nil {
    return err
  }

  for _, h := range hl.Hosts {
    if _, err := fmt.Fprintln(out, h); err != nil {
      return err
    }
  }

  return nil
}
```

This function creates an instance of the HostsList type provided by the package scan you created before. Then, it loads the content of the hostsFile into the hosts list instance and iterates over each entry, printing each item into the io.Writer interface as a new line. If an error occurs when printing the results, it returns the error; otherwise, it returns nil.

The list command is ready. Let's implement the add subcommand now. Save this file and edit the file cmd/add.go. Update the import section. This file uses the same packages you used to implement the list subcommand:

cobra/pScan.v3/cmd/add.go
```
import (
  "fmt"
  "io"
  "os"

  "github.com/spf13/cobra"
  "pragprog.com/rggo/cobra/pScan/scan"
)
```

Now, update the addCmd command instance properties. First, update the Use property. By default, this property only shows the command name. In our case, this command allows the user to provide additional arguments as series of strings each representing a host to add to the list. Update the Use property to represent that:

```
Use:          "add <host1>...<hostn>",
```

Next, add an alias called a to this command:

```
Aliases:      []string{"a"},
```

Update the Short description to Add new host(s) to the list and delete the Long description:

```
Short:        "Add new host(s) to list",
```

Cobra can also validate the arguments provided to a command. It provides some validation functions out-of-the-box, such as a minimum or maximum number of arguments, among others. For more complex scenarios, you can implement your custom validation function. This command requires at least one argument to work, otherwise, it has no hosts to add to the list. Use the function cobra.MinimumNArgs(1) as the value for the Args property to ensure the user provides at least one argument:

```
Args:          cobra.MinimumNArgs(1),
```

If the user provides an invalid number of arguments, Cobra returns an error. By default, Cobra also shows the command usage when an error occurs. In this case, it may be confusing for the user to understand what's wrong. Let's prevent the automatic usage display by setting the property SilenceUsage to true. The user can still see the command usage by providing the flag -h for help.

```
SilenceUsage: true,
```

Finally, implement the command's action by replacing the property Run with RunE similarly to what you did for the list command. This function handles the command-line flags and then calls the external function addAction() that executes the command action. The complete addCmd definition is this:

cobra/pScan.v3/cmd/add.go
```
var addCmd = &cobra.Command{
  Use:          "add <host1>...<hostn>",
  Aliases:      []string{"a"},
  Short:        "Add new host(s) to list",
  SilenceUsage: true,
  Args:         cobra.MinimumNArgs(1),
  RunE: func(cmd *cobra.Command, args []string) error {
    hostsFile, err := cmd.Flags().GetString("hosts-file")
    if err != nil {
      return err
    }

    return addAction(os.Stdout, hostsFile, args)
  },
}
```

Now, implement the function addAction() to execute the command's action. It takes the same input parameters as the listAction() function. In this case, it uses the args parameter that represents the arguments the user provided to the command. This function also returns a potential error:

cobra/pScan.v3/cmd/add.go
```
func addAction(out io.Writer, hostsFile string, args []string) error {
  hl := &scan.HostsList{}
```

```
  if err := hl.Load(hostsFile); err != nil {
    return err
  }

  for _, h := range args {
    if err := hl.Add(h); err != nil {
      return err
    }

    fmt.Fprintln(out, "Added host:", h)
  }

  return hl.Save(hostsFile)
}
```

This function creates an empty instance of scan.HostsList and uses the method Load() to load the contents of hostsFile into the list. Then it iterates over each item of the slice args, using the method Add() to add them to the list. Finally, it saves the file, returning an error if one occurs.

Finally, implement the delete subcommand. Save the file cmd/add.go and edit the file cmd/delete.go. Start by updating the import section. It uses the same packages as the two previous commands:

cobra/pScan.v3/cmd/delete.go
```
import (
  "fmt"
  "io"
  "os"

  "github.com/spf13/cobra"
  "pragprog.com/rggo/cobra/pScan/scan"
)
```

Next, update the deleteCmd command instance, like this:

cobra/pScan.v3/cmd/delete.go
```
var deleteCmd = &cobra.Command{
  Use:          "delete <host1>...<host n>",
  Aliases:      []string{"d"},
  Short:        "Delete hosts(s) from list",
  SilenceUsage: true,
  Args:         cobra.MinimumNArgs(1),
  RunE: func(cmd *cobra.Command, args []string) error {
    hostsFile, err := cmd.Flags().GetString("hosts-file")
    if err != nil {
      return err
    }

    return deleteAction(os.Stdout, hostsFile, args)
  },
}
```

This command uses d as the alias. The options are similar to the ones used for the addCmd command, with the exception of the descriptions. The function specified in RunE calls the deleteAction() function.

Now, implement the deleteAction() function. It works much the same as the addAction() function but uses the Remove() method in the loop to remove hosts instead. At the end, it saves the file, returning the error if it occurs.

cobra/pScan.v3/cmd/delete.go
```
func deleteAction(out io.Writer, hostsFile string, args []string) error {
  hl := &scan.HostsList{}

  if err := hl.Load(hostsFile); err != nil {
    return err
  }

  for _, h := range args {
    if err := hl.Remove(h); err != nil {
      return err
    }

    fmt.Fprintln(out, "Deleted host:", h)
  }

  return hl.Save(hostsFile)
}
```

This completes the code for the hosts management. Save the file cmd/delete.go. Next, you'll implement some tests for your command-line tool.

Testing the Manage Hosts Subcommands

Using boilerplate code that Cobra generated for your project makes it a little bit harder to write tests for your application. You gain development speed at the expense of flexibility since you're constrained by the generator's choices. To overcome this restriction while still benefiting from the generated code, you developed the application using action functions such as listAction() and deleteAction(). Because these functions are independent from the generated code, you have the flexibility to test them. By doing this, you won't be testing the part of the code generated by Cobra, but this is acceptable because we trust it was tested by Cobra's developers.

The action functions accept the parameters required to test them properly. You're using the same pattern you used before in Using Interfaces to Automate Tests, on page 58. These functions take as input an instance of the io.Writer interface as the command's output destination. In the main code, you use the os.Stdout type when calling the functions, so the output goes to the user's screen. For your tests, you'll use the type bytes.Buffer to capture the output and test it.

Start your tests by creating and editing a file cmd/actions_test.go under your application's cmd directory. Define the package and the import section. For these tests, you'll use the bytes package to use the type bytes.Buffer to capture output, the fmt package for formatted output, the io package to use the io.Writer interface, the ioutil package to create temporary files, the os package to delete temporary files, the strings package to manipulate string data, the testing package for the testing functionality, and the scan package you created before to help add items to the list for testing:

cobra/pScan.v4/cmd/actions_test.go

```go
package cmd

import (
  "bytes"
  "fmt"
  "io"
  "io/ioutil"
  "os"
  "strings"
  "testing"

  "pragprog.com/rggo/cobra/pScan/scan"
)
```

Since this application saves the hosts list to a file, these tests require temporary files. Let's create an auxiliary function to set up the test environment. This includes creating a temporary file and initializing a list if required. This function accepts as input an instance of the type testing.T, a slice of strings representing hosts to initialize a list, and a bool to indicate whether the list should be initialized. It returns the name of the temporary file as string and a cleanup function that deletes the temporary file after it was used:

cobra/pScan.v4/cmd/actions_test.go

```go
func setup(t *testing.T, hosts []string, initList bool) (string, func()) {
  // Create temp file
  tf, err := ioutil.TempFile("", "pScan")
  if err != nil {
    t.Fatal(err)
  }
  tf.Close()

  // Inititialize list if needed
  if initList {
    hl := &scan.HostsList{}

    for _, h := range hosts {
      hl.Add(h)
    }
```

```
    if err := hl.Save(tf.Name()); err != nil {
      t.Fatal(err)
    }
  }

  // Return temp file name and cleanup function
  return tf.Name(), func() {
    os.Remove(tf.Name())
  }
}
```

This function uses the TempFile() function from the ioutil package to create a temporary file with the pscan prefix. It stops the tests immediately by using t.Fatal() if it can't create the file. Then it closes the file since the calling function only needs the name. Next, it initializes a list if required and saves it into the temporary file. Finally, it returns the file's name and the cleanup function.

Now, define your first test function TestHostActions() to test the action functions:

cobra/pScan.v4/cmd/actions_test.go
```
func TestHostActions(t *testing.T) {
```

For this test, use the table-driven testing approach you first used in Testing with Table-Driven Testing, on page 82. First, define a slice of strings representing some hosts for the tests:

cobra/pScan.v4/cmd/actions_test.go
```
// Define hosts for actions test
hosts := []string{
  "host1",
  "host2",
  "host3",
}
```

Then define the test cases using the table-driven approach. Each test has a name as string, a list of arguments args to pass to the action function, an expected output expectedOut, a bool initList that indicates whether the list must be initialized before the test, and the actionFunction that represents which action function to test. This property accepts any function with the signature func(io.Writer, string, []string) error, which allows you to use any of the action functions you developed:

cobra/pScan.v4/cmd/actions_test.go
```
// Test cases for Action test
testCases := []struct {
  name           string
  args           []string
  expectedOut    string
  initList       bool
  actionFunction func(io.Writer, string, []string) error
}{
```

```
{
    name:           "AddAction",
    args:           hosts,
    expectedOut:    "Added host: host1\nAdded host: host2\nAdded host: host3\n",
    initList:       false,
    actionFunction: addAction,
},
{
    name:           "ListAction",
    expectedOut:    "host1\nhost2\nhost3\n",
    initList:       true,
    actionFunction: listAction,
},
{
    name:           "DeleteAction",
    args:           []string{"host1", "host2"},
    expectedOut:    "Deleted host: host1\nDeleted host: host2\n",
    initList:       true,
    actionFunction: deleteAction,
},
}
```

Next, start the test loop, iterating over each test case:

cobra/pScan.v4/cmd/actions_test.go
```
for _, tc := range testCases {
  t.Run(tc.name, func(t *testing.T) {
```

For each test case, run the setup() function you defined before and defer the execution of the cleanup() function to ensure the file is deleted after the tests:

cobra/pScan.v4/cmd/actions_test.go
```
// Setup Action test
tf, cleanup := setup(t, hosts, tc.initList)
defer cleanup()
```

Then, define a variable of type bytes.Buffer to capture the output of the action function, and execute the action function with the required parameters. If the function returns an error, fail the test immediately:

cobra/pScan.v4/cmd/actions_test.go
```
// Define var to capture Action output
var out bytes.Buffer

// Execute Action and capture output
if err := tc.actionFunction(&out, tf, tc.args); err != nil {
  t.Fatalf("Expected no error, got %q\n", err)
}
```

Finally, compare the output of the action function with the expected output, failing the test if they don't match:

cobra/pScan.v4/cmd/actions_test.go
```
    // Test Actions output
    if out.String() != tc.expectedOut {
      t.Errorf("Expected output %q, got %q\n", tc.expectedOut, out.String())
    }
  })
  }
}
```

This completes the TestHostActions() test. Let's add an integration test now. The goal is to execute all commands in sequence, simulating what a user would do with the tool. For this test, we'll simulate a flow where the user adds three hosts to the list, prints them out, deletes a host from the list, and prints the list again. Start by defining the test function:

cobra/pScan.v4/cmd/actions_test.go
```
func TestIntegration(t *testing.T) {
```

Then add the slice of strings with some hosts to add to the list:

cobra/pScan.v4/cmd/actions_test.go
```
// Define hosts for integration test
hosts := []string{
  "host1",
  "host2",
  "host3",
}
```

Next, set up the test using your setup() function:

cobra/pScan.v4/cmd/actions_test.go
```
// Setup integration test
tf, cleanup := setup(t, hosts, false)
defer cleanup()
```

Create a variable to hold the name of the host that will be deleted with the delete operation and another that represents the end state of the list of hosts after the delete operation:

cobra/pScan.v4/cmd/actions_test.go
```
delHost := "host2"

hostsEnd := []string{
  "host1",
  "host3",
}
```

Next, define a variable of type bytes.Buffer to capture output for the integrated test:

```
cobra/pScan.v4/cmd/actions_test.go
// Define var to capture output
var out bytes.Buffer
```

Now, define the expected output by concatenating the output of all the operations that'll be executed during this test. First, loop through the hosts slice to create the output for the add operation, then join the items of the hosts slice with a newline character \n as the output of the list operation, use a formatted print to include the output for the delete operation, and repeat the list output:

```
cobra/pScan.v4/cmd/actions_test.go
// Define expected output for all actions
expectedOut := ""
for _, v := range hosts {
  expectedOut += fmt.Sprintf("Added host: %s\n", v)
}
expectedOut += strings.Join(hosts, "\n")
expectedOut += fmt.Sprintln()
expectedOut += fmt.Sprintf("Deleted host: %s\n", delHost)
expectedOut += strings.Join(hostsEnd, "\n")
expectedOut += fmt.Sprintln()
```

Next, execute all the operations in the defined sequence add -> list -> delete -> list, using the proper parameters for each. Use the same buffer variable out to capture the output of all operations. If any of these operations results in an error, fail the test immediately:

```
cobra/pScan.v4/cmd/actions_test.go
// Add hosts to the list
if err := addAction(&out, tf, hosts); err != nil {
  t.Fatalf("Expected no error, got %q\n", err)
}

// List hosts
if err := listAction(&out, tf, nil); err != nil {
  t.Fatalf("Expected no error, got %q\n", err)
}

// Delete host2
if err := deleteAction(&out, tf, []string{delHost}); err != nil {
  t.Fatalf("Expected no error, got %q\n", err)
}

// List hosts after delete
if err := listAction(&out, tf, nil); err != nil {
  t.Fatalf("Expected no error, got %q\n", err)
}
```

Finally, compare the output of all the operations with the expected output, failing the test if they don't match:

```
cobra/pScan.v4/cmd/actions_test.go
  // Test integration output
  if out.String() != expectedOut {
    t.Errorf("Expected output %q, got %q\n", expectedOut, out.String())
  }
}
```

Save this file and execute the tests. If you're not in the cmd directory, change to it and then execute the tests:

```
$ cd cmd
$ pwd
/home/ricardo/pragprog.com/rggo/cobra/pScan.v4/cmd
$ go test -v
=== RUN    TestHostActions
=== RUN    TestHostActions/AddAction
=== RUN    TestHostActions/ListAction
=== RUN    TestHostActions/DeleteAction
--- PASS: TestHostActions (0.00s)
    --- PASS: TestHostActions/AddAction (0.00s)
    --- PASS: TestHostActions/ListAction (0.00s)
    --- PASS: TestHostActions/DeleteAction (0.00s)
=== RUN    TestIntegration
--- PASS: TestIntegration (0.00s)
PASS
ok      pragprog.com/rggo/cobra/pScan/cmd      0.006s
```

Once all the tests pass, you can try your application. Switch back to the application's root directory and build it with go build:

```
$ cd ..
$ pwd
/home/ricardo/pragprog.com/rggo/cobra/pScan.v4
$ go build
$ ls
cmd  go.mod  go.sum  LICENSE  main.go  pScan  scan
```

The go build command created your application's executable file pScan. If you execute it with no parameters, you'll see the same default help you got in Adding the First Subcommand to Your Application, on page 220. Execute it with the hosts command to see the list of subcommands you can use:

```
$ ./pScan hosts
Manages the hosts lists for pScan

Add hosts with the add command
Delete hosts with the delete command
List hosts with the list command.
```

```
Usage:
  pScan hosts [command]

Available Commands:
  add          Add new host(s) to list
  delete       Delete hosts(s) from list
  list         List hosts in hosts list

Flags:
  -h, --help    help for hosts

Global Flags:
      --config string       config file (default is $HOME/.pScan.yaml)
  -f, --hosts-file string   pScan hosts file (default "pScan.hosts")

Use "pScan hosts [command] --help" for more information about a command.
```

You can also see the help information for one of its subcommands by supplying the flag -h with that subcommand:

```
$ ./pScan hosts add -h
Add new host(s) to list

Usage:
  pScan hosts add <host1>...<hostn> [flags]

Aliases:
  add, a

Flags:
  -h, --help    help for add

Global Flags:
      --config string       config file (default is $HOME/.pScan.yaml)
  -f, --hosts-file string   pScan hosts file (default "pScan.hosts")
```

Now, add a host to the list:

```
$ ./pScan hosts add localhost
Added host: localhost
```

Or you can use the alias a instead of add:

```
$ ./pScan hosts a myhost
Added host: myhost
```

Since you did not specify the --hosts-file flag, the pScan command automatically saved your list in the file pScan.hosts. List the hosts in the file with the list command:

```
$ ./pScan hosts list
localhost
myhost
```

Check the file created by the pScan tool:

```
$ ls pScan.hosts
pScan.hosts
$ cat pScan.hosts
localhost
myhost
```

Before moving on to the next section, explore some of the other options such as the delete command or the --hosts-file flag. The hosts management capability is ready. Next, let's add the port scanning functionality to the tool.

Adding the Port Scanning Functionality

Your application is coming along nicely. You can manage hosts on which to execute a port scan. Let's implement the port scanning functionality now. Let's start by adding the functionality to the scan package. After that, we'll implement the subcommand on the command-line tool. Switch to the scan subdirectory:

```
$ cd scan
$ pwd
/home/ricardo/pragprog.com/rggo/cobra/pScan/scan
```

Create and edit the file scanHosts.go to hold the code related to the scan functionality. Add the package definition and the import list. For this functionality, you'll use the package fmt for formatted printing, the package net for network-related functions, and the package time to define timeouts:

```
cobra/pScan.v5/scan/scanHosts.go
// Package scan provides types and functions to perform TCP port
// scans on a list of hosts
package scan

import (
  "fmt"
  "net"
  "time"
)
```

Next, define a new custom type PortState that represents the state for a single TCP port. This struct has two fields: Port of type int that corresponds to the TCP port and Open of type state that indicates whether the port is open or closed. You'll define the type state shortly:

```
cobra/pScan.v5/scan/scanHosts.go
// PortState represents the state of a single TCP port
type PortState struct {
  Port int
  Open state
}
```

Define the custom type state as a wrapper on the bool type. This type uses true or false to indicate whether a port is open or closed. By creating a custom type, we can associate methods to it. In this case, define the method String() to this type to return open or closed instead of true or false when printing this value:

cobra/pScan.v5/scan/scanHosts.go

```
type state bool

// String converts the boolean value of state to a human readable string
func (s state) String() string {
  if s {
    return "open"
  }

  return "closed"
}
```

By implementing the String() method on the state type, you satisfy the Stringer interface, which allows you to use this type directly with print functions. You used this technique before in Improving the List Output Format, on page 33.

Next, implement the scanPort() function to perform a port scan on a single TCP port. This function takes as input the host as string and the port as an integer number. It returns an instance of the type PortState you defined before:

cobra/pScan.v5/scan/scanHosts.go

```
// scanPort performs a port scan on a single TCP port
func scanPort(host string, port int) PortState {
```

In the function's body, start by defining an instance p of the type PortState. Assign the port number as the value for the property Port. You don't need to assign a value for the Open property as it's automatically initialized to false as the zero value for a Boolean:

cobra/pScan.v5/scan/scanHosts.go

```
p := PortState{
  Port: port,
}
```

To verify if the given port is open or closed, you'll use the function DialTimeout() from the net package. This function attempts to connect to a network address within a given time. If it can't connect to the address within the specified time, it returns an error. For the purpose of this tool, assume that an error means the port is closed. If the connection attempt succeeds, consider the port to be open. This is a naive approach, but it works well enough for this example.

Use the function net.JoinHostPort() from the net package to define the network address based on the host and port you want to scan. Using this function is recommended over concatenating the values directly as it takes care of corner cases, such as the IPv6 value:

```
cobra/pScan.v5/scan/scanHosts.go
address := net.JoinHostPort(host, fmt.Sprintf("%d", port))
```

Now use the address value with the net.DialTimeout() function to perform the connection attempt. This function takes three input parameters, the network type, the address, and the timeout. For this example, run a TCP scan only by specifying the network type as tcp and hard-code the timeout as 1 second:

```
cobra/pScan.v5/scan/scanHosts.go
scanConn, err := net.DialTimeout("tcp", address, 1*time.Second)
```

Next, verify if the function returned an error. If it did, assume the port is closed and return the PortState variable p as is, since it has the default value false for the Open property.

```
cobra/pScan.v5/scan/scanHosts.go
if err != nil {
   return p
}
```

When the connection succeeds, close the connection using the scanConn.Close() method, set the property value Open to true, and then return p:

```
cobra/pScan.v5/scan/scanHosts.go
   scanConn.Close()
   p.Open = true
   return p
}
```

The function scanPort() is complete. Notice that we defined this function as private, with a lowercase letter as the first letter of its name. We don't want users of this package to use this function directly. Let's define an exported function Run() that performs a port scan on the hosts list. The Run() function uses the scanPort() function to perform the scan on each port.

Before defining the Run() function, add a new custom type Results that represents the scan result for a host. The Run() function returns a slice of Results, one for each host in the list:

```
cobra/pScan.v5/scan/scanHosts.go
// Results represents the scan results for a single host
type Results struct {
   Host        string
   NotFound    bool
   PortStates []PortState
}
```

This new type has three fields: Host as string representing a host, NotFound as a bool indicating whether the host can be resolved to a valid IP Address in the network, and PortStates as a slice of the type PortState indicating the status for each port scanned.

Now, define the Run() function that performs a port scan on the hosts list. This function takes a pointer to a HostsList type and a slice of integers representing the ports to scan. It returns a slice of Results:

```
cobra/pScan.v5/scan/scanHosts.go
// Run performs a port scan on the hosts list
func Run(hl *HostsList, ports []int) []Results {
```

Initialize the slice of Results as a variable res with the capacity set to the number of hosts in the list. You'll append the results for each host into this slice and return it at the end:

```
cobra/pScan.v5/scan/scanHosts.go
res := make([]Results, 0, len(hl.Hosts))
```

Now loop through the list of hosts and define an instance of Results for each host:

```
cobra/pScan.v5/scan/scanHosts.go
for _, h := range hl.Hosts {
  r := Results{
    Host: h,
  }
```

Next, use the net.LookupHost() function from the net package to resolve the host name into a valid IP address. If it returns an error, the host can't be found, in which case you set the property NotFound to true, append the result to the slice res and skip the port scan on this host by using the continue statement to process the next item in the loop:

```
cobra/pScan.v5/scan/scanHosts.go
if _, err := net.LookupHost(h); err != nil {
  r.NotFound = true
  res = append(res, r)
  continue
}
```

If the host was found, execute the port scan by looping through each port in the ports slice, using the function scanPort() you defined before. Append the returned PortState into the PortStates slice. Finally, append the current result r into the Results slice res and return it when the loop finishes processing all hosts:

cobra/pScan.v5/scan/scanHosts.go
```
    for _, p := range ports {
      r.PortStates = append(r.PortStates, scanPort(h, p))
    }

    res = append(res, r)
  }

  return res
}
```

The code for the new scan functionality is complete. Next, let's write some tests to ensure it works. Save this file and create and edit a new file scan-Hosts_test.go for the tests. Define the package package scan_test to test the exposed API only, as you did with the hosts tests:

cobra/pScan.v5/scan/scanHosts_test.go
```
package scan_test
```

Then, add the import section. For these tests, you'll use the net package to create a local TCP server, the package strconv to convert strings to integer numbers, the testing package for the testing function, and the scan package that you're testing:

cobra/pScan.v5/scan/scanHosts_test.go
```
import (
  "net"
  "strconv"
  "testing"

  "pragprog.com/rggo/cobra/pScan/scan"
)
```

Now, add your first test function TestStateString() to test the String() method of the state type. We want to ensure it returns open or closed:

cobra/pScan.v5/scan/scanHosts_test.go
```
func TestStateString(t *testing.T) {
  ps := scan.PortState{}

  if ps.Open.String() != "closed" {
    t.Errorf("Expected %q, got %q instead\n", "closed", ps.Open.String())
  }

  ps.Open = true

  if ps.Open.String() != "open" {
    t.Errorf("Expected %q, got %q instead\n", "open", ps.Open.String())
  }
}
```

For this test, you're defining an instance of the type scan.PortState. By default, the value of its Open property is false, so you're testing that the String() method returns closed. Then, you are switching the Open value to true and testing that it returns open.

Next, add a test function TestRunHostFound() to test the Run() function when the host exists. To ensure that the host exists, you'll use localhost as the host. This test has two cases, open port and closed port.

```
cobra/pScan.v5/scan/scanHosts_test.go
func TestRunHostFound(t *testing.T) {
  testCases := []struct {
    name        string
    expectState string
  }{
    {"OpenPort", "open"},
    {"ClosedPort", "closed"},
  }
```

Local Network and Firewalls

Since you're using the host localhost, this test should work on most machines. But network configurations may vary. Check your network configuration to ensure localhost is configured.

Most local firewalls allow traffic to localhost by default. If this test fails, ensure your firewall allows this traffic.

Create an instance of the scan.HostsList and add localhost to it:

```
cobra/pScan.v5/scan/scanHosts_test.go
host := "localhost"
hl := &scan.HostsList{}

hl.Add(host)
```

Since this test involves testing TCP ports, ensure it's reproducible in different machines. If you try to use a fixed port number, you could have a conflict as each machine environment is different. To overcome this challenge, use the port number 0 (zero) when executing the function net.Listen(). This ensures that the function uses a port that's available on the host. Then you extract the port from the Listener address using its Addr() method and add it to a ports slice that we can use later as an argument to the Run() function we're testing:

```
cobra/pScan.v5/scan/scanHosts_test.go
ports := []int{}

// Init ports, 1 open, 1 closed
for _, tc := range testCases {
  ln, err := net.Listen("tcp", net.JoinHostPort(host, "0"))
  if err != nil {
    t.Fatal(err)
  }
```

```
  defer ln.Close()

  _, portStr, err := net.SplitHostPort(ln.Addr().String())
  if err != nil {
    t.Fatal(err)
  }

  port, err := strconv.Atoi(portStr)
  if err != nil {
    t.Fatal(err)
  }

  ports = append(ports, port)

  if tc.name == "ClosedPort" {
    ln.Close()
  }
}
```

For the ClosedPort case, we're closing the port immediately after opening it, using the ln.Close() method. This ensures that we're using an available port and that it's closed for the test.

Now, execute the Run() method using the ports slice as an argument. Since the Run() function accepts a slice of ports, you don't need to execute the tests for each case.

cobra/pScan.v5/scan/scanHosts_test.go
```
res := scan.Run(hl, ports)
```

Next, test the results. There should be only one element in the Results slice returned by the Run() function. The host name in the result should match the variable host, and the property NotFound should be false since we expect this host to exist:

cobra/pScan.v5/scan/scanHosts_test.go
```
// Verify results for HostFound test
if len(res) != 1 {
  t.Fatalf("Expected 1 results, got %d instead\n", len(res))
}

if res[0].Host != host {
  t.Errorf("Expected host %q, got %q instead\n", host, res[0].Host)
}

if res[0].NotFound {
  t.Errorf("Expected host %q to be found\n", host)
}
```

Then, verify that two ports are present in the PortStates slice:

```
cobra/pScan.v5/scan/scanHosts_test.go
if len(res[0].PortStates) != 2 {
  t.Fatalf("Expected 2 port states, got %d instead\n", len(res[0].PortStates))
}
```

Finally, verify each port state by looping through each test case and that the port number and state match the expected values:

```
cobra/pScan.v5/scan/scanHosts_test.go
  for i, tc := range testCases {
    if res[0].PortStates[i].Port != ports[i] {
      t.Errorf("Expected port %d, got %d instead\n", ports[0],
        res[0].PortStates[i].Port)
    }

    if res[0].PortStates[i].Open.String() != tc.expectState {
      t.Errorf("Expected port %d to be %s\n", ports[i], tc.expectState)
    }
  }
}
```

The test for whether the host is found is done. Add another function to test the case when the host isn't found:

```
cobra/pScan.v5/scan/scanHosts_test.go
func TestRunHostNotFound(t *testing.T) {
```

Create an instance of the scan.HostsList and add the host 389.389.389.389 to it. Name resolution on this host should fail unless you have it on your DNS:

```
cobra/pScan.v5/scan/scanHosts_test.go
host := "389.389.389.389"
hl := &scan.HostsList{}

hl.Add(host)
```

Now execute the Run() method using an empty slice as the ports argument. Since the host doesn't exist, the ports are irrelevant as the function shouldn't execute the scan.

```
cobra/pScan.v5/scan/scanHosts_test.go
res := scan.Run(hl, []int{})
```

To finish the test, verify the results. There should be only one element in the Results slice returned by the Run() function. The host name in the result should match the variable host, the property NotFound should be true since we don't expect this host to exist, and the PortStates slice should contain no elements as the scan should be skipped for this host:

cobra/pScan.v5/scan/scanHosts_test.go
```
  // Verify results for HostNotFound test
  if len(res) != 1 {
    t.Fatalf("Expected 1 results, got %d instead\n", len(res))
  }

  if res[0].Host != host {
    t.Errorf("Expected host %q, got %q instead\n", host, res[0].Host)
  }

  if !res[0].NotFound {
    t.Errorf("Expected host %q NOT to be found\n", host)
  }

  if len(res[0].PortStates) != 0 {
    t.Fatalf("Expected 0 port states, got %d instead\n", len(res[0].PortStates))
  }
}
```

Save the file and execute the tests to ensure the new functionality works as designed:

```
$ go test -v
=== RUN    TestAdd
=== RUN    TestAdd/AddNew
=== RUN    TestAdd/AddExisting
--- PASS: TestAdd (0.00s)
    --- PASS: TestAdd/AddNew (0.00s)
    --- PASS: TestAdd/AddExisting (0.00s)
=== RUN    TestRemove
=== RUN    TestRemove/RemoveExisting
=== RUN    TestRemove/RemoveNotFound
--- PASS: TestRemove (0.00s)
    --- PASS: TestRemove/RemoveExisting (0.00s)
    --- PASS: TestRemove/RemoveNotFound (0.00s)
=== RUN    TestSaveLoad
--- PASS: TestSaveLoad (0.00s)
=== RUN    TestLoadNoFile
--- PASS: TestLoadNoFile (0.00s)
=== RUN    TestStateString
--- PASS: TestStateString (0.00s)
=== RUN    TestRunHostFound
--- PASS: TestRunHostFound (0.00s)
=== RUN    TestRunHostNotFound
--- PASS: TestRunHostNotFound (0.00s)
PASS
ok      pragprog.com/rggo/cobra/pScan/scan      0.014s
```

The tests pass, which means the new functionality of the scan package is complete. Let's implement the command-line functionality now. Switch back to the root directory of your application:

```
$ cd ..
$ pwd
/home/ricardo/pragprog.com/rggo/cobra/pScan
```

Use the cobra add generator to add the scan subcommand to your tool:

```
$ cobra add scan
Using config file: /home/ricardo/.cobra.yaml
scan created at /home/ricardo/pragprog.com/rggo/cobra/pScan
```

Switch to the cmd directory and edit the file scan.go:

```
$ cd cmd
$ pwd
/home/ricardo/pragprog.com/rggo/cobra/pScan/cmd
```

Edit the import section and add the io package to use the io.Writer interface, the os package to use the os.Stdout, and your scan package for the port scan functionality:

cobra/pScan.v5/cmd/scan.go
```
import (
    "fmt"
➤    "io"
➤    "os"
➤
    "github.com/spf13/cobra"
➤    "pragprog.com/rggo/cobra/pScan/scan"
)
```

Then edit the init() function to include a local flag --ports or -p to allow the user to specify a slice of ports to be scanned. Use the method Flags() of the type scanCmd to create a flag that is available only for this command:

cobra/pScan.v5/cmd/scan.go
```
func init() {
  rootCmd.AddCommand(scanCmd)
➤    scanCmd.Flags().IntSliceP("ports", "p", []int{22, 80, 443}, "ports to scan")
}
```

In this function, you're using the method IntSliceP() to create a flag that takes a slice of integer numbers. By default, this flag sets the ports to be scanned as 22, 80, and 443.

Now, edit the scanCmd type definition according to the command requirements. Update the short description to Run a port scan on the hosts and remove the long description:

```
cobra/pScan.v5/cmd/scan.go
var scanCmd = &cobra.Command{
  Use:   "scan",
  Short: "Run a port scan on the hosts",
```

Implement the action by replacing the Run property with RunE as you did when
you implemented the hosts commands. This function handles both the hosts-
file and ports command-line flags and then calls the external function scanAction()
to execute the command action:

```
cobra/pScan.v5/cmd/scan.go
  RunE: func(cmd *cobra.Command, args []string) error {
    hostsFile, err := cmd.Flags().GetString("hosts-file")
    if err != nil {
      return err
    }

    ports, err := cmd.Flags().GetIntSlice("ports")
    if err != nil {
      return err
    }

    return scanAction(os.Stdout, hostsFile, ports)
  },
}
```

Now, define the scanAction() function. This function takes as input an io.Writer
interface representing where to print output to, the string hostsFile which contains
the name of the file to load the hosts list from, and a slice of integers ports
representing the ports to scan. It returns a potential error:

```
cobra/pScan.v5/cmd/scan.go
func scanAction(out io.Writer, hostsFile string, ports []int) error {
  hl := &scan.HostsList{}

  if err := hl.Load(hostsFile); err != nil {
    return err
  }

  results := scan.Run(hl, ports)

  return printResults(out, results)
}
```

This function creates an instance of the HostsList type provided by the package
scan you created before. Then, it loads the content of the hostsFile into the hosts
list instance and executes the port scan by calling the function scan.Run().
Finally, it calls the function printResults(), which you'll define shortly, to print
the results to the output assigned to the variable out, returning any errors
from it.

To complete this command's functionality, define the function printResults() to print the results out. This function takes the io.Writer interface and a slice of scan.Results as input, and it returns an error:

cobra/pScan.v5/cmd/scan.go
```
func printResults(out io.Writer, results []scan.Results) error {
```

In the function's body, define an empty string variable message to compose the output message:

cobra/pScan.v5/cmd/scan.go
```
message := ""
```

Then loop through each result in the results slice. For each host, add the host name and the list of ports with each status to the message variable. If the host was not found, add Host not found after the host name to the message and move to the next iteration of the loop:

cobra/pScan.v5/cmd/scan.go
```
for _, r := range results {
  message += fmt.Sprintf("%s:", r.Host)

  if r.NotFound {
    message += fmt.Sprintf(" Host not found\n\n")
    continue
  }

  message += fmt.Sprintln()

  for _, p := range r.PortStates {
    message += fmt.Sprintf("\t%d: %s\n", p.Port, p.Open)
  }

  message += fmt.Sprintln()
}
```

Finally, print the contents of message to the io.Writer interface and return the error:

cobra/pScan.v5/cmd/scan.go
```
  _, err := fmt.Fprint(out, message)
  return err
}
```

The code is done, so let's update the test file to include tests for the scan functionality. Save and close the scan.go file and edit the actions_test.go test file. Start by updating the import section to include two additional packages: net to create a network listener and strconv to convert string data to integer numbers:

```
cobra/pScan.v5/cmd/actions_test.go
import (
  "bytes"
  "fmt"
  "io"
  "io/ioutil"
  "net"
  "os"
  "strconv"
  "strings"
  "testing"

  "pragprog.com/rggo/cobra/pScan/scan"
)
```

Next, add another test function TestScanAction() to this file to test the scanAction() function:

```
cobra/pScan.v5/cmd/actions_test.go
func TestScanAction(t *testing.T) {
```

Define a list of hosts for this test that includes localhost and a host that doesn't exist in your network, for example, unknownhostoutthere:

```
cobra/pScan.v5/cmd/actions_test.go
// Define hosts for scan test
hosts := []string{
  "localhost",
  "unknownhostoutthere",
}
```

Then use the setup() helper function to set up the tests using this list of hosts as input:

```
cobra/pScan.v5/cmd/actions_test.go
// Setup scan test
tf, cleanup := setup(t, hosts, true)
defer cleanup()
```

Next, initialize the ports for the localhost test, similar to what you did when testing the scan package before:

```
cobra/pScan.v5/cmd/actions_test.go
ports := []int{}

// Init ports, 1 open, 1 closed
for i := 0; i < 2; i++ {
  ln, err := net.Listen("tcp", net.JoinHostPort("localhost", "0"))
  if err != nil {
    t.Fatal(err)
  }
```

```
  defer ln.Close()

  _, portStr, err := net.SplitHostPort(ln.Addr().String())
  if err != nil {
    t.Fatal(err)
  }

  port, err := strconv.Atoi(portStr)
  if err != nil {
    t.Fatal(err)
  }

  ports = append(ports, port)

  if i == 1 {
    ln.Close()
  }
}
```

Define the expected output expectedOut variable. For this test, we expect the localhost host to have two ports, one open and one closed, and the host unknownhostoutthere not to be found:

cobra/pScan.v5/cmd/actions_test.go
```
// Define expected output for scan action
expectedOut := fmt.Sprintln("localhost:")
expectedOut += fmt.Sprintf("\t%d: open\n", ports[0])
expectedOut += fmt.Sprintf("\t%d: closed\n", ports[1])
expectedOut += fmt.Sprintln()
expectedOut += fmt.Sprintln("unknownhostoutthere: Host not found")
expectedOut += fmt.Sprintln()
```

Now, define a variable out of type bytes.Buffer to capture the output, execute the scanAction() function, and compare its captured output with the expected output, failing the test if they don't match:

cobra/pScan.v5/cmd/actions_test.go
```
  // Define var to capture scan output
  var out bytes.Buffer

  // Execute scan and capture output
  if err := scanAction(&out, tf, ports); err != nil {
    t.Fatalf("Expected no error, got %q\n", err)
  }

  // Test scan output
  if out.String() != expectedOut {
    t.Errorf("Expected output %q, got %q\n", expectedOut, out.String())
  }
}
```

This completes this test case. Now update the integration test to include the hosts scan step. First, update the expected output. We expect the two hosts, host1 and host3, that are in the final hosts list, to not exist:

```
cobra/pScan.v5/cmd/actions_test.go
// Define expected output for all actions
expectedOut := ""
for _, v := range hosts {
  expectedOut += fmt.Sprintf("Added host: %s\n", v)
}
expectedOut += strings.Join(hosts, "\n")
expectedOut += fmt.Sprintln()
expectedOut += fmt.Sprintf("Deleted host: %s\n", delHost)
expectedOut += strings.Join(hostsEnd, "\n")
expectedOut += fmt.Sprintln()
for _, v := range hostsEnd {
  expectedOut += fmt.Sprintf("%s: Host not found\n", v)
  expectedOut += fmt.Sprintln()
}
```

Then include the scanAction() function as the last step in the test execution, capturing its output in the same variable out:

```
cobra/pScan.v5/cmd/actions_test.go
  // List hosts after delete
  if err := listAction(&out, tf, nil); err != nil {
    t.Fatalf("Expected no error, got %q\n", err)
  }

  // Scan hosts
  if err := scanAction(&out, tf, nil); err != nil {
    t.Fatalf("Expected no error, got %q\n", err)
  }

  // Test integration output
  if out.String() != expectedOut {
    t.Errorf("Expected output %q, got %q\n", expectedOut, out.String())
  }
}
```

Save and close the actions_test.go file and execute the tests to ensure the new command works as designed:

```
$ go test -v
=== RUN   TestHostActions
=== RUN   TestHostActions/AddAction
=== RUN   TestHostActions/ListAction
=== RUN   TestHostActions/DeleteAction
--- PASS: TestHostActions (0.00s)
    --- PASS: TestHostActions/AddAction (0.00s)
    --- PASS: TestHostActions/ListAction (0.00s)
    --- PASS: TestHostActions/DeleteAction (0.00s)
```

```
=== RUN    TestScanAction
--- PASS: TestScanAction (0.01s)
=== RUN    TestIntegration
--- PASS: TestIntegration (0.01s)
PASS
ok      pragprog.com/rggo/cobra/pScan/cmd        0.018s
```

Your tests pass, so give your application a try. Switch back to the root directory of your application and build it:

```
$ cd ..
$ pwd
/home/ricardo/pragprog.com/rggo/cobra/pScan
$ go build
```

Execute it with the hosts list subcommand to see if you have any hosts in the list:

```
$ ./pScan hosts list
```

If you don't have any hosts, use hosts add to add some hosts, for example, localhost. To make it more useful, add some hosts that exist on your local network, so you can scan their ports. Your list and output will be different from mine:

```
$ ./pScan hosts add localhost 192.168.0.199
Added host: localhost
Added host: 192.168.0.199
```

Now execute a port scan on these hosts using the scan subcommand. You can pass some ports that you expect to be open using the --ports flag:

```
$ ./pScan scan --ports 22,80,443,6060
localhost:
        22: closed
        80: closed
        443: closed
        6060: open

192.168.0.199:
        22: open
        80: closed
        443: closed
        6060: closed
```

In this case, port 6060 is open on localhost while port 22 is open on host 192.168.0.199. Your output will be different from this.

You have a working port scan application. Next, you'll use Viper to increase the flexibility of your tool, allowing the user to configure it in different ways.

Using Viper for Configuration Management

When you use the Cobra generator to create the boilerplate code for your application, it automatically enables Viper. Viper is a configuration management solution for Go applications which allows you to specify configuration options for your application in several ways, including configuration files, environment variables, and command-line flags.

Cobra enables Viper by running the function initConfig() when initializing the application. This function is defined in the cmd/root.go file:

```
cobra/pScan.v6/cmd/root.go
func initConfig() {
  if cfgFile != "" {
    // Use config file from the flag.
    viper.SetConfigFile(cfgFile)
  } else {
    // Find home directory.
    home, err := homedir.Dir()
    if err != nil {
      fmt.Println(err)
      os.Exit(1)
    }

    // Search config in home directory with name ".pScan" (without extension).
    viper.AddConfigPath(home)
    viper.SetConfigName(".pScan")
  }

  viper.AutomaticEnv() // read in environment variables that match

  // If a config file is found, read it in.
  if err := viper.ReadInConfig(); err == nil {
    fmt.Println("Using config file:", viper.ConfigFileUsed())
  }
}
```

If the user specifies a config file using the flag --config, Viper sets it as the configuration file for the application. If not, it sets the configuration file as the file $HOME/.pScan.yaml. Then it uses the function viper.AutomaticEnv() to read the configuration from environment variables that match any expected configuration keys. Finally, if the configuration file exists, Viper reads the configuration from it.

Even though Viper is enabled by default, it doesn't set any configuration key. Since your application already sets its options using flags, you can create Viper configuration keys by binding them to those flags. Let's bind a configuration key hosts-file to the persistent flag hosts-file, allowing users to specify the hosts file name using the configuration file or environment variables. Edit the file cmd/root.go, and update the import section to include the package strings to manipulate string data:

```
cobra/pScan.v6/cmd/root.go
import (
  "fmt"
  "os"

➤ "strings"

  "github.com/spf13/cobra"

  homedir "github.com/mitchellh/go-homedir"
  "github.com/spf13/viper"
)
```

Then add these lines into the init() function to bind the configuration with the hosts-file flag and allow the user to specify it as an environment variable:

```
cobra/pScan.v6/cmd/root.go
func init() {
  cobra.OnInitialize(initConfig)

  // Here you will define your flags and configuration settings.
  // Cobra supports persistent flags, which, if defined here,
  // will be global for your application.

  rootCmd.PersistentFlags().StringVar(&cfgFile, "config", "",
    "config file (default is $HOME/.pScan.yaml)")

  rootCmd.PersistentFlags().StringP("hosts-file", "f", "pScan.hosts",
    "pScan hosts file")
➤ replacer := strings.NewReplacer("-", "_")
➤ viper.SetEnvKeyReplacer(replacer)
➤ viper.SetEnvPrefix("PSCAN")
➤
➤ viper.BindPFlag("hosts-file", rootCmd.PersistentFlags().Lookup("hosts-file"))

  versionTemplate := `{{printf "%s: %s - version %s\n" .Name .Short .Version}}`
  rootCmd.SetVersionTemplate(versionTemplate)
}
```

On some operating systems, you can't use the dash (-) character in the environment variable name, so you need to use a strings.Replacer to replace the dash with the underscore character. You're also setting the prefix PSCAN to the environment variables. In this case, the user can specify the hosts file name by setting the environment variable PSCAN_HOSTS_FILE. Then, you bind the hosts-file key to the flag --hosts-file by using the function viper.BindPFlag().

The initial setup for Viper is complete. Save and close the cmd/root.go file.

Next, you need to update the commands that use the hosts-file flag to use the Viper configuration key instead. Start with the add command. Edit the file cmd/add.go. Include the package github.com/spf13/viper in the import section:

cobra/pScan.v6/cmd/add.go
```
import (
  "fmt"
  "io"
  "os"

  "github.com/spf13/cobra"
➤  "github.com/spf13/viper"
  "pragprog.com/rggo/cobra/pScan/scan"
)
```

Replace all the lines you used to obtain the value of the hosts-file flag in the RunE property with this line to obtain the value from Viper:

cobra/pScan.v6/cmd/add.go
```
RunE: func(cmd *cobra.Command, args []string) error {
➤  hostsFile := viper.GetString("hosts-file")

  return addAction(os.Stdout, hostsFile, args)
},
```

That's it, the add command is ready. Save and close the cmd/add.go file, and repeat this process with the other files: cmd/list.go, cmd/delete.go, and cmd/scan.go.

Since you didn't make any changes to the action functions, there's no impact on the tests. Just in case, execute the tests again to ensure the application still works as designed:

```
$ go test -v ./cmd
=== RUN    TestHostActions
=== RUN    TestHostActions/AddAction
=== RUN    TestHostActions/ListAction
=== RUN    TestHostActions/DeleteAction
--- PASS: TestHostActions (0.00s)
    --- PASS: TestHostActions/AddAction (0.00s)
    --- PASS: TestHostActions/ListAction (0.00s)
    --- PASS: TestHostActions/DeleteAction (0.00s)
=== RUN    TestScanAction
--- PASS: TestScanAction (0.01s)
=== RUN    TestIntegration
--- PASS: TestIntegration (0.01s)
PASS
ok      pragprog.com/rggo/cobra/pScan/cmd        (cached)
```

Build the application again using go build:

```
$ go build
```

If you still have the hosts file pScan.hosts from the previous example, you can list the hosts. If not, add a few hosts to the default file:

```
$ ./pScan hosts list
localhost
192.168.0.199
```

Now use the environment variable PSCAN_HOSTS_FILE to set a new hosts file name, and list the hosts:

```
$ PSCAN_HOSTS_FILE=newFile.hosts ./pScan hosts list
```

It returns nothing because the file newFile.hosts doesn't exist. Add some hosts to this new file:

```
$ PSCAN_HOSTS_FILE=newFile.hosts ./pScan hosts add host01 host02
Added host: host01
Added host: host02
$ PSCAN_HOSTS_FILE=newFile.hosts ./pScan hosts list
host01
host02
```

You have two hosts files in your directory now:

```
$ ls *.hosts
newFile.hosts   pScan.hosts
```

You can also specify the hosts file name using a configuration file. Create a configuration file config.yaml and add the key hosts-file with value newFile.hosts to it:

cobra/pScan.v6/config.yaml
```
hosts-file: newFile.hosts
```

Now execute the list command again, using the flag --config to specify config.yaml as the configuration file:

```
$ ./pScan hosts list --config config.yaml
Using config file: config.yaml
host01
host02
```

The command listed the hosts in the hosts file named newFile.hosts as specified in the configuration file.

By using Viper, you added some flexibility to your tool, enabling your users to configure it in different ways. Next, let's use Cobra to generate command completion and documentation for your application.

Generating Command Completion and Documentation

Two features that improve your user experience are command completion and documentation. Command completion guides the user by providing contextual suggestions when they press the TAB key. Documentation instructs users by providing additional information, context, and examples about using the application.

Let's add two new subcommands to your tool allowing the users to generate command completion and documentation for it. Start with the command completion subcommand completion. Use the Cobra generator again to add this subcommand to your application:

```
$ cobra add completion
Using config file: /home/ricardo/.cobra.yaml
completion created at /home/ricardo/pragprog.com/rggo/cobra/pScan
```

Then edit the generated file cmd/completion.go. Update the import section by removing the fmt package as this command doesn't use it. Also, add the io package to use the io.Writer interface and the os package to use the file os.Stdout to print the command completion to STDOUT.

```
cobra/pScan.v7/cmd/completion.go
import (
➤    "io"
➤    "os"
➤
     "github.com/spf13/cobra"
)
```

Next, update the completionCmd definition by updating the Short description, including an example of how to use this feature in the Long description and replacing the property Run with RunE for the action the same way you did with other commands:

```
cobra/pScan.v7/cmd/completion.go
var completionCmd = &cobra.Command{
  Use:   "completion",
  Short: "Generate bash completion for your command",
  Long: `To load your completions run
source <(pScan completion)

To load completions automatically on login, add this line to you .bashrc file:
$ ~/.bashrc
source <(pScan completion)
`,
```

```
  RunE: func(cmd *cobra.Command, args []string) error {
    return completionAction(os.Stdout)
  },
}
```

The function assigned to the property RunE calls the function completionAction() to perform the action. The completionAction() function uses the method rootCmd.GenBash-Completion() from Cobra on the rootCmd command to generate command completion for the entire application. It prints the completion to an io.Writer interface:

```
cobra/pScan.v7/cmd/completion.go
func completionAction(out io.Writer) error {
  return rootCmd.GenBashCompletion(out)
}
```

Bash Completion

In this example, you're adding command completion for the Bash shell only.

To test this example on the Windows operating system, you need access to a Bash shell. You can use programs like Git Bash[6] or the Windows Subsystem for Linux WSL.[7] This book doesn't cover the installation of these tools.

Alternatively, you can use Cobra to generate command completion for Powershell[8] in addition to Bash.

Save and close the file cmd/completion.go and build your application:

```
$ go build
```

Now, open a Bash shell session and enable the command completion as suggested in the example you added to the completion command:

```
$ source <(./pScan completion)
```

Then, execute the application. Press the TAB key after typing its name to see the suggestions:

```
$ ./pScan <TAB>
completion    hosts       scan
$ ./pScan hosts <TAB>
add     delete  list
$ ./pScan hosts add --<TAB>
--config       --config=       --hosts-file    --hosts-file=
```

---

6. gitforwindows.org/
7. docs.microsoft.com/en-us/windows/wsl/install-win10
8. godoc.org/github.com/spf13/cobra#Command.GenPowerShellCompletion

As you type subcommands and options, if you press TAB, Bash suggests relevant ways to continue to use the application.

Next, let's add the command docs to your application, allowing the user to generate Markdown documentation for the tool. In addition to Markdown, Cobra generates Linux man pages, REST pages, or YAML documentation. It uses the package cobra/doc to generate documentation. For more information about this package, consult its GitHub page.[9]

Use the Cobra generator one more time to add the docs subcommand to your application:

```
$ cobra add docs
Using config file: /home/ricardo/.cobra.yaml
docs created at /home/ricardo/pragprog.com/rggo/cobra/pScan
```

Then edit the generated file cmd/docs.go. Modify the import section by adding the following packages: io to use the io.Writer interface, io/ioutil to create temporary files, os to use operating system functionality, and github.com/spf13/cobra/doc to generate command documentation:

cobra/pScan.v7/cmd/docs.go
```
import (
    "fmt"
➤   "io"
➤   "io/ioutil"
➤   "os"
➤

    "github.com/spf13/cobra"
➤   "github.com/spf13/cobra/doc"
)
```

Update the init() function to add a local flag --dir, allowing the user to specify the target directory to place the generated docs:

cobra/pScan.v7/cmd/docs.go
```
func init() {
    rootCmd.AddCommand(docsCmd)

➤   docsCmd.Flags().StringP("dir", "d", "", "Destination directory for docs")
}
```

Edit the docsCmd definition by changing the Short description, deleting the Long description, and updating the RunE function the same as you did for the other subcommands:

---

9. github.com/spf13/cobra/tree/master/doc

cobra/pScan.v7/cmd/docs.go

```
var docsCmd = &cobra.Command{
  Use:    "docs",
  Short: "Generate documentation for your command",
  RunE: func(cmd *cobra.Command, args []string) error {
    dir, err := cmd.Flags().GetString("dir")
    if err != nil {
      return err
    }

    if dir == "" {
      if dir, err = ioutil.TempDir("", "pScan"); err != nil {
        return err
      }
    }

    return docsAction(os.Stdout, dir)
  },
}
```

The function associated with the property RunE obtains the value for the --dir flag. If the user didn't provide this flag, it creates a temporary file as the destination directory. Then it calls the function docsAction() using this value as input.

Now, define the function docsAction() to generate the documentation. This function uses the function doc.GenMarkdownTree() from the cobra/doc package to generate the documentation for the entire command tree starting from rootCmd in the given directory dir. Finally, it prints a message confirming where the user can find the documentation returning any potential errors:

cobra/pScan.v7/cmd/docs.go

```
func docsAction(out io.Writer, dir string) error {
  if err := doc.GenMarkdownTree(rootCmd, dir); err != nil {
    return err
  }

  _, err := fmt.Fprintf(out, "Documentation successfully created in %s\n", dir)
  return err
}
```

Save and close this file. It's a good idea to write a test for this function since it prints output, but we won't do it here for brevity. You can write it as an exercise.

Try out the new functionality. Rebuild your application using go build:

```
$ go build
```

Then create a directory docs for the documentation and execute the application with the docs command and this directory as the value for the --dir flag:

```
$ mkdir docs
$ ./pScan docs --dir ./docs
Documentation successfully created in ./docs
$ ls docs
pScan_completion.md   pScan_docs.md   pScan_hosts_add.md   pScan_hosts_delete.md
pScan_hosts_list.md   pScan_hosts.md   pScan.md   pScan_scan.md
```

Verify the generated markdown documentation. For example, take a look at the hosts command documentation:

cobra/pScan.v7/docs/pScan_hosts.md
```
## pScan hosts

Manage the hosts list

### Synopsis

Manages the hosts lists for pScan

Add hosts with the add command
Delete hosts with the delete command
List hosts with the list command.

### Options

```
  -h, --help    help for hosts
```

Options inherited from parent commands

```
      --config string      config file (default is $HOME/.pScan.yaml)
  -f, --hosts-file string   pScan hosts file (default "pScan.hosts")
```

SEE ALSO

* [pScan](pScan.md)   - Fast TCP port scanner
* [pScan hosts add](pScan_hosts_add.md) - Add new host(s) to list
* [pScan hosts delete](pScan_hosts_delete.md)   - Delete hosts(s) from list
* [pScan hosts list](pScan_hosts_list.md)   - List hosts in hosts list

Auto generated by spf13/cobra on 14-May-2020
```

Since this is Markdown, your users can improve or add more information to the documentation and upload it to a documentation server or version control system.

Your application is complete, and it includes command completion and documentation to ensure users have the information and guidance they need to use it correctly.

Exercises

Before you move on, you should build on the skills and techniques you explored in this chapter. Here are some suggestions:

- Allow the user to provide port ranges, such as 1-1024, in addition to specific ports for scan.

- Validate the provided port numbers are within the proper range for TCP ports from 1 to 65535.

- Allow the user to execute UDP port scans in addition to TCP. Update the scan package and the command-line tool accordingly.

- Add a new flag to the scan subcommand allowing the user to specify a filter to show only open or closed ports.

- Add a new flag to the scan subcommand allowing the user to specify a custom timeout for the scan.

Wrapping Up

You used Cobra to create a command-line application that looks professional. Your application includes detailed help and usage information, POSIX-compatible flags, configuration files, command completion, and documentation. You also used the Cobra generator to create the boilerplate code for these features allowing you to focus on your business logic to create a functional TCP port scanner for your network.

In the next chapter, you'll use Cobra again to develop a command-line application that connects to web services using the REST standard.

## CHAPTER 8

Talking to REST APIs

Web services that use the representational state transfer (REST) format provide a flexible and agnostic way of exchanging data between computers and different programming languages. Many applications and services on the Internet use this clear and concise format to expose their data to other applications. Using Go to interact with REST APIs opens the door to a large number of services that provide many resources for your command-line tools. It allows you to create flexible tools that were previously challenging to develop by integrating information from multiple sources.

In this chapter, you'll apply the concepts you learned in Chapter 7, Using the Cobra CLI Framework, on page 213, to design a command-line tool that connects to a REST API using Go's net/http package. You'll explore more advanced concepts such as the http.Client and http.Request types to fine-tune specific connection parameters like headers and timeouts, and you'll use the encoding/json package to parse JSON response data.

You need access to a REST API to explore how to build a CLI that works with one. You could use one of the many web services available on the Internet. But because these services can change, there's no guarantee they'll be available by the time you're reading this book. Instead, you'll design and develop your own REST API server so you have a local server to test. This is also a good opportunity to explore the concepts of dealing with network and HTTP requests using Go. You'll apply the same concepts to develop the command-line client in Developing the Initial Client for the REST API, on page 300, later in this chapter.

Finally, you'll use several testing techniques to test your API server as well as your command-line client application, including local tests, simulated responses, mock servers, and integration tests.

Let's begin by developing the REST API server.

Developing a REST API Server

Let's build an API for our command-line tool to talk to. To save some time, you'll create a REST API server that exposes data from the to-do API you developed in Defining the To-Do API, on page 12. It will let users view, add, and modify to-do items using HTTP methods. You'll reuse the code you developed before by importing the package todo from the module pragprog.com/rggo/interacting/todo.

Start by creating the directory structure for the server under your book's root directory:

```
$ mkdir -p $HOME/pragprog.com/rggo/apis/todoServer
$ cd $HOME/pragprog.com/rggo/apis/todoServer
```

Then, initialize the Go module for this project:

```
$ cd $HOME/pragprog.com/rggo/apis/todoServer
$ go mod init pragprog.com/rggo/apis/todoServer
go: creating new go.mod: module pragprog.com/rggo/apis/todoServer
```

Next, you need to add the pragprog.com/rggo/interacting/todo module dependency to the go.mod file. In a normal workflow, with a module that's available in a public repository, you don't need to take additional actions. As explained in Go Modules, on page xxiii, by running the go build or go test tools, Go would automatically download the module and add the dependency to the go.mod file. But because we're using a package that's only available locally, you need to make changes to the go.mod file to ensure it can locate the package in your local machine. You can do this by editing the file directly or by using the go mod edit command. Let's use the command. First, add the dependency:

```
$ go mod edit -require=pragprog.com/rggo/interacting/todo@v0.0.0
```

Since the module you're importing isn't versioned, you're setting the version to v0.0.0. If you try to list the module dependencies at this time, it fails as Go can't find the module online:

```
$ go list -m all
go: pragprog.com/rggo/interacting/todo@v0.0.0: unrecognized import path
"pragprog.com/rggo/interacting/todo" (parse
https://pragprog.com/rggo/interacting/todo?go-get=1: no go-import meta tags ())
```

To ensure that Go can find the module in the local machine, use the replace directive to replace the module path with the local path. You can use absolute or relative paths. Assuming the todo module is rooted in the book's root directory, use a relative path:

```
$ go mod edit -replace=pragprog.com/rggo/interacting/todo=../../interacting/todo
```

Your go.mod file now looks like this:

```
$ cat go.mod
module pragprog.com/rggo/apis/todoServer

go 1.16

require pragprog.com/rggo/interacting/todo v0.0.0

replace pragprog.com/rggo/interacting/todo => ../../interacting/todo/
```

Now Go can find the module dependency in the local path:

```
$ go list -m all
pragprog.com/rggo/apis/todoServer
pragprog.com/rggo/interacting/todo v0.0.0 => ../../interacting/todo/
```

With the to-do dependency sorted out, you can develop the REST API server. For now, you'll create the basic structure of the server and the root route. You'll add the remaining routes to complete the *CRUD* (create, read, update, and delete) operations later.

Start by creating the file main.go in the todoServer directory. Edit the file and add the package definition and the import list. For this file, you're importing the following packages: flag to handle command-line flags, fmt to format output, net/http to handle HTTP connections, os for operating system–related functions, and time to define variables based on time to handle timeouts:

apis/todoServer/main.go
```
package main

import (
  "flag"
  "fmt"
  "net/http"
  "os"
  "time"
)
```

Then, define the function main() as the program entry point. Define three command-line flags to handle server options: h for the server hostname, p for the server listening port, and f for the file name to save the to-do list. Parse the flags using the function flag.Parse() so you can use them in the program:

apis/todoServer/main.go
```
func main() {
  host := flag.String("h", "localhost", "Server host")
  port := flag.Int("p", 8080, "Server port")
  todoFile := flag.String("f", "todoServer.json", "todo JSON file")
  flag.Parse()
```

Next, create an instance of the http.Server type to serve HTTP content. The net/http package provides the function ListenAndServe() that allows you to serve HTTP without creating a custom server instance. But it's a good practice to create your own custom instance so you have more control over server options such as read and write timeouts. The timeout options are particularly important to prevent issues with slow clients that could hang connections and extinguish server resources.

The http.Server type takes many parameters. For now, you'll set these four options:

Addr: The HTTP server listening address. This is a combination of hostname host and listening port port.

Handler: The handler to dispatch routes. You'll create a custom multiplexer function newMux() that accepts the name of the file where you'll save the to-do list as input. By doing this you avoid passing the file name as a global variable. You'll define this function momentarily.

ReadTimeout: The time limit to read the entire request including the body if available.

WriteTimeout: The time limit to send the response back to the client.

Instantiate a new HTTP server s like this:

```
apis/todoServer/main.go
s := &http.Server{
    Addr:         fmt.Sprintf("%s:%d", *host, *port),
    Handler:      newMux(*todoFile),
    ReadTimeout:  10 * time.Second,
    WriteTimeout: 10 * time.Second,
}
```

Then, execute the method s.ListenAndServe() from the type http.Server to listen for incoming requests at the provided listening address. If errors occur, display them and exit the program with exit code 1:

```
apis/todoServer/main.go
    if err := s.ListenAndServe(); err != nil {
        fmt.Fprintln(os.Stderr, err)
        os.Exit(1)
    }
}
```

You could also control how the HTTP server behaves when a connection closes, or you could gracefully stop it. We don't need to worry about those options since we're using this server for testing and not for handling real workload. Save and close the main.go file.

Next design the multiplexer function newMux() and the handlers for the different routes. A multiplexer function, or Mux for short, maps incoming requests to the proper handlers based on the URL of the request. The handler function handles the request and responds to it. The net/http package provides a default multiplexer named DefaultServeMux. For security reasons, it's a good practice to provide your own since the default Mux register routes globally. This could allow third-party packages to register routes that you may not be aware of, leading to accidental data exposure. In addition, writing your own custom multiplexer allows you to add dependencies for the routes, including file names or database connections. Finally, a custom multiplexer allows integrated testing.

Create a new file called server.go and open it in your editor. Add the package definition and the import section. We're using the package net/http to respond to HTTP requests:

apis/todoServer/server.go
```go
package main

import (
  "net/http"
)
```

Now define the new multiplexer function newMux(). This function takes as input the name of the file to save the to-do list to, and it returns a type that satisfies the http.Handler interface. An http.Handler is a type that responds to an HTTP request. It does this by implementing the function ServeHTTP(http.ResponseWriter, *http.Request), which takes a ResponseWriter to write the response to and a pointer to a Request that provides details about the incoming request.

apis/todoServer/server.go
```go
func newMux(todoFile string) http.Handler {
```

In the function's body, instantiate a new http.ServeMux by calling the function NewServerMux(). The type http.ServMux provides a multiplexer that satisfies the http.Handler interface and allows us to map routes to handler functions:

apis/todoServer/server.go
```go
m := http.NewServeMux()
```

Then, attach the first route to the multiplexer m by using the method m.HandleFunc(). This function maps the route / to the function that handles its response rootHandler(). You'll implement the handler function shortly:

apis/todoServer/server.go
```
m.HandleFunc("/", rootHandler)
```

For now, this is the only route we'll handle. To complete the custom mux function, return the http.ServeMux instance m:

apis/todoServer/server.go
```
    return m
}
```

Save the file and create a new file handlers.go to create the handler functions. Add the package definition and the import section. For now, we'll use only the net/http package to deal with HTTP requests and responses:

apis/todoServer/handlers.go
```
package main

import (
  "net/http"
)
```

Next, define the function rootHandler(w http.ResponseWriter, r *http.Request) to handle requests to the server root. Go provides an adapter type http.HandlerFunc that allows you to use any functions with the signature func(http.ResponseWriter, *http.Request) as a handler that responds to HTTP requests automatically:

apis/todoServer/handlers.go
```
func rootHandler(w http.ResponseWriter, r *http.Request) {
```

In the function's body, first check if the client requested the root path / explicitly. If not, use the function http.NotFound() to respond with an HTTP Not Found error:

apis/todoServer/handlers.go
```
if r.URL.Path != "/" {
  http.NotFound(w, r)
  return
}
```

If the client requested the root path, reply with the content *There's an API here* indicating that the server is up and running. Instead of adding the code to respond with the content directly, let's use a custom function replyTextContent() to write the response. By doing this, you can reuse the code in other places that require responding with text content later:

apis/todoServer/handlers.go
```
  content := "There's an API here"
  replyTextContent(w, r, http.StatusOK, content)
}
```

Save this file and open the server.go file again to create the custom replyTextContent() function. This function takes four input parameters: w of type http.ResponseWriter to write the response to, r of type *http.Request with details about the request, status which is an integer representing the HTTP status code, and content as string:

apis/todoServer/server.go
```
func replyTextContent(w http.ResponseWriter, r *http.Request,
  status int, content string) {
```

To respond with text content, set the response header *Content-Type* as *text/plain*, write the headers with the given status code, and then write the body response by converting the variable content to a slice of bytes:

apis/todoServer/server.go
```
  w.Header().Set("Content-Type", "text/plain")
  w.WriteHeader(status)
  w.Write([]byte(content))
}
```

Save the file to complete the initial version of the server. Verify the code is working by running the server with go run . (and be sure to include the dot):

```
$ go run .
```

You won't see any output. Your terminal will be blocked, indicating the server is running. By default, your server uses port 8080 to listen to requests. If this port is already in use by another process on your machine, you'll see an error that says listen tcp 127.0.0.1:8080: bind: address already in use. In this case, rerun the sever specifying an alternative port using the -p option:

```
$ go run . -p 9090
```

Check the server by using the curl command in a different terminal. When requesting the root path on the server, you'll see the response *There's an API here*:

```
$ curl http://localhost:8080
There's an API here
```

If you try any other paths, you'll get the *404 page not found* response:

```
$ curl http://localhost:8080/todo
404 page not found
```

When you're done checking the server, finish it by using Ctrl+C on the same terminal where you're running the server.

Next, let's automate testing the server.

Testing the REST API Server

In addition to manually checking the server with curl, let's add some structured tests using Go's testing package. Go provides the package net/http/httptest with additional types and functions for testing HTTP servers.

One approach for testing HTTP servers is testing each handler function individually by using the type httptest.ResponseRecorder. This type allows the recording of an HTTP response for analysis or tests. This approach is useful if you're using the DefaultServeMux as the server multiplexer.

Because you implemented your own multiplexer function, newMux(), you can use a different approach that allows integrated testing, including the route dispatching. You'll use the type httptest.Server and instantiate a test server providing the multiplexer function as input. This approach creates a test server with an URL that simulates your server, allowing you to make requests similarly to using curl on the actual server. Then you can analyze and test the responses to ensure the server works as designed.

Since you're going to create this test server multiple times, add a helper function to the test file to help with that. First, create a new test file server_test.go, edit it, and add the package and import sections. For these tests, we'll use the following packages: io/ioutil to help read the response body, net/http to deal with HTTP requests and responses, net/http/httptest which provides HTTP testing utilities, strings to compare strings, and testing which provides testing utilities:

apis/todoServer/server_test.go
```go
package main

import (
  "io/ioutil"
  "net/http"
  "net/http/httptest"
  "strings"
  "testing"
)
```

Now add the helper function setupAPI() similarly to what you did in Testing with the Help of Test Helpers, on page 89. This function takes the testing.T type as input, returns the server URL as a string, and uses a function to clean up the test server after you complete the tests:

apis/todoServer/server_test.go
```go
func setupAPI(t *testing.T) (string, func()) {
```

Mark this function as a test helper with t.Helper(), and then create a new test server using the function httptest.NewServer() from the httptest package. Provide your custom multiplexer function newMux() as input with a blank string for the to-do file name as we're not using it yet:

apis/todoServer/server_test.go
```
t.Helper()

ts := httptest.NewServer(newMux(""))
```

Complete this function by returning the test server URL and an anonymous function that closes the server when executed:

apis/todoServer/server_test.go
```
  return ts.URL, func() {
    ts.Close()
  }
}
```

Next, add the test function TestGet() to test the HTTP GET method on the server's root. Use the table-driven testing approach we first discussed in Testing with Table-Driven Testing, on page 82, so you can add more tests later. The test cases for this test have these parameters: name, path representing the server URL path to test, expCode representing the expected return code from the server, expItems as the expected number of items returned when querying the to-do API, and expContent with the expected body content of the response:

apis/todoServer/server_test.go
```
func TestGet(t *testing.T) {
  testCases := []struct {
    name       string
    path       string
    expCode    int
    expItems   int
    expContent string
  }{
    {name: "GetRoot", path: "/",
      expCode:    http.StatusOK,
      expContent: "There's an API here",
    },
    {name: "NotFound", path: "/todo/500",
      expCode: http.StatusNotFound,
    },
  }
```

For now, we're testing two cases: the response from the server's root and the *Not Found* error in case we query a route that's not defined. Note that for the expected return code we're using the constants provided by the net/http package, such as http.StatusOK, instead of the number 200. This makes the code more readable and easier to maintain.

Instantiate a new test server using the helper function setupAPI(). Defer the execution of the cleanup() function to ensure Go closes the server at the end of the tests:

apis/todoServer/server_test.go
```
url, cleanup := setupAPI(t)
defer cleanup()
```

Loop through each case, executing the tests. For each test, obtain the response from the server using the function http.Get() from the net/http package. Use the variable url to access the test server URL and tc.path to test the specific test case path. Check and fail the test if any errors are returned from the call to Get():

apis/todoServer/server_test.go
```
for _, tc := range testCases {
  t.Run(tc.name, func(t *testing.T) {
    var (
      body []byte
      err  error
    )

    r, err := http.Get(url + tc.path)
    if err != nil {
      t.Error(err)
    }
```

Defer closing the response's body to ensure Go frees its resource at the end of the function execution:

apis/todoServer/server_test.go
```
defer r.Body.Close()
```

Then, validate the returned status code:

apis/todoServer/server_test.go
```
if r.StatusCode != tc.expCode {
  t.Fatalf("Expected %q, got %q.", http.StatusText(tc.expCode),
    http.StatusText(r.StatusCode))
}
```

Next, use a switch case to check the response's content type. Use the method r.Header.Get("Content-Type") to obtain the content type from the response's headers. For now, we're only expecting the content as plain text. Read the entire content of the body and test whether it contains the expected content:

apis/todoServer/server_test.go
```
switch {
case strings.Contains(r.Header.Get("Content-Type"), "text/plain"):
  if body, err = ioutil.ReadAll(r.Body); err != nil {
    t.Error(err)
  }
```

```
  if !strings.Contains(string(body), tc.expContent) {
    t.Errorf("Expected %q, got %q.", tc.expContent,
      string(body))
  }
```

Later you'll use the same switch statement to check for other content types. Finally, use a default case to fail the test in case we receive any other content type:

apis/todoServer/server_test.go
```
    default:
      t.Fatalf("Unsupported Content-Type: %q", r.Header.Get("Content-Type"))
    }

  })
  }
}
```

The test code is complete. Save the file and execute the tests with go test -v:

```
$ go test -v
=== RUN    TestGet
=== RUN    TestGet/GetRoot
=== RUN    TestGet/NotFound
--- PASS: TestGet (0.00s)
    --- PASS: TestGet/GetRoot (0.00s)
    --- PASS: TestGet/NotFound (0.00s)
PASS
ok        pragprog.com/rggo/apis/todoServer        0.009s
```

The API server works, but it doesn't return anything useful. Let's make it work with the to-do API now.

Completing the REST API Server

With the general structure of your API server ready, let's add the CRUD operations for the to-do list. You'll use the to-do API you developed in Defining the To-Do API, on page 12.

Your to-do REST API supports these operations:

Method	URL	Description
GET	/todo	Retrieve all to-do items
GET	/todo/{number}	Retrieve a to-do item {number}
POST	/todo	Create a to-do item
PATCH	/todo/{number}?complete	Mark a to-do item {number} as completed
DELETE	/todo/{number}	Delete a to-do item {number}

Table 1—To-Do REST API Operations

The REST API serves all to-do–related content using the /todo URL path. It handles different operations based on the HTTP method, path, and parameters. The path may include a number for operations that act on a single to-do item. For example, to delete the third item from the list, the user sends a DELETE request to the URL path /todo/3.

The first two GET operations on the list retrieve items from the list. For this example, the REST API responds with JSON data. Besides the to-do items, we want to include additional information with the response, such as the current date and the number of results included. A sample response for multiple items looks like this:

```
{
  "results": [
    {
      "Task": "Task Number 1",
      "Done": true,
      "CreatedAt": "2019-10-13T11:16:00.756817096-04:00",
      "CompletedAt": "2019-10-13T21:25:30.008877148-04:00"
    },
    {
      "Task": "Task Number 2",
      "Done": false,
      "CreatedAt": "2019-10-14T15:55:48.273514272-04:00",
      "CompletedAt": "0001-01-01T00:00:00Z"
    }
  ],
  "date": 1575922413,
  "total_results": 2
}
```

The response includes the field results that wraps the to-do list. Let's create a new type todoResponse to wrap the list. In the same directory where you have main.go, create a new file todoResponse.go. Add the package definition and the import section. For this file, we're using the following packages: encoding/json to customize JSON output, time to work with time functions, and pragprog.com/rggo/interacting/todo that you developed in Defining the To-Do API, on page 12, to use the to-do API:

apis/todoServer.v1/todoResponse.go
```go
package main

import (
	"encoding/json"
	"time"

	"pragprog.com/rggo/interacting/todo"
)
```

Then, add the new struct type todoResponse to wrap the todo.List type:

```
apis/todoServer.v1/todoResponse.go
type todoResponse struct {
  Results todo.List `json:"results"`
}
```

In this struct type, the field name Results is exported with the first character of its name capitalized. This ensures that it's exported as JSON when using Go's JSON encoding. We're using a struct tag to change the name to results in the resulting JSON as it's common to have all fields in JSON spelled with lowercase characters.

Using struct tags is the best way to do simple JSON customizations in Go. You can change the spelling of the fields, remap them to other fields, or even omit them. But if you need more complex customizations, then you need to associate a custom MarshalJSON() method to your type. In this case, let's associate this custom method to the todoResponse type to add the fields date and total_results to the JSON output while having them calculated dynamically at the time of using them:

```
apis/todoServer.v1/todoResponse.go
func (r *todoResponse) MarshalJSON() ([]byte, error) {
  resp := struct {
    Results      todo.List `json:"results"`
    Date         int64     `json:"date"`
    TotalResults int       `json:"total_results"`
  }{
    Results:      r.Results,
    Date:         time.Now().Unix(),
    TotalResults: len(r.Results),
  }

  return json.Marshal(resp)
}
```

In this method, we're creating an anonymous struct providing the original Results field. We're also defining the Date field using the current time in Unix format and the TotalResults field by calculating the number of results in the list using the built-in len() function on the original Results field. In addition, we're using struct tags to encode their names with common JSON patterns such as snake case.

Save and close the todoResponse.go file. Before we dive into routing for the /todo path, let's add a couple of helper functions to prevent repetitive code when replying to requests. These are similar to the function replyTextContent() you wrote in Developing a REST API Server, on page 274. Open the server.go file and update the import list to include the packages encoding/json to convert data to JSON and log to log errors:

apis/todoServer.v1/server.go
```
"encoding/json"
"log"
```

Then, create the function replyJSONContent() to reply to a request using JSON data:

apis/todoServer.v1/server.go
```
func replyJSONContent(w http.ResponseWriter, r *http.Request,
  status int, resp *todoResponse) {

  body, err := json.Marshal(resp)
  if err != nil {
    replyError(w, r, http.StatusInternalServerError, err.Error())
    return
  }

  w.Header().Set("Content-Type", "application/json")
  w.WriteHeader(status)
  w.Write(body)
}
```

Next, add the function replyError() to log an error and reply to the request with an appropriate HTTP error:

apis/todoServer.v1/server.go
```
func replyError(w http.ResponseWriter, r *http.Request,
  status int, message string) {

  log.Printf("%s %s: Error: %d %s", r.URL, r.Method, status, message)
  http.Error(w, http.StatusText(status), status)
}
```

To handle the requests to the /todo path, we need to associate the path to an http.Handler or http.HandlerFunc like the one we used to handle requests to the API root. The issue is that, by default, Go only handles requests based on the URL path, not on the HTTP method. Moreover, we would like to pass additional parameters to this function so it can deal with to-do lists. These include the file name to save the to-do list. Because handler functions require a specific function signature func(http.ResponseWriter, *http.Request), we'll apply Go's functional nature as well as the concept of closures to develop a custom function that makes an http.HandlerFunc. Then, you'll use its output to route the requests to the /todo route.

Save the file server.go and open the file handlers.go. Include new packages in the import list. You'll use the following packages: encoding/json to work with JSON data, errors to define and handle errors, fmt to print formatted output, strconv to convert strings to integer numbers, sync to use the type sync.Mutex to prevent racing conditions when accessing the to-do save file concurrently, and finally, todo to manipulate to-do items:

apis/todoServer.v1/handlers.go
```go
import (

    "encoding/json"
    "errors"
    "fmt"

    "net/http"
    "strconv"
    "sync"

    "pragprog.com/rggo/interacting/todo"
)
```

Define two error values to indicate possible errors that need to be handled internally:

apis/todoServer.v1/handlers.go
```go
var (
  ErrNotFound = errors.New("not found")
  ErrInvalidData = errors.New("invalid data")
)
```

Now, define the routing function named todoRouter(). This function looks at the incoming request and dispatches to the appropriate replying function. This function takes two input parameters: the file name to save the list todoFile as string and an instance of interface sync.Locker I. This interface accepts any types that implement the methods Lock() and Unlock() such as sync.Mutex. This routing function returns another function of type http.HandlerFunc so you can use its output as a handling function in the newMux() function:

apis/todoServer.v1/handlers.go
```go
func todoRouter(todoFile string, l sync.Locker) http.HandlerFunc {
```

Then, in the function's body, return an anonymous function with the http. HandlerFunc signature:

apis/todoServer.v1/handlers.go
```go
return func(w http.ResponseWriter, r *http.Request) {
```

Next, define a variable list as an empty todo.List and load the contents of the todoFile into it using the method list.Get() from the todo package. If errors occur, use the previously defined function replyError() to respond to the request with the HTTP Internal Server Error:

```
apis/todoServer.v1/handlers.go
list := &todo.List{}

l.Lock()
defer l.Unlock()
if err := list.Get(todoFile); err != nil {
  replyError(w, r, http.StatusInternalServerError, err.Error())
  return
}
```

For this example, you're using the method l.Lock() from the sync.Locker interface to lock the entire request handling. This prevents concurrent access to the file represented by the variable todoFile which could lead to data loss. This is acceptable in this example as we're not expecting any high load to the API. In a production scenario, this isn't the ideal solution. But in a production scenario, you wouldn't likely be saving the data directly to a file like this.

Now, you need to route the request appropriately. This decision is based on the path of the request and the HTTP method. First, check the request path. For this API, users can make a request to the /todo root to get all items or to create a new item, or they can make a request for an individual item by providing the item ID with the path, like /todo/1. To make it easier to evaluate the path, you'll strip the /todo prefix from the path before calling this function. So the path will either be an empty string for the /todo root path or an item number for an individual request.

First, handle the /todo root path case by checking whether the path matches an empty string. Then, use a switch statement to route the request to the appropriate function based on the HTTP method. Go provides constant values for identifying the method, such as http.MethodGet for the GET method. Use them instead of the string value for cleaner and more maintainable code:

```
apis/todoServer.v1/handlers.go
if r.URL.Path == "" {
  switch r.Method {
  case http.MethodGet:
    getAllHandler(w, r, list)
  case http.MethodPost:
    addHandler(w, r, list, todoFile)
  default:
    message := "Method not supported"
    replyError(w, r, http.StatusMethodNotAllowed, message)
  }
  return
}
```

The return statement at the end of switch ensures that we finish processing any requests to the /todo root. From now on, we know the request contains a value.

Use the validateID() function to ensure that this value is an integer number that matches an existing *todo* item. You'll write this function shortly. If errors occur, return the appropriate status code using the replyError() function. Finally, complete this function by checking the request method to dispatch the request to the correct handling function as you did before:

apis/todoServer.v1/handlers.go
```
    id, err := validateID(r.URL.Path, list)
    if err != nil {
      if errors.Is(err, ErrNotFound) {
        replyError(w, r, http.StatusNotFound, err.Error())
        return
      }
      replyError(w, r, http.StatusBadRequest, err.Error())
      return
    }

    switch r.Method {
    case http.MethodGet:
      getOneHandler(w, r, list, id)
    case http.MethodDelete:
      deleteHandler(w, r, list, id, todoFile)
    case http.MethodPatch:
      patchHandler(w, r, list, id, todoFile)
    default:
      message := "Method not supported"
      replyError(w, r, http.StatusMethodNotAllowed, message)
    }
  }
}
```

Now define the handling functions for each case. Start with the getAllHandler() function to obtain all to-do items. This function wraps the current todo.List in a todoResponse type and then uses the function replyJSONContent() to encode it into JSON and reply to the request:

apis/todoServer.v1/handlers.go
```
func getAllHandler(w http.ResponseWriter, r *http.Request, list *todo.List) {
  resp := &todoResponse{
    Results: *list,
  }
  replyJSONContent(w, r, http.StatusOK, resp)
}
```

Next, define the function getOneHandler() to reply with a single item. This is similar to the getAllHandler() function, but it slices the original list into a list containing a single element by using the variable id and the slice expression (*list)[id-1: id]:

apis/todoServer.v1/handlers.go
```go
func getOneHandler(w http.ResponseWriter, r *http.Request,
  list *todo.List, id int) {

  resp := &todoResponse{
    Results: (*list)[id-1 : id],
  }
  replyJSONContent(w, r, http.StatusOK, resp)
}
```

Then, define the function deleteHandler() to delete the item represented by the variable id:

apis/todoServer.v1/handlers.go
```go
func deleteHandler(w http.ResponseWriter, r *http.Request,
  list *todo.List, id int, todoFile string) {

  list.Delete(id)
  if err := list.Save(todoFile); err != nil {
    replyError(w, r, http.StatusInternalServerError, err.Error())
    return
  }

  replyTextContent(w, r, http.StatusNoContent, "")
}
```

Next, define the patchHandler() function to complete a specific item. This function uses the method r.URL.Query() to look for query parameters. If it finds the query parameter complete, it completes the item represented by id. Otherwise, it replies with the HTTP Bad Request error:

apis/todoServer.v1/handlers.go
```go
func patchHandler(w http.ResponseWriter, r *http.Request,
  list *todo.List, id int, todoFile string) {

  q := r.URL.Query()

  if _, ok := q["complete"]; !ok {
    message := "Missing query param 'complete'"
    replyError(w, r, http.StatusBadRequest, message)
    return
  }

  list.Complete(id)
  if err := list.Save(todoFile); err != nil {
    replyError(w, r, http.StatusInternalServerError, err.Error())
    return
  }

  replyTextContent(w, r, http.StatusNoContent, "")
}
```

Define the function addHandler() to add a new item to the list. This function reads the request body, expecting a JSON object with a single variable task representing the task name to include in the list. It decodes the JSON into an anonymous struct and uses it to add the new item. It replies with the HTTP Status Created if successful or an appropriate error status if errors occur:

```
apis/todoServer.v1/handlers.go
func addHandler(w http.ResponseWriter, r *http.Request,
  list *todo.List, todoFile string) {

  item := struct {
    Task string `json:"task"`
  }{}

  if err := json.NewDecoder(r.Body).Decode(&item); err != nil {
    message := fmt.Sprintf("Invalid JSON: %s", err)
    replyError(w, r, http.StatusBadRequest, message)
    return
  }

  list.Add(item.Task)
  if err := list.Save(todoFile); err != nil {
    replyError(w, r, http.StatusInternalServerError, err.Error())
    return
  }

  replyTextContent(w, r, http.StatusCreated, "")
}
```

Then define the function validateID() to ensure the ID provided by the user is valid. This function converts the string value to an integer number and validates that the number represents an existing item in the list. It returns the ID if successful or an appropriate error otherwise:

```
apis/todoServer.v1/handlers.go
func validateID(path string, list *todo.List) (int, error) {
  id, err := strconv.Atoi(path)
  if err != nil {
    return 0, fmt.Errorf("%w: Invalid ID: %s", ErrInvalidData, err)
  }

  if id < 1 {
    return 0, fmt.Errorf("%w, Invalid ID: Less than one", ErrInvalidData)
  }

  if id > len(*list) {
    return id, fmt.Errorf("%w: ID %d not found", ErrNotFound, id)
  }

  return id, nil
}
```

Next, update the function rootHandler() to use the replyError() function when replying with an error instead of calling the http.NotFound() function directly, like this:

```
apis/todoServer.v1/handlers.go
func rootHandler(w http.ResponseWriter, r *http.Request) {
  if r.URL.Path != "/" {
    replyError(w, r, http.StatusNotFound, "")
    return
  }

  content := "There's an API here"
  replyTextContent(w, r, http.StatusOK, content)
}
```

Now update the newMux() function to route the requests for the /todo path. Save the file handlers.go and open the file server.go. Update the function newMux() by defining a new variable mu as a pointer to a sync.Mutex type. The pointer to Mutex implements the interface sync.Locker, so you can use it as an input to the todoRouter() function. Then use the variables mu and todoFile to run the function todoRouter(), assigning its output to a variable t. Finally, use the variable t in the function http.StripPrefix() to strip the /todo prefix from the URL path, passing its output to the method m.Handle() to handle requests to the /todo route. The complete, new version of newMux() is this:

```
apis/todoServer.v1/server.go
func newMux(todoFile string) http.Handler {
  m := http.NewServeMux()
  mu := &sync.Mutex{}

  m.HandleFunc("/", rootHandler)

  t := todoRouter(todoFile, mu)

  m.Handle("/todo", http.StripPrefix("/todo", t))
  m.Handle("/todo/", http.StripPrefix("/todo/", t))

  return m
}
```

In this function, you're also routing the requests to the path /todo/ using the same routing function. This way users get the same result with or without the trailing slash.

Before saving the file, make sure to include the package sync in the import list to use the type sync.Mutex:

```
apis/todoServer.v1/server.go
"sync"
```

Now the code is complete. Let's add more tests to ensure it does what we expect. Save the file server.go and edit the file server_test.go. Update the import section to include the new required packages. You'll use the bytes package to capture output in a buffer, the encoding/json package to encode and decode JSON data, the fmt package to print formatted output, the log package to change logging options, the os package to handle operating system operations, and the prag-prog.com/rggo/interacting/todo package to deal with to-do lists:

apis/todoServer.v1/server_test.go
```go
import (
➤    "bytes"
➤    "encoding/json"
➤    "fmt"
➤
     "io/ioutil"
➤    "log"
     "net/http"
     "net/http/httptest"

➤    "os"
     "strings"
     "testing"

➤    "pragprog.com/rggo/interacting/todo"
)
```

Then, update the function setupAPI() to include a test to-do file and a few items for testing. Use the ioutil.TempFile() function to create a temporary file to use when calling the newMux() function to instantiate the test server. Then, use a for loop to add three test items using the server API. At the end, include a line in the cleanup function to remove the temporary file when you're done with the tests:

apis/todoServer.v1/server_test.go
```go
func setupAPI(t *testing.T) (string, func()) {
  t.Helper()
➤  tempTodoFile, err := ioutil.TempFile("", "todotest")
➤  if err != nil {
➤    t.Fatal(err)
➤  }
➤
➤  ts := httptest.NewServer(newMux(tempTodoFile.Name()))
➤
➤  // Adding a couple of items for testing
➤  for i := 1; i < 3; i++ {
➤    var body bytes.Buffer
➤    taskName := fmt.Sprintf("Task number %d.", i)
➤    item := struct {
➤      Task string `json:"task"`
➤    }{
➤      Task: taskName,
➤    }
➤
```

```go
        if err := json.NewEncoder(&body).Encode(item); err != nil {
            t.Fatal(err)
        }

        r, err := http.Post(ts.URL+"/todo", "application/json", &body)
        if err != nil {
            t.Fatal(err)
        }

        if r.StatusCode != http.StatusCreated {
            t.Fatalf("Failed to add initial items: Status: %d", r.StatusCode)
        }
    }

    return ts.URL, func() {
        ts.Close()
        os.Remove(tempTodoFile.Name())
    }
}
```

Next, update the test function TestGet() to include tests for the /todo route. You'll add one test case for getting all items and another test to get a single item:

```go
apis/todoServer.v1/server_test.go
func TestGet(t *testing.T) {
    testCases := []struct {
        name        string
        path        string
        expCode     int
        expItems    int
        expContent  string
    }{
        {name: "GetRoot", path: "/",
            expCode:    http.StatusOK,
            expContent: "There's an API here",
        },
        {name: "GetAll", path: "/todo",
            expCode:    http.StatusOK,
            expItems:   2,
            expContent: "Task number 1.",
        },
        {name: "GetOne", path: "/todo/1",
            expCode:    http.StatusOK,
            expItems:   1,
            expContent: "Task number 1.",
        },
        {name: "NotFound", path: "/todo/500",
            expCode: http.StatusNotFound,
        },
    }

    url, cleanup := setupAPI(t)
```

Now, define a variable resp as an anonymous struct with the response format:

apis/todoServer.v1/server_test.go

```go
var (
    resp struct {
        Results      todo.List `json:"results"`
        Date         int64     `json:"date"`
        TotalResults int       `json:"total_results"`
    }
    body []byte
    err  error
)
```

Finally, add a case statement to the switch block to handle the situation where the response content type is *application/json*. Decode the response body into the resp variable and test whether the returned content matches the expected content in the test cases:

apis/todoServer.v1/server_test.go

```go
switch {
case r.Header.Get("Content-Type") == "application/json":
    if err = json.NewDecoder(r.Body).Decode(&resp); err != nil {
        t.Error(err)
    }
    if resp.TotalResults != tc.expItems {
        t.Errorf("Expected %d items, got %d.", tc.expItems, resp.TotalResults)
    }
    if resp.Results[0].Task != tc.expContent {
        t.Errorf("Expected %q, got %q.", tc.expContent,
            resp.Results[0].Task)
    }
case strings.Contains(r.Header.Get("Content-Type"), "text/plain"):
    if body, err = ioutil.ReadAll(r.Body); err != nil {
        t.Error(err)
    }

    if !strings.Contains(string(body), tc.expContent) {
        t.Errorf("Expected %q, got %q.", tc.expContent,
            string(body))
    }
default:
```

Next, include a test to add new items to the list. Use two subtests: one to add the item and the other to ensure it was added correctly:

apis/todoServer.v1/server_test.go

```go
func TestAdd(t *testing.T) {
    url, cleanup := setupAPI(t)
    defer cleanup()

    taskName := "Task number 3."
    t.Run("Add", func(t *testing.T) {
```

```go
    var body bytes.Buffer
    item := struct {
      Task string `json:"task"`
    }{
      Task: taskName,
    }

    if err := json.NewEncoder(&body).Encode(item); err != nil {
      t.Fatal(err)
    }

    r, err := http.Post(url+"/todo", "application/json", &body)
    if err != nil {
      t.Fatal(err)
    }

    if r.StatusCode != http.StatusCreated {
      t.Errorf("Expected %q, got %q.",
        http.StatusText(http.StatusCreated), http.StatusText(r.StatusCode))
    }
  })

  t.Run("CheckAdd", func(t *testing.T) {
    r, err := http.Get(url + "/todo/3")
    if err != nil {
      t.Error(err)
    }

    if r.StatusCode != http.StatusOK {
      t.Fatalf("Expected %q, got %q.",
        http.StatusText(http.StatusOK), http.StatusText(r.StatusCode))
    }

    var resp todoResponse
    if err := json.NewDecoder(r.Body).Decode(&resp); err != nil {
      t.Fatal(err)
    }
    r.Body.Close()

    if resp.Results[0].Task != taskName {
      t.Errorf("Expected %q, got %q.", taskName, resp.Results[0].Task)
    }
  })
}
```

Then, include a test for the delete operation:

apis/todoServer.v1/server_test.go
```go
func TestDelete(t *testing.T) {
  url, cleanup := setupAPI(t)
  defer cleanup()

  t.Run("Delete", func(t *testing.T) {
    u := fmt.Sprintf("%s/todo/1", url)
    req, err := http.NewRequest(http.MethodDelete, u, nil)
```

```
    if err != nil {
      t.Fatal(err)
    }

    r, err := http.DefaultClient.Do(req)
    if err != nil {
      t.Error(err)
    }

    if r.StatusCode != http.StatusNoContent {
      t.Fatalf("Expected %q, got %q.",
        http.StatusText(http.StatusNoContent), http.StatusText(r.StatusCode))
    }
  })

  t.Run("CheckDelete", func(t *testing.T) {
    r, err := http.Get(url + "/todo")
    if err != nil {
      t.Error(err)
    }

    if r.StatusCode != http.StatusOK {
      t.Fatalf("Expected %q, got %q.",
        http.StatusText(http.StatusOK), http.StatusText(r.StatusCode))
    }

    var resp todoResponse
    if err := json.NewDecoder(r.Body).Decode(&resp); err != nil {
      t.Fatal(err)
    }
    r.Body.Close()

    if len(resp.Results) != 1 {
      t.Errorf("Expected 1 item, got %d.", len(resp.Results))
    }

    expTask := "Task number 2."
    if resp.Results[0].Task != expTask {
      t.Errorf("Expected %q, got %q.", expTask, resp.Results[0].Task)
    }
  })
}
```

Finally, include a test for the complete operation:

```
apis/todoServer.v1/server_test.go
func TestComplete(t *testing.T) {
  url, cleanup := setupAPI(t)
  defer cleanup()

  t.Run("Complete", func(t *testing.T) {
    u := fmt.Sprintf("%s/todo/1?complete", url)
    req, err := http.NewRequest(http.MethodPatch, u, nil)
```

```go
    if err != nil {
      t.Fatal(err)
    }

    r, err := http.DefaultClient.Do(req)
    if err != nil {
      t.Error(err)
    }

    if r.StatusCode != http.StatusNoContent {
      t.Fatalf("Expected %q, got %q.",
        http.StatusText(http.StatusNoContent), http.StatusText(r.StatusCode))
    }
  })

  t.Run("CheckComplete", func(t *testing.T) {
    r, err := http.Get(url + "/todo")
    if err != nil {
      t.Error(err)
    }

    if r.StatusCode != http.StatusOK {
      t.Fatalf("Expected %q, got %q.",
        http.StatusText(http.StatusOK), http.StatusText(r.StatusCode))
    }

    var resp todoResponse
    if err := json.NewDecoder(r.Body).Decode(&resp); err != nil {
      t.Fatal(err)
    }
    r.Body.Close()
    if len(resp.Results) != 2 {
      t.Errorf("Expected 2 items, got %d.", len(resp.Results))
    }

    if !resp.Results[0].Done {
      t.Error("Expected Item 1 to be completed")
    }

    if resp.Results[1].Done {
      t.Error("Expected Item 2 not to be completed")
    }
  })
}
```

Save the file server_test.go, and execute the tests using go test -v:

```
$ go test -v
=== RUN   TestGet
=== RUN   TestGet/GetRoot
=== RUN   TestGet/GetAll
=== RUN   TestGet/GetOne
=== RUN   TestGet/NotFound
2019/12/16 21:44:51 500 GET: Error: 404 ID 500 not found
```

```
--- PASS: TestGet (0.01s)
    --- PASS: TestGet/GetRoot (0.00s)
    --- PASS: TestGet/GetAll (0.00s)
    --- PASS: TestGet/GetOne (0.00s)
    --- PASS: TestGet/NotFound (0.00s)
=== RUN    TestAdd
=== RUN    TestAdd/Add
=== RUN    TestAdd/CheckAdd
--- PASS: TestAdd (0.00s)
    --- PASS: TestAdd/Add (0.00s)
    --- PASS: TestAdd/CheckAdd (0.00s)
=== RUN    TestDelete
=== RUN    TestDelete/Delete
=== RUN    TestDelete/CheckDelete
--- PASS: TestDelete (0.00s)
    --- PASS: TestDelete/Delete (0.00s)
    --- PASS: TestDelete/CheckDelete (0.00s)
=== RUN    TestComplete
=== RUN    TestComplete/Complete
=== RUN    TestComplete/CheckComplete
--- PASS: TestComplete (0.00s)
    --- PASS: TestComplete/Complete (0.00s)
    --- PASS: TestComplete/CheckComplete (0.00s)
PASS
ok      pragprog.com/rggo/apis/todoServer       0.020s
```

Because you're using the default logger from the log package, the log output from the server shows up in the test results. This can clutter the results and make it harder to read them. If you want to get rid of the log output, add a TestMain() function to your server_test.go file and set the default log output for the tests to the ioutil.Discard variable, like this:

apis/todoServer.v1/server_test.go
```
func TestMain(m *testing.M) {
  log.SetOutput(ioutil.Discard)
  os.Exit(m.Run())
}
```

Rerun the tests and verify that the log output is gone:

```
$ go test -v
=== RUN    TestGet
=== RUN    TestGet/GetRoot
=== RUN    TestGet/GetAll
=== RUN    TestGet/GetOne
=== RUN    TestGet/NotFound
--- PASS: TestGet (0.01s)
    --- PASS: TestGet/GetRoot (0.00s)
    --- PASS: TestGet/GetAll (0.00s)
```

```
--- PASS: TestGet/GetOne (0.00s)
    --- PASS: TestGet/NotFound (0.00s)
=== RUN    TestAdd
=== RUN    TestAdd/Add
=== RUN    TestAdd/CheckAdd
--- PASS: TestAdd (0.00s)
    --- PASS: TestAdd/Add (0.00s)
    --- PASS: TestAdd/CheckAdd (0.00s)
=== RUN    TestDelete
=== RUN    TestDelete/Delete
=== RUN    TestDelete/CheckDelete
--- PASS: TestDelete (0.00s)
    --- PASS: TestDelete/Delete (0.00s)
    --- PASS: TestDelete/CheckDelete (0.00s)
=== RUN    TestComplete
=== RUN    TestComplete/Complete
=== RUN    TestComplete/CheckComplete
--- PASS: TestComplete (0.00s)
    --- PASS: TestComplete/Complete (0.00s)
    --- PASS: TestComplete/CheckComplete (0.00s)
PASS
ok        pragprog.com/rggo/apis/todoServer        0.018s
```

You completed your REST API server example.

Let's develop the API client command line next.

Developing the Initial Client for the REST API

With the to-do REST API server in place, you can now build a command-line application that uses the API to query, add, complete, and delete items.

Start by creating the directory structure for your REST API client under your book's root directory:

```
$ mkdir -p $HOME/pragprog.com/rggo/apis/todoClient
$ cd $HOME/pragprog.com/rggo/apis/todoClient
```

For this application, you'll use the Cobra framework generator again as you did in Chapter 7, Using the Cobra CLI Framework, on page 213, to generate some of the boilerplate code for your application.

Initialize a Cobra application in this directory:

```
$ cobra init --pkg-name pragprog.com/rggo/apis/todoClient
Using config file: /home/ricardo/.cobra.yaml
Your Cobra application is ready at
/home/ricardo/pragprog.com/rggo/apis/todoClient
```

Cobra Config File

⚠️ This command assumes you have a Cobra configuration file in your home directory. If you executed the examples in Chapter 7, Using the Cobra CLI Framework, on page 213, you should have this file. Otherwise, take a look at Starting Your Cobra Application, on page 214, to create the configuration file.

You can also initialize the application without the configuration file. Cobra uses its default options, so the LICENSE and comments in your code will be different from these examples.

Next, initialize the Go module for this project:

```
$ cd $HOME/pragprog.com/rggo/apis/todoClient
$ go mod init pragprog.com/rggo/apis/todoClient
go: creating new go.mod: module pragprog.com/rggo/apis/todoClient
```

Then, add a requirement to go.mod to ensure you're using Cobra v1.1.3, which is what this book's code uses. Again you can use a later version, but you may need to change the code a bit. Run go mod tidy to download the required dependencies:

```
$ go mod edit --require github.com/spf13/cobra@v1.1.3
$ go mod tidy
```

This command-line application will have five subcommands:

add <task>: Followed by a task string, adds a new task to the list.

list: Lists all items in the list.

complete <n>: Completes item number n.

del <n>: Deletes item number n from the list.

view <n>: Views details about item number n.

Let's develop the skeleton for the application and implement the first operation, list, to list all items. You'll implement the other operations later.

Start by modifying the root command of your application generated by Cobra. Edit the file cmd/root.go and update the import section. Include the package strings to deal with string values:

apis/todoClient/cmd/root.go
```
import (
    "fmt"
    "os"

➤   "strings"
```

```
    "github.com/spf13/cobra"

    homedir "github.com/mitchellh/go-homedir"
    "github.com/spf13/viper"
)
```

Next, update the rootCmd command definition according to your tool's requirements. Update the Short description and delete the Long description:

apis/todoClient/cmd/root.go
```
var rootCmd = &cobra.Command{
    Use:    "todoClient",
    Short: "A Todo API client",
    // Uncomment the following line if your bare application
    // has an action associated with it:
    //  Run: func(cmd *cobra.Command, args []string) { },
}
```

Then, modify the init() function to include a new command-line flag --api-root
that allows users to specify the URL for the to-do REST API. Use Viper to bind
it to an environment variable TODO_API_ROOT by setting a replacer and a prefix,
as you did in Using Viper for Configuration Management, on page 262:

apis/todoClient/cmd/root.go
```
func init() {
    cobra.OnInitialize(initConfig)

    // Here you will define your flags and configuration settings.
    // Cobra supports persistent flags, which, if defined here,
    // will be global for your application.

    rootCmd.PersistentFlags().StringVar(&cfgFile, "config", "",
        "config file (default is $HOME/.todoClient.yaml)")

➤   rootCmd.PersistentFlags().String("api-root",
➤       "http://localhost:8080", "Todo API URL")
➤
➤   replacer := strings.NewReplacer("-", "_")
➤   viper.SetEnvKeyReplacer(replacer)
➤   viper.SetEnvPrefix("TODO")
➤
➤   viper.BindPFlag("api-root", rootCmd.PersistentFlags().Lookup("api-root"))
}
```

Save and close this file. Now, let's define the logic to connect to the to-do REST
API to retrieve to-do items. Create and edit the file cmd/client.go in the cmd
directory. Add the package definition and the import list. For this file, you're
using the following packages: encoding/json to encode and decode JSON data,
errors to define error values, fmt for formatted printing, ioutil to read the HTTP
response body, net/http to handle HTTP connections, and time to define timeouts
and time constants:

```
apis/todoClient/cmd/client.go
package cmd

import (
  "encoding/json"
  "errors"
  "fmt"
  "io/ioutil"
  "net/http"
  "time"
)
```

Define the required error values to use throughout the package. You'll use these errors to wrap errors coming from the API and during test validation:

```
apis/todoClient/cmd/client.go
var (
  ErrConnection = errors.New("Connection error")
  ErrNotFound = errors.New("Not found")
  ErrInvalidResponse = errors.New("Invalid server response")
  ErrInvalid = errors.New("Invalid data")
  ErrNotNumber = errors.New("Not a number")
)
```

Next, define two custom types to obtain the results from the REST API calls. For this example, you should assume that you don't control the actual API server, since this is what happens when you're using a third-party API. You'll have to consult the API documentation to understand what values it returns so that you can create the appropriate types. For the to-do REST API example, create one type to represent an item and another type to represent the API response:

```
apis/todoClient/cmd/client.go
type item struct {
  Task        string
  Done        bool
  CreatedAt   time.Time
  CompletedAt time.Time
}

type response struct {
  Results      []item `json:"results"`
  Date         int    `json:"date"`
  TotalResults int    `json:"total_results"`
}
```

To send an HTTP request to a server using Go, you need an instance of type http.Client. Go provides a default client that you can use for simple requests. But it's recommended that you instantiate your own client so you can adjust parameters relevant to your requirements. One of the most important parameters is the connection timeout. The default client has no timeout set, which means your application could take a long time to return or hang forever if the server has an issue. Let's define a function to instantiate a new client with a timeout of 10 seconds. If you want, you could make this value customizable. For now, we'll keep it hardcoded:

apis/todoClient/cmd/client.go
```go
func newClient() *http.Client {
  c := &http.Client{
    Timeout: 10 * time.Second,
  }

  return c
}
```

The http.Client is safe to be reused for multiple connections so you shouldn't create one every time. In our case, the command-line application executes a single task and then quits, so we don't need to worry about adding more code to reuse it.

Next, define a function to retrieve to-do items from the REST API using the client. Because we want to be able to retrieve a single item or all items from the list, create a function that works for both cases named getItems(). This function takes as input the URL as string, and it returns a slice of item and a potential error. Later, you'll wrap this function with another function to retrieve all items or a single item:

apis/todoClient/cmd/client.go
```go
func getItems(url string) ([]item, error) {
```

In the function's body, instantiate a new http.Client using the newClient() function. Because this function returns a pointer to the http.Client type, chain the method Get() using the url as input to execute a GET request to the REST API on a single line. Verify and return potential errors for that operation:

apis/todoClient/cmd/client.go
```go
r, err := newClient().Get(url)
if err != nil {
  return nil, fmt.Errorf("%w: %s", ErrConnection, err)
}
```

If successful, you'll need to read the content from the response body. To ensure you close the body after reading it, defer the call to its Close() method:

apis/todoClient/cmd/client.go
```go
defer r.Body.Close()
```

For our REST API example, we expect that successfully retrieving to-do items returns an HTTP status of 200 or OK. Use the http.StatusOK constant instead of the literal value for more readable and maintainable code. If that's not the case, the GET operation was successful but the API returned an error. Read the response's body content to retrieve the error message, and return it as a new error wrapping one of the error values you defined before. If the HTTP status code matches http.StatusNotFound, wrap the error ErrNotFound, otherwise, wrap ErrInvalidResponse. This API returns errors as plain text, so you don't need to decode data. In case you can't read the body, return a new error with the message *Cannot read body* wrapping the original error:

apis/todoClient/cmd/client.go
```go
if r.StatusCode != http.StatusOK {
  msg, err := ioutil.ReadAll(r.Body)
  if err != nil {
    return nil, fmt.Errorf("Cannot read body: %w", err)
  }
  err = ErrInvalidResponse
  if r.StatusCode == http.StatusNotFound {
    err = ErrNotFound
  }
  return nil, fmt.Errorf("%w: %s", err, msg)
}
```

If successful, the body contains JSON data that matches the response type you defined before. Create a new variable resp of type response and decode the body into it using the Decode() method from the type Decoder provided by the package encoding/json:

apis/todoClient/cmd/client.go
```go
var resp response

if err := json.NewDecoder(r.Body).Decode(&resp); err != nil {
  return nil, err
}
```

Verify that the response contains items by checking the TotalResults field. If no items exist, return an appropriate error:

apis/todoClient/cmd/client.go
```go
if resp.TotalResults == 0 {
  return nil, fmt.Errorf("%w: No results found", ErrNotFound)
}
```

Otherwise, return the list of items from the resp.Results field and the value nil indicating no error exists:

apis/todoClient/cmd/client.go
```go
  return resp.Results, nil
}
```

Finally, define the function getAll() wrapping up the function getItems(). Use the function fmt.Sprintf() to append the correct URL path /todo to the variable apiRoot, which is needed to obtain all the items from the REST API. Then use the new value to call the function getItems():

apis/todoClient/cmd/client.go
```
func getAll(apiRoot string) ([]item, error) {
  u := fmt.Sprintf("%s/todo", apiRoot)

  return getItems(u)
}
```

Save the file cmd/client.go to complete the code.

Now you can use these functions to implement the first command list to list all to-do items from the API. Use the Cobra generator to add the list command to your application:

```
$ cobra add list
Using config file: /home/ricardo/.cobra.yaml
list created at /home/ricardo/pragprog.com/rggo/apis/todoClient
```

Edit the file cmd/list.go and update the import section to include the following packages: io to use the io.Writer interface for flexible output, os to use the os.Stdout for output, text/tabwriter to print formatted tabulated data, and github.com/spf13/viper to obtain configuration values:

apis/todoClient/cmd/list.go
```
import (
  "fmt"
  "io"
  "os"
  "text/tabwriter"

  "github.com/spf13/cobra"
  "github.com/spf13/viper"
)
```

Then edit the command instance definition. Delete the Long description, update the Short description, and set the property SilenceUsage to true to prevent automatic usage display with errors. For the command action, replace the property Run with RunE, which returns an error. This is the same pattern you used in Creating the Subcommands to Manage Hosts, on page 230:

apis/todoClient/cmd/list.go
```
var listCmd = &cobra.Command{
  Use:          "list",
  Short:        "List todo items",
  SilenceUsage: true,
  RunE: func(cmd *cobra.Command, args []string) error {
```

```
    apiRoot := viper.GetString("api-root")

    return listAction(os.Stdout, apiRoot)
  },
}
```

In the body of the function defined by the RunE, we're using Viper to obtain the value for the api-root configuration that represents the base URL for the to-do REST API. Then, we're calling the listAction() function that executes the action.

Now define the function listAction() to execute the command action. In the function's body, obtain all to-do items from the REST API, using the function getAll() that you created before. Then, print all items using the function printAll(), which you'll define shortly:

apis/todoClient/cmd/list.go
```
func listAction(out io.Writer, apiRoot string) error {
  items, err := getAll(apiRoot)
  if err != nil {
    return err
  }

  return printAll(out, items)
}
```

Finally, define the function printAll() to print all items from the list. It takes the io.Writer interface as the output destination and a slice of item as input, and it returns an error:

apis/todoClient/cmd/list.go
```
func printAll(out io.Writer, items []item) error {
```

Use the standard library package text/tabwriter to print tabulated data. This package uses an algorithm that takes into account the minimum column width and adds padding to ensure the output columns are properly aligned. For more information about this package, consult its documentation.[1]

Create an instance of the type tabwriter.Writer by using the function tabwriter.NewWriter(). Set the final output to the given out variable. Set the minimum column width to 3 characters, the tabwidth to 2 characters, the padding to 0, the pad character to a space, and the value 0 to disable additional flags:

apis/todoClient/cmd/list.go
```
w := tabwriter.NewWriter(out, 3, 2, 0, ' ', 0)
```

The function tabwriter.NewWriter() returns a type that implements the io.Writer interface. It expects the input to be tabulated data separated by the \t tab character.

---

1.   golang.org/pkg/text/tabwriter/

Print all the items to this io.Writer by looping through the slice of items and printing each one using the fmt.Fprintf() function. Verify the property Done of each item, and, if the item is done, print the character X at the beginning of the line:

apis/todoClient/cmd/list.go
```
for k, v := range items {
  done := "-"
  if v.Done {
    done = "X"
  }
  fmt.Fprintf(w, "%s\t%d\t%s\t\n", done, k+1, v.Task)
}
```

When the loop is done, use the method w.Flush() to flush the output to the underlying io.Writer interface:

apis/todoClient/cmd/list.go
```
  return w.Flush()
}
```

This completes the code for the list command. Let's write some tests for it next.

Testing the Client Without Connecting to the API

Testing your API client by connecting to the real API is hard because you don't always have full control over the API or the network. Even testing on your local server can be tricky because each test can impact the next. On a real live API, it's even harder to ensure the tests are reproducible. You may also be unable to test error conditions such as invalid responses or empty lists.

In addition, it's not nice to hit someone else's server to test your code, especially if this is part of an automated test pipeline that runs periodically, for example, when using a continuous integration platform.

To overcome these challenges, you mock the API locally for your tests, simulating the expected responses by using the httptest.Server type. This is similar to the approach you used to test the server implementation in Testing the REST API Server, on page 280.

But this approach isn't perfect. The challenge here is to ensure that the mock data you use to simulate the API response is up-to-date with the actual API. Otherwise, your tests may work locally but your application will fail when connecting to the live API.

The recommended approach is to have a balance between those two cases. For this application, you'll use the mock API to run unit tests locally since these tests run often and you don't want to hit the live API frequently. Later, in Executing Integration Tests, on page 336, you'll add integration tests to your application to execute some final tests to ensure the application works with the live API before shipping it. The key is running the integration tests sporadically.

Start by defining the resources to mock the API locally. Create and edit the file cmd/mock_test.go. It's a good practice to use the suffix _test to name files used only during tests to prevent them from being compiled into the final application binary. Add the package definition and the import list. For this file, you'll use the packages net/http to handle HTTP requests and net/http/httptest to instantiate an HTTP test server:

apis/todoClient/cmd/mock_test.go
```
package cmd

import (
  "net/http"
  "net/http/httptest"
)
```

Add a variable testResp with some mock response data. This variable is of type map and maps a string key representing the data name to a struct that contains the properties Status as an integer and Body as string. The Status property represents the expected HTTP response status, while the Body contains the JSON or text response data. For these tests, define five keys (resultsMany, resultsOne, noResults, root, and notFound) with their respective data:

apis/todoClient/cmd/mock_test.go
```
var testResp = map[string]struct {
  Status int
  Body   string
}{
  "resultsMany": {
    Status: http.StatusOK,
    Body: `{
  "results": [
    {
      "Task": "Task 1",
      "Done": false,
      "CreatedAt": "2019-10-28T08:23:38.310097076-04:00",
      "CompletedAt": "0001-01-01T00:00:00Z"
    },
    {
      "Task": "Task 2",
      "Done": false,
      "CreatedAt": "2019-10-28T08:23:38.323447798-04:00",
      "CompletedAt": "0001-01-01T00:00:00Z"
    }
  ],
```

```
    "date": 1572265440,
    "total_results": 2
}`,
  },
  "resultsOne": {
    Status: http.StatusOK,
    Body: `{
    "results": [
      {
        "Task": "Task 1",
        "Done": false,
        "CreatedAt": "2019-10-28T08:23:38.310097076-04:00",
        "CompletedAt": "0001-01-01T00:00:00Z"
      }
    ],
    "date": 1572265440,
    "total_results": 1
}`,
  },

  "noResults": {
    Status: http.StatusOK,
    Body: `{
    "results": [],
    "date": 1572265440,
    "total_results": 0
}`,
  },

  "root": {
    Status: http.StatusOK,
    Body:    "There's an API here",
  },

  "notFound": {
    Status: http.StatusNotFound,
    Body:    "404 - not found",
  },
}
```

Then add the function mockServer() to create an HTTP server instance that will be used to execute tests. To make the implementation flexible and allow a variety of tests, this function takes as input a function of type http.HandlerFunc. You used this type earlier when you implemented the HTTP server in Developing a REST API Server, on page 274. This allows you to provide a custom response when instantiating the test server to test different cases. This function returns the URL for the test server and a cleanup function to close the server after the tests:

```
apis/todoClient/cmd/mock_test.go
func mockServer(h http.HandlerFunc) (string, func()) {
  ts := httptest.NewServer(h)

  return ts.URL, func() {
    ts.Close()
  }
}
```

Now write the unit tests for the listAction() function. Save and close the file cmd/mock_test.go. Create and edit a new file for the tests, cmd/actions_test.go. Add the package definition and the import list. For these tests, you'll use the following packages: bytes to capture output, errors to check errors, fmt for formatted printing, net/http to deal with HTTP connections, and testing for the testing utilities:

```
apis/todoClient/cmd/actions_test.go
package cmd

import (
  "bytes"
  "errors"
  "fmt"
  "net/http"
  "testing"
)
```

Add the test function TestListAction() to test the listAction() function. Use the table-driven testing approach you used in Testing with Table-Driven Testing, on page 82, to test different cases. Each test case has a name, an expected error expError, an expected output expOut, a response resp that you'll use to create the response function for the test server, and a flag closeServer indicating whether to close the server immediately to test error conditions:

```
apis/todoClient/cmd/actions_test.go
func TestListAction(t *testing.T) {
  testCases := []struct {
    name       string
    expError   error
    expOut     string
    resp       struct {
      Status int
      Body   string
    }
    closeServer bool
  }{
    {name: "Results",
      expError: nil,
      expOut:   "-  1  Task 1\n-  2  Task 2\n",
      resp:     testResp["resultsMany"],
    },
```

```
    {name: "NoResults",
      expError: ErrNotFound,
      resp:        testResp["noResults"]},
    {name: "InvalidURL",
      expError:    ErrConnection,
      resp:        testResp["noResults"],
      closeServer: true},
  }
```

For these tests, you're defining three cases: one to test a response with results, another to test a valid response with no results, and an error condition where the server is unreachable. Each case associates a corresponding key from the testResp map you created before.

Next, loop through each case and execute it as a subtest using the tc.name property to identify the test:

apis/todoClient/cmd/actions_test.go
```
for _, tc := range testCases {
  t.Run(tc.name, func(t *testing.T) {
```

Instantiate a test server using the mockServer() function you created before. Provide an anonymous function of type func(w http.ResponseWriter, r *http.Request) as input. This function works as an HTTP handler, and the test server uses this function to respond to any income requests. Use the values from tc.resp to reply with the correct HTTP status and data:

apis/todoClient/cmd/actions_test.go
```
url, cleanup := mockServer(
  func(w http.ResponseWriter, r *http.Request) {
    w.WriteHeader(tc.resp.Status)
    fmt.Fprintln(w, tc.resp.Body)
  })
```

Defer the execution of the cleanup() function to ensure the server closes after the tests. If the tc.closeServer flag is true, close the server immediately to test error conditions:

apis/todoClient/cmd/actions_test.go
```
defer cleanup()

if tc.closeServer {
  cleanup()
}
```

Next, define a variable out of type bytes.Buffer to capture the output, and execute the listAction() function providing the test server URL url as input. Capture the error and output:

```
apis/todoClient/cmd/actions_test.go
var out bytes.Buffer

err := listAction(&out, url)
```

Finally, complete the tests by comparing the actual values with the expected values, failing the test if they don't match:

```
apis/todoClient/cmd/actions_test.go
      if tc.expError != nil {
        if err == nil {
          t.Fatalf("Expected error %q, got no error.", tc.expError)
        }

        if ! errors.Is(err, tc.expError) {
          t.Errorf("Expected error %q, got %q.", tc.expError, err)
        }
        return
      }

      if err != nil {
        t.Fatalf("Expected no error, got %q.", err)
      }

      if tc.expOut != out.String() {
        t.Errorf("Expected output %q, got %q", tc.expOut, out.String())
      }
    })
  }
}
```

Save and close this file, and execute the tests to ensure the list commands work as expected:

```
$ go test -v ./cmd
=== RUN    TestListAction
=== RUN    TestListAction/Results
=== RUN    TestListAction/NoResults
=== RUN    TestListAction/InvalidURL
--- PASS: TestListAction (0.00s)
    --- PASS: TestListAction/Results (0.00s)
    --- PASS: TestListAction/NoResults (0.00s)
    --- PASS: TestListAction/InvalidURL (0.00s)
PASS
ok      pragprog.com/rggo/apis/todoClient/cmd   0.013s
```

Now try the new command with the actual REST API. If you don't have your API server running, open a new terminal window, navigate to the server application's root directory, and build the todoServer application:

```
$ cd $HOME/pragprog.com/rggo/apis/todoServer
$ go build
```

Then execute the server using a temporary file to ensure you're starting with an empty list:

```
$ ./todoServer -f /tmp/testtodoclient01.json
```

This is going to block your terminal while the server is running. In a different terminal add some items to your list. Since the application doesn't have that functionality yet, use the curl command to make a request to the server to add two new items:

```
$ curl -L -XPOST -d '{"task":"Task 1"}' -H 'Content-Type: application/json' \
> http://localhost:8080/todo
$ curl -L -XPOST -d '{"task":"Task 2"}' -H 'Content-Type: application/json' \
> http://localhost:8080/todo
```

If you're in a different terminal, switch to your todoClient application directory, build your application, and execute it with the list command to see the items from the REST API:

```
$ cd $HOME/pragprog.com/rggo/apis/todoClient
$ go build
$ ./todoClient list
-  1  Task 1
-  2  Task 2
```

The list command works. Let's add another command to view details about a single item next.

Viewing a Single Item

At this point, your application can query the to-do REST API for all items. Let's add the ability to get details for a specific item.

The to-do REST API returns information about a single item by querying the URL /todo/id using the HTTP Get method. The id is a numeric identifier that represents an item from the list. You can find the item id using the list command. When you're working with an API you're unfamiliar with, consult the REST API documentation to understand how to make queries for particular resources that you're interested in.

To obtain a single item from the REST API, first add a new function to the cmd/client.go file. This function wraps the getItems() function similarly to the getAll() function you developed for the list command, but providing the proper URL endpoint to query one item only. Name this function getOne(). It takes as input the apiRoot and the integer id that represents the item identifier. It returns an instance of the item type and an error:

apis/todoClient.v1/cmd/client.go
```go
func getOne(apiRoot string, id int) (item, error) {
  u := fmt.Sprintf("%s/todo/%d", apiRoot, id)

  items, err := getItems(u)
  if err != nil {
    return item{}, err
  }

  if len(items) != 1 {
    return item{}, fmt.Errorf("%w: Invalid results", ErrInvalid)
  }

  return items[0], nil
}
```

In this function, you're using the input parameters apiRoot and id to compose the correct URL endpoint to query a single item. Then we query the REST API using the getItems() function and check for errors. If successful, we're returning the item.

When printing details about the item, you'll print the time the task was created and completed. The item type uses the type time.Time to represent the time data. If you print the time data without any formatting, it prints a long string including every detail about the time. While this may be useful in some situations, some of this information is irrelevant for our users. To print a shorter version of the time data including only the month, day, hour, and minute, define a constant timeFormat, which you'll use later to format the time output. For more information about customizing the time format, consult the package time documentation:[2]

apis/todoClient.v1/cmd/client.go
```go
const timeFormat = "Jan/02 @15:04"
```

Save and close this file, and then use the Cobra generator to add the view command to your application:

```
$ cobra add view
Using config file: /home/ricardo/.cobra.yaml
view created at /home/ricardo/pragprog.com/rggo/apis/todoClient
```

Edit the generated file cmd/view.go. Update the import section to include the following packages: io to use the io.Writer interface, os to use os.Stdout for output, strconv to convert string to integer, text/tabwriter to print tabulated data, and github.com/spf13/viper to get the api-root configuration value:

---

2. pkg.go.dev/time#pkg-constants

```
apis/todoClient.v1/cmd/view.go
import (
  "fmt"
  "io"
  "os"
  "strconv"
  "text/tabwriter"

  "github.com/spf13/cobra"
  "github.com/spf13/viper"
)
```

Then update the viewCmd command definition. Update the Use definition to include the id argument, edit the Short description, delete the Long description, and prevent automatic usage display by setting the property SilenceUsage to true:

```
apis/todoClient.v1/cmd/view.go
var viewCmd = &cobra.Command{
  Use:          "view <id>",
  Short:        "View details about a single item",
  SilenceUsage: true,
```

Since this command requires a single argument id, validate that the user provides only one argument by setting the property Args to the validation function cobra.ExactArgs(1). This function returns an error if the user doesn't provide the exact number of arguments, in this case 1.

```
apis/todoClient.v1/cmd/view.go
Args:          cobra.ExactArgs(1),
```

Following the same pattern you used to define previous command actions, replace the Run property with RunE and implement the function to obtain the api-root configuration value from Viper and execute the action function viewAction():

```
apis/todoClient.v1/cmd/view.go
  RunE: func(cmd *cobra.Command, args []string) error {
    apiRoot := viper.GetString("api-root")

    return viewAction(os.Stdout, apiRoot, args[0])
  },
}
```

Next, implement the action function viewAction(). This function takes as input the io.Writer interface to print the output to, the apiRoot, and the arg argument as string provided by the user when executing the command. It returns an error. This function converts the argument arg from string to int using the function strconv.Atoi() from the strconv package, returning an error if the user provided an argument that's not an integer number. Then it queries the REST API using the getOne() function you defined before, and it prints details about the item using the function printOne(), which you'll define shortly:

apis/todoClient.v1/cmd/view.go
```go
func viewAction(out io.Writer, apiRoot, arg string) error {
  id, err := strconv.Atoi(arg)
  if err != nil {
    return fmt.Errorf("%w: Item id must be a number", ErrNotNumber)
  }

  i, err := getOne(apiRoot, id)
  if err != nil {
    return err
  }

  return printOne(out, i)
}
```

Now, define the function printOne() to print the details about the to-do item. This function takes the io.Writer interface as the output destination and the item. It returns an error. Use the package tabwriter again to ensure the columns align correctly. Print details about the task such as its name and creation date. If the task is completed, print its completion date also:

apis/todoClient.v1/cmd/view.go
```go
func printOne(out io.Writer, i item) error {
  w := tabwriter.NewWriter(out, 14, 2, 0, ' ', 0)
  fmt.Fprintf(w, "Task:\t%s\n", i.Task)
  fmt.Fprintf(w, "Created at:\t%s\n", i.CreatedAt.Format(timeFormat))
  if i.Done {
    fmt.Fprintf(w, "Completed:\t%s\n", "Yes")
    fmt.Fprintf(w, "Completed At:\t%s\n", i.CompletedAt.Format(timeFormat))
    return w.Flush()
  }

  fmt.Fprintf(w, "Completed:\t%s\n", "No")
  return w.Flush()
}
```

In this function, you're using the method Format() on the instances of time.Time types such as CreatedAt and CompletedAt to format the date and time according to the constant timeFormat you defined in the file client.go.

The expected output for a completed item looks like this:

```
Task:         Task 1
Created at:   Oct/26 @17:37
Completed:    Yes
Completed At: Nov/12 @01:09
```

Let's write some tests for the new command. Save and close the file cmd/view.go, and edit the file cmd/actions_test.go. Add a new test function TestViewAction() to test the viewAction() function using the table-driven testing approach. This function is essentially the same as the TestListAction() you created before. Define the testCases type with three test cases:

apis/todoClient.v1/cmd/actions_test.go

```go
func TestViewAction(t *testing.T) {
  // testCases for ViewAction test
  testCases := []struct {
    name     string
    expError error
    expOut   string
    resp     struct {
      Status int
      Body   string
    }
    id string
  }{
    {name: "ResultsOne",
      expError: nil,
      expOut: `Task:          Task 1
Created at:    Oct/28 @08:23
Completed:     No
`,
      resp: testResp["resultsOne"],
      id:   "1",
    },
    {name: "NotFound",
      expError: ErrNotFound,
      resp:     testResp["notFound"],
      id:       "1",
    },
    {name: "InvalidID",
      expError: ErrNotNumber,
      resp:     testResp["noResults"],
      id:       "a"},
  }
```

The type testCases() is similar to the one you used for the listAction() test except that we don't need to test the server error condition, so we're removing the flag closeServer and adding a new parameter id of type string to specify the item id for the test.

Loop through each test case, executing the function viewAction() and comparing the results with the expected values:

apis/todoClient.v1/cmd/actions_test.go

```go
  // Execute ViewAction test
  for _, tc := range testCases {
    t.Run(tc.name, func(t *testing.T) {
      url, cleanup := mockServer(
        func(w http.ResponseWriter, r *http.Request) {
          w.WriteHeader(tc.resp.Status)
          fmt.Fprintln(w, tc.resp.Body)
        })
      defer cleanup()

      var out bytes.Buffer

      err := viewAction(&out, url, tc.id)

      if tc.expError != nil {
        if err == nil {
          t.Fatalf("Expected error %q, got no error.", tc.expError)
        }

        if ! errors.Is(err, tc.expError) {
          t.Errorf("Expected error %q, got %q.", tc.expError, err)
        }
        return
      }

      if err != nil {
        t.Fatalf("Expected no error, got %q.", err)
      }

      if tc.expOut != out.String() {
        t.Errorf("Expected output %q, got %q", tc.expOut, out.String())
      }
    })
  }
}
```

Save and close the actions_test.go file. Execute the tests with go test -v:

```
$ go test -v ./cmd
=== RUN   TestListAction
=== RUN   TestListAction/Results
=== RUN   TestListAction/NoResults
=== RUN   TestListAction/InvalidURL
--- PASS: TestListAction (0.00s)
    --- PASS: TestListAction/Results (0.00s)
    --- PASS: TestListAction/NoResults (0.00s)
    --- PASS: TestListAction/InvalidURL (0.00s)
=== RUN   TestViewAction
=== RUN   TestViewAction/ResultsOne
=== RUN   TestViewAction/NotFound
=== RUN   TestViewAction/InvalidID
```

```
--- PASS: TestViewAction (0.00s)
    --- PASS: TestViewAction/ResultsOne (0.00s)
    --- PASS: TestViewAction/NotFound (0.00s)
    --- PASS: TestViewAction/InvalidID (0.00s)
PASS
ok        pragprog.com/rggo/apis/todoClient/cmd    0.015s
```

All tests passed, so test the new functionality with the actual API. If you still have the todoServer process running, execute the commands directly. If not, start the server as you did in Testing the Client Without Connecting to the API, on page 308.

Build the new version of the client using go build:

```
$ go build
```

With the server running, list all to-do items with the list command, and then view the details about item number 1 using the view command:

```
$ ./todoClient list
-  1  Task 1
-  2  Task 2
$ ./todoClient view 1
Task:        Task 1
Created at:  May/19 @23:35
Completed:   No
```

You can view the details about to-do items from the REST API using the view command. Next, let's include the ability to add new items to the list.

Adding an Item

So far, your to-do REST API client is able to get all the items from the list and view details about specific items. Let's include the ability to add new items to the list so users can track their new tasks.

To add new tasks to the to-do list using your REST API, the client must send an HTTP POST request to the /todo endpoint containing the task as a JSON payload. For details, consult Completing the REST API Server, on page 283. As usual, obtain this information from the API's documentation to understand their requirements.

Let's define the logic to send the HTTP POST requests in the cmd/client.go file. Edit this file and update the import section by including two new dependencies: the bytes package to use a buffer of bytes as the content body and the io package to use the io.Reader interface:

```
apis/todoClient.v2/cmd/client.go
import (
  "bytes"
  "encoding/json"
  "errors"
  "fmt"

  "io"
  "io/ioutil"
  "net/http"
  "time"
)
```

To create an item, you have to send the HTTP POST request to add a new item, but in Completing and Deleting Items, on page 330, you'll also send other types of requests to complete and delete items. Instead of defining a function that sends the POST request only, you'll use the same approach you used to develop the getItems() function in Developing the Initial Client for the REST API, on page 300, by defining a more generic function sendRequest() that can send many different requests and then using it in a more specific function addItem() that sends the specific request to add a new item to the list.

Define the function sendRequest(). It takes as input the url as string to send the request to, the method also as string representing the HTTP method to use in the request, the contentType as string representing the type of body content to send, the expected HTTP status expStatus as an integer to verify if the response is correct, and the actual content body as the interface io.Reader. It returns a potential error:

```
apis/todoClient.v2/cmd/client.go
func sendRequest(url, method, contentType string,
  expStatus int, body io.Reader) error {
```

The type http.Client we're using to connect to the REST API can issue POST requests directly with its Post() method. But since we're developing a function that can also issue other types of requests, instead of using that method, we'll use the method Do() that can send any type of request. Specify the request's details by instantiating the type http.Request using the function NewRequest() from the http package. Provide the HTTP Method, the target URL, and the request body as inputs:

```
apis/todoClient.v2/cmd/client.go
req, err := http.NewRequest(method, url, body)
if err != nil {
  return err
}
```

By using the Request type, you can also specify additional request headers. If the variable contentType isn't an empty string, set the Content-Type header to its value:

```
apis/todoClient.v2/cmd/client.go
if contentType != "" {
  req.Header.Set("Content-Type", contentType)
}
```

The property Header of the type http.Request is of type http.Header. This type maps a string key, representing the HTTP header to one or more string values. You can use it to set any headers your API call requires. A common use case is setting a header with the API token if the API requires authentication. Consult your API documentation to understand the requirements.

Execute the request by instantiating a new client and using its Do() method, all in a single line. Provide the request req variable that you defined before as input. Check and return any errors that might have occurred:

```
apis/todoClient.v2/cmd/client.go
r, err := newClient().Do(req)
if err != nil {
  return err
}
defer r.Body.Close()
```

If the request is successful, the Do() method returns a pointer to an instance of the type http.Response. We're ensuring the response body will close by deferring the call to its Close() method.

Next, verify the status code received with the Response matches the expected status code expStatus. If not, return the content of the response body as the error message wrapping your predefined error value ErrInvalidResponse or ErrNotFound if the HTTP status is http.StatusNotFound. Return cannot read body if an error reading the body occurs. If the status code matches the expected value, return nil, indicating the function completed successfully.

```
apis/todoClient.v2/cmd/client.go
  if r.StatusCode != expStatus {
    msg, err := ioutil.ReadAll(r.Body)
    if err != nil {
      return fmt.Errorf("Cannot read body: %w", err)
    }
    err = ErrInvalidResponse
    if r.StatusCode == http.StatusNotFound {
      err = ErrNotFound
    }
    return fmt.Errorf("%w: %s", err, msg)
  }

  return nil
}
```

Now define the function addItem() to add the new item to the list. This function takes two input parameters: the apiRoot as string and the task to add to the list also as string. The function also returns an error:

apis/todoClient.v2/cmd/client.go
```
func addItem(apiRoot, task string) error {
```

In the function's body, compose the endpoint URL for this call by adding the suffix /todo to the apiRoot:

apis/todoClient.v2/cmd/client.go
```
// Define the Add endpoint URL
u := fmt.Sprintf("%s/todo", apiRoot)
```

Next, you need to define the body for the request. The to-do API expects to receive the task to add into the list as JSON with a single key-value pair where the key is task and the value is the task to add, like this:

```
{
   "task": "A task to add"
}
```

To encode the JSON, create an anonymous struct type with a single field Task with the value set to the given parameter task. Use the struct tag `json:"task"` to ensure the field is encoded with the proper name, as you did in Completing the REST API Server, on page 283:

apis/todoClient.v2/cmd/client.go
```
item := struct {
   Task string `json:"task"`
}{
   Task: task,
}
```

Because this payload contains a single field, you can use an anonymous struct to represent it. For more complex payloads or if you need to reuse it, you should define a custom type.

Create a variable called body of type bytes.Buffer to encode the payload. This type is a good fit here since it implements both the interface io.Writer required by the JSON NewEncoder() function and the io.Reader interface we need to use as an input for the function sendRequest() you defined before:

apis/todoClient.v2/cmd/client.go
```
var body bytes.Buffer
```

Then, encode the anonymous item struct into JSON by using the Encode() method of the json.Encoder type. Obtain this type by using the NewEncoder() function with the address of the variable &body as input to encode the JSON into this variable. Chain the method calls to execute them all in a single line, returning any errors:

apis/todoClient.v2/cmd/client.go
```
if err := json.NewEncoder(&body).Encode(item); err != nil {
  return err
}
```

Finally, call the function sendRequest() to send the POST request. Use the variable u as the URL, the constant http.MethodPost to specify the HTTP POST method, the value application/json as the content type, the constant http.StatusCreated as the expected response status code, and the address of the variable &body as the request body:

apis/todoClient.v2/cmd/client.go
```
    return sendRequest(u, http.MethodPost, "application/json",
      http.StatusCreated, &body)
}
```

This completes the client code to add a new item. Now, let's implement the command-line option. Save the file cmd/client.go and use the Cobra generator to add a new command add to your tool:

```
$ cobra add add
Using config file: /home/ricardo/.cobra.yaml
add created at /home/ricardo/pragprog.com/rggo/apis/todoClient
```

Edit the generated file cmd/add.go. Update the import section to include the following packages: io to use the io.Writer interface, os to use os.Stdout for output, strings to manipulate string data, and github.com/spf13/viper to get the api-root configuration value:

apis/todoClient.v2/cmd/add.go
```
import (
  "fmt"
➤ "io"
➤ "os"
➤ "strings"
➤
  "github.com/spf13/cobra"
➤ "github.com/spf13/viper"
)
```

Next, update the addCmd command definition according to the command's requirements. Update the Use property and the Short description, remove the Long description, set SilenceUsage to true, and ensure the user provides at least one argument by setting the property Args to cobra.MinimumNArgs(1):

apis/todoClient.v2/cmd/add.go
```
var addCmd = &cobra.Command{
  Use:           "add <task>",
  Short:         "Add a new task to the list",
  SilenceUsage: true,
  Args:          cobra.MinimumNArgs(1),
```

Implement the command's action the same way you've been doing for other Cobra commands. Replace the property Run with RunE to return an error, get the apiRoot value using Viper, and call the addAction() function to execute the action:

apis/todoClient.v2/cmd/add.go
```
  RunE: func(cmd *cobra.Command, args []string) error {
    apiRoot := viper.GetString("api-root")

    return addAction(os.Stdout, apiRoot, args)
  },
}
```

Now define the function addAction() to add the new task to the list. This function joins all given arguments with a space using the strings.Join() function, makes the request to the REST API using the function addItem() you defined before, and if successful then prints a confirmation message using the printAdd() function:

apis/todoClient.v2/cmd/add.go
```
func addAction(out io.Writer, apiRoot string, args []string) error {
  task := strings.Join(args, " ")

  if err := addItem(apiRoot, task); err != nil {
    return err
  }

  return printAdd(out, task)
}
```

Finally, define the function printAdd() to print the confirmation message that the item was included:

apis/todoClient.v2/cmd/add.go
```
func printAdd(out io.Writer, task string) error {
  _, err := fmt.Fprintf(out, "Added task %q to the list.\n", task)
  return err
}
```

The code for adding a new task to the list is complete. Next, let's write the test for it.

Testing HTTP Requests Locally

So far, the tests that you've added to this application focused on the response you obtained from the REST API. This is acceptable as the requests were less complex than the responses for the commands list and view.

For the add command, the scenario is reversed. The simple response has a status and no body, but the request has more details, including a JSON payload and additional headers. We want our tests to ensure the application sends a valid request so we're confident it's going to work properly.

If you were testing this application by connecting directly to the actual API server, it wouldn't be an issue since the server would throw an error if the request was invalid. But since you're testing this locally using a mock HTTP server, the server doesn't validate the request's content.

The mock HTTP server accepts a function as input. Let's use Go's functional nature again and the concept of closures to include the required checks in the function we use when instantiating a new test server. You used a similar concept in Completing the REST API Server, on page 283, to define the todoRouter() function that included the file name to save the list.

Before you do that, edit the file cmd/mock_test.go to include the simulated response for the add operation into the testResp map:

```
apis/todoClient.v2/cmd/mock_test.go
  "notFound": {
    Status: http.StatusNotFound,
    Body:   "404 - not found",
  },

  "created": {
    Status: http.StatusCreated,
    Body:    "",
  },
}
```

Save and close this file, and edit the cmd/actions_test.go file. Add the package io/ioutil to the import list. You'll use this package to read the request's body:

```
apis/todoClient.v2/cmd/actions_test.go
import (
  "bytes"
  "errors"
  "fmt"
```

➤
```
    "io/ioutil"
    "net/http"
    "testing"
)
```

Next, define the test function TestAddAction() to test the add command action. Add the expected values for the request and the arguments variable args to use in the test:

apis/todoClient.v2/cmd/actions_test.go
```
func TestAddAction(t *testing.T) {
  expURLPath := "/todo"
  expMethod := http.MethodPost
  expBody := "{\"task\":\"Task 1\"}\n"
  expContentType := "application/json"
  expOut := "Added task \"Task 1\" to the list.\n"
  args := []string{"Task", "1"}
```

Then use the function mockServer() to instantiate a new test server, providing as input an anonymous function that's compatible with the http.HandlerFunc type, as you did before:

apis/todoClient.v2/cmd/actions_test.go
```
// Instantiate a test server for Add test
url, cleanup := mockServer(
  func(w http.ResponseWriter, r *http.Request) {
```

In this function, before responding to the request, verify the request parameters match the expected values. You can do this because this anonymous function closes on the outside scope, making those variables (such as the *testing.T t) and the expected values available inside the anonymous function.

Start by validating the request URL path r.URL.Path matches the expected value:

apis/todoClient.v2/cmd/actions_test.go
```
if r.URL.Path != expURLPath {
  t.Errorf("Expected path %q, got %q", expURLPath, r.URL.Path)
}
```

Then validate that the request method matches the expected value, in this case, a POST request:

apis/todoClient.v2/cmd/actions_test.go
```
if r.Method != expMethod {
  t.Errorf("Expected method %q, got %q", expMethod, r.Method)
}
```

Next, use the ReadAll() function from the ioutil package to read the entire content of the request body r.Body and verify that it matches the expected body. Close the body after reading it:

```
apis/todoClient.v2/cmd/actions_test.go
body, err := ioutil.ReadAll(r.Body)
if err != nil {
  t.Fatal(err)
}
r.Body.Close()

if string(body) != expBody {
  t.Errorf("Expected body %q, got %q", expBody, string(body))
}
```

Verify that the request header Content-Type matches the expected value application/json. Get the request header by using the method r.Header.Get():

```
apis/todoClient.v2/cmd/actions_test.go
contentType := r.Header.Get("Content-Type")
if contentType != expContentType {
  t.Errorf("Expected Content-Type %q, got %q",
    expContentType, contentType)
}
```

Finally, respond to the request with the content of the created response from the testResp map you defined before:

```
apis/todoClient.v2/cmd/actions_test.go
    w.WriteHeader(testResp["created"].Status)
    fmt.Fprintln(w, testResp["created"].Body)
  })
defer cleanup()
```

Now create a variable out of type bytes.Buffer to capture the output and execute the tests by running the function addAction() and verifying the output matches the expected output. When you execute the addAction() function, it will connect to the test server, executing a handler function that includes the request tests you defined before.

```
apis/todoClient.v2/cmd/actions_test.go
  // Execute Add test
  var out bytes.Buffer

  if err := addAction(&out, url, args); err != nil {
    t.Fatalf("Expected no error, got %q.", err)
  }

  if expOut != out.String() {
    t.Errorf("Expected output %q, got %q", expOut, out.String())
  }
}
```

Save and close the file, and run the tests to ensure the application works as intended:

```
$ go test -v ./cmd
=== RUN    TestListAction
=== RUN    TestListAction/Results
=== RUN    TestListAction/NoResults
=== RUN    TestListAction/InvalidURL
--- PASS: TestListAction (0.00s)
    --- PASS: TestListAction/Results (0.00s)
    --- PASS: TestListAction/NoResults (0.00s)
    --- PASS: TestListAction/InvalidURL (0.00s)
=== RUN    TestViewAction
=== RUN    TestViewAction/ResultsOne
=== RUN    TestViewAction/NotFound
=== RUN    TestViewAction/InvalidID
--- PASS: TestViewAction (0.00s)
    --- PASS: TestViewAction/ResultsOne (0.00s)
    --- PASS: TestViewAction/NotFound (0.00s)
    --- PASS: TestViewAction/InvalidID (0.00s)
=== RUN    TestAddAction
--- PASS: TestAddAction (0.00s)
PASS
ok      pragprog.com/rggo/apis/todoClient/cmd    0.012s
```

The add command works. Let's try it out if you still have the todoServer running from the previous section. If not, start the REST API server now.

Build the client again:

```
$ go build
```

List the current tasks from the server:

```
$ ./todoClient list
-   1   Task 1
-   2   Task 2
```

Add a new task to the list using the new add command:

```
$ ./todoClient add A New Task
Added task "A New Task" to the list.
```

List all the tasks again to verify that the new task was added:

```
$ ./todoClient list
-   1   Task 1
-   2   Task 2
-   3   A New Task
```

The task was added successfully. Next, you'll add the ability to complete and delete tasks from the list.

Completing and Deleting Items

Let's complete the application functionality by adding the two missing features: the complete command to mark an item as done and the del command to delete an item from the list.

According to the to-do REST API requirements, to complete an item you must send an HTTP PATCH request to the endpoint /todo/id?complete, where id is an integer number representing the item in the list. To delete an item from the list, send an HTTP DELETE request to the endpoint /todo/id, where id is again a number that represents the item. For more information on this API's requirements, see Table 1, To-Do REST API Operations, on page 283.

To send those requests, you'll reuse the function sendRequest() you implemented for the add command in Adding an Item, on page 320. Open and edit the file cmd/client.go. Define a new function completeItem() that takes two parameters, the apiRoot as string and id as int. It returns an error. This function uses those two parameters to compose the final URL for the request and then uses the sendRequest() function to send the request to the server:

```
apis/todoClient.v3/cmd/client.go
func completeItem(apiRoot string, id int) error {
  u := fmt.Sprintf("%s/todo/%d?complete", apiRoot, id)

  return sendRequest(u, http.MethodPatch, "", http.StatusNoContent, nil)
}
```

In this function, you use the constant http.MethodPatch as the HTTP method and the constant http.StatusNoContent as the expected HTTP status. This request doesn't require a body, so you set the content type to an empty string and the body as nil.

Define an analogous function deleteItem() to delete the item. Compose the proper URL according to the requirements and use the constant http.MethodDelete to send an HTTP DELETE request:

```
apis/todoClient.v3/cmd/client.go
func deleteItem(apiRoot string, id int) error {
  u := fmt.Sprintf("%s/todo/%d", apiRoot, id)

  return sendRequest(u, http.MethodDelete, "", http.StatusNoContent, nil)
}
```

Now implement the command-line options. Save and close the cmd/client.go file, and use the Cobra generator to add the complete command to your application:

```
$ cobra add complete
Using config file: /home/ricardo/.cobra.yaml
complete created at /home/ricardo/pragprog.com/rggo/apis/todoClient
```

Then edit the generated file cmd/complete.go the same way you did for the previous commands. Update the import section to include the following packages: io to use the io.Writer interface, os to use os.Stdout for output, strconv to convert string to integer, and github.com/spf13/viper to get the api-root configuration value:

apis/todoClient.v3/cmd/complete.go
```go
import (
  "fmt"
➤  "io"
➤  "os"
➤  "strconv"
➤
  "github.com/spf13/cobra"
➤  "github.com/spf13/viper"
)
```

Update the completeCmd command type definition according to the command's requirements. Because this command requires the id to identify the task to complete, the options are similar to the view command you defined in Viewing a Single Item, on page 314. Use the function completeAction() as the action function in the RunE property:

apis/todoClient.v3/cmd/complete.go
```go
var completeCmd = &cobra.Command{
  Use:          "complete <id>",
  Short:        "Marks an item as completed",
  SilenceUsage: true,
  Args:         cobra.ExactArgs(1),
  RunE: func(cmd *cobra.Command, args []string) error {
    apiRoot := viper.GetString("api-root")

    return completeAction(os.Stdout, apiRoot, args[0])
  },
}
```

Next, define the function completeAction() to execute the command action. This function converts the string arg to an integer representing the item id, uses the function completeItem() to make the API call to mark the item as completed, and prints the results using the function printComplete():

apis/todoClient.v3/cmd/complete.go
```go
func completeAction(out io.Writer, apiRoot, arg string) error {
  id, err := strconv.Atoi(arg)
  if err != nil {
    return fmt.Errorf("%w: Item id must be a number", ErrNotNumber)
  }

  if err := completeItem(apiRoot, id); err != nil {
    return err
  }

  return printComplete(out, id)
}
```

Finally, define the function printComplete() to print the results of the complete action:

apis/todoClient.v3/cmd/complete.go
```go
func printComplete(out io.Writer, id int) error {
  _, err := fmt.Fprintf(out, "Item number %d marked as completed.\n", id)
  return err
}
```

Now implement the del command to delete items from the list. Save and close the file cmd/complete.go, and use the Cobra generator one more time to add the command:

```
$ cobra add del
Using config file: /home/ricardo/.cobra.yaml
del created at /home/ricardo/pragprog.com/rggo/apis/todoClient
```

Edit the generated file cmd/del.go the same way you did for the complete command. Update the import section to include the same packages:

apis/todoClient.v3/cmd/del.go
```go
import (
    "fmt"
➤   "io"
➤   "os"
➤   "strconv"
➤
    "github.com/spf13/cobra"
➤   "github.com/spf13/viper"
)
```

Update the delCmd command according to its requirements. This is almost the same as for the completeCmd command with the proper descriptions. Use the function delAction() as the action function:

```
apis/todoClient.v3/cmd/del.go
var delCmd = &cobra.Command{
  Use:          "del <id>",
  Short:        "Deletes an item from the list",
  SilenceUsage: true,
  Args:         cobra.ExactArgs(1),
  RunE: func(cmd *cobra.Command, args []string) error {
    apiRoot := viper.GetString("api-root")

    return delAction(os.Stdout, apiRoot, args[0])
  },
}
```

Next, define the function delAction() to execute the delete action. This function converts the string arg to an integer, uses the function deleteItem() to make the REST API call to delete the item, and prints the results using the function printDel():

```
apis/todoClient.v3/cmd/del.go
func delAction(out io.Writer, apiRoot, arg string) error {
  id, err := strconv.Atoi(arg)
  if err != nil {
    return fmt.Errorf("%w: Item id must be a number", ErrNotNumber)
  }

  if err := deleteItem(apiRoot, id); err != nil {
    return err
  }

  return printDel(out, id)
}
```

Complete this command by defining the function printDel() to print the results of the delete action:

```
apis/todoClient.v3/cmd/del.go
func printDel(out io.Writer, id int) error {
  _, err := fmt.Fprintf(out, "Item number %d deleted.\n", id)
  return err
}
```

Save and close the cmd/del.go file. Let's add the tests for the two new commands.

Both of the new API calls expect a response with the status No Content. Open the file cmd/mock_test.go in your editor and add a new value to the testResp map to simulate this response:

```
apis/todoClient.v3/cmd/mock_test.go
"created": {
  Status: http.StatusCreated,
  Body:    "",
},
```

```
    "noContent": {
      Status: http.StatusNoContent,
      Body:    "",
    },
  }
```

Save and close this file, and edit the cmd/actions_test.go file. Add a new test function TestCompleteAction() to test the complete action. This test function applies the same concept as in Testing HTTP Requests Locally, on page 326, by using a closure to test and ensure the request has the correct parameters:

apis/todoClient.v3/cmd/actions_test.go
```
func TestCompleteAction(t *testing.T) {
  expURLPath := "/todo/1"
  expMethod := http.MethodPatch
  expQuery := "complete"
  expOut := "Item number 1 marked as completed.\n"
  arg := "1"
```

Instantiate the mock API server with the closure function to test the request parameters. In the anonymous function's body, verify the URL path and the request HTTP method, as you did for the add command test. The API request to complete the item includes an URL query parameter. Verify if this expected query parameter exists by using the *comma ok* idiom.[3] Obtain the map with the query parameters by using the method r.URL.Query() of the http.Request type:

apis/todoClient.v3/cmd/actions_test.go
```
// Instantiate a test server for Complete test
url, cleanup := mockServer(
  func(w http.ResponseWriter, r *http.Request) {
    if r.URL.Path != expURLPath {
      t.Errorf("Expected path %q, got %q", expURLPath, r.URL.Path)
    }

    if r.Method != expMethod {
      t.Errorf("Expected method %q, got %q", expMethod, r.Method)
    }

    if _, ok := r.URL.Query()[expQuery]; !ok {
      t.Errorf("Expected query %q not found in URL", expQuery)
    }

    w.WriteHeader(testResp["noContent"].Status)
    fmt.Fprintln(w, testResp["noContent"].Body)
  })
defer cleanup()
```

---

3. golang.org/doc/effective_go.html#maps

Test the function by defining a variable out to capture the output, execute the completeAction() function, and verify the output matches the expected value, failing the test if it doesn't:

apis/todoClient.v3/cmd/actions_test.go
```go
  // Execute Complete test
  var out bytes.Buffer

  if err := completeAction(&out, url, arg); err != nil {
    t.Fatalf("Expected no error, got %q.", err)
  }

  if expOut != out.String() {
    t.Errorf("Expected output %q, got %q", expOut, out.String())
  }
}
```

Finally, add a test function TestDelAction() to test the delete action by applying the same concept. Use the constant http.MethodDelete as the expected method and Item number 1 deleted.\n as the expected output:

apis/todoClient.v3/cmd/actions_test.go
```go
func TestDelAction(t *testing.T) {
  expURLPath := "/todo/1"
  expMethod := http.MethodDelete
  expOut := "Item number 1 deleted.\n"
  arg := "1"

  // Instantiate a test server for Del test
  url, cleanup := mockServer(
    func(w http.ResponseWriter, r *http.Request) {
      if r.URL.Path != expURLPath {
        t.Errorf("Expected path %q, got %q", expURLPath, r.URL.Path)
      }

      if r.Method != expMethod {
        t.Errorf("Expected method %q, got %q", expMethod, r.Method)
      }

      w.WriteHeader(testResp["noContent"].Status)
      fmt.Fprintln(w, testResp["noContent"].Body)
    })
  defer cleanup()
  // Execute Del test
  var out bytes.Buffer

  if err := delAction(&out, url, arg); err != nil {
    t.Fatalf("Expected no error, got %q.", err)
  }

  if expOut != out.String() {
    t.Errorf("Expected output %q, got %q", expOut, out.String())
  }
}
```

Save and close the file cmd/actions_test.go and run the tests using go test:

```
$ go test -v ./cmd
=== RUN    TestListAction
=== RUN    TestListAction/Results
=== RUN    TestListAction/NoResults
=== RUN    TestListAction/InvalidURL
--- PASS: TestListAction (0.00s)
    --- PASS: TestListAction/Results (0.00s)
    --- PASS: TestListAction/NoResults (0.00s)
    --- PASS: TestListAction/InvalidURL (0.00s)
=== RUN    TestViewAction
=== RUN    TestViewAction/ResultsOne
=== RUN    TestViewAction/NotFound
=== RUN    TestViewAction/InvalidID
--- PASS: TestViewAction (0.00s)
    --- PASS: TestViewAction/ResultsOne (0.00s)
    --- PASS: TestViewAction/NotFound (0.00s)
    --- PASS: TestViewAction/InvalidID (0.00s)
=== RUN    TestAddAction
--- PASS: TestAddAction (0.00s)
=== RUN    TestCompleteAction
--- PASS: TestCompleteAction (0.00s)
=== RUN    TestDelAction
--- PASS: TestDelAction (0.00s)
PASS
ok      pragprog.com/rggo/apis/todoClient/cmd    0.015s
```

The local tests passed and the application is almost done. Before we complete it, we need to ensure it works with the actual API by running integration tests.

Executing Integration Tests

As you learned in Testing the Client Without Connecting to the API, on page 308, executing the unit tests locally allows you to execute these tests frequently without touching the actual REST API. This is particularly useful when you're working on a disconnected environment or when using third-party APIs. It also provides a controlled and repeatable environment where you can test different conditions that may not be possible with the actual API, such as error conditions.

This approach has a downside. If you missed a detail about the API or if the API changed, the application may not work properly, but the local tests will make you think it does. To overcome this challenge, you'll run an integration test that connects to the actual API as the last step in your testing process. To ensure that this test doesn't run all the time, you'll use a Go build constraint. You'll learn more about build constraints in Chapter 11, Distributing

Your Tool, on page 433, so, for now, think of a build constraint as a condition that defines whether to include a file when building or testing the application.[4]

For this example, you'll create a new test file cmd/integration_test.go with the build constraint *integration*. This prevents Go from selecting this file and consequently running this test unless you explicitly use the parameter -tags integration when running the tests.

Create and edit a new file called cmd/integration_test.go. Define the build constraint as a comment at the top of the file, before the package definition. Include the package definition as well:

apis/todoClient.v3/cmd/integration_test.go
```
// +build integration

package cmd
```

Add the import list. For this test, you'll use the following packages: bufio to read lines from the output, bytes to create buffers to capture output, fmt to define formatted strings, math/rand to help create a random task name for the test, os to read environment variables, strings to manipulate string data, testing that provides the testing features, and time to deal with time data:

apis/todoClient.v3/cmd/integration_test.go
```
import (
    "bufio"
    "bytes"
    "fmt"
    "math/rand"
    "os"
    "strings"
    "testing"
    "time"
)
```

One of the major challenges when testing with a live REST API is ensuring the test is reproducible. You want to avoid conflicts with existing data exposed by the API, as well as conflicts with other test data. In some cases, you may have control over the REST API, or you may have a separate development environment you can use to test. For this example, we're assuming that you're using a third-party API that you don't control. To deal with this situation, you'll create a random task name that will be different each time you execute the test.

Define a new helper function randomTaskName() that uses the math/rand package and the strings.Builder() type to generate a random 32-character–long string. The

---

4. golang.org/pkg/go/build/#hdr-Build_Constraints

number 32 is arbitrary but should provide enough uniqueness to guarantee no conflict occurs with the existing data or other tests:

apis/todoClient.v3/cmd/integration_test.go
```
func randomTaskName(t *testing.T) string {
  t.Helper()
  const chars = "abcdefghijklmnopqrstuvwxyzABCDEFGHIJKLMNOPQRSTUVWXYZ0123456789"

  r := rand.New(rand.NewSource(time.Now().UnixNano()))

  var p strings.Builder
  for i := 0; i < 32; i++ {
    p.WriteByte(chars[r.Intn(len(chars))])
  }

  return p.String()
}
```

Add the test function TestIntegration() to define the integration test:

apis/todoClient.v3/cmd/integration_test.go
```
func TestIntegration(t *testing.T) {
```

Create a variable called apiRoot with a default value for the REST API root URL, and allow the user to change it by setting the environment variable TODO_API_ROOT:

apis/todoClient.v3/cmd/integration_test.go
```
apiRoot := "http://localhost:8080"

if os.Getenv("TODO_API_ROOT") != "" {
  apiRoot = os.Getenv("TODO_API_ROOT")
}
```

Then define a variable called today that contains the current date formatted with month and day. You'll use this variable to check if the date format in the task details is correct. The task details also include the timestamp hour and minute, but it's tricky to test those if you execute the test when the minute changes. By checking the day only, you minimize that risk, unless you execute the test around midnight:

apis/todoClient.v3/cmd/integration_test.go
```
today := time.Now().Format("Jan/02")
```

Define the task name by using the randomTaskName() function you defined before. Then define an empty variable taskId for setting the task ID later after the task is created using the API:

apis/todoClient.v3/cmd/integration_test.go
```
task := randomTaskName(t)
taskId := ""
```

You're ready to start executing the tests. The integration test workflow is:

1. AddTask
2. ListTasks
3. ViewTask
4. CompleteTask
5. ListCompletedTask
6. DeleteTask
7. ListDeletedTask

Organize each step of the integration test workflow as a subtest using the t.Run() method. Define the first subtest AddTask:

apis/todoClient.v3/cmd/integration_test.go
```go
t.Run("AddTask", func(t *testing.T) {
  args := []string{task}
  expOut := fmt.Sprintf("Added task %q to the list.\n", task)

  // Execute Add test
  var out bytes.Buffer

  if err := addAction(&out, apiRoot, args); err != nil {
    t.Fatalf("Expected no error, got %q.", err)
  }

  if expOut != out.String() {
    t.Errorf("Expected output %q, got %q", expOut, out.String())
  }
})
```

Then define the ListTasks test. Because we don't control the API, we don't know how many items are in the list before the test, so we can't test the number of items or the full command output. Use the bufio.Scanner type to look for the test task name in the list. Fail the test if the task you created in the previous subtest isn't in the list. If the task is in the list, use the function strings.Fields() to split the output by spaces and verify the task isn't completed. Use the same function to extract the task ID to use in the following tests:

apis/todoClient.v3/cmd/integration_test.go
```go
t.Run("ListTasks", func(t *testing.T) {
  var out bytes.Buffer
  if err := listAction(&out, apiRoot); err != nil {
    t.Fatalf("Expected no error, got %q.", err)
  }

  outList := ""
  scanner := bufio.NewScanner(&out)
  for scanner.Scan() {
    if strings.Contains(scanner.Text(), task) {
      outList = scanner.Text()
```

```
        break
    }
  }

  if outList == "" {
    t.Errorf("Task %q is not in the list", task)
  }

  taskCompleteStatus := strings.Fields(outList)[0]

  if taskCompleteStatus != "-" {
    t.Errorf("Expected status %q, got %q", "-", taskCompleteStatus)
  }

  taskId = strings.Fields(outList)[1]
})
```

Now define the ViewTask subtest to view the task details. Capture its return value, assigning it to the variable vRes. Later, you'll use this output to decide whether to continue the tests. Use the taskId variable you set in the previous test. Split the output by line using the function strings.Split(), and then verify that the content of each line corresponds to the expected output, including the task name, date, and completion status. Fail the test using the t.Fatalf() function to stop the subtest immediately:

apis/todoClient.v3/cmd/integration_test.go
```
vRes := t.Run("ViewTask", func(t *testing.T) {
  var out bytes.Buffer
  if err := viewAction(&out, apiRoot, taskId); err != nil {
    t.Fatalf("Expected no error, got %q.", err)
  }

  viewOut := strings.Split(out.String(), "\n")

  if !strings.Contains(viewOut[0], task) {
    t.Fatalf("Expected task %q, got %q", task, viewOut[0])
  }

  if !strings.Contains(viewOut[1], today) {
    t.Fatalf("Expected creation day/month %q, got %q", today, viewOut[1])
  }

  if !strings.Contains(viewOut[2], "No") {
    t.Fatalf("Expected completed status %q, got %q", "No", viewOut[2])
  }
})
```

Verify that the previous subtest failed to complete, and fail the test here to prevent the rest of the subtests from running. This is a safeguard to ensure the next test doesn't update or delete the incorrect item:

```
apis/todoClient.v3/cmd/integration_test.go
if !vRes {
  t.Fatalf("View task failed. Stopping integration tests.")
}
```

Next, define the CompleteTask test to mark the item as completed. Verify the output and fail the test if it doesn't match the expected value:

```
apis/todoClient.v3/cmd/integration_test.go
t.Run("CompleteTask", func(t *testing.T) {
  var out bytes.Buffer
  if err := completeAction(&out, apiRoot, taskId); err != nil {
    t.Fatalf("Expected no error, got %q.", err)
  }

  expOut := fmt.Sprintf("Item number %s marked as completed.\n", taskId)

  if expOut != out.String() {
    t.Fatalf("Expected output %q, got %q", expOut, out.String())
  }
})
```

Add the next subtest ListCompletedTask. This is similar to the previous ListTasks subtest, but it verifies that the task is completed instead. You don't need to set the task ID again:

```
apis/todoClient.v3/cmd/integration_test.go
t.Run("ListCompletedTask", func(t *testing.T) {
  var out bytes.Buffer
  if err := listAction(&out, apiRoot); err != nil {
    t.Fatalf("Expected no error, got %q.", err)
  }

  outList := ""
  scanner := bufio.NewScanner(&out)
  for scanner.Scan() {
    if strings.Contains(scanner.Text(), task) {
      outList = scanner.Text()
      break
    }
  }

  if outList == "" {
    t.Errorf("Task %q is not in the list", task)
  }

  taskCompleteStatus := strings.Fields(outList)[0]

  if taskCompleteStatus != "X" {
    t.Errorf("Expected status %q, got %q", "X", taskCompleteStatus)
  }
})
```

Then add the subtest DeleteTask to delete the task from the list. Since this is a destructive test, ensure safeguards are around it to prevent any data loss. In our case, we would stop the test before this point if the task details don't match the expected values. In other cases, you may need to perform additional checks before running this type of test:

```
apis/todoClient.v3/cmd/integration_test.go
t.Run("DeleteTask", func(t *testing.T) {
  var out bytes.Buffer
  if err := delAction(&out, apiRoot, taskId); err != nil {
    t.Fatalf("Expected no error, got %q.", err)
  }

  expOut := fmt.Sprintf("Item number %s deleted.\n", taskId)

  if expOut != out.String() {
    t.Fatalf("Expected output %q, got %q", expOut, out.String())
  }
})
```

Finally, define the subtest ListDeletedTask. This is a modified version of the List-Tasks subtest, but, this time, you're expecting to not find the item in the list:

```
apis/todoClient.v3/cmd/integration_test.go
t.Run("ListDeletedTask", func(t *testing.T) {
  var out bytes.Buffer
  if err := listAction(&out, apiRoot); err != nil {
    t.Fatalf("Expected no error, got %q.", err)
  }

  scanner := bufio.NewScanner(&out)
  for scanner.Scan() {
    if strings.Contains(scanner.Text(), task) {
      t.Errorf("Task %q is still in the list", task)
      break
    }
  }
})
```

This completes the definition of the integration tests. In some situations, you may need to perform additional cleanup actions after your tests. In our scenario, since your tests delete the task, you don't need to do anything else.

Before executing the integration tests, let's add a build constraint to the local tests to prevent them from executing when running the integration tests. Save and close the cmd/integration_test.go file, and edit the cmd/actions_test.go file. Add the build constraint // +build !integration as the first line in the file. The exclamation point ! character before the constraint name integration negates it. In this case, this file isn't included in the build (or tests) when using the tag integration:

apis/todoClient.v3/cmd/actions_test.go
```
// +build !integration

package cmd
```

Save and close the file cmd/actions_test.go, and execute the integration tests using the go test command with the -tags integration option to include the integration tests and exclude the local tests:

```
$ go test -v ./cmd -tags integration
=== RUN    TestIntegration
=== RUN    TestIntegration/AddTask
=== RUN    TestIntegration/ListTasks
=== RUN    TestIntegration/ViewTask
=== RUN    TestIntegration/CompleteTask
=== RUN    TestIntegration/ListCompletedTask
=== RUN    TestIntegration/DeleteTask
=== RUN    TestIntegration/ListDeletedTask
--- PASS: TestIntegration (0.01s)
    --- PASS: TestIntegration/AddTask (0.00s)
    --- PASS: TestIntegration/ListTasks (0.00s)
    --- PASS: TestIntegration/ViewTask (0.00s)
    --- PASS: TestIntegration/CompleteTask (0.00s)
    --- PASS: TestIntegration/ListCompletedTask (0.00s)
    --- PASS: TestIntegration/DeleteTask (0.00s)
    --- PASS: TestIntegration/ListDeletedTask (0.00s)
PASS
ok      pragprog.com/rggo/apis/todoClient/cmd    0.016s
```

If you execute the tests a second time, Go provides cached results to improve the speed if the code didn't change since the first test execution. You can see this when the test results include the word (cached):

```
$ go test ./cmd -tags integration
ok      pragprog.com/rggo/apis/todoClient/cmd    (cached)
```

While this is a useful feature when running unit tests, it may not be desired when running the integration tests, as you want to touch the API to ensure it didn't change. To make sure Go doesn't provide cached results for the integration tests, append the option -count=1 to the go test command:

```
$ go test ./cmd -tags integration -count=1
ok      pragprog.com/rggo/apis/todoClient/cmd    0.013s
```

If you execute the tests without the -tags integration option, Go executes only the local tests. Since this is the default, you can control when to execute the integration tests:

```
$ go test -v ./cmd
=== RUN     TestListAction
=== RUN     TestListAction/Results
=== RUN     TestListAction/NoResults
=== RUN     TestListAction/InvalidURL
--- PASS: TestListAction (0.00s)
    --- PASS: TestListAction/Results (0.00s)
    --- PASS: TestListAction/NoResults (0.00s)
    --- PASS: TestListAction/InvalidURL (0.00s)
=== RUN     TestViewAction
=== RUN     TestViewAction/ResultsOne
=== RUN     TestViewAction/NotFound
=== RUN     TestViewAction/InvalidID
--- PASS: TestViewAction (0.00s)
    --- PASS: TestViewAction/ResultsOne (0.00s)
    --- PASS: TestViewAction/NotFound (0.00s)
    --- PASS: TestViewAction/InvalidID (0.00s)
=== RUN     TestAddAction
--- PASS: TestAddAction (0.00s)
=== RUN     TestCompleteAction
--- PASS: TestCompleteAction (0.00s)
=== RUN     TestDelAction
--- PASS: TestDelAction (0.00s)
PASS
ok      pragprog.com/rggo/apis/todoClient/cmd    (cached)
```

Try your application now. Build it with go build:

```
$ go build
```

This assumes the todoServer from the previous section is still running. If not, start it now:

```
$ cd $HOME/pragprog.com/rggo/apis/todoServer
$ ./todoServer -f /tmp/testtodoclient01.json
```

In a different terminal, list the existing tasks:

```
$ cd $HOME/pragprog.com/rggo/apis/todoClient
$ ./todoClient list
-  1  Task 1
-  2  Task 2
-  3  A New Task
```

Complete task number 2:

```
$ ./todoClient complete 2
Item number 2 marked as completed.
$ ./todoClient list
-  1  Task 1
X  2  Task 2
-  3  A New Task
```

Delete item number 3:

```
$ ./todoClient del 3
Item number 3 deleted.
$ ./todoClient list
-  1  Task 1
X  2  Task 2
```

This completes your REST API client command-line application.

Exercises

Before you move on, you may want to expand the skills and techniques you've explored in this chapter. Here are some suggestions:

* Add a flag --active to the list command to display only active tasks that aren't completed.

* Create a command-line tool that queries data from an API over the Internet using the principles you learned in this chapter. Some good starting points are the Movie DB[5] or the Open Weather API.[6]

Wrapping Up

In this chapter, you used the Cobra framework and the net/http package to develop a command-line application that interacts with a remote REST API using different techniques and options. You also used the encoding/json package to parse JSON data. These skills allow you to gather data from a variety of sources on the Internet or from your environment to create powerful and flexible tools.

You also explored and applied several techniques for testing your API server and your command-line client implementation. By combining unit tests with simulated responses and test servers, you can execute constant local tests while using integration tests sporadically to ensure your application works reliably across different environments.

In the next chapter, you'll develop an interactive terminal application.

---

5. www.themoviedb.org/documentation/api
6. openweathermap.org/api

## CHAPTER 9

Developing Interactive Terminal Tools

So far, you've built applications that run mostly unattended. This is one of the major benefits of command-line tools: you provide the required parameters, the tool performs some actions, and it then provides you with the results. But some applications are better suited for an interactive workflow where the user provides or receives feedback continuously, like the kinds of applications in a graphical user interface (GUI).

In this chapter, you'll develop an interactive Pomodoro timer application. The Pomodoro[1] is a time management approach that allows you to focus on tasks by defining a short time interval to concentrate on it, called Pomodoro, followed by short and long breaks to allow you to rest and reprioritize tasks. In general, a Pomodoro interval lasts 25 minutes while breaks are typically 5 and 15 minutes.

Instead of developing a full GUI, you'll design and implement an interactive CLI application that runs directly on a terminal. Compared to full GUI applications, interactive CLI apps use fewer resources, and often require fewer dependencies, making them more portable. Examples of this type of application include system monitoring applications, such as top or htop, and interactive disk utilities, such as ncdu.

For your Pomodoro application, you'll implement the Repository pattern[2] to abstract the data source, decoupling the business logic from the data. This way you can implement different data stores according to your requirements. For instance, in this chapter, you'll implement an in-memory data store for this application. Later in Chapter 10, Persisting Data in a SQL Database, on page 395, you'll expand this application by implementing another repository backed up by a SQL database.

---

1. en.wikipedia.org/wiki/Pomodoro_Technique
2. martinfowler.com/eaaCatalog/repository.html

At the end of this chapter, your Pomodoro tool will look like Figure 12:

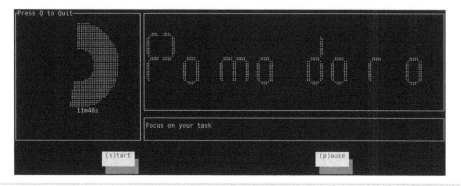

Figure 12—Pomodoro Screen

After you add the summary widgets in Chapter 10, Persisting Data in a SQL Database, on page 395, the complete tool will look like Figure 13:

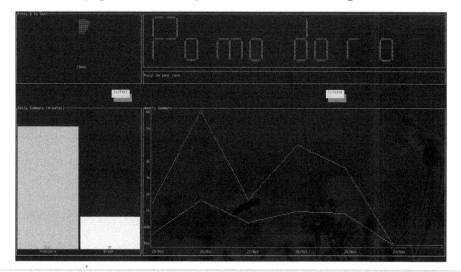

Figure 13—Pomodoro Screen with Summary

Let's start by developing the business logic for the application.

Initializing the Pomodoro Application

Start by creating the directory structure for your Pomodoro application under your book's root directory:

```
$ mkdir -p $HOME/pragprog.com/rggo/interactiveTools/pomo
$ cd $HOME/pragprog.com/rggo/interactiveTools/pomo
```

Next, initialize the Go module for this project:

```
$ cd $HOME/pragprog.com/rggo/interactiveTools/pomo
$ go mod init pragprog.com/rggo/interactiveTools/pomo
go: creating new go.mod: module pragprog.com/rggo/interactiveTools/pomo
```

Let's start this application by developing the pomodoro package that contains the business logic to create and use the pomodoro timer. By creating a separate package for the business logic, you can test it independently of the user interface and use the same package in other projects. Create the subdirectory pomodoro in your project directory and switch to it:

```
$ mkdir -p $HOME/pragprog.com/rggo/interactiveTools/pomo/pomodoro
$ cd $HOME/pragprog.com/rggo/interactiveTools/pomo/pomodoro
```

In this directory, create the file interval.go, which is where you'll put the timer functionality. The Pomodoro technique records time in intervals that can be of different types such as *Pomodoro, short breaks,* or *long breaks*. Open this file in your text editor and add the package definition and import section. You'll use the following packages: context to carry context and cancellation signals from the user interface, errors to define custom errors, fmt to format output, and time to handle time-related data:

interactiveTools/pomo/pomodoro/interval.go
```
package pomodoro

import (
  "context"
  "errors"
  "fmt"
  "time"
)
```

Next, define two sets of constants to represent the different categories and states for a Pomodoro interval. Start with the category. As mentioned before, a Pomodoro interval can be one of three categories: *Pomodoro, short break,* or *long break*. Create a set of constants CategoryPomodoro, CategoryShortBreak, and CategoryLongBreak to represent them:

interactiveTools/pomo/pomodoro/interval.go
```
// Category constants
const (
  CategoryPomodoro   = "Pomodoro"
  CategoryShortBreak = "ShortBreak"
  CategoryLongBreak  = "LongBreak"
)
```

Then, add the constant set for the state. Represent the state as an integer number to save space when saving this data in a database. This isn't critical for this specific application, but we'll use it as an example of a different data type later in Chapter 10, Persisting Data in a SQL Database, on page 395. Your pomodoro interval can be one of five states: StateNotStarted, StateRunning, StatePaused, StateDone, or StateCancelled. Use the iota operator to define sequential values like this:

interactiveTools/pomo/pomodoro/interval.go
```
// State constants
const (
  StateNotStarted = iota
  StateRunning
  StatePaused
  StateDone
  StateCancelled
)
```

By using the iota operator, Go automatically increases the number for each line, resulting in a set of constants from zero (0) for StateNotStarted to five (5) for StateCancelled. Now define a custom struct type named Interval to represent the pomodoro interval:

interactiveTools/pomo/pomodoro/interval.go
```
type Interval struct {
  ID               int64
  StartTime        time.Time
  PlannedDuration  time.Duration
  ActualDuration   time.Duration
  Category         string
  State            int
}
```

As you saw in this chapter's introduction, you'll use the Repository pattern for this application, starting in Storing Data with the Repository Pattern, on page 356. To allow for that, abstract the data source by defining the Repository interface here. This interface defines the methods Create() to create an interval, Update() to update the interval, ByID() to retrieve an interval by its ID, Last() to find the last interval, and Breaks() to retrieve intervals of type break. Define the interface like this:

interactiveTools/pomo/pomodoro/interval.go
```
type Repository interface {
  Create(i Interval) (int64, error)
  Update(i Interval) error
  ByID(id int64) (Interval, error)
  Last() (Interval, error)
  Breaks(n int) ([]Interval, error)
}
```

Then define new error values for this package representing particular errors that it may return. For this application, we're especially interested in verifying errors that might occur in the business logic or during tests. For brevity, this isn't a comprehensive set:

interactiveTools/pomo/pomodoro/interval.go
```go
var (
  ErrNoIntervals = errors.New("No intervals")
  ErrIntervalNotRunning = errors.New("Interval not running")
  ErrIntervalCompleted = errors.New("Interval is completed or cancelled")
  ErrInvalidState = errors.New("Invalid State")
  ErrInvalidID = errors.New("Invalid ID")
)
```

Next, define the custom type IntervalConfig representing the configuration required to instantiate an interval. This type allows users to provide the desired duration for each interval type and the data store repository to use:

interactiveTools/pomo/pomodoro/interval.go
```go
type IntervalConfig struct {
  repo              Repository
  PomodoroDuration  time.Duration
  ShortBreakDuration time.Duration
  LongBreakDuration  time.Duration
}
```

Add a new function NewConfig() to instantiate a new IntervalConfig. This function uses the values provided by the user or sets default values for each interval type in case the user doesn't provide them:

interactiveTools/pomo/pomodoro/interval.go
```go
func NewConfig(repo Repository, pomodoro, shortBreak,
  longBreak time.Duration) *IntervalConfig {

  c := &IntervalConfig{
    repo:              repo,
    PomodoroDuration:  25 * time.Minute,
    ShortBreakDuration: 5 * time.Minute,
    LongBreakDuration:  15 * time.Minute,
  }

  if pomodoro > 0 {
    c.PomodoroDuration = pomodoro
  }

  if shortBreak > 0 {
    c.ShortBreakDuration = shortBreak
  }

  if longBreak > 0 {
    c.LongBreakDuration = longBreak
  }

  return c
}
```

Next, you'll create a set of functions and methods to deal with the main Interval type. Start with the internal, non-exported functions. The first function, nextCategory(), takes a reference to the repository as input and returns the next interval category as a string or an error:

interactiveTools/pomo/pomodoro/interval.go

```
func nextCategory(r Repository) (string, error) {
  li, err := r.Last()
  if err != nil && err == ErrNoIntervals {
    return CategoryPomodoro, nil
  }
  if err != nil {
    return "", err
  }

  if li.Category == CategoryLongBreak || li.Category == CategoryShortBreak {
    return CategoryPomodoro, nil
  }

  lastBreaks, err := r.Breaks(3)
  if err != nil {
    return "", err
  }

  if len(lastBreaks) < 3 {
    return CategoryShortBreak, nil
  }

  for _, i := range lastBreaks {
    if i.Category == CategoryLongBreak {
      return CategoryShortBreak, nil
    }
  }

  return CategoryLongBreak, nil
}
```

This function retrieves the last interval from the repository and determines the next interval category based on the Pomodoro Technique rules. After each Pomodoro interval, there's a short break, and after four Pomodoros, there's a long break. If the function can't find the last interval, for example, for the first execution, it returns the category CategoryPomodoro.

Next comes the tick() function that controls the timer for each interval's execution. Controlling time is the main goal of a Pomodoro application, but doing only this isn't useful. We want to provide a way for callers of this package to perform tasks while the interval executes. These tasks are useful for providing feedback to users, such as updating a screen with a timer or another visual indicator, or notifying the users about something. To enable this functionality, this package allows callers to pass callback functions to execute during the interval. Before defining the tick() function, define a new exported type Callback with the underlying type func(Interval). The Callback function accepts an instance of type Interval as input and returns no values:

interactiveTools/pomo/pomodoro/interval.go

```
type Callback func(Interval)
```

Now define the tick() function to control the interval timer. This function takes as input an instance of context.Context that indicates a cancellation, the id of the Interval to control, an instance of the configuration IntervalConfig, and three Callback functions that you defined before (one to execute at the start, one at the end, and one periodically). This function returns an error:

interactiveTools/pomo/pomodoro/interval.go

```
func tick(ctx context.Context, id int64, config *IntervalConfig,
  start, periodic, end Callback) error {

  ticker := time.NewTicker(time.Second)
  defer ticker.Stop()

  i, err := config.repo.ByID(id)
  if err != nil {
    return err
  }
  expire := time.After(i.PlannedDuration - i.ActualDuration)

  start(i)

  for {
    select {
    case <-ticker.C:
      i, err := config.repo.ByID(id)
      if err != nil {
        return err
      }

      if i.State == StatePaused {
        return nil
      }

      i.ActualDuration += time.Second
      if err := config.repo.Update(i); err != nil {
        return err
      }
      periodic(i)
    case <-expire:
      i, err := config.repo.ByID(id)
      if err != nil {
        return err
      }
      i.State = StateDone
      end(i)
      return config.repo.Update(i)
```

```
      case <-ctx.Done():
        i, err := config.repo.ByID(id)
        if err != nil {
          return err
        }
        i.State = StateCancelled
        return config.repo.Update(i)
      }
    }
  }
```

This function uses the time.Ticker type and a loop to execute actions every
second while the interval time progresses. It uses a select statement to take
actions, executing periodically when the time.Ticker goes off, finishing successfully when the interval time expires, or canceling when a signal is received
from Context.

The last non-exported function in this package, newInterval(), takes an instance
of the config IntervalConfig and returns a new Interval instance with the appropriate
category and values:

interactiveTools/pomo/pomodoro/interval.go
```
func newInterval(config *IntervalConfig) (Interval, error) {
  i := Interval{}
  category, err := nextCategory(config.repo)
  if err != nil {
    return i, err
  }

  i.Category = category

  switch category {
  case CategoryPomodoro:
    i.PlannedDuration = config.PomodoroDuration
  case CategoryShortBreak:
    i.PlannedDuration = config.ShortBreakDuration
  case CategoryLongBreak:
    i.PlannedDuration = config.LongBreakDuration
  }

  if i.ID, err = config.repo.Create(i); err != nil {
    return i, err
  }

  return i, nil
}
```

Once you have the private functions in place, define the API for the Interval
type. It consists of three exported functions: GetInterval(), Start(), and Pause().
First, define the GetInterval() function, which takes an instance of IntervalConfig
as input, and returns either an instance of the Interval type or an error:

interactiveTools/pomo/pomodoro/interval.go
```go
func GetInterval(config *IntervalConfig) (Interval, error) {
  i := Interval{}
  var err error

  i, err = config.repo.Last()

  if err != nil && err != ErrNoIntervals {
    return i, err
  }

  if err == nil && i.State != StateCancelled && i.State != StateDone {
    return i, nil
  }

  return newInterval(config)
}
```

This function attempts to retrieve the last interval from the repository, returning it if it's active or returning an error when there's an issue accessing the repository. If the last interval is inactive or unavailable, this function returns a new interval using the previously defined function newInterval().

Next, define the Start() method that callers use to start the interval timer. This function checks the state of the current interval setting the appropriate options and then calls the tick() function to time the interval. This function takes the same input parameters as the tick() function, including the callbacks to pass to tick() when required. It returns an error:

interactiveTools/pomo/pomodoro/interval.go
```go
func (i Interval) Start(ctx context.Context, config *IntervalConfig,
  start, periodic, end Callback) error {

  switch i.State {
  case StateRunning:
    return nil
  case StateNotStarted:
    i.StartTime = time.Now()
    fallthrough
  case StatePaused:
    i.State = StateRunning
    if err := config.repo.Update(i); err != nil {
      return err
    }
    return tick(ctx, i.ID, config, start, periodic, end)
  case StateCancelled, StateDone:
    return fmt.Errorf("%w: Cannot start", ErrIntervalCompleted)
  default:
    return fmt.Errorf("%w: %d", ErrInvalidState, i.State)
  }
}
```

Finally, define the Pause() method that callers use to pause a running interval. This function takes an instance of IntervalConfig as input and returns an error. It verifies whether the instance of Interval is running and pauses it by setting the state to StatePaused:

```
interactiveTools/pomo/pomodoro/interval.go
func (i Interval) Pause(config *IntervalConfig) error {
  if i.State != StateRunning {
    return ErrIntervalNotRunning
  }

  i.State = StatePaused

  return config.repo.Update(i)
}
```

This completes the business logic for the Pomodoro timer. Next, you'll implement a data source to save data using the Repository pattern.

Storing Data with the Repository Pattern

Let's implement a data store for Pomodoro intervals using the Repository pattern. With this approach, you decouple the data store implementation from the business logic, granting you flexibility for how you'll store data. You can modify the implementation later or switch to a different database entirely, without impacting the business logic.

For instance, you'll implement two different data stores with this application: an in-memory data store and another data store backed up by a SQLite database. Later you can implement another data store backed up by a different database such as PostgreSQL if you want.

The Repository pattern requires two components. One is an interface that specifies all the methods that a given type must implement to qualify as a repository for this application. The other is a custom type which implements that interface working as the repository.

First, define the repository interface, in the same package where you use it. For this case, you already defined the Repository interface in Initializing the Pomodoro Application, on page 348. As a reminder, the Repository interface specifies these methods:

- Create(): Creates/saves a new Interval in the data store.
- Update(): Updates details about an Interval in the data store.
- Last(): Retrieves the last Interval from the data store.
- ByID(): Retrieves a specific Interval from the data store by its ID.

- Breaks(): Retrieves a given number of Interval items from the data store that matches CategoryLongBreak or CategoryShortBreak.

Let's implement the in-memory data store, which will store the data using Go slices. With this method, the data doesn't persist when the application stops. This is useful for testing or as an initial example, but you can also use it to store data that you don't need to keep between sessions.

Implement the repository using a separate package to avoid duplication and potential circular dependencies. Create a directory for the repository package under the pomodoro directory:

```
$ mkdir -p $HOME/pragprog.com/rggo/interactiveTools/pomo/pomodoro/repository
$ cd $HOME/pragprog.com/rggo/interactiveTools/pomo/pomodoro/repository
```

Create and edit the file inMemory.go in this directory. Begin by defining the package definition and the import list. For this file, you'll use the fmt package to format errors, the sync package to prevent conflicts when executing this code concurrently, and the pomodoro package you created before to use the Interval type:

interactiveTools/pomo/pomodoro/repository/inMemory.go
```go
package repository

import (
  "fmt"
  "sync"

  "pragprog.com/rggo/interactiveTools/pomo/pomodoro"
)
```

Now define the inMemoryRepo type that represents your in-memory repository. You'll implement all the Repository methods on this type to use it as a repository for the Pomodoro app. This type has one field, intervals of type slice of pomodoro. Interval, to store the intervals in memory. In addition, this type embeds the sync.RWMutex type, which lets you access its methods directly from the inMemoryRepo type. You'll use mutexes to prevent concurrent access to the data store:

interactiveTools/pomo/pomodoro/repository/inMemory.go
```go
type inMemoryRepo struct {
  sync.RWMutex
  intervals []pomodoro.Interval
}
```

This type has no exported fields, and it's not exported itself. By doing this, you ensure that callers can only access it through the exported methods that compose the Repository interface, guaranteeing data consistency.

Next, create the NewInMemoryRepo() function that instantiates a new inMemoryRepo type with an empty slice of pomodoro.Interval:

```
interactiveTools/pomo/pomodoro/repository/inMemory.go
func NewInMemoryRepo() *inMemoryRepo {
  return &inMemoryRepo{
    intervals: []pomodoro.Interval{},
  }
}
```

Then implement all the methods that compose the Repository interface. Start with the Create() method that takes an instance of pomodoro.Interval as input, saves its values to the data store, and returns the ID of the saved entry:

```
interactiveTools/pomo/pomodoro/repository/inMemory.go
func (r *inMemoryRepo) Create(i pomodoro.Interval) (int64, error) {
  r.Lock()
  defer r.Unlock()

  i.ID = int64(len(r.intervals)) + 1

  r.intervals = append(r.intervals, i)

  return i.ID, nil
}
```

Because slices are not concurrent-safe, we're using the mutex lock to prevent concurrent access to the data store while making changes to it. You'll do the same for all methods.

Next, define the Update() method that updates the values of an existing entry in the data store:

```
interactiveTools/pomo/pomodoro/repository/inMemory.go
func (r *inMemoryRepo) Update(i pomodoro.Interval) error {
  r.Lock()
  defer r.Unlock()
  if i.ID == 0 {
    return fmt.Errorf("%w: %d", pomodoro.ErrInvalidID, i.ID)
  }

  r.intervals[i.ID-1] = i
  return nil
}
```

Implement the ByID() method to retrieve and return an item by its ID:

```
interactiveTools/pomo/pomodoro/repository/inMemory.go
func (r *inMemoryRepo) ByID(id int64) (pomodoro.Interval, error) {
  r.RLock()
  defer r.RUnlock()
  i := pomodoro.Interval{}
  if id == 0 {
    return i, fmt.Errorf("%w: %d", pomodoro.ErrInvalidID, id)
  }
```

```
    i = r.intervals[id-1]
    return i, nil
}
```

Add the method Last() to retrieve and return the last Interval from the data store:

interactiveTools/pomo/pomodoro/repository/inMemory.go
```
func (r *inMemoryRepo) Last() (pomodoro.Interval, error) {
  r.RLock()
  defer r.RUnlock()
  i := pomodoro.Interval{}
  if len(r.intervals) == 0 {
    return i, pomodoro.ErrNoIntervals
  }

  return r.intervals[len(r.intervals)-1], nil
}
```

Finally, implement the Breaks() method to retrieve a given number n of Intervals of category break:

interactiveTools/pomo/pomodoro/repository/inMemory.go
```
func (r *inMemoryRepo) Breaks(n int) ([]pomodoro.Interval, error) {
  r.RLock()
  defer r.RUnlock()
  data := []pomodoro.Interval{}
  for k := len(r.intervals) - 1; k >= 0; k-- {
    if r.intervals[k].Category == pomodoro.CategoryPomodoro {
      continue
    }

    data = append(data, r.intervals[k])

    if len(data) == n {
      return data, nil
    }
  }

  return data, nil
}
```

Your first implementation of the repository is ready. Now it's time to write some tests for the Pomodoro package.

Testing the Pomodoro Functionality

Now that you have both implementations for the Pomodoro business logic and the in-memory repository, let's write some tests for the business logic.

For brevity, you'll add tests for the business logic only, which will indirectly test the repository when it's used. For a real production application, we recommend that you write unit tests for the repository implementation as well.

Some of these tests require access to the repository. Because you can have different implementations of the repository, first let's create a helper function getRepo() to get an instance of the repository. You can implement different versions of this function for the different repository implementations without changing the test code. To do this, switch back to the pomodoro package directory and create a file named inmemory_test.go:

```
$ cd $HOME/pragprog.com/rggo/interactiveTools/pomo/pomodoro
```

Open the inmemory_test.go file in your editor to write the specific function for this repository implementation. Add the package definition and import section. You'll use the testing package for the testing-related functions, and you'll also use pomodoro and repository so you can use the repository:

interactiveTools/pomo/pomodoro/inmemory_test.go
```go
package pomodoro_test

import (
  "testing"

  "pragprog.com/rggo/interactiveTools/pomo/pomodoro"
  "pragprog.com/rggo/interactiveTools/pomo/pomodoro/repository"
)
```

Finally, define the function getRepo() that returns the repository instance and a cleanup function. The in-memory repository doesn't require a cleanup function so return an empty function:

interactiveTools/pomo/pomodoro/inmemory_test.go
```go
func getRepo(t *testing.T) (pomodoro.Repository, func()) {
  t.Helper()

  return repository.NewInMemoryRepo(), func() {}
}
```

Save and close this file. Create and edit the main test file interval_test.go. Add the package and import definitions. For these tests, you'll use the following packages: context to define contexts that carry cancellation signals, fmt to format errors and output, testing for the test-related functions, time to handle and compare time-related data, and pomodoro to access Pomodoro's functionality for testing:

interactiveTools/pomo/pomodoro/interval_test.go
```go
package pomodoro_test

import (
  "context"
  "errors"
  "fmt"
  "testing"
  "time"
```

```
    "pragprog.com/rggo/interactiveTools/pomo/pomodoro"
)
```

Add the first test, TestNewConfig(), to test the NewConfig() function. For this test, you'll use the table-driven approach you first used in Testing with Table-Driven Testing, on page 82. Declare the function, and then add the anonymous struct with three test cases: *Default* to test setting the default values, *SingleInput* to test that the function takes a single input and sets the config accordingly, and *MultiInput* to test that it sets all the input values:

interactiveTools/pomo/pomodoro/interval_test.go
```go
func TestNewConfig(t *testing.T) {
  testCases := []struct {
    name    string
    input   [3]time.Duration
    expect  pomodoro.IntervalConfig
  }{
    {name: "Default",
      expect: pomodoro.IntervalConfig{
        PomodoroDuration:   25 * time.Minute,
        ShortBreakDuration: 5 * time.Minute,
        LongBreakDuration:  15 * time.Minute,
      },
    },
    {name: "SingleInput",
      input: [3]time.Duration{
        20 * time.Minute,
      },
      expect: pomodoro.IntervalConfig{
        PomodoroDuration:   20 * time.Minute,
        ShortBreakDuration: 5 * time.Minute,
        LongBreakDuration:  15 * time.Minute,
      },
    },
    {name: "MultiInput",
      input: [3]time.Duration{
        20 * time.Minute,
        10 * time.Minute,
        12 * time.Minute,
      },
      expect: pomodoro.IntervalConfig{
        PomodoroDuration:   20 * time.Minute,
        ShortBreakDuration: 10 * time.Minute,
        LongBreakDuration:  12 * time.Minute,
      },
    },
  }
}
```

Next, execute the tests by looping through all the test cases and by using the method t.Run() to execute each test. For each case, use the function pomodoro. NewConfig() to instantiate a new configuration using the input values from the test case. Then, assert that the config has the correct values, failing the test if it doesn't:

interactiveTools/pomo/pomodoro/interval_test.go
```go
// Execute tests for NewConfig
for _, tc := range testCases {
  t.Run(tc.name, func(t *testing.T) {
    var repo pomodoro.Repository
    config := pomodoro.NewConfig(
      repo,
      tc.input[0],
      tc.input[1],
      tc.input[2],
    )

    if config.PomodoroDuration != tc.expect.PomodoroDuration {
      t.Errorf("Expected Pomodoro Duration %q, got %q instead\n",
        tc.expect.PomodoroDuration, config.PomodoroDuration)
    }
    if config.ShortBreakDuration != tc.expect.ShortBreakDuration {
      t.Errorf("Expected ShortBreak Duration %q, got %q instead\n",
        tc.expect.ShortBreakDuration, config.ShortBreakDuration)
    }
    if config.LongBreakDuration != tc.expect.LongBreakDuration {
      t.Errorf("Expected LongBreak Duration %q, got %q instead\n",
        tc.expect.LongBreakDuration, config.LongBreakDuration)
    }
  })
}
```

Now add the test for the GetInterval() function. This function obtains the current interval or creates a new one when needed. To test it, you'll execute the Get-Interval() function 16 times to ensure it gets the interval with the proper category. You'll need access to a repository to store the intervals so the function can determine the correct categories. Start by defining the function and obtaining the repository, using the getRepo() function you created before:

interactiveTools/pomo/pomodoro/interval_test.go
```go
func TestGetInterval(t *testing.T) {
  repo, cleanup := getRepo(t)
  defer cleanup()
```

For this test, you'll need to start and complete each interval to allow the Get-Interval() function to obtain the next category. Define a Pomodoro configuration with a short duration of a few milliseconds so the test runs quickly:

interactiveTools/pomo/pomodoro/interval_test.go
```
const duration = 1 * time.Millisecond
config := pomodoro.NewConfig(repo, 3*duration, duration, 2*duration)
```

Next, start the loop to execute the test 16 times. The expected category and duration depend on each iteration of the loop. Use a switch statement to define them. We expect a Pomodoro interval for every odd iteration, a long break for every eight iterations, and a short break for any other even number:

interactiveTools/pomo/pomodoro/interval_test.go
```
for i := 1; i <= 16; i++ {
  var (
    expCategory string
    expDuration time.Duration
  )

  switch {
  case i%2 != 0:
    expCategory = pomodoro.CategoryPomodoro
    expDuration = 3 * duration
  case i%8 == 0:
    expCategory = pomodoro.CategoryLongBreak
    expDuration = 2 * duration
  case i%2 == 0:
    expCategory = pomodoro.CategoryShortBreak
    expDuration = duration
  }
```

Then define a test name based on the iteration number and expected category, and execute the tests using the t.Run() method. For each test, start the interval and test that the category and expected duration matches the expected values, failing the test if they don't match. Because we're not interested in what happens during the interval execution, define an empty function to use as a callback and use an empty context as the context:

interactiveTools/pomo/pomodoro/interval_test.go
```
testName := fmt.Sprintf("%s%d", expCategory, i)
t.Run(testName, func(t *testing.T) {
  res, err := pomodoro.GetInterval(config)

  if err != nil {
    t.Errorf("Expected no error, got %q.\n", err)
  }
```

```
      noop := func(pomodoro.Interval) {}

      if err := res.Start(context.Background(), config,
        noop, noop, noop); err != nil {
        t.Fatal(err)
      }

      if res.Category != expCategory {
        t.Errorf("Expected category %q, got %q.\n",
          expCategory, res.Category)
      }

      if res.PlannedDuration != expDuration {
        t.Errorf("Expected PlannedDuration %q, got %q.\n",
          expDuration, res.PlannedDuration)
      }

      if res.State != pomodoro.StateNotStarted {
        t.Errorf("Expected State = %q, got %q.\n",
          pomodoro.StateNotStarted, res.State)
      }

      ui, err := repo.ByID(res.ID)
      if err != nil {
        t.Errorf("Expected no error. Got %q.\n", err)
      }

      if ui.State != pomodoro.StateDone {
        t.Errorf("Expected State = %q, got %q.\n",
          pomodoro.StateDone, res.State)
      }
    })
  }
}
```

Now add a test for the Pause() method. This test also needs to start the interval but, unlike the previous test, it can't finish quickly. You need to set a duration that allows the tick() function to check the status change, which happens every second. So set the duration to two seconds, allowing the check but still not taking long to complete the test. Add the test definition, set the required values to create an interval, and add two test cases using the table-driven testing approach: one case to test the method when the interval isn't running and another to pause a running interval:

interactiveTools/pomo/pomodoro/interval_test.go
```
func TestPause(t *testing.T) {
  const duration = 2 * time.Second

  repo, cleanup := getRepo(t)
  defer cleanup()

  config := pomodoro.NewConfig(repo, duration, duration, duration)
```

```
testCases := []struct {
  name         string
  start        bool
  expState     int
  expDuration time.Duration
}{
  {name: "NotStarted", start: false,
    expState: pomodoro.StateNotStarted, expDuration: 0},
  {name: "Paused", start: true,
    expState: pomodoro.StatePaused, expDuration: duration / 2},
}

expError := pomodoro.ErrIntervalNotRunning
```

Next, execute the tests in the loop with the t.Run() method. For each test, use the pomodoro.Callback function to execute actions and tests during the interval run. Use the *end* callback to test that nothing runs at the end, since the interval will be paused, and use the periodic callback to pause the interval. Verify that the values for the interval parameters match the expected values, failing the tests in case they don't match:

interactiveTools/pomo/pomodoro/interval_test.go

```
  // Execute tests for Pause
  for _, tc := range testCases {
    t.Run(tc.name, func(t *testing.T) {
      ctx, cancel := context.WithCancel(context.Background())

      i, err := pomodoro.GetInterval(config)
      if err != nil {
        t.Fatal(err)
      }

      start := func(pomodoro.Interval) {}
      end := func(pomodoro.Interval) {
        t.Errorf("End callback should not be executed")
      }
      periodic := func(i pomodoro.Interval) {
        if err := i.Pause(config); err != nil {
          t.Fatal(err)
        }
      }

      if tc.start {
        if err := i.Start(ctx, config, start, periodic, end); err != nil {
          t.Fatal(err)
        }
      }

      i, err = pomodoro.GetInterval(config)
      if err != nil {
        t.Fatal(err)
      }
```

```go
      err = i.Pause(config)
      if err != nil {
        if ! errors.Is(err, expError) {
          t.Fatalf("Expected error %q, got %q", expError, err)
        }
      }

      if err == nil {
        t.Errorf("Expected error %q, got nil", expError)
      }

      i, err = repo.ByID(i.ID)
      if err != nil {
        t.Fatal(err)
      }

      if i.State != tc.expState {
        t.Errorf("Expected state %d, got %d.\n",
          tc.expState, i.State)
      }

      if i.ActualDuration != tc.expDuration {
        t.Errorf("Expected duration %q, got %q.\n",
          tc.expDuration, i.ActualDuration)
      }
      cancel()
    })
  }
}
```

Finally, add a test for the Start() method similar to the Pause() method test. Define a duration of two seconds to execute the interval, giving it time to run the callback functions. Define two test cases, one that executes until it finishes and another to cancel the run in the middle:

interactiveTools/pomo/pomodoro/interval_test.go
```go
func TestStart(t *testing.T) {
  const duration = 2 * time.Second

  repo, cleanup := getRepo(t)
  defer cleanup()

  config := pomodoro.NewConfig(repo, duration, duration, duration)

  testCases := []struct {
    name        string
    cancel      bool
    expState    int
    expDuration time.Duration
  }{

    {name: "Finish", cancel: false,
      expState: pomodoro.StateDone, expDuration: duration},
```

```
  {name: "Cancel", cancel: true,
    expState: pomodoro.StateCancelled, expDuration: duration / 2},
}
```

Now execute the test cases following the table-driven test approach loop.
Again, use pomodoro.Callback functions to perform actions and execute tests
during the interval execution. Use a start callback to check for the interval
status and duration while executing, the end callback to verify the end state,
and the periodic callback to cancel the interval during the Cancel test case.
Fail the tests if current values don't match the expected ones:

interactiveTools/pomo/pomodoro/interval_test.go
```go
// Execute tests for Start
for _, tc := range testCases {
  t.Run(tc.name, func(t *testing.T) {
    ctx, cancel := context.WithCancel(context.Background())

    i, err := pomodoro.GetInterval(config)
    if err != nil {
      t.Fatal(err)
    }

    start := func(i pomodoro.Interval) {
      if i.State != pomodoro.StateRunning {
        t.Errorf("Expected state %d, got %d.\n",
          pomodoro.StateRunning, i.State)
      }
      if i.ActualDuration >= i.PlannedDuration {
        t.Errorf("Expected ActualDuration %q, less than Planned %q.\n",
          i.ActualDuration, i.PlannedDuration)
      }
    }

    end := func(i pomodoro.Interval) {
      if i.State != tc.expState {
        t.Errorf("Expected state %d, got %d.\n",
          tc.expState, i.State)
      }
      if tc.cancel {
        t.Errorf("End callback should not be executed")
      }
    }

    periodic := func(i pomodoro.Interval) {
      if i.State != pomodoro.StateRunning {
        t.Errorf("Expected state %d, got %d.\n",
          pomodoro.StateRunning, i.State)
      }
      if tc.cancel {
        cancel()
      }
    }
```

```
    if err := i.Start(ctx, config, start, periodic, end); err != nil {
      t.Fatal(err)
    }

    i, err = repo.ByID(i.ID)
    if err != nil {
      t.Fatal(err)
    }

    if i.State != tc.expState {
      t.Errorf("Expected state %d, got %d.\n",
        tc.expState, i.State)
    }
    if i.ActualDuration != tc.expDuration {
      t.Errorf("Expected ActualDuration %q, got %q.\n",
        tc.expDuration, i.ActualDuration)
    }
    cancel()
  })
  }
}
```

These are all the tests for this package. Save and close the file. Then, execute the tests:

```
$ go test -v .
=== RUN   TestNewConfig
=== RUN   TestNewConfig/Default
=== RUN   TestNewConfig/SingleInput
=== RUN   TestNewConfig/MultiInput
---- TRUNCATED OUTPUT ------
PASS
ok      pragprog.com/rggo/interactiveTools/pomo/pomodoro      5.045s
```

Once all the tests pass, the business logic for your Pomodoro application is ready. Next, let's build the initial version of the terminal GUI for the application.

Building the Interface Widgets

Now that the business logic is ready and tested, you can build the terminal interface for your Pomodoro application. You'll create the basic interface that has the controls required to run and display the Pomodoro status. When you are done, the interface will look like the image shown in Figure 14 on page 369.

To create this interface, you'll use the Termdash[3] dashboard library. Termdash is a good option because it's cross-platform, it's under active development, and it has a good set of features. Among these features, Termdash provides

---

3.   github.com/mum4k/termdash

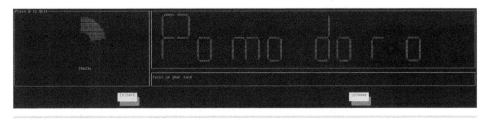

Figure 14—Pomodoro Basic Screen

a variety of graphical widgets, dashboard resizing, customizable layout, and handling of mouse and keyboard events. For more information about Termdash with a complete list of features, consult the project's page. Termdash relies on other libraries to run as back end. For these examples, you'll use the Tcell back-end library as it's currently being developed and maintained.

Before we dive into designing the interface, let's review each of its four main sections as shown in the following images:

1.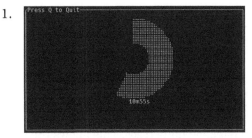

    The Timer section presents the time left in the current interval both in text form and in a graphical donut shape that fills up as time progresses.

    You'll implement the donut interface using the Donut Termdash widget and the text timer using Termdash's Text widget.

2.

    The Type section displays the current interval's type or category. You'll implement this section using the SegmentDisplay widget from Termdash.

3. Focus on your task

    The Info section presents relevant user messages and statuses. You'll implement this item with the Text widget.

4.

The Buttons section displays two buttons, Start and Pause, used to start and pause the interval respectively. You will implement them using Termdash's Button widget.

Termdash is in constant development and new versions may introduce breaking changes with its API. The examples in this chapter use Termdash v0.13.0. Use Go modules to specify this version as a dependency to ensure the examples work correctly:

```
$ cd $HOME/pragprog.com/rggo/interactiveTools/pomo
$ go mod edit -require github.com/mum4k/termdash@v0.13.0
```

Your go.mod file now has this content:

```
$ cat go.mod
module pragprog.com/rggo/interactiveTools/pomo

go 1.14

require github.com/mum4k/termdash v0.13.0
```

Now let's design the interface. Create a new subdirectory app under the main directory and switch to it:

```
$ mkdir $HOME/pragprog.com/rggo/interactiveTools/pomo/app
$ cd $HOME/pragprog.com/rggo/interactiveTools/pomo/app
```

Develop the interface code in a new Go package named app. This allows the code to be self-contained and easier to maintain. Start by adding the main widgets to the interface. Create and edit the file widgets.go. Add the package definition and the import section. For this file, you'll use the context package to pass a context that carries a cancellation signal to the widgets, the termdash/cell package to modify widgets' properties such as color, the termdash/donut package to add a Donut widget, the termdash/segmentdisplay package to add a SegmentDisplay widget, and the termdash/text package to add a Text widget:

interactiveTools/pomo/app/widgets.go
```go
package app

import (
  "context"

  "github.com/mum4k/termdash/cell"
  "github.com/mum4k/termdash/widgets/donut"
  "github.com/mum4k/termdash/widgets/segmentdisplay"
  "github.com/mum4k/termdash/widgets/text"
)
```

Next, define a new private custom type called widgets to represent a collection of widgets. This type defines a pointer to the four main status widgets in your application: donTimer for the Donut widget in the Timer section, txtTimer for the Text widget in the Timer section, disType for the SegmentDisplay widget in the Type section, and txtInfo for the Text widget in the Info section. It also includes four Go channels that you'll use to update those widgets concurrently:

interactiveTools/pomo/app/widgets.go
```
type widgets struct {
  donTimer          *donut.Donut
  disType           *segmentdisplay.SegmentDisplay
  txtInfo           *text.Text
  txtTimer          *text.Text
  updateDonTimer chan []int
  updateTxtInfo  chan string
  updateTxtTimer chan string
  updateTxtType  chan string
}
```

Then add an update() method to the widgets type to update the widgets with new data. This method will take five input parameters: timer of type []int to update the timer Donut, txtType to update the SegmentDisplay, txtInfo and txtTimer to update Text widgets for Info and Timer, and redrawCh which is a channel of bool that indicates when the app should redraw the screen. This method sends the update data to the respective widget channel if that value isn't blank or empty:

interactiveTools/pomo/app/widgets.go
```
func (w *widgets) update(timer []int, txtType, txtInfo, txtTimer string,
  redrawCh chan<- bool) {

  if txtInfo != "" {
    w.updateTxtInfo <- txtInfo
  }

  if txtType != "" {
    w.updateTxtType <- txtType
  }

  if txtTimer != "" {
    w.updateTxtTimer <- txtTimer
  }

  if len(timer) > 0 {
    w.updateDonTimer <- timer
  }

  redrawCh <- true
}
```

Next, create the function newWidgets() to initialize the widgets type. This function calls other functions to instantiate each widget. You'll write those functions shortly. The initializing functions are similar, so call each of them to initialize the corresponding widget and pass context for cancellation, the appropriate channel to update the widget, and an error channel to send errors to when running concurrently:

interactiveTools/pomo/app/widgets.go

```go
func newWidgets(ctx context.Context, errorCh chan<- error) (*widgets, error) {
  w := &widgets{}
  var err error

  w.updateDonTimer = make(chan []int)
  w.updateTxtType = make(chan string)
  w.updateTxtInfo = make(chan string)
  w.updateTxtTimer = make(chan string)

  w.donTimer, err = newDonut(ctx, w.updateDonTimer, errorCh)
  if err != nil {
    return nil, err
  }

  w.disType, err = newSegmentDisplay(ctx, w.updateTxtType, errorCh)
  if err != nil {
    return nil, err
  }

  w.txtInfo, err = newText(ctx, w.updateTxtInfo, errorCh)
  if err != nil {
    return nil, err
  }

  w.txtTimer, err = newText(ctx, w.updateTxtTimer, errorCh)
  if err != nil {
    return nil, err
  }

  return w, nil
}
```

Now, create the functions to initialize each widget type. Each of those widget-initializing functions will follow a similar formula where you pass the context for cancellation, a channel to update the widget, and an error channel to send errors to when running concurrently. In each function, you'll initialize the widget and then launch a new goroutine to update the widget when it receives data in the update channel.

Start with the newText() function, which will initialize a new Text widget. Define the function with the required input parameters. This function returns a pointer to an instance of Termdash text.Text type and a potential error:

interactiveTools/pomo/app/widgets.go
```
func newText(ctx context.Context, updateText <-chan string,
  errorCh chan<- error) (*text.Text, error) {
```

Instantiate the text.Text widget using the text.New() function, assigning the result to a variable txt. Execute text.New() without any arguments, since this widget doesn't require any configuration. Check and return any errors:

interactiveTools/pomo/app/widgets.go
```
txt, err := text.New()
if err != nil {
  return nil, err
}
```

By default, Termdash runs the dashboard components concurrently. To update each widget, you'll use Go's concurrency features such as goroutines and channels. Use an anonymous function to create a closure and launch it as a new goroutine. By doing this, you can use the variable txt defined outside the closure to update the widget. This goroutine listens on the given update channel for new data and then updates the widget with it. If it receives a context cancellation, use return to exit the function and finish it. Use a select statement to block waiting for input on the channel or the context cancellation:

interactiveTools/pomo/app/widgets.go
```
// Goroutine to update Text
go func() {
  for {
    select {
    case t := <-updateText:
      txt.Reset()
      errorCh <- txt.Write(t)
    case <-ctx.Done():
      return
    }
  }
}()
```

In the goroutine, you're using the method txt.Reset() to reset the text in the widget and then the method txt.Write() to write the new value obtained from the update channel. Because this function runs concurrently, you can't return an error, so forward any errors to the error channel errorCh. You'll write the error-handling mechanism later.

To complete the newText() function, return the widget instance txt and nil as the error.

```
  return txt, nil
}
```

Next, create a similar function to initialize the Donut widget for the Timer section:

```
func newDonut(ctx context.Context, donUpdater <-chan []int,
  errorCh chan<- error) (*donut.Donut, error) {
```

Within the function's body, use the function donut.New() from Termdash to instantiate a new Donut widget. Unlike the Text widget, you'll set options to change its behavior and appearance. The donut.New() function accepts any number of options as input parameters. Termdash represents options using an interface, in this case donut.Option. It implements different options by providing functions that return a value that implements this interface. You can see a complete list of options in Termdash's documentation.[4]

For this case, set two options. Use donut.Clockwise() to make the donut progress in a clockwise direction and use the donut.CellOpts() to change its color to blue. To set the color using the Tcell back end, use the cell.FgColor() function with the constant value cell.ColorBlue:

```
don, err := donut.New(
  donut.Clockwise(),
  donut.CellOpts(cell.FgColor(cell.ColorBlue)),
)

if err != nil {
  return nil, err
}
```

Then implement the goroutine that updates the Donut widget the same way you implemented the Text update. Use the method don.Absolute() to set an absolute value for the Donut progress because it represents the absolute value of Interval duration at runtime:

```
go func() {
  for {
    select {
    case d := <-donUpdater:
      if d[0] <= d[1] {
        errorCh <- don.Absolute(d[0], d[1])
      }
```

---

4.   godoc.org/github.com/mum4k/termdash/widgets/donut

```
    case <-ctx.Done():
      return
    }
  }
}()
```

Complete the newDonut() function by returning the widget instance don and nil as the error.

interactiveTools/pomo/app/widgets.go
```
  return don, nil
}
```

Next, add the newSegmentDisplay() function to instantiate the SegmentDisplay widget, similar to the other two widget instantiating functions. Use Termdash's segmentdisplay.New() function to instantiate a new SegmentDisplay and a goroutine closure to update it. Return the new instance at the end:

interactiveTools/pomo/app/widgets.go
```
func newSegmentDisplay(ctx context.Context, updateText <-chan string,
  errorCh chan<- error) (*segmentdisplay.SegmentDisplay, error) {

  sd, err := segmentdisplay.New()
  if err != nil {
    return nil, err
  }

  // Goroutine to update SegmentDisplay
  go func() {
    for {
      select {
      case t := <-updateText:
        if t == "" {
          t = " "
        }

        errorCh <- sd.Write([]*segmentdisplay.TextChunk{
          segmentdisplay.NewChunk(t),
        })
      case <-ctx.Done():
        return
      }
    }
  }()

  return sd, nil
}
```

To update the SegmentDisplay widget, you use the method sd.Write(), passing a slice of values of type segmentdisplay.TextChunk which allows passing multiple text segments to display. In our case, because we're displaying a single segment, you're passing a slice literal that contains a single element using the segment-display.NewChunk() function with the text value obtained from the channel.

Now that you added the main widgets, you can create the buttons to start and pause Pomodoro intervals. To make it easier to maintain and update the code, you'll add the buttons in a different file. Save and close the widgets.go file and open a new file buttons.go for editing.

Start by adding the package definition and the import list. For this file, you'll use the following packages: context to carry cancellation signals, fmt to format strings, termdash/cell that provides customization options for widgets, termdash/widgets/button to define a button widget, and the pomodoro that you created with the business logic:

interactiveTools/pomo/app/buttons.go
```
package app

import (
  "context"
  "fmt"

  "github.com/mum4k/termdash/cell"
  "github.com/mum4k/termdash/widgets/button"
  "pragprog.com/rggo/interactiveTools/pomo/pomodoro"
)
```

Then define a new custom type, buttonSet, that includes the btStart and btPause fields of type button.Button, which represents a Termdash button:

interactiveTools/pomo/app/buttons.go
```
type buttonSet struct {
  btStart *button.Button
  btPause *button.Button
}
```

Next, add the function newButtonSet() to instantiate a buttonSet. This function takes the following inputs: a Context to carry cancellation signals, an instance of pomodoro.IntervalConfig to call Pomodoro functions, a pointer to the widgets type you created before to update widgets, and the channels redrawCh and errorCh to send data to the app signaling a screen redraw or an error respectively. It returns a pointer to a buttonSet or an error:

interactiveTools/pomo/app/buttons.go
```
func newButtonSet(ctx context.Context, config *pomodoro.IntervalConfig,
  w *widgets, redrawCh chan<- bool, errorCh chan<- error) (*buttonSet, error) {
```

When you create a Termdash button, you provide its action through a callback function. Termdash executes this function every time the user presses the button. Because the user can press the button many times, this function has to be lightweight. It also has to be nonblocking to allow the other components of the interface to update and redraw if necessary.

You can implement the button action in many ways. For example, you could implement a short callback that updates a value and finishes its execution and then another function could pick that value up and execute additional tasks. You could also use a channel to update another goroutine executing the code. Your choice of implementation depends on your requirements.

In our example, you'll implement the button action by spawning a new goroutine that attempts to start or pause the interval using the corresponding method from the pomodoro.Interval type, from within the button callback. By executing a new goroutine, you ensure the code is non-blocking. The Pomodoro business logic returns back to the calling function quickly if the action isn't required, allowing the user to press the button many times without restarting or pausing the interval many times.

Let's begin by defining the action function to start an interval and assign it to a variable startInterval, making it easier to read and maintain, instead of having several layers of functions within functions. Define the function and use the pomodoro.GetInterval() function to obtain the current interval. Because this function executes concurrently, it can't return errors. Send any errors to the error channel errorCh for further processing:

interactiveTools/pomo/app/buttons.go
```
startInterval := func() {
  i, err := pomodoro.GetInterval(config)
  errorCh <- err
```

Then define the three callbacks required to call the Interval.Start() method to start the Pomodoro interval. First, define the start callback. At the start of the interval, change the message displayed in the Info section of the application, depending on the type of interval. Use the method widgets.update() you defined before, to update the Info message and the Type section according to the interval category:

interactiveTools/pomo/app/buttons.go
```
start := func(i pomodoro.Interval) {
  message := "Take a break"
  if i.Category == pomodoro.CategoryPomodoro {
    message = "Focus on your task"
  }
  w.update([]int{}, i.Category, message, "", redrawCh)
}
```

Next define the end callback to execute at the end of the interval, setting the Info message to Nothing running...:

interactiveTools/pomo/app/buttons.go
```go
end := func(pomodoro.Interval) {
  w.update([]int{}, "", "Nothing running...", "", redrawCh)
}
```

Define the periodic callback that executes every second. For this callback, use the widgets.update() method to update the Timer section with the current interval time:

interactiveTools/pomo/app/buttons.go
```go
periodic := func(i pomodoro.Interval) {
  w.update(
    []int{int(i.ActualDuration), int(i.PlannedDuration)},
    "", "",
    fmt.Sprint(i.PlannedDuration-i.ActualDuration),
    redrawCh,
  )
}
```

To complete this function, attempt to start the interval by calling the i.Start() method, and send any errors to the error channel errorCh for handling:

interactiveTools/pomo/app/buttons.go
```go
  errorCh <- i.Start(ctx, config, start, periodic, end)
}
```

Now define the action function to pause the interval and assign it to the pause-Interval variable. In this function, obtain the current interval and attempt to pause it using the i.Pause() method. If it can't pause the interval, use the return statement to terminate the function without taking any further action. If the pause succeeds, use the widgets.update() method to update the Info message section of the interface. Send any errors to the error channel for further processing:

interactiveTools/pomo/app/buttons.go
```go
pauseInterval := func() {
  i, err := pomodoro.GetInterval(config)
  if err != nil {
    errorCh <- err
    return
  }

  if err := i.Pause(config); err != nil {
    if err == pomodoro.ErrIntervalNotRunning {
      return
    }
    errorCh <- err
    return
  }
  w.update([]int{}, "", "Paused... press start to continue", "", redrawCh)
}
```

With the two action functions completed, instantiate the buttons by using Termdash's button.New() function. First, add the Start button by passing the button text (s)tart, the callback function that spawns a new goroutine using the start-Interval() function you created before, and the button options. If errors occur, return nil for the button set and the error:

```
interactiveTools/pomo/app/buttons.go
btStart, err := button.New("(s)tart", func() error {
  go startInterval()
  return nil
},
  button.GlobalKey('s'),
  button.WidthFor("(p)ause"),
  button.Height(2),
)

if err != nil {
  return nil, err
}
```

You're setting three options for this button:

- button.GlobalKey('s'): Setting global key to s, allowing the users to use the button by pressing s on the keyboard.

- button.WidthFor("(p)ause"): Setting the button width to the length of string (p)ause matching the width of the next button. This is useful for keeping all buttons with the same size.

- button.Height(2): Setting the button height to two cells.

Add the pause button in a similar way. Set the global key to p and height to two cells. Use the function button.FillColor() to change the button color to the color number 220 by using the Tcell function cell.ColorNumber(). This gives this button a shade of yellow to differentiate it from the standard blue you're using for the Start button:

```
interactiveTools/pomo/app/buttons.go
btPause, err := button.New("(p)ause", func() error {
  go pauseInterval()
  return nil
},
  button.FillColor(cell.ColorNumber(220)),
  button.GlobalKey('p'),
  button.Height(2),
)

if err != nil {
  return nil, err
}
```

Setting the color to 220 assumes that your user's terminal supports 256 colors, which is common for modern terminal emulators. Set the color appropriately if you are targeting terminals that support fewer colors.

Complete this function by instantiating the type buttonSet, using the buttons you just created, and returning its address with the value nil for the error:

interactiveTools/pomo/app/buttons.go
```
  return &buttonSet{btStart, btPause}, nil
}
```

This completes the code for the buttons. Save and close this file. You have all the widgets ready for the initial interface. Let's define the interface layout and functionality next.

Organizing the Interface's Layout

Once you have all the widgets for your interface, you need to organize and lay them out logically to compose the user interface.

In Termdash you define the dashboard layout using containers represented by the type container.Container. Termdash requires at least one container to start the application. You can use multiple containers to split the screen and organize the widgets.

You can create the containers in two different ways: using the container package to split containers resulting in a binary tree layout; or using the grid package to define a grid of rows and columns. You can find more information about the Container API on the Termdash wiki.[5]

For this application, you'll organize the layout using the grid method, as it's easier to organize the code to compose a layout like the one in Pomodoro Application Screen on page 348. The application layout consists of three main rows. The first row is split in two columns, which are further split in two additional rows. The second row has two columns, as well as the third row. For now, you'll build the first two rows, leaving the third row as a placeholder for the summary widgets that you'll design in Displaying a Summary to the Users, on page 416.

Start by adding and editing the file grid.go under the app subdirectory in your application directory. Add the package definition and import section. You'll use the termdash/align package to align widgets in containers, the container package to use the Container API, the container/grid package to define a grid layout, the

---

termdash/linestyle package to define the container border's line style, and the terminalapi package which you need to create Termdash containers:

interactiveTools/pomo/app/grid.go
```go
package app

import (
  "github.com/mum4k/termdash/align"
  "github.com/mum4k/termdash/container"
  "github.com/mum4k/termdash/container/grid"
  "github.com/mum4k/termdash/linestyle"
  "github.com/mum4k/termdash/terminal/terminalapi"
)
```

Next, define the function newGrid() to define a new grid layout. This function takes as input a pointer to a buttonSet, a pointer to widgets, and an instance of Termdash terminalapi.Terminal. It returns a pointer to a container.Container and a potential error:

interactiveTools/pomo/app/grid.go
```go
func newGrid(b *buttonSet, w *widgets,
  t terminalapi.Terminal) (*container.Container, error) {
```

Termdash uses the grid.Builder type to build grid layouts. After you complete the layout, use the method Build() to generate the corresponding container options to create a new container with the desired layout. Define a new grid.Builder by using the function grid.New():

interactiveTools/pomo/app/grid.go
```go
builder := grid.New()
```

Use the method builder.Add() to add the first row. This method takes any number of values of type grid.Element. A grid element can be a row, a column, or a widget. Use rows and columns to subdivide the container and then place a widget within the container. You can create rows and columns with fixed lengths or by using a percentage of the parent container space. For this project you'll use percentages to allow dynamic resizing of the application. Add the first row, which will occupy 30% of the terminal's height, using the function grid.RowHeightPerc():

interactiveTools/pomo/app/grid.go
```go
// Add first row
builder.Add(
  grid.RowHeightPerc(30,
```

Within this row, add a column to the left that will occupy 30% of the available space. Use the function grid.ColWidthPercWithOpts() to specify additional options for this column, such as the line style and the title Press Q to Quit informing the user what they have to do to quit the application:

interactiveTools/pomo/app/grid.go

```
grid.ColWidthPercWithOpts(30,
  []container.Option{
    container.Border(linestyle.Light),
    container.BorderTitle("Press Q to Quit"),
  },
```

In the left column, define a row that takes 80% of the space and add the w.donTimer donut widget in it:

interactiveTools/pomo/app/grid.go

```
// Add inside row
grid.RowHeightPerc(80,
  grid.Widget(w.donTimer)),
```

Then add another row taking the remaining 20% of the column and add the w.txtTimer text widget with options to align it in the middle of the column:

interactiveTools/pomo/app/grid.go

```
  grid.RowHeightPercWithOpts(20,
    []container.Option{
      container.AlignHorizontal(align.HorizontalCenter),
    },
    grid.Widget(w.txtTimer,
      container.AlignHorizontal(align.HorizontalCenter),
      container.AlignVertical(align.VerticalMiddle),
      container.PaddingLeftPercent(49),
    ),
  ),
),
```

Now, add the column to the right using the remaining 70% of the first row. Add two rows in it, using 80% and 20% of the space, respectively. Add the w.disType segment display widget in the top row and the w.txtInfo info text widget in the bottom row. Use a light line-style border on both widgets:

interactiveTools/pomo/app/grid.go

```
    grid.ColWidthPerc(70,
      grid.RowHeightPerc(80,
        grid.Widget(w.disType, container.Border(linestyle.Light)),
      ),
      grid.RowHeightPerc(20,
        grid.Widget(w.txtInfo, container.Border(linestyle.Light)),
      ),
    ),
  ),
)
```

This completes the first row. Now add the second row using 10% of the space. Add two columns with the same size, with each taking 50% of the available space, and add the Start and Pause buttons on each:

interactiveTools/pomo/app/grid.go

```
// Add second row
builder.Add(
  grid.RowHeightPerc(10,
    grid.ColWidthPerc(50,
      grid.Widget(b.btStart),
    ),
    grid.ColWidthPerc(50,
      grid.Widget(b.btPause),
    ),
  ),
)
```

Next, add the placeholder for the third line, using the remaining 60% of the screen space:

interactiveTools/pomo/app/grid.go

```
// Add third row
builder.Add(
  grid.RowHeightPerc(60),
)
```

Now that you have the initial layout complete, use the builder.Build() method to build the layout and create the container options required to instantiate a container following the desired layout. Return the error from builder.Build() if it fails to execute:

interactiveTools/pomo/app/grid.go

```
gridOpts, err := builder.Build()
if err != nil {
  return nil, err
}
```

Use the generated container options to instantiate the container using the method container.New(). In addition to the container options, this function takes an instance of type terminalapi.Terminal, which is received as an input parameter by function newGrid():

interactiveTools/pomo/app/grid.go

```
c, err := container.New(t, gridOpts...)
if err != nil {
  return nil, err
}
```

Then, complete your newGrid() function by returning the newly created container c and nil for the error, indicating a successful completion:

interactiveTools/pomo/app/grid.go
```
  return c, nil
}
```

Building the Interactive Interface

Now that you have the widgets and layout ready, let's put everything together to create an app that launches and manages the interface. Termdash provides two ways to run dashboard applications:

1. termdash.Run(): Starts and manages the application automatically. Using this function, Termdash periodically redraws the screen and handles resizing for you.

2. termdash.NewController(): Creates a new instance of termdash.Controller that allows you to manually manage your application's redrawing and resizing processes.

It's easier to get started with Termdash by using termdash.Run() since Termdash manages the application for you. But due to the periodic screen redraw, it continuously consumes system resources. This is fine if you have an application that provides constant feedback, such as a system dashboard or monitoring application. For the Pomodoro application you're developing, this isn't ideal because the application would consume system resources when it's stopped or paused. For this reason, you'll use an instance of termdash.Controller to manage this application.

Ensure that you're in the app subdirectory under your application directory:

```
$ cd $HOME/pragprog.com/rggo/interactiveTools/pomo/app
```

Create and edit the file app.go. Include the package definition and import section. For this file, you'll use the following packages: context to handle cancellation contexts, image to use 2D geometry functions necessary to resize the screen, time to use time-related types, the Termdash related termdash, terminal/tcell, and terminal/terminalapi to draw the interface on the terminal, and your pomodoro to access the Pomodoro configuration:

interactiveTools/pomo/app/app.go
```
package app

import (
  "context"
  "image"
  "time"
```

```
    "github.com/mum4k/termdash"
    "github.com/mum4k/termdash/terminal/tcell"
    "github.com/mum4k/termdash/terminal/terminalapi"
    "pragprog.com/rggo/interactiveTools/pomo/pomodoro"
)
```

Now define the exported type App that callers will use to instantiate and control the interface. This new type includes private fields required to control, redraw, and resize the interface:

interactiveTools/pomo/app/app.go
```
type App struct {
    ctx        context.Context
    controller *termdash.Controller
    redrawCh   chan bool
    errorCh    chan error
    term       *tcell.Terminal
    size       image.Point
}
```

These fields are private because you'll control the behavior through a set of methods. Before adding the methods, define a function New() to instantiate a new App. This function instantiates the required widgets, buttons, and grid, and puts them together in a new instance of termdash.Controller. Start by defining the function:

interactiveTools/pomo/app/app.go
```
func New(config *pomodoro.IntervalConfig) (*App, error) {
```

Within the function's body, define a new cancellation context that you'll use to close all widgets when the application closes:

interactiveTools/pomo/app/app.go
```
ctx, cancel := context.WithCancel(context.Background())
```

Next, define the function quitter() to map the keyboard key Q q to the context cancel() function, allowing the user to quit the application by pressing Q. You'll provide this function as an input parameter when instantiating termdash.Controller later:

interactiveTools/pomo/app/app.go
```
quitter := func(k *terminalapi.Keyboard) {
  if k.Key == 'q' || k.Key == 'Q' {
    cancel()
  }
}
```

Define two channels to control the application's asynchronous redrawing redrawCh and errorCh:

interactiveTools/pomo/app/app.go
```
redrawCh := make(chan bool)
errorCh := make(chan error)
```

Then instantiate the widgets and buttons that compose your interface using the newWidgets() and newButtonSet() functions that you defined before:

interactiveTools/pomo/app/app.go
```
w, err := newWidgets(ctx, errorCh)
if err != nil {
  return nil, err
}

b, err := newButtonSet(ctx, config, w, redrawCh, errorCh)
if err != nil {
  return nil, err
}
```

Define a new instance of tcell.Terminal to use as the back end for the application. Then use it to instantiate a new termdash.Container using the grid layout you defined before:

interactiveTools/pomo/app/app.go
```
term, err := tcell.New()
if err != nil {
  return nil, err
}

c, err := newGrid(b, w, term)
if err != nil {
  return nil, err
}
```

With all the components defined, use the termdash.NewController() function to instantiate a new termdash.Controller to control your application. Provide the tcell.Terminal instance term, the container c, and a new keyboard subscriber, using the quitter() function you defined before, as input parameters:

interactiveTools/pomo/app/app.go
```
controller, err := termdash.NewController(term, c,
  termdash.KeyboardSubscriber(quitter))
if err != nil {
  return nil, err
}
```

Complete the New() function by returning a pointer to an instance of type App using the instances you defined within the function's body:

interactiveTools/pomo/app/app.go
```go
  return &App{
    ctx:        ctx,
    controller: controller,
    redrawCh:   redrawCh,
    errorCh:    errorCh,
    term:       term,
  }, nil
}
```

Next, define the resize() method to resize the interface if needed. We'll run this function periodically to verify whether the application requires a resize. Use the method Eq() from the image package to check if the underlying terminal size has changed. To avoid using too many system resources, return immediately if a resize isn't required. In case the terminal size has changed, store the new size in the size field for future comparison and then resize the terminal by using the terminal method Clear() to clear the terminal, followed by calling the method controller.Redraw() to redraw the widgets:

interactiveTools/pomo/app/app.go
```go
func (a *App) resize() error {
  if a.size.Eq(a.term.Size()) {
    return nil
  }

  a.size = a.term.Size()
  if err := a.term.Clear(); err != nil {
    return err
  }

  return a.controller.Redraw()
}
```

Define the exported method Run() to run and control the application:

interactiveTools/pomo/app/app.go
```go
func (a *App) Run() error {
```

Within the function's body, defer closing the controller and terminal to clean up resources when the application finishes:

interactiveTools/pomo/app/app.go
```go
defer a.term.Close()
defer a.controller.Close()
```

Define a new time.Ticker with a two seconds interval to periodically check if a resize is needed. Defer stopping ticker when the application finishes:

interactiveTools/pomo/app/app.go
```go
ticker := time.NewTicker(2 * time.Second)
defer ticker.Stop()
```

Then, run the main loop using a select statement to take actions based on data arriving in one of the four channels:

- a.redrawCh: Redraw the application by calling termdash.Controller method a.controller.Redraw().

- a.errorCh: Return the error received by the channel finishing the application.

- a.ctx.Done: Data received in this channel indicates the main context was cancelled by the user typing q. Return nil as error, finishing the application successfully.

- ticker.C: The ticker timer expired. Use the method a.resize() to resize the application if required.

interactiveTools/pomo/app/app.go
```go
for {
  select {
  case <-a.redrawCh:
    if err := a.controller.Redraw(); err != nil {
      return err
    }
  case err := <-a.errorCh:
    if err != nil {
      return err
    }
  case <-a.ctx.Done():
    return nil
  case <-ticker.C:
    if err := a.resize(); err != nil {
      return err
    }
  }
 }
}
```

Save and close this file to complete the code for your application's interactive interface. Next, you'll add code to launch the application.

Initializing the CLI with Cobra

Now that the interface and the back-end code are ready, you need a way to launch your application. You'll use the Cobra framework again to have a standard way to handle command-line parameters and configuration files. Switch back to your application's root directory and use the Cobra framework generator as you did in Chapter 7, Using the Cobra CLI Framework, on page 213, to generate the initial boilerplate code:

```
$ cd $HOME/pragprog.com/rggo/interactiveTools/pomo
$ cobra init --pkg-name pragprog.com/rggo/interactiveTools/pomo
Using config file: /home/ricardo/.cobra.yaml
Your Cobra application is ready at
/home/ricardo/pragprog.com/rggo/interactiveTools/pomo
```

Cobra Config File

> ⚠ This command uses the default Cobra configuration file in your home directory. You created this configuration file in Chapter 7, Using the Cobra CLI Framework, on page 213. If you need to create it again, take a look at Starting Your Cobra Application, on page 214.
>
> You can also initialize the application without a configuration file. In that case, Cobra will use its default options for LICENSE and comments. The contents of your files will be different from these examples.

Then, add a requirement to go.mod to ensure you're using Cobra v1.1.3, which is what the book's code uses. Again, you can use a later version but you may need to change the code somewhat. Run go mod tidy to download the required dependencies:

```
$ go mod edit --require github.com/spf13/cobra@v1.1.3
$ go mod tidy
```

After initializing the application, Cobra created the subdirectory cmd and three files: LICENSE, main.go, and cmd/root.go. This application doesn't require subcommands, so you only need to update cmd/root.go to start it.

To start this application, you'll need the instance of pomodoro.IntervalConfig, which is required to create an instance of your app.App type. To create a new configuration, you also need an instance of pomodoro.Repository. To make this application extensive, let's create a getRepo() function to get the repository. Later you can implement different versions of this function to obtain different repositories. First, switch to the cmd subdirectory:

```
$ cd $HOME/pragprog.com/rggo/interactiveTools/pomo/cmd
```

Then create and open the file repoinmemory.go. Add the package definition and import section; you'll use your pomodoro and pomodoro/repository packages to instantiate and return a new repository:

interactiveTools/pomo/cmd/repoinmemory.go
```go
package cmd

import (
    "pragprog.com/rggo/interactiveTools/pomo/pomodoro"
    "pragprog.com/rggo/interactiveTools/pomo/pomodoro/repository"
)
```

Add the function getRepo(), which returns an instance of pomodoro.Repository and an error. For the in-memory repository, the error is always nil, but you may use this value later for other repositories:

interactiveTools/pomo/cmd/repoinmemory.go
```go
func getRepo() (pomodoro.Repository, error) {
  return repository.NewInMemoryRepo(), nil
}
```

Save and close this file. Then open the cmd/root.go file Cobra's generator created. Include the io package to use the io.Writer interface, the time package to create time-related types and variables, your app package to instantiate the application interface, and the pomodoro package to access the Pomodoro configuration:

interactiveTools/pomo/cmd/root.go
```go
import (
  "fmt"
  "io"
  "os"
  "time"

  "github.com/spf13/cobra"
  "pragprog.com/rggo/interactiveTools/pomo/app"
  "pragprog.com/rggo/interactiveTools/pomo/pomodoro"

  homedir "github.com/mitchellh/go-homedir"
  "github.com/spf13/viper"
)
```

Then edit the init() function to include three command-line parameters, allowing users to customize the Pomodoro, short break, and long break interval durations. Set default values and associate them with the Viper configuration, enabling the setting of these options in a configuration file automatically:

interactiveTools/pomo/cmd/root.go
```go
func init() {
  cobra.OnInitialize(initConfig)

  rootCmd.PersistentFlags().StringVar(&cfgFile, "config", "",
    "config file (default is $HOME/.pomo.yaml)")

  rootCmd.Flags().DurationP("pomo", "p", 25*time.Minute,
                    "Pomodoro duration")
  rootCmd.Flags().DurationP("short", "s", 5*time.Minute,
                    "Short break duration")
  rootCmd.Flags().DurationP("long", "l", 15*time.Minute,
                    "Long break duration")

  viper.BindPFlag("pomo", rootCmd.Flags().Lookup("pomo"))
  viper.BindPFlag("short", rootCmd.Flags().Lookup("short"))
  viper.BindPFlag("long", rootCmd.Flags().Lookup("long"))
}
```

Next, update the rootCmd command definition to customize it according to your requirements. Delete the Long description and include a Short description, Interactive Pomodoro Timer, to help users. By default, Cobra's root command doesn't run any actions, but—since this tool doesn't have any subcommands—add the RunE property and assign it to an anonymous action function. This function obtains the repository by calling the function getRepo(), creates a new Pomodoro configuration using pomodoro.NewConfig(), and then calls the function rootAction() to start the application. You'll define rootAction() shortly:

interactiveTools/pomo/cmd/root.go
```go
var rootCmd = &cobra.Command{
  Use:   "pomo",
  Short: "Interactive Pomodoro Timer",
  // Uncomment the following line if your bare application
  // has an action associated with it:
  //  Run: func(cmd *cobra.Command, args []string) { },
  RunE: func(cmd *cobra.Command, args []string) error {
    repo, err := getRepo()
    if err != nil {
      return err
    }

    config := pomodoro.NewConfig(
      repo,
      viper.GetDuration("pomo"),
      viper.GetDuration("short"),
      viper.GetDuration("long"),
    )
    return rootAction(os.Stdout, config)
  },
}
```

Finally, define the function rootAction() to start the application. Create a new App instance by using the function app.New(), providing the Pomodoro configuration as input. Then run the app by using its a.Run() method:

interactiveTools/pomo/cmd/root.go
```go
func rootAction(out io.Writer, config *pomodoro.IntervalConfig) error {
  a, err := app.New(config)
  if err != nil {
    return err
  }

  return a.Run()
}
```

Save and close the file. Switch back to your application's root directory and use go build to build it:

```
$ cd $HOME/pragprog.com/rggo/interactiveTools/pomo
$ go build
```

Run your application by executing the pomo binary directly, for default interval durations:

```
$ ./pomo
```

You'll see your application interface onscreen. Use the Start and Pause buttons to start and pause your intervals. When you're done, press Q to quit the application. For a quicker test, change the default interval duration by providing command-line parameters. You can see all the options by using --help:

```
$ ./pomo --help
Interactive Pomodoro Timer

Usage:
  pomo [flags]

Flags:
      --config string     config file (default is $HOME/.pomo.yaml)
  -h, --help              help for pomo
  -l, --long duration     Long break duration (default 15m0s)
  -p, --pomo duration     Pomodoro duration (default 25m0s)
  -s, --short duration    Short break duration (default 5m0s)
```

Because you used Viper to bind configuration options, you can also set them in a configuration file. For example, you can permanently modify your Pomodoro application's behavior by setting the Pomodoro interval to 10 minutes, the short break to 2 minutes, and the long break to 4 minutes, using the configuration file $HOME/.pomo.yaml with this content:

```
pomo: 10m
short: 2m
long: 4m
```

When you start the application now, it uses your configuration file and sets the corresponding options. You can see it's using the configuration file after starting the application as it displays the file name, as shown in Figure 15 on page 393.

```
$ ./pomo
Using config file: /home/ricardo/.pomo.yaml
```

Your interactive Pomodoro timer application is complete. Run it a few times to understand how the several timers work. Because you're using an in-memory repository, the interval resets to a Pomodoro interval every time you start the application. You'll improve its functionality in the next chapter by saving your history to a SQL database. You can also test the resizing functionality by changing the size of your terminal window. The application will resize accordingly.

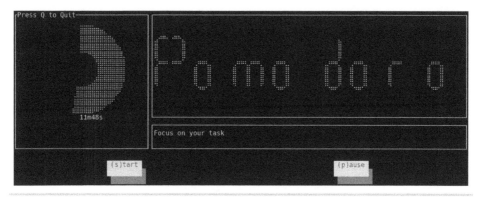

Figure 15—The completed Pomodoro application

Exercises

Before moving on, exercise the skills you learned in this chapter. Here are some suggestions:

- Investigate some of the other widgets available with Termdash to understand what's available for future projects.

- In the next chapter, you'll use two more widgets: BarChart and LineChart to add an activity summary for this application. Before then, test some of the other widgets. For example, replace the Donut widget with the Gauge widget to represent the time elapsed in the interval.

- Use a SegmentDisplay widget to represent the time instead of the text widget.

Wrapping Up

You developed your first interactive CLI application that displays and controls a Pomodoro timer. You designed an application that provides constant user feedback and allows users to control its flow interactively by starting and pausing the timer at will.

In this version of the application, you applied different interactive widgets to compose your application, and you employed concurrent Go techniques to control the application flow asynchronously.

In the next chapter, you'll expand this application by allowing users to save its data to a Structured Query Language (SQL) database. By running queries on saved data, you'll implement two additional widgets for your application, providing the user with the ability to see how much time they spend focusing on their tasks daily and weekly.

## CHAPTER 10

Persisting Data in a SQL Database

In Chapter 9, Developing Interactive Terminal Tools, on page 347, you developed a Pomodoro timer application. It's a fully functional application, but it doesn't persist data. It doesn't keep track of previous intervals, so it always begins at the first Pomodoro interval every time you start it.

In this chapter, you'll improve the *pomo* tool by persisting data to a relational database using Structured Query Language (SQL).[1]

Because you developed this application using the Repository pattern, you can integrate a new data store by adding a new repository without changing the business logic and application. This is a powerful resource that allows your applications to persist data in different ways according to different requirements. For example, you could implement an in-memory data store for tests and a database engine for production. For more details on how you implement the Repository pattern, take a look at Storing Data with the Repository Pattern, on page 356.

The Pomodoro application is a personal application, making it a good candidate for an embedded database. You'll implement a data store using SQLite,[2] which is a popular choice for embeddable databases. SQLite is fast, small, and supports multiple operating systems.

Once your Pomodoro application is capable of saving data, you'll implement two additional widgets to show users a summary of historical data in daily and weekly summaries. When you're done, the new version of your application will look like Figure 16 on page 396.

---

1. en.wikipedia.org/wiki/SQL

2. https://www.sqlite.org/index.html

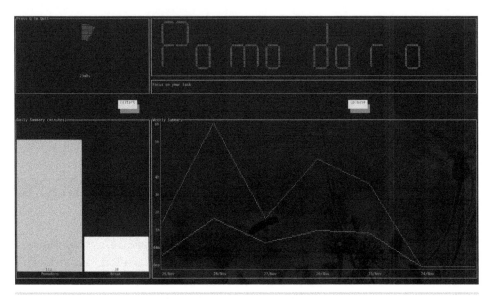

Figure 16—Pomodoro Screen

To make it easier to follow the examples in the book, you can copy the existing version of your Pomodoro application to a new working environment. By doing this, your application source files will match the description provided in this chapter. This isn't strictly necessary, and you can continue to develop your application in its original directory. If you prefer this alternative, ensure you're changing the appropriate files and adding new files to the correct path relative to the original directory.

First, switch to your book's root directory and create the directory persistentDataSQL for the new version of your application:

```
$ cd $HOME/pragprog.com/rggo/
$ mkdir -p $HOME/pragprog.com/rggo/persistentDataSQL
```

Then copy the directory pomo from the original directory $HOME/pragprog.com/rggo/interactiveTools to the newly created directory recursively, and switch to it:

```
$ cp -r $HOME/pragprog.com/rggo/interactiveTools/pomo \
  $HOME/pragprog.com/rggo/persistentDataSQL
$ cd $HOME/pragprog.com/rggo/persistentDataSQL/pomo
```

Once you switch to the new directory, you'll be able to continue developing your application from the same point. Because you're using Go modules, you don't need to take any extra actions. Go modules will resolve the modules to the current directory for you automatically.

Now that the application is ready for you to continue developing it, let's install SQLite.

Getting Started with SQLite

SQLite implements both a library to access the database and a file format to store the data. To use it with other applications, you need SQLite installed on your system.

If you're running Linux, there's a good chance you already have SQLite installed, since many applications use it to store data. You can use your distribution's package manager to check for and install SQLite if it's not installed yet. SQLite is available with most popular Linux distributions. For more details, consult your distribution's documentation and package repositories.

If you're using macOS, install SQLite by using Homebrew:[3]

```
$ brew install sqlite3
```

In Windows, you can download a precompiled version of SQLite from its download page,[4] or use Chocolatey:[5]

```
C:\> choco install SQLite
```

Once SQLite is installed, ensure it works correctly. First, switch to your application directory:

```
$ cd $HOME/pragprog.com/rggo/persistentDataSQL/pomo
```

SQLite databases consist of a single file that uses the .db extension by convention. Saving the entire database in a single file makes it more portable, and is one of SQLite's main benefits. Start the SQLite client with the command sqlite3, followed by the filename pomo.db to save the database in:

```
$ sqlite3 pomo.db
SQLite version 3.34.1 2021-01-20 14:10:07
Enter ".help" for usage hints.
sqlite>
```

The SQLite client launches. You can run SQLite commands by prepending them with a period (.). For example, to see a list of tables, type .tables, and to quit the client interface, type .quit. Type .help for an exhaustive list of available commands.

---

3. brew.sh/
4. www.sqlite.org/download.html
5. chocolatey.org/

Try to list existing tables:

```
sqlite> .tables
sqlite>
```

Since this is a newly created database, it has no tables yet. Let's create a new table. You can execute database queries and statements by typing them directly into the client and followed by a semicolon ; character. SQLite allows multiline input to keep your queries organized and readable. Create a table interval to hold data for your Pomodoro application using the CREATE TABLE SQL statement:

```
sqlite> CREATE TABLE "interval" (
   ...> "id"    INTEGER,
   ...> "start_time"    DATETIME NOT NULL,
   ...> "planned_duration"      INTEGER DEFAULT 0,
   ...> "actual_duration"       INTEGER DEFAULT 0,
   ...> "category"  TEXT NOT NULL,
   ...> "state" INTEGER DEFAULT 1,
   ...> PRIMARY KEY("id")
   ...> );
sqlite>
```

List the tables again to confirm the table was created:

```
sqlite> .tables
interval
```

The table was created but it has no data. Add a few entries in the table using the INSERT SQL statement. Provide a value for each field of the database. Use NULL as a value for the id column to allow it to autoincrement and the function date('now') to insert the current date in the start_time column:

```
sqlite> INSERT INTO interval VALUES(NULL, date('now'),25,25,"Pomodoro",3);
sqlite> INSERT INTO interval VALUES(NULL, date('now'),5,5,"ShortBreak",3);
sqlite> INSERT INTO interval VALUES(NULL, date('now'),15,15,"LongBreak",3);
```

Now, use SQL SELECT statements to select data from the table. For example, to see all rows and columns, use SELECT *:

```
sqlite> SELECT * FROM interval;
1|2021-02-16|25|25|Pomodoro|3
2|2021-02-16|5|5|ShortBreak|3
3|2021-02-16|15|15|LongBreak|3
```

You can also limit the rows of your query using the WHERE statement followed by a condition. For example, query all rows where the category column matches Pomodoro:

```
sqlite> SELECT * FROM interval WHERE category='Pomodoro';
1|2021-02-16|25|25|Pomodoro|3
```

Once you're done testing, delete the data from the table using the DELETE statement. Use a WHERE statement to limit the rows. Always pay attention when using DELETE because the default behavior, without a WHERE condition, deletes all the data from table. In this case, you can delete all the rows since the application will manage the data within the table:

```
sqlite> DELETE FROM interval;
sqlite> SELECT COUNT(*) FROM interval;
0
sqlite> .quit
```

To get more familiar with SQL and how to use it with SQLite, consult SQLite's documentation.[6]

You'll use some of these queries and statements later when developing the integration between your application and SQLite, but your application will manage the data within the database. To accomplish that, first, let's connect Go to SQLite.

Go, SQL, and SQLite

Go talks to SQL databases using the package database/sql. This package provides a generic interface to databases that use SQL. It allows you to connect to and interface with different databases by providing the queries and statements to execute.

The database/sql package provides a balance between a low-level and high-level interface. It abstracts data types, connections, and other lower-level aspects of connecting to a database engine, but it still requires you to execute queries through SQL statements. It allows great flexibility for developing applications that rely on databases but requires writing your own functions to process data.

In addition to the package database/sql, you need access to a specific driver to connect to the required database. The driver works together with the database/sql package, implementing the details to interface with the desired database engine. These database drivers are not part of Go's standard library and are generally developed and maintained by the open source community. For a complete list of available drivers, consult Go's SQL database drivers wiki.[7]

---

6. www.sqlite.org/docs.html
7. github.com/golang/go/wiki/SQLDrivers

For this application, you'll use the go-sqlite3 driver.[8] This driver uses C bindings to connect to SQLite, so you need to have CGO[9] enabled and a C compiler available. CGO is part of the Go tools and the standard way to call C/C++ libraries from Go.

For Linux, you can use gcc, which is available with most Linux distributions by default. If it isn't installed, install it using your distribution's package manager. For macOS, install XCode[10] to have access to Apple's C compiler and other developer tools.

For Windows, you need to install a C compiler and toolchain, such as TDM-GCC[11] or MINGW.[12] If you use Chocolatey, you can install the MINGW gcc toolchain directly from it, like this:

```
C:\> choco install mingw
```

After installing a gcc toolchain, ensure that it's available on the system PATH so the Go compiler can access it.

Before downloading and building the driver, ensure that CGO is enabled using go env:

```
$ go env CGO_ENABLED
1
```

If CGO isn't enabled, you can enable it permanently by using go env, like this:

```
$ go env -w CGO_ENABLED=1
$ go env CGO_ENABLED
1
```

If you prefer to temporarily enable CGO to build the SQLite driver, use the shell export command instead:

```
$ export CGO_ENABLED=1
```

At the time of writing this book, there's an issue with SQLite libraries and GCC 10 or greater that causes the driver to display warning messages every time you connect to a database. These messages aren't critical, but they disrupt the application flow and interface. You can prevent this from happening by setting the GCC flag -Wno-return-local-addr before installing the driver:

```
$ go env -w CGO_CFLAGS="-g -O2 -Wno-return-local-addr"
```

---

8. github.com/mattn/go-sqlite3
9. https://golang.org/cmd/go/#hdr-Calling_between_Go_and_C
10. en.wikipedia.org/wiki/Xcode
11. https://sourceforge.net/projects/tdm-gcc/
12. sourceforge.net/projects/mingw-w64

Now download and install go-sqlite3 using the go command:

```
$ go get github.com/mattn/go-sqlite3
$ go install github.com/mattn/go-sqlite3
```

By installing the driver, you compile and cache the library, which lets you use it to build your application without requiring GCC again and without recompiling every time, which saves you time, especially while developing and testing your application.

Your environment is ready. Next, let's add the new SQLite repository to your Pomodoro application.

Persisting Data in the Database

Now that your environment is ready, you'll add a new repository to save *pomo's* application data into SQLite. Currently, the application supports only the inMemory repository. When you add more repositories, you need to provide a way for your users to choose how to store data. You can do this at compile time or run time.

Providing this choice at run time makes your application more flexible, allowing users to choose which data store to use for every execution. To do this, you need to compile your application with support for all required data stores and allow the user to choose one, using command-line parameters or configuration options.

You can also compile the application with support for a specific data store, creating a binary file with fewer dependencies and a smaller size. The application will be less flexible but more efficient. To do this, you include specific files in your build according to different criteria. The criteria depend on your requirements. For example, you can include different data stores for testing, production environments, or when compiling for an operating system that doesn't support a required dependency.

For this example, you'll take the second approach and define the data store at compile time so you can build this application and test it using the inMemory repository in case you are unable to install SQLite. You'll do this by including specific files in your build using build tags. You used them in Executing Integration Tests, on page 336, to execute integration tests when using a specific tag. You'll learn more about build tags in Chapter 11, Distributing Your Tool, on page 433.

Since saving the data to the database gives the application more functionality, let's make it the default option, so when you build the application without any tags, it will include the SQLite repository and not the inMemory one. When you want to build the application with support for inMemory storage, you'll use the build tag *inmemory*.

Update the files related to the inMemory repository with the inmemory build tag by adding the line // +build inmemory at the top of each file. First, edit pomodoro/repository/inMemory.go:

persistentDataSQL/pomo/pomodoro/repository/inMemory.go
```
// +build inmemory

package repository
```

It's critical to leave a blank line between the build tag comment and the package definition. If you don't, Go will consider it to be a regular comment and will ignore the build tag.

Next, include the same build tag for the remaining two files: pomodoro/inmemory_test.go and cmd/repoinmemory.go:

persistentDataSQL/pomo/pomodoro/inmemory_test.go
```
// +build inmemory

package pomodoro_test
```

persistentDataSQL/pomo/cmd/repoinmemory.go
```
// +build inmemory

package cmd
```

Create a new file called sqlite3.go in the repository package directory pomodoro/repository, which will contain the code for the SQLite repository. Open the file in your editor and add the build tag to include this file when the tag inmemory isn't available. Use the character ! to negate the tag:

persistentDataSQL/pomo/pomodoro/repository/sqlite3.go
```
// +build !inmemory
```

Then add the package definition and the import list. For this file, you'll use the database/sql package to interface with a SQL database, the sync package to use a mutex to prevent concurrent access to the database, the time package to use time and date functions, the SQLite driver package github.com/mattn/go-sqlite3, and your pomodoro package that contains the repository interface definition:

persistentDataSQL/pomo/pomodoro/repository/sqlite3.go
```
package repository

import (
  "database/sql"
  "sync"
  "time"
```

```
  // Blank import for sqlite3 driver only
  _ "github.com/mattn/go-sqlite3"
  "pragprog.com/rggo/interactiveTools/pomo/pomodoro"
)
```

You import the SQLite driver using the blank identifier _ to ensure Go doesn't throw a build error because you're not using any functions directly from that package. You import this package to enable the database/sql package to interface with the desired database.

Next, define a constant string to represent the SQL statement required to create the interval table where you'll store the Pomodoro interval data. You'll use this constant later to initialize the database with a single table. This statement is similar to the one you used when testing the SQLite database before, but it uses CREATE TABLE IF NOT EXISTS to create the table only if it's not already created, avoiding additional checks.

When you were testing SQLite, you created the table manually, but it's not a good user experience to make your users do that. Generally speaking, you want to initialize your database with the required structure and, in some cases, with data. You have different options for doing that. Because SQLite stores databases in a single file, you could provide the database file directly, but that's another file for you to maintain and package.

Another common practice is to provide scripts or migration files to initialize your databases. For large and complex applications, you may need several files, and it's worth managing and version controlling them separately.

Since you're creating a small application that uses a single table, you can provide the table initialization statement as a constant within your source code.

persistentDataSQL/pomo/pomodoro/repository/sqlite3.go
```
const (
  createTableInterval string = `CREATE TABLE IF NOT EXISTS "interval" (
        "id"     INTEGER,
        "start_time"    DATETIME NOT NULL,
        "planned_duration"     INTEGER DEFAULT 0,
        "actual_duration"      INTEGER DEFAULT 0,
        "category"   TEXT NOT NULL,
        "state" INTEGER DEFAULT 1,
        PRIMARY KEY("id")
);`
)
```

The database table structure represents the pomodoro/Interval type, with columns matching each of the Interval's fields, according to the table on page 404.

Field	Field Type	Column	Column Data Type	Comment
ID	int64	id	INTEGER	This is the table's PRIMARY KEY. SQLite automatically sets autoincrement for a PRIMARY KEY column of type INTEGER.
StartTime	time.Time	start_time	DATE-TIME	The sqlite3 driver automatically handles conversion between Go's time.Time type and SQLite DATETIME.
Planned-Duration	time.Dura-tion	planned_duration	INTEGER	The driver handles the conversion between the data types implicitly.
Actual-Duration	time.Dura-tion	actual_duration	INTEGER	The driver handles the conversion between the data types implicitly.
Category	string	category	TEXT	Setting the NOT NULL constraint as category is always required.
State	int	state	INTEGER	

Next, define the dbRepo type that represents your SQLite repository. To use it as a repository, you'll implement the methods from the pomodoro.Repository interface. This type has a single unexported field, db, which is a pointer to the sql.DB type, representing the database handle. It also embeds the sync.Mutex type, allowing you to access its fields as methods directly from instances of your type. You'll use mutexes to prevent concurrent access to the database.

persistentDataSQL/pomo/pomodoro/repository/sqlite3.go
```
type dbRepo struct {
  db *sql.DB
  sync.RWMutex
}
```

Define a constructor function NewSQLite3Repo() to instantiate a new dbRepo. This function takes a dbfile string parameter representing the database file to connect to and returns a pointer to the dbRepo instance or an error.

persistentDataSQL/pomo/pomodoro/repository/sqlite3.go
```
func NewSQLite3Repo(dbfile string) (*dbRepo, error) {
```

To connect to the database, use the function sql.Open() from the database/sql package, providing the driver name sqlite3 and the connection string, which in this case is the path to the database file represented by the dbfile parameter. Return an error if necessary:

```
persistentDataSQL/pomo/pomodoro/repository/sqlite3.go
db, err := sql.Open("sqlite3", dbfile)
if err != nil {
  return nil, err
}
```

For more complex applications, you can pass additional database parameters using the connection string, including authentication, encryption, cache options, and more. For a full list, consult the sqlite3 driver documentation.[13]

The driver also takes care of connection details, such as opening an existing database file or creating a new one if necessary, so you don't need to worry about that.

After opening the database connection, you can use the db handler to specify additional connection options such as the maximum number of open connections or the database connection's maximum lifetime. Correctly adjusting these parameters may improve your program's performance or its use of system resources. For this application, these considerations are not critical but, as an example, use db.SetConnMaxLifetime to set the maximum connection time to 30 minutes, and set the maximum number of connections, db.SetMaxOpenConns to one because this is a single-user application:

```
persistentDataSQL/pomo/pomodoro/repository/sqlite3.go
db.SetConnMaxLifetime(30 * time.Minute)
db.SetMaxOpenConns(1)
```

Verify that the connection with the DB was established by using the Ping() method. In this example, for brevity, return the error if necessary. For more complex applications, you'll include additional logic to handle the issue or retry the connection a few times if required:

```
persistentDataSQL/pomo/pomodoro/repository/sqlite3.go
if err := db.Ping(); err != nil {
  return nil, err
}
```

Next, initialize the database using the constant statement createTableInterval, which you defined before. Since your statement uses the instruction CREATE

---

13. github.com/mattn/go-sqlite3#connection-string

TABLE IF NOT EXISTS, it's safe to run it every time as it will create the table only if needed:

persistentDataSQL/pomo/pomodoro/repository/sqlite3.go
```
if _, err := db.Exec(createTableInterval); err != nil {
  return nil, err
}
```

After completing the setup, return a pointer to a new dbRepo type, setting the field db to your database handler:

persistentDataSQL/pomo/pomodoro/repository/sqlite3.go
```
  return &dbRepo{
    db: db,
  }, nil
}
```

Now implement the methods required to make dbRepo act like a pomodoro. Repository. You defined this interface in Storing Data with the Repository Pattern, on page 356, with these methods:

```
type Repository interface {
  Create(i Interval) (int64, error)
  Update(i Interval) error
  ByID(id int64) (Interval, error)
  Last() (Interval, error)
  Breaks(n int) ([]Interval, error)
}
```

First, implement the Create() method to add a new interval to the repository. This method receives an instance of type pomodoro.Interval, attempts to add it to the repository, and returns its id if it succeeded or an error if it failed. Define the method with the signature required by the Repository interface, associating it with the dbRepo type by setting it as the method receiver:

persistentDataSQL/pomo/pomodoro/repository/sqlite3.go
```
func (r *dbRepo) Create(i pomodoro.Interval) (int64, error) {
```

Then, within the method's body, use the embedded function Lock() from the sync package to lock the repository, preventing concurrent access to it. Since this is a single-user application and performance isn't a concern, locking the repository prevents concurrency issues and avoids adding more logic to handle it. Defer the Unlock() execution to ensure the repository is unlocked when the function returns:

```
persistentDataSQL/pomo/pomodoro/repository/sqlite3.go
// Create entry in the repository
r.Lock()
defer r.Unlock()
```

Next, prepare the INSERT SQL statement to insert data into the database. Preparing a statement sends the statement with placeholders for the parameters to the database. The database compiles and caches the statement, allowing you to execute the same query multiple times with different parameters more efficiently. Prepared statements can also improve security by preventing SQL injection issues.[14] Since this is a local application, performance and security aren't major concerns, so using prepared statements isn't strictly necessary. It's still cleaner than concatenating strings and parameters to define query statements. Add the following code to define the prepared statement:

```
persistentDataSQL/pomo/pomodoro/repository/sqlite3.go
// Prepare INSERT statement
insStmt, err := r.db.Prepare("INSERT INTO interval VALUES(NULL, ?,?,?,?,?)")
if err != nil {
  return 0, err
}
defer insStmt.Close()
```

SQLite uses the question mark character ? as the placeholder for parameters. Other database engines use different characters, so check your database documentation for specific details. In this block, you're also deferring closing the prepared statements to ensure Go cleans up resources.

Next, execute the query using the prepared statement passing all required parameters you want to insert into the database and storing the results in a variable named res of the type sql.Results. Check for any issues and return an error if something went wrong:

```
persistentDataSQL/pomo/pomodoro/repository/sqlite3.go
// Exec INSERT statement
res, err := insStmt.Exec(i.StartTime, i.PlannedDuration,
  i.ActualDuration, i.Category, i.State)
if err != nil {
  return 0, err
}
```

Then use the method res.LastInsertId() from the sql.Results type to obtain the ID of the row you inserted. Return this ID to complete the method:

---

14. en.wikipedia.org/wiki/SQL_injection

persistentDataSQL/pomo/pomodoro/repository/sqlite3.go
```go
  // INSERT results
  var id int64
  if id, err = res.LastInsertId(); err != nil {
    return 0, err
  }

  return id, nil
}
```

Next, define the Update() method to modify an existing Interval entry in the repository. This method follows the same structure as the Create() method you just defined. This method uses an UPDATE SQL statement to update a single row based on the existing record's ID, using the condition WHERE id=?. It then uses the method res.RowsAffected() from sql.Results to check for errors:

persistentDataSQL/pomo/pomodoro/repository/sqlite3.go
```go
func (r *dbRepo) Update(i pomodoro.Interval) error {
  // Update entry in the repository
  r.Lock()
  defer r.Unlock()

  // Prepare UPDATE statement
  updStmt, err := r.db.Prepare(
    "UPDATE interval SET start_time=?, actual_duration=?, state=? WHERE id=?")
  if err != nil {
    return err
  }
  defer updStmt.Close()

  // Exec UPDATE statement
  res, err := updStmt.Exec(i.StartTime, i.ActualDuration, i.State, i.ID)
  if err != nil {
    return err
  }

  // UPDATE results
  _, err = res.RowsAffected()
  return err
}
```

Now define the method ByID(), which returns a single interval from the repository based on its ID:

persistentDataSQL/pomo/pomodoro/repository/sqlite3.go
```go
func (r *dbRepo) ByID(id int64) (pomodoro.Interval, error) {
```

Lock the database for reading by using the embedded function RLock() from the package sync. This lock blocks and waits if the database is locked for writing, providing safe concurrent read and write operations, while allowing multiple reads to improve performance:

```
persistentDataSQL/pomo/pomodoro/repository/sqlite3.go
// Search items in the repository by ID
r.RLock()
defer r.RUnlock()
```

The database/sql package provides a series of methods for executing database queries that return rows. Use the method QueryRow() to execute a SELECT query that returns a single row based on its ID:

```
persistentDataSQL/pomo/pomodoro/repository/sqlite3.go
// Query DB row based on ID
row := r.db.QueryRow("SELECT * FROM interval WHERE id=?", id)
```

The method QueryRow returns a single result of type sql.Row. Use its Scan() method to parse the returned columns into pointers to Interval field values. Scan() expects a number of parameters that match the number of returned rows in the same order that they are returned:

```
persistentDataSQL/pomo/pomodoro/repository/sqlite3.go
// Parse row into Interval struct
i := pomodoro.Interval{}
err := row.Scan(&i.ID, &i.StartTime, &i.PlannedDuration,
  &i.ActualDuration, &i.Category, &i.State)
```

The Scan() method converts columns to Go types automatically for most of Go's built-in types such as string or int. For a complete list of supported types and rules, consult the documentation.[15] In addition to built-in types, the sqlite3 driver converts the SQLite DATETIME column to Go's time.Time automatically.

Complete your method by returning the Interval and any errors:

```
persistentDataSQL/pomo/pomodoro/repository/sqlite3.go
  return i, err
}
```

Next, follow a similar structure to implement the Last() method, which queries and returns the last Interval from the repository:

```
persistentDataSQL/pomo/pomodoro/repository/sqlite3.go
func (r *dbRepo) Last() (pomodoro.Interval, error) {
  // Search last item in the repository
  r.RLock()
  defer r.RUnlock()

  // Query and parse last row into Interval struct
  last := pomodoro.Interval{}
```

---

15. pkg.go.dev/database/sql#Rows.Scan

```
err := r.db.QueryRow("SELECT * FROM interval ORDER BY id desc LIMIT 1").Scan(
  &last.ID, &last.StartTime, &last.PlannedDuration,
  &last.ActualDuration, &last.Category, &last.State,
)

if err == sql.ErrNoRows {
  return last, pomodoro.ErrNoIntervals
}

if err != nil {
  return last, err
}

return last, nil
}
```

Now add the method Breaks() to query and return n intervals, which category matches to either ShortBreak or LongBreak:

persistentDataSQL/pomo/pomodoro/repository/sqlite3.go
```
func (r *dbRepo) Breaks(n int) ([]pomodoro.Interval, error) {
```

Lock the database for reading and define the SELECT query to search for breaks. Use the SQL LIKE operator and the percent sign % to query a pattern that ends with Break:

persistentDataSQL/pomo/pomodoro/repository/sqlite3.go
```
// Search last n items of type break in the repository
r.RLock()
defer r.RUnlock()

// Define SELECT query for breaks
stmt := `SELECT * FROM interval WHERE category LIKE '%Break'
ORDER BY id DESC LIMIT ?`

// Query DB for breaks
rows, err := r.db.Query(stmt, n)
if err != nil {
  return nil, err
}
defer rows.Close()

// Parse data into slice of Interval
data := []pomodoro.Interval{}
for rows.Next() {
  i := pomodoro.Interval{}
  err = rows.Scan(&i.ID, &i.StartTime, &i.PlannedDuration,
    &i.ActualDuration, &i.Category, &i.State)
  if err != nil {
    return nil, err
  }

  data = append(data, i)
}
```

```
  err = rows.Err()
  if err != nil {
    return nil, err
  }

  // Return data
  return data, nil
}

func (r *dbRepo) CategorySummary(day time.Time,
  filter string) (time.Duration, error) {

  // Return a daily summary
  r.RLock()
  defer r.RUnlock()

  // Define SELECT query for daily summary
  stmt := `SELECT sum(actual_duration) FROM interval
  WHERE category LIKE ? AND
  strftime('%Y-%m-%d', start_time, 'localtime')=
  strftime('%Y-%m-%d', ?, 'localtime')`

  var ds sql.NullInt64
  err := r.db.QueryRow(stmt, filter, day).Scan(&ds)

  var d time.Duration
  if ds.Valid {
    d = time.Duration(ds.Int64)
  }

  return d, err
}
```

This will look different on your system because here the query statement is broken into two lines to keep the lines within the book's margins.

Execute the query using the Query() method that returns multiple rows, providing the parameter n to replace the query statement placeholder. This method returns rows using the type sql.Rows. Defer executing rows.Close() to ensure Go releases resources at the end of the function:

persistentDataSQL/pomo/pomodoro/repository/sqlite3.go
```
// Query DB for breaks
rows, err := r.db.Query(stmt, n)
if err != nil {
  return nil, err
}
defer rows.Close()
```

Parse the results into a slice of Interval. Use the rows.Next() method to iterate through the returned rows. This method returns true when results are present to be processed, or false when no more results exist or an error occurs. Within the loop, use Scan() to parse each row the same way you used it for the other methods:

persistentDataSQL/pomo/pomodoro/repository/sqlite3.go
```go
// Parse data into slice of Interval
data := []pomodoro.Interval{}
for rows.Next() {
  i := pomodoro.Interval{}
  err = rows.Scan(&i.ID, &i.StartTime, &i.PlannedDuration,
    &i.ActualDuration, &i.Category, &i.State)
  if err != nil {
    return nil, err
  }

  data = append(data, i)
}
err = rows.Err()
if err != nil {
  return nil, err
}
```

After the loop, the code checks for an error using rows.Err() to ensure the loop processed all the results.

Complete the method by returning the data:

persistentDataSQL/pomo/pomodoro/repository/sqlite3.go
```go
  // Return data
  return data, nil
}
```

Your SQLite repository is complete. Save and close this file. Now, let's test the pomodoro package using this repository.

Testing the Repository with SQLite

In Testing the Pomodoro Functionality, on page 359, you wrote tests for the pomodoro package using a helper function getRepo() to obtain the repository. At that time, only the inMemory repository was available. Now that you've added the sqlite3 repository, you'll provide an alternative version of this function that returns the new repository. You can control when to use each by applying build tags. Switch back to the pomodoro package directory and create a file named sqlite3_test.go:

```
$ cd $HOME/pragprog.com/rggo/persistentDataSQL/pomo/pomodoro
```

Open the sqlite3_test.go file in your editor to write the specific function for this repository implementation. Add the build tag +build !inmemory to use this file unless you provide the tag inmemory, in which case it'll include the file inmemory_test.go instead. You already added the equivalent build tag to that file. Skip a line and add the package definition:

persistentDataSQL/pomo/pomodoro/sqlite3_test.go
```
//+build !inmemory

package pomodoro_test
```

Next, add the import section. You'll use the io/ioutil package to create a temporary file, the os package to delete the file, the testing package for the testing-related functions, and your pomodoro and repository packages to use the repository interface:

persistentDataSQL/pomo/pomodoro/sqlite3_test.go
```
import (
  "io/ioutil"
  "os"
  "testing"

  "pragprog.com/rggo/interactiveTools/pomo/pomodoro"
  "pragprog.com/rggo/interactiveTools/pomo/pomodoro/repository"
)
```

Finally, define the function getRepo(), which will return the repository instance and a cleanup function. Use ioutil.TempFile() to create a temporary file and use its name to define a new sqlite3 repository. Return this repository and a cleanup function that deletes the file:

persistentDataSQL/pomo/pomodoro/sqlite3_test.go
```
func getRepo(t *testing.T) (pomodoro.Repository, func()) {
  t.Helper()

  tf, err := ioutil.TempFile("", "pomo")
  if err != nil {
    t.Fatal(err)
  }
  tf.Close()

  dbRepo, err := repository.NewSQLite3Repo(tf.Name())

  if err != nil {
    t.Fatal(err)
  }

  return dbRepo, func() {
    os.Remove(tf.Name())
  }
}
```

Save and close the file, and execute the tests again to test the new repository:

```
$ go test
PASS
ok          pragprog.com/rggo/interactiveTools/pomo/pomodoro          5.075s
```

To execute the tests using the inMemory repository, provide the inmemory tag to the test command:

```
$ go test -tags=inmemory
PASS
ok          pragprog.com/rggo/interactiveTools/pomo/pomodoro          5.043s
```

The test result doesn't show which repository back end it uses, because the test relies on the higher-level Repository interface. If you want to make sure the test is using the SQLite repository, you can monitor the temp directory to verify it creates temporary database files following the pattern pomo211866403; or you can print a message, such as Using SQLite repository, using the method t.Log() in the getRepo() function to provide some quick visual feedback.

Now that the new repository tests pass, let's update the application to use it.

Updating the Application to Use the SQLite Repository

Once the SQLite repository is available, you need to update the *Pomo* application to use it. Start by switching into the cmd directory:

```
$ cd $HOME/pragprog.com/rggo/persistentDataSQL/pomo/cmd
```

Edit the file root.go to add a new command-line parameter that lets the user specify the database file to use. Bind that flag with viper so the user can set it in the configuration file as well:

persistentDataSQL/pomo/cmd/root.go
```
func init() {
  cobra.OnInitialize(initConfig)

  rootCmd.PersistentFlags().StringVar(&cfgFile, "config", "",
    "config file (default is $HOME/.pomo.yaml)")

➤  rootCmd.Flags().StringP("db", "d", "pomo.db", "Database file")

  rootCmd.Flags().DurationP("pomo", "p", 25*time.Minute,
                           "Pomodoro duration")
  rootCmd.Flags().DurationP("short", "s", 5*time.Minute,
                           "Short break duration")
  rootCmd.Flags().DurationP("long", "l", 15*time.Minute,
                           "Long break duration")
➤  viper.BindPFlag("db", rootCmd.Flags().Lookup("db"))
  viper.BindPFlag("pomo", rootCmd.Flags().Lookup("pomo"))
  viper.BindPFlag("short", rootCmd.Flags().Lookup("short"))
  viper.BindPFlag("long", rootCmd.Flags().Lookup("long"))
}
```

Save and close this file. Create a new file called reposqlite.go, which will contain the function getRepo() used to obtain a SQLite repository instance. To use this file as the default, add the build tag +build !inmemory. You already added the counterpart build tag to that file. Then skip a line and add the package definition:

persistentDataSQL/pomo/cmd/reposqlite.go
```
// +build !inmemory

package cmd
```

Add the import section. You'll use the viper package to obtain the database file name and your pomodoro and repository packages to use the repository interface:

persistentDataSQL/pomo/cmd/reposqlite.go
```
import (
  "github.com/spf13/viper"
  "pragprog.com/rggo/interactiveTools/pomo/pomodoro"
  "pragprog.com/rggo/interactiveTools/pomo/pomodoro/repository"
)
```

Finally, define the getRepo() function to return the repository instance based on the configured database file name:

persistentDataSQL/pomo/cmd/reposqlite.go
```
func getRepo() (pomodoro.Repository, error) {
  repo, err := repository.NewSQLite3Repo(viper.GetString("db"))
  if err != nil {
    return nil, err
  }

  return repo, nil
}
```

Save this file, switch back to the application's root directory, and build your application to test it using the new repository:

```
$ cd ..
$ go build
```

Run the application with --help to see the new --db option. By default, if not specified, *pomo* creates and uses a database file pomo.db:

```
$ ./pomo --help
Interactive Pomodoro Timer

Usage:
  pomo [flags]

Flags:
      --config string   config file (default is $HOME/.pomo.yaml)
  -d, --db string       Database file (default "pomo.db")
  -h, --help            help for pomo
```

```
-l, --long duration     Long break duration (default 15m0s)
-p, --pomo duration     Pomodoro duration (default 25m0s)
-s, --short duration    Short break duration (default 5m0s)
```

Execute your application to see that it creates this file:

```
$ ./pomo
```

Open a new terminal, switch into your application's root directory, and check that the file pomo.db exists:

```
$ cd $HOME/pragprog.com/rggo/persistentDataSQL/pomo
$ ls podmo.db
pomo.db
```

Use the sqlite3 client to connect to this database. Execute a SELECT query on interval. It should return no results as the application has just created this database and table:

```
$ sqlite3 pomo.db
SQLite version 3.34.1 2021-01-20 14:10:07
Enter ".help" for usage hints.
sqlite> select * from interval;
sqlite>
```

Switch back to your original terminal and start an interval using the application's Start button. Switch back to the terminal running the sqlite3 client, and reexecute the same query to see that a new entry now exists:

```
sqlite> select * from interval;
1|2021-02-20 15:05:43.998875893-05:00|10000000000|1000000000|Pomodoro|1
sqlite> select * from interval;
1|2021-02-20 15:05:43.998875893-05:00|10000000000|10000000000|Pomodoro|3
```

Your results may vary a little depending on your Pomodoro configuration and interval state when you run the queries.

Your application is now capable of saving historical data about your intervals in a database. Let's use the historical data to display a summary of the activities to the users.

Displaying a Summary to the Users

One of the benefits of having the data stored in a SQL database is that you can use its expressive power to query and summarize the data in many ways. Let's use that to present a summary of the users' activities in the application.

To display the data to the users, you'll add two new sections to your application's interface as shown in the figures on page 417.

1.

```
┌Daily Summary (minutes)─────────────────────────────┐
│                                                    │
│                                                    │
│                                                    │
│                                                    │
│                                                    │
│                                                    │
│                                                    │
│                                                    │
│                                                    │
│                                                    │
│                                                    │
│                                                    │
│                                                    │
│                          ┌──────────────────────┐  │
│                          │                      │  │
│          112             │          30          │  │
│        Pomodoro          │        Break         │  │
└────────────────────────────────────────────────────┘
```

The Daily Summary section presents a summary of the current day's activities in minutes broken down by Pomodoro and Breaks.

You'll implement the Daily Summary interface using the BarChart Termdash widget.

2.

The Weekly Summary section displays the current week's activities broken down by Pomodoro and Breaks, using the Termdash LineChart widget.

These widgets require data to display. You can extract the required data using a single SQL query with the appropriate filters. You'll add a single method to the Repository interface to query the data and then use a pair of functions to transform the data according to each widget's requirements.

Start by modifying the Repository interface. Switch to directory pomodoro under your application's root directory:

```
$ cd $HOME/pragprog.com/rggo/persistentDataSQL/pomo/pomodoro
```

Edit the file interval.go and add a new method called CategorySummary() to the Repository interface:

persistentDataSQL/pomo/pomodoro/interval.go
```go
type Repository interface {
  Create(i Interval) (int64, error)
  Update(i Interval) error
  ByID(id int64) (Interval, error)
  Last() (Interval, error)
  Breaks(n int) ([]Interval, error)
➤ CategorySummary(day time.Time, filter string) (time.Duration, error)
}
```

This method takes two inputs: a time.Time type representing the day to summarize and a string filter to filter the category. It returns a value of type time.Duration as a sum of the time spent on that category for a given day.

You need to implement this new method on both repositories, so start with the inMemory repository. Open the file repository/inMemory.go and add the new method CategorySummary() with the same signature as the one defined in the interface:

persistentDataSQL/pomo/pomodoro/repository/inMemory.go
```go
func (r *inMemoryRepo) CategorySummary(day time.Time,
  filter string) (time.Duration, error) {

  // Return a daily summary
  r.RLock()
  defer r.RUnlock()

  var d time.Duration

  filter = strings.Trim(filter, "%")

  for _, i := range r.intervals {
    if i.StartTime.Year() == day.Year() &&
      i.StartTime.YearDay() == day.YearDay() {
      if strings.Contains(i.Category, filter) {
        d += i.ActualDuration
      }
    }
  }

  return d, nil
}
```

This is similar to the other function in this repository. You iterate over all the entries, and, if the StartTime matches the given year and day and the Category matches the given filter, add the ActualDuration to the total. You return the total at the end.

Next, implement the method for the sqlite3 repository. Save and close the inMemory file and open repository/sqlite3.go. Add the method's definition following the required signature:

```
func (r *dbRepo) CategorySummary(day time.Time,
  filter string) (time.Duration, error) {
```

Within the method's body, first lock the repository for reading as you did for other querying methods:

```
// Return a daily summary
r.RLock()
defer r.RUnlock()
```

Then define the SQL SELECT statement to retrieve the required data. Start by defining the stmt variable and use a raw literal string with the backtick character to write the query on multiple lines. Use the SQL aggregation function sum() to add the values directly in the database:

```
// Define SELECT query for daily summary
stmt := `SELECT sum(actual_duration) FROM interval
```

Next, define the WHERE condition to limit the entries queried. The first condition is category LIKE, followed by an expression. Leave the question mark as a placeholder for the query. You use the given filter as this value during the actual query.

```
WHERE category LIKE ? AND
```

For the next condition, compare the record date with the given variable day. Use the SQL function strftime() with the parameter '%Y-%m-%d' to extract the date part and ignore the time, allowing it to query all records for the same day. Use the SQL column start_time for the first side of the comparison, and leave the ? placeholder for the second. Use the parameter localtime to ensure SQLite doesn't convert the time to UTC, which would result in shifting some dates:

```
strftime('%Y-%m-%d', start_time, 'localtime')=
strftime('%Y-%m-%d', ?, 'localtime')`
```

When you execute this query, the result will be NULL if you're querying a day or category for which there's no data. When using the database/sql package, you need to handle potential NULL values explicitly as Go won't perform automatic conversion. This package provides a series of types that you can use to represent values from the database that can be NULL. For this program, create a variable called ds of type sql.NullInt64, which is an int64 that can be NULL:

```
var ds sql.NullInt64
```

Then execute the query using the method QueryRow() since we expect only one result with the sum of all values. Provide the given input parameters filter and day to replace the placeholders, and scan the results into the nullable variable ds:

persistentDataSQL/pomo/pomodoro/repository/sqlite3.go
```
err := r.db.QueryRow(stmt, filter, day).Scan(&ds)
```

Now use the ds variable to verify whether the value is NULL. Create a variable d of type time.Duration that Go initializes as zero. Use the field ds.Valid to check that ds contains a valid int64 instead of NULL. In this case, extract the value using the field ds.Int64, convert it to time.Duration, and assign it to d.

persistentDataSQL/pomo/pomodoro/repository/sqlite3.go
```
var d time.Duration
if ds.Valid {
  d = time.Duration(ds.Int64)
}
```

If ds contains a NULL value, the variable d won't be updated, and it'll still be set to zero. Return this variable and the error to finish the method:

persistentDataSQL/pomo/pomodoro/repository/sqlite3.go
```
  return d, err
}
```

Save and close this file. Next, you'll add two functions to generate data in the format the widgets need. You'll add these two functions to the pomodoro package since the repository isn't exported.

Create and edit a new file called summary.go under the pomodoro directory. Add the package definition and import section, and use the fmt package to format strings and the time package to use time and date functions:

persistentDataSQL/pomo/pomodoro/summary.go
```
package pomodoro

import (
  "fmt"
  "time"
)
```

Each widget requires different data. The bar chart widget requires a slice of integers, with each element representing a bar in the chart. For this app, you'll have two bars: one representing Pomodoro time and another representing Breaks. Define the function DailySummary() that takes a time.Time type representing the day and a pointer to IntervalConfig to access the repository. It returns a slice of time.Duration and an error.

```
persistentDataSQL/pomo/pomodoro/summary.go
func DailySummary(day time.Time,
  config *IntervalConfig) ([]time.Duration, error) {
```

Even though the bar chart uses integers instead of time.Duration, you define the function with the latter type so that you can also use it to extract the data for the weekly summary. Later when you use this data in the bar chart widget, you'll convert it to integers.

Next, use the repository method CategorySummary() to extract data for the Pomodoro category. Use the constant value CategoryPomodoro as the filter:

```
persistentDataSQL/pomo/pomodoro/summary.go
dPomo, err := config.repo.CategorySummary(day, CategoryPomodoro)
if err != nil {
  return nil, err
}
```

Use the same approach to obtain the data for breaks. To sum both the long breaks and the short breaks in a single query, use the value %Break as the filter so the database searches for this pattern instead of the constant value:

```
persistentDataSQL/pomo/pomodoro/summary.go
dBreaks, err := config.repo.CategorySummary(day, "%Break")
if err != nil {
  return nil, err
}
```

Complete the function by returning both values as a slice of time.Duration values:

```
persistentDataSQL/pomo/pomodoro/summary.go
  return []time.Duration{
    dPomo,
    dBreaks,
  }, nil
}
```

The Line Chart widget needs a slice of float64 numbers representing each value on the chart's y-axis for each line. In addition to this slice, you'll also provide a map with dates to use as the x-axis label.

Define a new custom type LineSeries to represent this data:

```
persistentDataSQL/pomo/pomodoro/summary.go
type LineSeries struct {
  Name    string
  Labels map[int]string
  Values []float64
}
```

Then define the function RangeSummary() to obtain the data for the Line Chart widget. This function takes a time.Time instance representing the starting day, an integer n representing the number of days to look back from the start, and a pointer to IntervalConfig to access the repository. It returns a slice of LineSeries representing the data required for all lines in the line chart and an error. Add the following code to define the function:

persistentDataSQL/pomo/pomodoro/summary.go
```go
func RangeSummary(start time.Time, n int,
  config *IntervalConfig) ([]LineSeries, error) {
```

Then initialize two instances of LineSeries: one for Pomodoro data and another for Breaks data:

persistentDataSQL/pomo/pomodoro/summary.go
```go
pomodoroSeries := LineSeries{
  Name:   "Pomodoro",
  Labels: make(map[int]string),
  Values: make([]float64, n),
}

breakSeries := LineSeries{
  Name:   "Break",
  Labels: make(map[int]string),
  Values: make([]float64, n),
}
```

Next, iterate over the number of days n to extract. For each iteration of the loop, subtract n days from the start date using the AddDate() method with a negative number for the days parameter. Use your function DailySummary() to extract the data for the given day, create the label for that date, and assign the values to the corresponding elements of each series. Use the number of seconds as the y-axis values.

persistentDataSQL/pomo/pomodoro/summary.go
```go
for i := 0; i < n; i++ {
  day := start.AddDate(0, 0, -i)
  ds, err := DailySummary(day, config)
  if err != nil {
    return nil, err
  }

  label := fmt.Sprintf("%02d/%s", day.Day(), day.Format("Jan"))

  pomodoroSeries.Labels[i] = label
  pomodoroSeries.Values[i] = ds[0].Seconds()

  breakSeries.Labels[i] = label
  breakSeries.Values[i] = ds[1].Seconds()
}
```

Finally, return the slice of LineSeries including both series to conclude the function:

persistentDataSQL/pomo/pomodoro/summary.go
```
  return []LineSeries{
    pomodoroSeries,
    breakSeries,
  }, nil
}
```

Save and close this file. Now, let's update the application interface to display the two new widgets. Switch to the app directory:

```
$ cd ../app
```

Create and edit a new file called summaryWidgets.go to define the new widgets. Add the package definition and import list. You'll use the context package to define a cancellation context to close the widgets, the math package to use some mathematical functions, the time package to deal with times and dates, the cell, widgets/barchart, and widgets/linechart packages to create the required widgets, and your pomodoro package to access the repository:

persistentDataSQL/pomo/app/summaryWidgets.go
```
package app

import (
  "context"
  "math"
  "time"

  "github.com/mum4k/termdash/cell"
  "github.com/mum4k/termdash/widgets/barchart"
  "github.com/mum4k/termdash/widgets/linechart"
  "pragprog.com/rggo/interactiveTools/pomo/pomodoro"
)
```

Create a custom type summary as a collection of summary widgets. This is similar to how you defined the other widgets in Building the Interface Widgets, on page 368. You'll use this type to connect the widgets to the app and update them:

persistentDataSQL/pomo/app/summaryWidgets.go
```
type summary struct {
  bcDay        *barchart.BarChart
  lcWeekly     *linechart.LineChart
  updateDaily  chan bool
  updateWeekly chan bool
}
```

Define an update() method for the summary type, which will update all summary widgets by sending a value to the update channels. Each widget will have a goroutine waiting for data coming from this channel to update. This is the same approach you used for all the previous widgets:

persistentDataSQL/pomo/app/summaryWidgets.go
```go
func (s *summary) update(redrawCh chan<- bool) {
  s.updateDaily <- true
  s.updateWeekly <- true
  redrawCh <- true
}
```

Now define a newSummary() function that initializes both widgets and returns an instance of summary with them. You'll define the widget initialization functions shortly:

persistentDataSQL/pomo/app/summaryWidgets.go
```go
func newSummary(ctx context.Context, config *pomodoro.IntervalConfig,
  redrawCh chan<- bool, errorCh chan<- error) (*summary, error) {

  s := &summary{}
  var err error

  s.updateDaily = make(chan bool)
  s.updateWeekly = make(chan bool)

  s.bcDay, err = newBarChart(ctx, config, s.updateDaily, errorCh)
  if err != nil {
    return nil, err
  }

  s.lcWeekly, err = newLineChart(ctx, config, s.updateWeekly, errorCh)
  if err != nil {
    return nil, err
  }

  return s, nil
}
```

Next, define the widget initialization functions newBarChart() and newLineChart(). You'll use the same pattern for both functions: you'll initialize the widget, define an update function, run a goroutine to update, and return the widget. This is similar to the approach you used to develop the other widgets. Start by defining the newBarChart() function to instantiate a new bar chart widget:

persistentDataSQL/pomo/app/summaryWidgets.go
```go
func newBarChart(ctx context.Context, config *pomodoro.IntervalConfig,
  update <-chan bool, errorCh chan<- error) (*barchart.BarChart, error) {
```

Then initialize a new bar chart using barchart.New() from Termdash. Set the colors for each bar, using blue for Pomodoros and yellow for breaks. Set the foreground value color to black and add the corresponding labels:

```
persistentDataSQL/pomo/app/summaryWidgets.go
// Initialize BarChart
bc, err := barchart.New(
  barchart.ShowValues(),
  barchart.BarColors([]cell.Color{
    cell.ColorBlue,
    cell.ColorYellow,
  }),
  barchart.ValueColors([]cell.Color{
    cell.ColorBlack,
    cell.ColorBlack,
  }),
  barchart.Labels([]string{
    "Pomodoro",
    "Break",
  }),
)
if err != nil {
  return nil, err
}
```

Define an anonymous function to update the widget. Use the function pomodoro.
DailySummary() that you developed to obtain the data. Set the values using the
barchart method bc.Values(). Convert the values to be integers. Set the maximum
value of the bars to the largest of both series plus 10% to leave a little space
above the chart for clarity. Otherwise, the bar would take all the widget's space:

```
persistentDataSQL/pomo/app/summaryWidgets.go
// Update function for BarChart
updateWidget := func() error {
  ds, err := pomodoro.DailySummary(time.Now(), config)
  if err != nil {
    return err
  }

  return bc.Values(
    []int{int(ds[0].Minutes()),
      int(ds[1].Minutes())},
    int(math.Max(ds[0].Minutes(),
      ds[1].Minutes())*1.1)+1,
  )
}
```

Next, execute an anonymous goroutine to update or close the widget depending
on which channel it receives data from. Use the select statement to block and
sleep until it receives data in one of the two channels:

persistentDataSQL/pomo/app/summaryWidgets.go
```go
// Update goroutine for BarChart
go func() {
  for {
    select {
    case <-update:
      errorCh <- updateWidget()
    case <-ctx.Done():
      return
    }
  }
}()
```

Run the updateWidget() function once to populate the widget when the application
starts and then return the new widget and a nil error to complete the function.

persistentDataSQL/pomo/app/summaryWidgets.go
```go
  // Force Update BarChart at start
  if err := updateWidget(); err != nil {
    return nil, err
  }

  return bc, nil
}
```

Next, define the function newLineChart() to instantiate a new Line Chart widget:

persistentDataSQL/pomo/app/summaryWidgets.go
```go
func newLineChart(ctx context.Context, config *pomodoro.IntervalConfig,
  update <-chan bool, errorCh chan<- error) (*linechart.LineChart, error) {
```

Initialize a new line chart using linechart.New() from Termdash. Set the axes
colors to red, the y-axis foreground to blue, and the x-axis foreground to
Cyan. Also set a dynamic formatter for the y-axis value, expecting a time.Duration
value rounded to 0 decimals:

persistentDataSQL/pomo/app/summaryWidgets.go
```go
// Initialize LineChart
lc, err := linechart.New(
  linechart.AxesCellOpts(cell.FgColor(cell.ColorRed)),
  linechart.YLabelCellOpts(cell.FgColor(cell.ColorBlue)),
  linechart.XLabelCellOpts(cell.FgColor(cell.ColorCyan)),
  linechart.YAxisFormattedValues(
    linechart.ValueFormatterSingleUnitDuration(time.Second, 0),
  ),
)
if err != nil {
  return nil, err
}
```

The dynamic axis formatter will update the y-axis labels depending on the values received, assuming they represent a time duration in seconds. It uses the appropriate unit to represent the current values. For example, initially, it can show seconds, switching to minutes or hours as values grow.

Next, define an anonymous function to update the widget. Use the function pomodoro.RangeSummary() that you developed before to obtain the data. Since you want to display a weekly summary, set the number of days to seven. Set the chart values using the linechart method lc.Series(). Set the series names and values from the custom LineSeries type you defined. The first slice element represents the Pomodoro series and the second represents the Breaks. Set the Pomodoro series line color to blue and the breaks line color to yellow, matching the bar chart. Finally, set the x-axis labels using data from the custom type:

persistentDataSQL/pomo/app/summaryWidgets.go
```go
// Update function for LineChart
updateWidget := func() error {
  ws, err := pomodoro.RangeSummary(time.Now(), 7, config)
  if err != nil {
    return err
  }

  err = lc.Series(ws[0].Name, ws[0].Values,
    linechart.SeriesCellOpts(cell.FgColor(cell.ColorBlue)),
    linechart.SeriesXLabels(ws[0].Labels),
  )
  if err != nil {
    return err
  }

  return lc.Series(ws[1].Name, ws[1].Values,
    linechart.SeriesCellOpts(cell.FgColor(cell.ColorYellow)),
    linechart.SeriesXLabels(ws[1].Labels),
  )
}
```

Then, like the previous function, run the update goroutine, force a chart update at start, and return the newly created widget:

persistentDataSQL/pomo/app/summaryWidgets.go
```go
// Update goroutine for LineChart
go func() {
  for {
    select {
    case <-update:
      errorCh <- updateWidget()
```

```
        case <-ctx.Done():
          return
        }
      }
    }()

    // Force Update LineChart at start
    if err := updateWidget(); err != nil {
      return nil, err
    }

    return lc, nil
}
```

The widgets are ready. Let's integrate them in the application now. Save and close this file.

Open the file grid.go and update the newGrid() definition to take in a collection of summary widgets in addition to all the other input parameters:

persistentDataSQL/pomo/app/grid.go
```
func newGrid(b *buttonSet, w *widgets, s *summary,
  t terminalapi.Terminal) (*container.Container, error) {
```

Then update the placeholder you left for the third row with the two new widgets you created. Split the row into two containers, placing the bar chart on the left with 30% of the space and the line chart on the right. Label the containers Daily Summary (minutes) and Weekly Summary, respectively:

persistentDataSQL/pomo/app/grid.go
```
// Add third row
builder.Add(
  grid.RowHeightPerc(60,
    grid.ColWidthPerc(30,
      grid.Widget(s.bcDay,
        container.Border(linestyle.Light),
        container.BorderTitle("Daily Summary (minutes)"),
      ),
    ),
    grid.ColWidthPerc(70,
      grid.Widget(s.lcWeekly,
        container.Border(linestyle.Light),
        container.BorderTitle("Weekly Summary"),
      ),
    ),
  ),
)
```

Save and close this file. Now open the file buttons.go to update the button definition. Start by including the summary collection as an input parameter for the newButtonSet() function:

```
persistentDataSQL/pomo/app/buttons.go
func newButtonSet(ctx context.Context, config *pomodoro.IntervalConfig,
  w *widgets, s *summary,
  redrawCh chan<- bool, errorCh chan<- error) (*buttonSet, error) {
```

Then update the summary widgets at the end of each interval by adding a call to s.update() in the end callback function:

```
persistentDataSQL/pomo/app/buttons.go
end := func(pomodoro.Interval) {
  w.update([]int{}, "", "Nothing running...", "", redrawCh)
➤  s.update(redrawCh)
}
```

Save and close this file and edit the file app.go to pull everything together. Update the New() function to instantiate a new collection of summary widgets after instantiating the other widgets. Then pass this collection to the function newButtonSet():

```
persistentDataSQL/pomo/app/app.go
w, err := newWidgets(ctx, errorCh)
if err != nil {
  return nil, err
}
➤ s, err := newSummary(ctx, config, redrawCh, errorCh)
➤ if err != nil {
➤   return nil, err
➤ }
➤
➤ b, err := newButtonSet(ctx, config, w, s, redrawCh, errorCh)
  if err != nil {
    return nil, err
  }

term, err := tcell.New()
```

Finally, update the call to newGrid() by adding the s parameter representing the summary collection:

```
persistentDataSQL/pomo/app/app.go
c, err := newGrid(b, w, s, term)
```

Save and close this file. Switch back to your application's root directory and build your new application to test it:

```
$ cd ..
$ go build
```

Run the application to see the new widgets. At first, they may be blank if you have no history saved. Run a few intervals to see that both widgets update with summary data at the end of each interval as seen in Figure 17 on page 430.

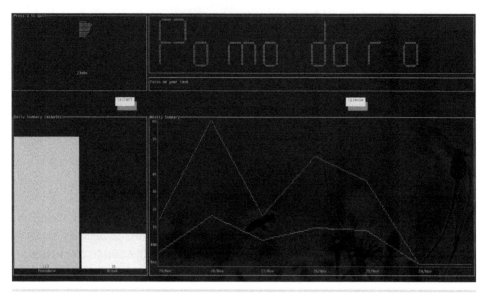

Figure 17—Pomodoro Final Screen

To compile your application using the in-memory data store, use the command-line parameter -tags=inmemory with go build. The application will display summarized data while it's open, but reset to blank if you close it since data in memory is lost.

Your Pomodoro application is complete. Using interactive widgets and SQL databases, you can build powerful command-line applications.

Exercises

Before moving to the final chapter, apply the skills you developed in this chapter by working on these exercises:

- Add tests for the functions DailySummary() and RangeSummary(). Create a helper function to instantiate a database and insert some data that you can use to query and test these functions.

- Integrate another database engine, such as PostgreSQL or MariaDB, with this application to understand what changes when connecting to different databases. You can reuse most of the code you developed to integrate with SQLite, but you'll need to update some queries according to the target database's specific syntax.

Wrapping Up

Your Pomodoro timer application is complete. It saves historical data into a SQL database and displays summarized data to the user using interactive charts.

You can use the concepts you applied in this chapter to develop other applications that interface with databases, whether to manage your application data or to query data for processing. The principles are the same. You can also use the package database/sql with the appropriate drivers to connect to other SQL databases such as PostgreSQL or MariaDB.

In the next chapter, you'll explore some options for building your application for multiple operating systems, and you'll learn how to make them available to your users.

## CHAPTER 11

Distributing Your Tool

By using what you've learned in this book, you can develop powerful tools that are flexible, fast, and well-tested. But the tools you build need to reach your users and work in their environment. As briefly discussed in Compiling Your Tool for Different Platforms, on page 8, one of the benefits of Go is that you can create command-line applications that run on multiple operating systems. You can even cross-compile an application for operating systems other than the one you're currently using.

In some cases, your tool may use libraries or programs that were built specifically for one particular operating system but may not work on another. In these situations, your command-line tool may not run in all required environments as is. In this chapter, you'll explore different options you can use to provide operating system–specific data and components for your applications.

To explore these concepts, you'll build a new package called notify to enable visual notifications for your applications, you'll apply techniques to include and exclude files from your builds, and you will include operating system–specific data, or operating system–specific files in your package. Then, you'll add notifications to the Pomodoro tool that you built in Chapter 9, Developing Interactive Terminal Tools, on page 347, and cross-compile this application for different operating systems.

Finally, you'll make this application available to your users using go get, and you'll distribute your application using Linux containers.

Let's start by creating the notify package and setting up the environment.

Starting the Notify Package

Unlike other applications you developed, notify won't be an executable application. It will be a library that allows you to include system notifications in other applications. You'll develop a naive but functional implementation that uses the os/exec package to call external programs that send a system notification. Because notifications vary according to the operating system, this is a practical example of how to use operating system–specific data and files in your applications. You'll provide support for three operating systems: Linux, macOS, and Windows.

To use this package, you need these tools installed on your system, according to your operating system:

Linux:

notify-send: Included as part of libnotify.[1] This package is usually available with many Linux distributions. Install it using your Linux distribution package manager.

Windows:

powershell.exe: You'll use Powershell to execute a custom script. Powershell is usually installed with Windows 10. If not, install it by following the official documentation.[2]

macOS:

terminal-notifier: It's a custom terminal notification application for macOS. Find more information on the project's GitHub page.[3] You can install it using Homebrew.

Once you have the prerequisite tool installed, create the directory structure for your notify package under your book's root directory:

```
$ mkdir -p $HOME/pragprog.com/rggo/distributing/notify
$ cd $HOME/pragprog.com/rggo/distributing/notify
```

Next, initialize the Go module for this project:

```
$ cd $HOME/pragprog.com/rggo/distributing/notify
$ go mod init pragprog.com/rggo/distributing/notify
go: creating new go.mod: module pragprog.com/rggo/distributing/notify
```

Now, create and edit the file notify.go. Add the package definition and the import section. For this file, you'll use the package runtime to check the running operating system and the package strings to execute operations with string values:

---

1.   developer.gnome.org/notification-spec/.
2.   docs.microsoft.com/en-us/powershell/scripting/install/installing-powershell-core-on-windows?view=powershell-7.1
3.   github.com/julienXX/terminal-notifier

distributing/notify/notify.go
```
package notify

import (
  "runtime"
  "strings"
)
```

Next, define a series of constants using the operator iota to represent the notification severities (SeverityLow, SeverityNormal, and SeverityUrgent):

distributing/notify/notify.go
```
const (
  SeverityLow = iota
  SeverityNormal
  SeverityUrgent
)
```

Define a custom type Severity with an underlying type int to represent the severity. By doing this, you can attach methods to this type. Later you'll define the method String() that returns the severity's string representation to use in the external tools:

distributing/notify/notify.go
```
type Severity int
```

Next, define the Notify type that represents a notification. This type has three non-exported fields: title, message, and severity. Define an initialization function for this type that returns a new Notify instance according to the values provided by the user:

distributing/notify/notify.go
```
type Notify struct {
  title    string
  message  string
  severity Severity
}

func New(title, message string, severity Severity) *Notify {
  return &Notify{
    title:    title,
    message:  message,
    severity: severity,
  }
}
```

Save the file, but leave it open. Next, you'll use the running operating system to return different string representations of the severity.

Including OS-Specific Data

Each one of the tools you're using to send the system notification has a different requirement for the notification severity. For example, on Linux notify-send expects severities as low, normal, or critical, while on Windows your script defines the type of icons such as Info, Warning, or Error. Finally, terminal-notifier on macOS doesn't use severities so you'll display the notification as text with the notification title.

The users of your package define the severity using a constant value of the Severity type. Let's write a method String() that converts the value to a string representation according to each tool's specific requirements based on the running operating system.

In Go, you can use the runtime package to obtain information from the Go runtime component about its environment, including the running operating system, through the constant GOOS. To obtain a list of possible values for GOOS, use the go tool command:

```
$ go tool dist list
aix/ppc64
android/386
... TRUNCATED ...
darwin/amd64
darwin/arm64
... TRUNCATED ...
linux/386
linux/amd64
linux/arm
linux/arm64
... TRUNCATED ...
windows/386
windows/amd64
windows/arm
```

The go tool command lists values grouped as Operating System/Architecture. For example, linux/amd64 is Linux for x86_64 architecture, while darwin/arm64 is macOS for ARM64. For this package you're only interested in the operating system's name, not the architecture.

Based on this output, define a method called String() for the Severity type that returns the correct string for the severity for each operating system by comparing runtime.GOOS with the target operating system. Use Linux as the default, so you don't need a comparison for it. For macOS capitalize the first letter to use it with the notification title:

distributing/notify/notify.go
```go
func (s Severity) String() string {
  sev := "low"

  switch s {
  case SeverityLow:
    sev = "low"
  case SeverityNormal:
    sev = "normal"
  case SeverityUrgent:
    sev = "critical"
  }

  if runtime.GOOS == "darwin" {
    sev = strings.Title(sev)
  }

  if runtime.GOOS == "windows" {
    switch s {
    case SeverityLow:
      sev = "Info"
    case SeverityNormal:
      sev = "Warning"
    case SeverityUrgent:
      sev = "Error"
    }
  }

  return sev
}
```

Using this method, you can make decisions and use different parameters and data depending on the operating system where your tool is running. You could also include a condition informing the user they're running on an unsupported platform if it doesn't match one of the expected operating system values.

Save and close this file. Next, you'll implement the Send() method of type Notify to send the notification for each operating system.

Including OS-Specific Files in the Build

Using runtime.GOOS to verify the current operating system is a practical way to include OS-specific parameters and data in your application. But it's not a good approach to include larger pieces of code because doing so may lead to convoluted code and it may not be possible in some cases to redefine the code within the condition block.

In these cases, you can use build constraints,[4] also known as build tags, which are a mechanism that lets you include and exclude files from your build and your tests according to different criteria.

In their most basic form, you can use build tags to tag Go source files and include them in your build when you provide the respective tag as a value to the parameter -tags=TAG when building or testing your code. You already used this concept in Executing Integration Tests, on page 336, to include integration test files when required.

Go also allows you to provide tags based on the operating system and architecture. For example, if you add the build constraint // +build linux, Go automatically includes this file in the build when targeting the Linux operating system.

Instead of providing the build tag, you can include the target operating system or architecture as a suffix in the file name, in front of the extension. For example, Go automatically includes the file notify_darwin.go when building your code for macOS. Using this technique simplifies the process because you don't have to maintain the build tag, and it's easier to identify which file will be included with the build by looking at its name.

Let's use this technique to define specific Send() methods for each operating system. You'll create three files: notify_linux.go, notify_darwin.go, and notify_windows.go. In each file, you'll implement the same method Send() using the same signature but the specific operating system implementation. Since Go will only include the file for the target operating system, there will be no conflict.

Start by creating and editing the Linux file notify_linux.go. Add the package definition and the import section. For this file, you'll use the os/exec package to execute an external command:

distributing/notify/notify_linux.go
```
package notify

import "os/exec"
```

Since this package uses external commands, you'll mock the command to execute tests simulating the command execution, as you did in Testing Commands with Mock Resources, on page 195. Define the variable command to substitute with the mock implementation during tests:

distributing/notify/notify_linux.go
```
var command = exec.Command
```

---

4. golang.org/pkg/go/build/#hdr-Build_Constraints

Then, define the method Send() for the type Notify. Use the os/exec module to create an instance of exec.Cmd using the function you saved in the variable command. For Linux, you're using the command notify-send with the parameters -u SEVERITY, TITLE, and MESSAGE. Execute the command and return the error to complete the function:

distributing/notify/notify_linux.go
```
func (n *Notify) Send() error {
  notifyCmdName := "notify-send"

  notifyCmd, err := exec.LookPath(notifyCmdName)
  if err != nil {
    return err
  }

  notifyCommand := command(notifyCmd, "-u", n.severity.String(),
    n.title, n.message)
  return notifyCommand.Run()
}
```

Save and close this file and then create and edit notify_darwin.go for macOS. Define the file's content similar to the notify_linux.go file. Use the terminal-notifier too with the options -title TITLE and -message MESSAGE. Because terminal-notifier doesn't support severity, add the severity to the title using fmt.Sprintf() to format the title string:

distributing/notify/notify_darwin.go
```
package notify

import (
  "fmt"
  "os/exec"
)

var command = exec.Command

func (n *Notify) Send() error {
  notifyCmdName := "terminal-notifier"

  notifyCmd, err := exec.LookPath(notifyCmdName)
  if err != nil {
    return err
  }

  title := fmt.Sprintf("(%s) %s", n.severity, n.title)

  notifyCommand := command(notifyCmd, "-title", title, "-message", n.message)
  return notifyCommand.Run()
}
```

Save and close this file. Now create and edit notify_windows.go for Windows. Define the package, import section, and the variable command like before:

distributing/notify/notify_windows.go
```go
package notify

import (
  "fmt"
  "os/exec"
)

var command = exec.Command
```

Then, define the Send() method and set the command name to powershell.exe. For Windows, you'll execute a Powershell script to send the notification.

distributing/notify/notify_windows.go
```go
func (n *Notify) Send() error {
  notifyCmdName := "powershell.exe"

  notifyCmd, err := exec.LookPath(notifyCmdName)
  if err != nil {
    return err
  }
```

Add the Powershell notification script. This script is loosely based on the BaloonTip script developed by Boe Prox.[5] Use fmt.Sprintf() to format the script by including values from the Notify fields n.severity, n.title, and n.message:

distributing/notify/notify_windows.go
```go
psscript := fmt.Sprintf(`Add-Type -AssemblyName System.Windows.Forms
  $notify = New-Object System.Windows.Forms.NotifyIcon
  $notify.Icon = [System.Drawing.SystemIcons]::Information
  $notify.BalloonTipIcon = %q
  $notify.BalloonTipTitle = %q
  $notify.BalloonTipText = %q
  $notify.Visible = $True
  $notify.ShowBalloonTip(10000)`,
  n.severity, n.title, n.message,
)
```

Define a slice of strings with the required Powershell arguments to run it silently:

distributing/notify/notify_windows.go
```go
args := []string{
  "-NoProfile",
  "-NonInteractive",
}
```

Append the script to the arguments slice to pass it to the function that creates the command:

---

5.   github.com/proxb/PowerShell_Scripts/blob/master/Invoke-BalloonTip.ps1

```
distributing/notify/notify_windows.go
args = append(args, psscript)
```

Then use the command and parameters slice to create and run the command. Return the potential error to complete the function:

```
distributing/notify/notify_windows.go
  notifyCommand := command(notifyCmd, args...)
  return notifyCommand.Run()
}
```

The code for this package is complete. Save and close this file. Next, you'll test the notification system.

Testing the Notify Package

Let's write some tests for this package. To fully test this package, you'll write unit tests and integration tests.

First, you'll write unit tests for the package functions and methods, using a test file within the same package notify. For these tests, you'll mock the command implementation using the same technique you applied in Testing Commands with Mock Resources, on page 195, allowing you to fully automate the unit tests without generating screen notifications.

Then, you'll also write integration tests to test the exposed API and ensure the notifications come up onscreen. This test is particularly important because this package doesn't produce an executable file to try it out. To avoid having notifications displayed every time, you'll limit the execution of these tests by providing the build tag +build integration. You'll only execute this test by providing the same tag to the go test tool.

Let's start by writing the unit tests. Create and edit the file notify_test.go for the unit tests. Add the build constraint +build !integration to execute this file without the integration build tag. Skip a line to ensure Go processes the comments as a build constraint instead of documentation, then add the package definition:

```
distributing/notify/notify_test.go
// +build !integration

package notify
```

Next, add the import section. For these tests, you'll use the following packages: fmt to process formatted strings, os to interact with the operating system, os/exec to mock external commands, runtime to obtain the current operating system, strings to format string values, and testing to use test-related functions:

distributing/notify/notify_test.go
```go
import (
  "fmt"
  "os"
  "os/exec"
  "runtime"
  "strings"
  "testing"
)
```

Add the first test function TestNew() to test the New() function. Use table-driven tests to test creating a new instance of type Notify with all severities:

distributing/notify/notify_test.go
```go
func TestNew(t *testing.T) {
  testCases := []struct {
    s Severity
  }{
    {SeverityLow},
    {SeverityNormal},
    {SeverityUrgent},
  }

  for _, tc := range testCases {
    name := tc.s.String()
    expMessage := "Message"
    expTitle := "Title"
    t.Run(name, func(t *testing.T) {
      n := New(expTitle, expMessage, tc.s)
      if n.message != expMessage {
        t.Errorf("Expected %q, got %q instead\n", expMessage, n.message)
      }
      if n.title != expTitle {
        t.Errorf("Expected %q, got %q instead\n", expTitle, n.title)
      }
      if n.severity != tc.s {
        t.Errorf("Expected %q, got %q instead\n", tc.s, n.severity)
      }
    })
  }
}
```

Next, test the method Severity.String() by using the table-driven testing approach again. Define one test case per severity per supported operating system. You won't be able to test all cases from the same operating system since the code depends on the constant runtime.GOOS. Therefore use the constant runtime.GOOS again to check the current operating system and call t.Skip() to skip the tests unless the expected operating system matches the current platform. This makes your test portable to all supported platforms:

```
distributing/notify/notify_test.go
func TestSeverityString(t *testing.T) {
  testCases := []struct {
    s   Severity
    exp string
    os  string
  }{
    {SeverityLow, "low", "linux"},
    {SeverityNormal, "normal", "linux"},
    {SeverityUrgent, "critical", "linux"},
    {SeverityLow, "Low", "darwin"},
    {SeverityNormal, "Normal", "darwin"},
    {SeverityUrgent, "Critical", "darwin"},
    {SeverityLow, "Info", "windows"},
    {SeverityNormal, "Warning", "windows"},
    {SeverityUrgent, "Error", "windows"},
  }

  for _, tc := range testCases {
    name := fmt.Sprintf("%s%d", tc.os, tc.s)
    t.Run(name, func(t *testing.T) {
      if runtime.GOOS != tc.os {
        t.Skip("Skipped: not OS", runtime.GOOS)
      }
      sev := tc.s.String()
      if sev != tc.exp {
        t.Errorf("Expected %q, got %q instead\n", tc.exp, sev)
      }
    })
  }
}
```

Then mock the command functionality to test the external command by creating the functions mockCmd() and TestHelperProcess() the same way you did in Testing Commands with Mock Resources, on page 195. In the TestHelperProcess() function, use a switch block to define the variable cmdName depending on the operating system. Assign the value corresponding to the expected external command that you would run for each platform. Then, use this value to compare with the value received by the function. If they match, the correct tool is used, in which case you can exit with code zero (0) representing a successful command execution. Otherwise, exit with code 1 otherwise.

```
distributing/notify/notify_test.go
func mockCmd(exe string, args ...string) *exec.Cmd {
  cs := []string{"-test.run=TestHelperProcess"}
  cs = append(cs, exe)
  cs = append(cs, args...)
  cmd := exec.Command(os.Args[0], cs...)
```

```go
  cmd.Env = []string{"GO_WANT_HELPER_PROCESS=1"}
  return cmd
}

func TestHelperProcess(t *testing.T) {
  if os.Getenv("GO_WANT_HELPER_PROCESS") != "1" {
    return
  }

  cmdName := ""

  switch runtime.GOOS {
  case "linux":
    cmdName = "notify-send"
  case "darwin":
    cmdName = "terminal-notifier"
  case "windows":
    cmdName = "powershell"
  }

  if strings.Contains(os.Args[2], cmdName) {
    os.Exit(0)
  }

  os.Exit(1)
}
```

Using this technique, you can simulate the command execution and check that the correct tool is used, without executing it. For a more complete test, you could also check for the parameters, but for brevity, we're only checking for the command name.

Finally, add the function TestSend() to test sending the notification using the mocked up command. Assign the function definition mockCmd() to the variable command to mock it instead of creating the real command. Execute the Send() method and verify that no errors occur. The test fails if the wrong external tool is used:

distributing/notify/notify_test.go
```go
func TestSend(t *testing.T) {
  n := New("test title", "test msg", SeverityNormal)

  command = mockCmd

  err := n.Send()

  if err != nil {
    t.Error(err)
  }
}
```

Save and close this file. Execute the tests with go test to ensure the package works correctly:

```
$ go test -v
=== RUN    TestNew
=== RUN    TestNew/low
=== RUN    TestNew/normal
=== RUN    TestNew/critical
--- PASS: TestNew (0.00s)
    --- PASS: TestNew/low (0.00s)
    --- PASS: TestNew/normal (0.00s)
    --- PASS: TestNew/critical (0.00s)
=== RUN    TestSeverityString
=== RUN    TestSeverityString/linux0
=== RUN    TestSeverityString/linux1
=== RUN    TestSeverityString/linux2
=== RUN    TestSeverityString/darwin0
    notify_test.go:63: Skipped: not OS linux
=== RUN    TestSeverityString/darwin1
    notify_test.go:63: Skipped: not OS linux
=== RUN    TestSeverityString/darwin2
    notify_test.go:63: Skipped: not OS linux
=== RUN    TestSeverityString/windows0
    notify_test.go:63: Skipped: not OS linux
=== RUN    TestSeverityString/windows1
    notify_test.go:63: Skipped: not OS linux
=== RUN    TestSeverityString/windows2
    notify_test.go:63: Skipped: not OS linux
--- PASS: TestSeverityString (0.00s)
    --- PASS: TestSeverityString/linux0 (0.00s)
    --- PASS: TestSeverityString/linux1 (0.00s)
    --- PASS: TestSeverityString/linux2 (0.00s)
    --- SKIP: TestSeverityString/darwin0 (0.00s)
    --- SKIP: TestSeverityString/darwin1 (0.00s)
    --- SKIP: TestSeverityString/darwin2 (0.00s)
    --- SKIP: TestSeverityString/windows0 (0.00s)
    --- SKIP: TestSeverityString/windows1 (0.00s)
    --- SKIP: TestSeverityString/windows2 (0.00s)
=== RUN    TestHelperProcess
--- PASS: TestHelperProcess (0.00s)
=== RUN    TestSend
--- PASS: TestSend (0.00s)
PASS
ok      pragprog.com/rggo/distributing/notify   0.005s
```

Note that the Go test tool skipped the severity tests for macOS and Windows because these tests ran on Linux.

Now create the integration test to test an actual notification execution. Create and edit the file integration_test.go. Add the build tag +build integration to execute this test when you pass the tag integration when you run the tests. Then define the package notify_test to test it as an external consumer, testing the exported API only:

distributing/notify/integration_test.go
```
// +build integration

package notify_test
```

Add the import section. For this test, you'll use the testing package to execute testing functions and the notify package that you're testing:

distributing/notify/integration_test.go
```
import (
  "testing"

  "pragprog.com/rggo/distributing/notify"
)
```

Then, add the test function TestSend() to test sending a notification. Create a new instance of type Notify using the function notify.New() passing test values. Send the notification using the method n.Send() and verify that no errors occur:

distributing/notify/integration_test.go
```
func TestSend(t *testing.T) {
  n := notify.New("test title", "test msg", notify.SeverityNormal)

  err := n.Send()

  if err != nil {
    t.Error(err)
  }
}
```

Note that you're not using the mock command. Because you're testing this as an external consumer and the variables required for mocking the test are private, it's not even possible to do that.

Now, save and close the file, and execute the tests using -tag=integration and assess whether the notification shows up:

```
$ go test -v -tags=integration
=== RUN    TestSend
--- PASS: TestSend (0.01s)
PASS
ok        pragprog.com/rggo/distributing/notify    0.009s
```

The test passed, which means the notification executed without errors. You'll also see the notification displayed if your system notification is enabled. The notification varies according to each operating system. On Linux it will be similar to the image shown in Figure 18 on page 447.

Your notification package is completed and tested. Next, you will use this package to add notifications to the Pomodoro tool.

Figure 18—Notification Test Linux

Conditionally Building Your Application

To keep the examples in this chapter clear and easier to follow, copy the existing version of your Pomodoro application to a new working environment. This ensures your application source files will match the description provided in this chapter. If you want to continue developing the Pomodoro application in its original directory, make sure you're changing the appropriate files and adding new files to the correct path relative to the original directory.

Copy the directory pomo from the directory $HOME/pragprog.com/rggo/persistentDataSQL to the current chapter directory recursively, and switch to it:

```
$ cp -r $HOME/pragprog.com/rggo/persistentDataSQL/pomo \
  $HOME/pragprog.com/rggo/distributing
$ cd $HOME/pragprog.com/rggo/distributing/pomo
```

Once you switch to the new directory, you can continue developing your application from the same point. Because you're using Go modules, you don't need to take any extra actions. Go modules will resolve the modules to the current directory for you automatically.

To use your notify package to send out notifications with the Pomodoro app, add the dependency to the file go.mod under the subdirectory pomo. Also, because your packages are local only, replace the path to the package pointing it to the local directory with its source code, by using the replace directive:

distributing/pomo/go.mod
```
module pragprog.com/rggo/interactiveTools/pomo

go 1.16

require (
  github.com/mattn/go-sqlite3 v1.14.5
  github.com/mitchellh/go-homedir v1.1.0
  github.com/mum4k/termdash v0.13.0
  github.com/spf13/cobra v1.1.1
  github.com/spf13/viper v1.7.1
  pragprog.com/rggo/distributing/notify v0.0.0
)

replace pragprog.com/rggo/distributing/notify => ../../distributing/notify
```

This last step wouldn't be necessary if your package was available on an external Git repository, as the Go tools would download it when required.

Now add the notification functionality in the package app, but let's make it optional. When the users are building the application, it will include the notification by default, but the user can disable it by providing the build tag disable_notification.

To do this, instead of calling package notify directly, you'll add a helper function send_notification(). By default, this function calls notify and sends out the notification. You'll also deploy a second version of this function that doesn't do anything in another file using the build tag disable_notification.

Go accepts multiple build tags for a single file. Separate the tags with spaces to evaluate them with an OR condition, which means Go includes the file if the user provides any of the tags. For an AND condition, separate the tags with a comma, in which case Go will include the file if the user provides all the tags.

Let's use this idea to build the notification integration. First, add the stub function that does nothing by adding a new file notification_stub.go under the directory pomo/app. Define the condition to include this file in the build by adding the build tags disable_notification and containers, separated by spaces:

distributing/pomo/app/notification_stub.go
```
// +build containers disable_notification

package app

func send_notification(msg string) {
  return
}
```

Save and close this file. Then create the file pomo/app/notification.go to enable notifications when building the application without providing the tags disable_notification AND containers:

distributing/pomo/app/notification.go
```
// +build !containers,!disable_notification

package app

import "pragprog.com/rggo/distributing/notify"

func send_notification(msg string) {
  n := notify.New("Pomodoro", msg, notify.SeverityNormal)

  n.Send()
}
```

Save and close the file. Now call this newly defined function from the Pomodoro application. Edit the file app/buttons.go and call send_notification() from the start callback to send a notification when an Interval starts:

distributing/pomo/app/buttons.go
```
start := func(i pomodoro.Interval) {
  message := "Take a break"
  if i.Category == pomodoro.CategoryPomodoro {
    message = "Focus on your task"
  }

  w.update([]int{}, i.Category, message, "", redrawCh)
➤ send_notification(message)
}
```

Call the function from the end callback to notify users when an interval finishes. Since the end() callback didn't have a message ready, include the instance i in the callback function call and use its field i.Category to inform the user which type of interval finished:

distributing/pomo/app/buttons.go
```
➤ end := func(i pomodoro.Interval) {
  w.update([]int{}, "", "Nothing running...", "", redrawCh)
  s.update(redrawCh)
➤ message := fmt.Sprintf("%s finished !", i.Category)
➤ send_notification(message)
}
```

Save and close this file. Rebuild your application without any tags to enable notifications. To disable notifications, rebuild the application providing either the disable_notification or containers tags.

When you run your application with notifications enabled it will display notifications when an interval starts or finishes. For example, in Linux you would see a notification like this when a Pomodoro interval starts:

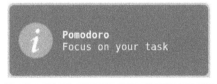

Figure 19—Notification Pomodoro Start

By using build constraints, you can create flexible tools that provide many build options for your users. For example, imagine that you wanted to provide a standard build targeted to run Pomodoro in a Linux container. To do this, you would use specific compilation options for containers, which you'll explore in Compiling Your Go Application for Containers, on page 456. For now, you'll define which application features will be included in the container build. To make it easier to run in an ephemeral environment, disable integration with SQLite and provide only the inMemory repository.

Edit the build tags in the repository files to include only inMemory when the user provides the tag containers. First, edit pomodoro/repository/inMemory.go and add the containers build tag with an OR condition:

distributing/pomo/pomodoro/repository/inMemory.go
```
// +build inmemory containers
```

Next, disable SQLite repository by adding the tag !containers to pomodoro/repository/sqlite3.go:

distributing/pomo/pomodoro/repository/sqlite3.go
```
// +build !inmemory,!containers
```

Do the same to include the inMemory repository by editing cmd/repoinmemory.go:

distributing/pomo/cmd/repoinmemory.go
```
// +build inmemory containers
```

Finally, disable the SQLite repository definition in cmd/reposqlite.go:

distributing/pomo/cmd/reposqlite.go
```
// +build !inmemory,!containers
```

In addition, containers won't have access to the system to run notifications, so you'll want to disable notifications. You're already doing that because you included the tag containers in the notification-related files.

To verify which files Go will include in a particular build according to the selected tags, use the go list command. This command is a powerful resource to help you understand the content of your packages, and it has many features. For a complete list of them, check the help with go help list. To list the source files included in a build, use the option -f to custom format the list providing the parameter '{{ .GoFiles }}' to list the source code files. For example, check which will be used to build the application without any build tags:

```
$ go list  -f '{{ .GoFiles }}' ./...
[main.go]
[app.go buttons.go grid.go notification.go summaryWidgets.go widgets.go]
[reposqlite.go root.go]
[interval.go summary.go]
[sqlite3.go]
```

Now execute the same command using the tag inmemory. Notice that the list of files changes, showing files related to the inMemory repository instead of SQLite. It still includes a notification with this build:

```
$ go list -tags=inmemory -f '{{ .GoFiles }}' ./...
[main.go]
[app.go buttons.go grid.go notification.go summaryWidgets.go widgets.go]
[repoinmemory.go root.go]
[interval.go summary.go]
[inMemory.go]
```

Execute the command one more time using the tag containers and verify that in addition to using the repository inMemory, it disabled notification by including the stub file.

```
$ go list -tags=containers -f '{{ .GoFiles }}' ./...
[main.go]
[app.go buttons.go grid.go notification_stub.go summaryWidgets.go widgets.go]
[repoinmemory.go root.go]
[interval.go summary.go]
[inMemory.go]
```

Using go list provides visibility of all the files included with a specific build option, making it easier to see if the application matches the requirements instead of compiling and executing it. Because go list provides textual output, you can also use it in tests to automate verification of build contents.

Next, you'll use these predefined build options to compile your application for multiple operating systems.

Cross-Compiling Your Application

Unlike interpreted languages such as Python or Nodejs, Go is a compiled language, which means it produces a binary executable file that contains all the requirements to run your application.

When you're planning to distribute your application, this is a major benefit as users can run your application by running the binary executable without having to install any interpreters or runtimes. This makes Go applications extremely portable.

When building the executable file, Go creates a file that contains instructions that are specific for a target operating system and architecture. Because of this, you can't take a file that is compiled for Linux and try to run it on Windows, or a file that was compiled for the Linux x86_64 architecture and try to run it on the Linux ARM system.

To help you with that, Go allows you to cross-compile or cross-build your applications. You can use the Go tools such as go build to compile a binary file for supported operating systems and architectures from a single platform. For example, if you're running Go on Linux, you can compile a binary for Linux but also for Windows, macOS, and different CPU architectures. To see a list of supported combinations of operating systems and architectures, use go tool dist list:

```
$ go tool dist list
aix/ppc64
android/386
... TRUNCATED ...
darwin/amd64
darwin/arm64
... TRUNCATED ...
linux/386
linux/amd64
linux/arm
linux/arm64
... TRUNCATED ...
windows/386
windows/amd64
windows/arm
```

By default, when you use go build to build your application, it compiles the application for the running platform, which is the combination of the running operating system and architecture. You can see which values Go uses by default in your Go environment by using the go env command. If you run this command without any parameters, it displays all configured Go environment values. You can provide specific variables to see their value. For example, verify the current operating system and architecture using go env like this:

```
$ go env GOOS
linux
$ go env GOARCH
amd64
```

Your results may be different depending on which platform you're running these examples.

Switch into the Pomodoro directory and run go build to build your application binary for the current platform.

```
$ cd $HOME/pragprog.com/rggo/distributing/pomo
$ go build
```

Then use the file command on Linux or macOS to inspect the file. Note that it shows the file is specific to Linux on the x86_64 architecture in the following example:

```
$ file pomo
pomo: ELF 64-bit LSB executable, x86-64, version 1 (SYSV),
  dynamically linked ...
```

Notice that by default, Go produces a binary that's *dynamically linked*, which means the binary will load any required shared libraries dynamically at run time. While this approach has many benefits, especially for system efficiency and memory management, it can cause the program to fail if the user executes it in a platform that doesn't support dynamically linked libraries. To make your application binary more portable, you can enable statically linked libraries by setting the variable CGO_ENABLED=0 before running go build:

```
$ CGO_ENABLED=0 go build
$ file pomo
pomo: ELF 64-bit LSB executable, x86-64, version 1 (SYSV),
  statically linked ...
```

To cross-compile your applications for different platforms, set the variables GOOS and GOARCH to the target operating system and platform before running go build. For example, to build the app for Windows running on the x86_64 architecture, use GOOS=windows and GOARCH=amd64:

```
$ GOOS=windows GOARCH=amd64 go build
```

But specifically for the Pomodoro tool, this command will fail. The reason is that the application by default uses the SQLite repository which requires you to compile a dependency with SQLite libraries written in C. You'll explore that example a little later in the chapter. For now, to test this command, use the build tag inmemory to use the inMemory repository that doesn't have external dependencies:

```
$ GOOS=windows GOARCH=amd64 go build -tags=inmemory
```

Use the file command again to inspect the produced binary file. Go automatically adds the .exe extension to Windows binaries:

```
$ file pomo.exe
pomo.exe: PE32+ executable (console) x86-64 (stripped to external PDB),
  for MS Windows
```

You can use this approach to release your application for your users in binary form, by building it to all platforms you support. Because these values are known, you create a program or script that automates the entire process for you. Let's create a Bash script that builds the Pomodoro application, using the inMemory repository for all the platforms we support: Linux, Windows, and macOS. In addition, imagine that we also want to support different architectures such as x86_64, ARM, and ARM64.

Create the subdirectory scripts under the Pomodoro root directory:

```
$ cd $HOME/pragprog.com/rggo/distributing/pomo
$ mkdir scripts
```

Then, add the script file cross_build.sh. The script file runs two loops, combining the supported operating systems and architectures. It excludes the invalid combinations windows/arm64 and darwin/arm. Then it runs go build, setting the cross-compile variable and the parameter -o to specify where to put the resulting binary, and organizing the output in subdirectories by operating system and architecture:

distributing/pomo/scripts/cross_build.sh
```bash
#!/bin/bash

OSLIST="linux windows darwin"
ARCHLIST="amd64 arm arm64"

for os in ${OSLIST}; do
  for arch in ${ARCHLIST}; do
    if [[ "$os/$arch" =~ ^(windows/arm64|darwin/arm)$ ]]; then continue; fi

    echo Building binary for $os $arch
    mkdir -p releases/${os}/${arch}
    CGO_ENABLED=0 GOOS=$os GOARCH=$arch go build -tags=inmemory \
      -o releases/${os}/${arch}/
  done
done
```

Now run the script to create binaries for all supported platforms under the releases subdirectory:

```
$ ./scripts/cross_build.sh
Building binary for linux amd64
Building binary for linux arm
Building binary for linux arm64
Building binary for windows amd64
Building binary for windows arm
Building binary for darwin amd64
Building binary for darwin arm64
```

You can also inspect the resulting binaries to ensure they match the correct platforms:

```
$ file release/*/*/*
releases/darwin/amd64/pomo:     Mach-O 64-bit x86_64 executable
releases/darwin/arm64/pomo:     Mach-O 64-bit arm64 executable,
      flags:<|DYLDLINK|PIE>
```

```
releases/linux/amd64/pomo:      ELF 64-bit LSB executable, x86-64, version 1
    (SYSV), statically linked, ...
releases/linux/arm64/pomo:      ELF 64-bit LSB executable, ARM aarch64,
                                 version 1
    (SYSV), statically linked, ...
releases/linux/arm/pomo:        ELF 32-bit LSB executable, ARM, EABI5
                                 version 1
    (SYSV), statically linked, ...
releases/windows/amd64/pomo.exe: PE32+ executable (console) x86-64
    (stripped to external PDB), for MS Windows
releases/windows/arm/pomo.exe:  PE32 executable (console) ARMv7 Thumb
    (stripped to external PDB), for MS Windows
```

Now, let's go back to the example of cross-compiling the Windows binary with support for the SQLite repository. Go also allows you to cross-build applications that depend on external C libraries. This process may vary for each application, so make sure to consult the documentation for the dependency you're using to understand its specific requirements.

For the go-sqlite3 package, you can cross-build your Windows binary by providing an alternative C compiler that supports Windows, such as MINGW.[6] To follow this example, install MINGW on your Linux system by using your distribution's package manager. This book won't cover specific installation details as they vary for each distribution. For more details, consult your distribution's documentation.

When you have the Windows C compiler toolchain installed, instruct Go build to use MINGW as the C compiler to cross-build the tool:

```
$ CGO_ENABLED=1 CC=x86_64-w64-mingw32-gcc CXX=x86_64-w64-mingw32-g++ \
> GOOS=windows GOARCH=amd64 go build
```

To run this code, you still need SQLite installed on the target operating system.

The Go toolchain is powerful and flexible, allowing you to use many combinations of parameters and tags to build different versions of your application to support your users' requirements, without requiring access to all the different target platforms.

If you're distributing your application in binary form to your users, you can take the resulting binary files and host them online to ensure your users can access them.

Next, let's compile the application to run in Linux containers.

---

6.   mingw-w64.org/doku.php/start

Compiling Your Go Application for Containers

Another alternative way to distribute your application that has become increasingly popular in recent years is allowing your users to run the application in Linux containers.[7] Containers package your application and all the required dependencies using a standard image format, and they run the application in isolation from other processes running on the same system. Containers use Linux kernel resources such as Namespaces and Cgroups to provide isolation and resource management.

There are different container runtimes available, such as Podman[8] and Docker.[9] If you're running these examples on a Linux system, you can use either one interchangeably. If you're running on Windows or macOS, Docker provides a desktop version that makes it easier to start. You can also use Podman on these operating systems, but you need to install a Virtual Machine to enable it. We'll not cover a container runtime installation process here. For more details, check the respective project's documentation.

To distribute your application as a container, you have to create a container image. You can do this in several ways, but a common way is by using a Dockerfile, which contains a recipe for how to create an image. Then you pass this file as input to docker or podman commands to build the image. For more details on how to create the Dockerfile, consult its documentation.[10]

The focus of this section is to provide some build options to optimize your application to run in containers. Go is a great choice for creating applications that run in containers because it generates a single binary file that you can add to the container image without additional runtimes or dependencies.

To make the binary file even more suitable to run in a container, you can pass additional build options. For example, you'll enable a statically linked binary by setting CGO_ENABLED=0, and you can pass additional linker options using the flag -ldflags. To reduce the binary size, use the options -ldflags="-s -w" to strip the binary of debug symbols. Before you get started, take a closer look at some of the build options that you'll use:

- CGO_ENABLED=0: Enables statically linked binaries to make the application more portable. It allows you to use the binary with source images that don't support shared libraries when building your container image.

---

7. opensource.com/resources/what-are-linux-containers
8. podman.io/
9. www.docker.com/get-started
10. docs.docker.com/engine/reference/builder/

- GOOS=linux: Since containers run Linux, set this option to enable repeatable builds even when building the application on a different platform.

- -ldflags="-s -w": The parameter -ldflags allows you to specify additional linker options that go build uses at the link stage of the build process. In this case, the option -s -w strips the binary of debugging symbols, decreasing its size. Without these symbols, it's harder to debug the application, but this is usually not a major concern when running in a container. To see all linker options you can use, run go tool link.

- -tags=containers: This is specific to your Pomodoro application. Build the application using the files specified with the container tag to remove dependency on SQLite and notifications as you did in Conditionally Building Your Application, on page 447.

Now build your binary using these options:

```
$ CGO_ENABLED=0 GOOS=linux go build -ldflags="-s -w" -tags=containers
```

Inspect this file to verify its properties and size:

```
$ ls -lh pomo
-rwxr-xr-x 1 ricardo users 7.2M Feb 28 12:06 pomo
$ file pomo
pomo: ELF 64-bit LSB executable, x86-64, version 1 (SYSV), statically linked,
 ... ... , stripped
```

Notice the file size is about 7MB and the file is statically linked and stripped.

Compare this with building the application without these options:

```
$ go build
$ ls -lh pomo
-rwxr-xr-x 1 ricardo users 13M Feb 28 12:09 pomo
$ file pomo
pomo: ELF 64-bit LSB executable, x86-64, version 1 (SYSV),
  dynamically linked,
interpreter /lib64/ld-linux-x86-64.so.2, ..., for GNU/Linux 4.4.0,
  not stripped
```

The binary file optimized for containers is almost 50% smaller than the original. It's also statically linked and stripped of debugging symbols.

Once you have the binary, you'll create a container image by using a Dockerfile. Switch back to the chapter's root directory and create a new subdirectory containers:

```
$ cd $HOME/pragprog.com/rggo/distributing
$ mkdir containers
```

Create and edit a file called Dockerfile in this subdirectory. Add the following contents to create a new image from the base image alpine:latest, create a regular user pomo to run the application, and copy the binary file pomo/pomo you built before to the image under directory /app:

distributing/containers/Dockerfile
```
FROM alpine:latest
RUN mkdir /app && adduser -h /app -D  pomo
WORKDIR /app
COPY --chown=pomo /pomo/pomo .
CMD ["/app/pomo"]
```

Build your image using the docker build command providing this Dockerfile as input:

```
$ docker build -t pomo/pomo:latest -f containers/Dockerfile .
STEP 1: FROM alpine:latest
STEP 2: RUN mkdir /app && adduser -h /app -D  pomo
--> 500286ad2c9
STEP 3: WORKDIR /app
--> 175d6b43663
STEP 4: COPY --chown=pomo /pomo/pomo .
--> 2b05fa6dbba
STEP 5: CMD ["/app/pomo"]
STEP 6: COMMIT pomo/pomo:latest
--> 998e1c2cc75
998e1c2cc75dc865f57890cb6294c2f25725da97ce8535909216ea27a4a56a38
```

This command creates an image tagged with pomo/pomo:latest. List it using docker images:

```
$ docker images
REPOSITORY                    TAG      IMAGE ID       CREATED          SIZE
localhost/pomo/pomo           latest   998e1c2cc75d   47 minutes ago   13.4 MB
docker.io/library/alpine      latest   e50c909a8df2   4 weeks ago      5.88 MB
```

Run your application using Docker, providing the -it flags to enable a terminal emulator, which is required to run Pomodoro's interactive CLI:

```
$ docker run --rm -it localhost/pomo/pomo
```

You can also use Docker to build the application with Go's official image and a multistage Dockerfile. A multistage Dockerfile instantiates a container to compile the application and then copies the resulting file to a second image, similar to the previous Dockerfile you created. Create a new file called Dockerfile.builder in the containers subdirectory. Define the multistage build using the following code:

distributing/containers/Dockerfile.builder
```
FROM golang:1.15 AS builder
RUN mkdir /distributing
```

```
WORKDIR /distributing
COPY notify/ notify/
COPY pomo/ pomo/
WORKDIR /distributing/pomo
RUN CGO_ENABLED=0 GOOS=linux go build -ldflags="-s -w" -tags=containers

FROM alpine:latest
RUN mkdir /app && adduser -h /app -D  pomo
WORKDIR /app
COPY --chown=pomo --from=builder /distributing/pomo/pomo .
CMD ["/app/pomo"]
```

Now use this image to build the binary and the container image for your application:

```
$ docker build -t pomo/pomo:latest -f containers/Dockerfile.builder .
STEP 1: FROM golang:1.15 AS builder
STEP 2: RUN mkdir /distributing
--> e8e2ea98b04
STEP 3: WORKDIR /distributing
--> 81cee711389
STEP 4: COPY notify/ notify/
--> ac86b302a7a
STEP 5: COPY pomo/ pomo/
--> 5353bc4d73e
STEP 6: WORKDIR /distributing/pomo
--> bfddd5217bf
STEP 7: RUN CGO_ENABLED=0 GOOS=linux go build -ldflags="-s -w" -tags=containers
go: downloading github.com/spf13/viper v1.7.1
go: downloading github.com/spf13/cobra v1.1.1
go: downloading github.com/mitchellh/go-homedir v1.1.0
go: downloading github.com/mum4k/termdash v0.13.0
go: downloading github.com/spf13/afero v1.1.2
go: downloading github.com/spf13/cast v1.3.0
go: downloading github.com/pelletier/go-toml v1.2.0
go: downloading gopkg.in/yaml.v2 v2.2.8
go: downloading github.com/mitchellh/mapstructure v1.1.2
go: downloading github.com/spf13/pflag v1.0.5
go: downloading golang.org/x/text v0.3.4
go: downloading github.com/subosito/gotenv v1.2.0
go: downloading github.com/magiconair/properties v1.8.1
go: downloading github.com/fsnotify/fsnotify v1.4.7
go: downloading github.com/mattn/go-runewidth v0.0.9
go: downloading github.com/spf13/jwalterweatherman v1.0.0
go: downloading github.com/hashicorp/hcl v1.0.0
go: downloading github.com/gdamore/tcell/v2 v2.0.0
go: downloading gopkg.in/ini.v1 v1.51.0
go: downloading golang.org/x/sys v0.0.0-20201113233024-12cec1faf1ba
go: downloading github.com/gdamore/encoding v1.0.0
go: downloading github.com/lucasb-eyer/go-colorful v1.0.3
--> de7b70a3753
```

```
STEP 8: FROM alpine:latest
STEP 9: RUN mkdir /app && adduser -h /app -D  pomo
--> Using cache 500286ad2c9f1242184343eedb016d53e36e1401675eb6769fb9c64146...
--> 500286ad2c9
STEP 10: WORKDIR /app
--> Using cache 175d6b43663f6db66fd8e61d80a82e5976b27078b79d59feebcc517d44...
--> 175d6b43663
STEP 11: COPY --chown=pomo --from=builder /distributing/pomo/pomo .
--> 0292f63c58f
STEP 12: CMD ["/app/pomo"]
STEP 13: COMMIT pomo/pomo:latest
--> 3c3ec9fafb8
3c3ec9fafb8f463aa2776f1e45c216dc60f7490df1875c133bb962ffcceab050
```

The result is the same image as before, but with this new Dockerfile, you don't have to compile the application manually before creating the image. The multistage build does everything for you in a repeatable and consistent way.

Go builds applications into single binaries; you can build them statically linked and can also create images that have no other files or dependencies. These tiny images are optimized for data transfer and are more secure since they contain only your application binary.

To create such an image, you'll use a multistage Dockerfile. So copy the file containers/Dockerfile.builder into a new file containers/Dockerfile.scratch, and edit this new file, replacing the second stage image on the FROM command with scratch. This image has no directories or users, so replace the remaining commands with a command to copy the binary to the root directory. When you're done, your Dockerfile will look like this:

```
distributing/containers/Dockerfile.scratch
FROM golang:1.15 AS builder
RUN mkdir /distributing
WORKDIR /distributing
COPY notify/ notify/
COPY pomo/ pomo/
WORKDIR /distributing/pomo
RUN CGO_ENABLED=0 GOOS=linux go build -ldflags="-s -w" -tags=containers

FROM scratch
WORKDIR /
COPY --from=builder /distributing/pomo/pomo .
CMD ["/pomo"]
```

Build your image using this Dockerfile as you did before:

```
$ docker build -t pomo/pomo:latest -f containers/Dockerfile.scratch .
STEP 1: FROM golang:1.15 AS builder
STEP 2: RUN mkdir /distributing
--> 9021735fd16
```

```
... TRUNCATED OUTPUT ...
STEP 8: FROM scratch
STEP 9: WORKDIR /
--> 00b6e665a3f
STEP 10: COPY --from=builder /distributing/pomo/pomo .
--> c6bbaccb87b
STEP 11: CMD ["/pomo"]
STEP 12: COMMIT pomo/pomo:latest
--> 4068859c281
```

Check your new image and notice that its size is close to the binary size because it's the only file in the image:

```
$ docker images
REPOSITORY                TAG      IMAGE ID      CREATED        SIZE
localhost/pomo/pomo       latest   4068859c281e  5 seconds ago  8.34 MB
```

Not all applications are good candidates to run in a container, but for the ones that are, this is another option to distribute your application for your users.

Next, let's explore go get to distribute your application with source code.

Distributing Your Application as Source Code

So far, you've explored some options for distributing your application as binary files that users can run directly on their system. Using this approach, users don't have to worry about building the application, and they can start using it right away.

But in some cases, you may want to distribute your application's source code and allow users to build it, selecting the options that meet their requirements. For example, for the Pomodoro application, users could build it using any of the available repositories, enabling or disabling notifications.

This provides users with additional flexibility but requires an extra step of building the application. Another benefit is that by having access to the source code, other developers can expand or add more features to the application, for example, by introducing an additional data store to meet their needs.

To distribute your application as source code, you need to host it in a publicly available location. Typical places include a hosted version control system, such as GitLab or GitHub. Another requirement is to have your application dependencies available for the end users. In general, you host any dependencies on a public platform as well.

When your source code is available, users can download it by using the go get tool. The general usage is go get REPOID where REPOID is the URL of your repository stripped of the http[s]:// prefix. For example, imagine that you're hosting your Pomodoro application in GitHub under your user ID and the repository name is pomo. Users could download this application with a command similar to go get github.com/USERID/pomo.

At the time of writing this book, the go get command automatically builds the application for you using standard options. If the root directory of your repository contains a file main.go, go get automatically builds the binary package and places it under the directory $GOPATH/bin. It also downloads any dependencies required to build the application. But this feature is deprecated and will be removed in a future Go release.

Users can download the source code without building the application by providing the flag -d to go get. After downloading the source code, they can build the application using go build or install it with go install, providing any additional options or flags to customize the application according to their requirements.

Distributing your application as source code is a flexible way to allow your users to build it according to their requirements. It can also foster collaboration and innovation by allowing them to extend the application if needed.

Exercises

Apply the skills you developed in this chapter by working on these exercises:

- Display an error to the user if they're trying to run the application on an operating system that's not in your list of supported platforms.

- Use the cross-compilation techniques to cross-build other applications you developed throughout the book. Some applications may require tuning or OS-specific data or files to work properly on multiple platforms.

- Use the Dockerfile examples provided in this chapter to build container images for other applications you developed in this book. For example, the REST API server you developed in Developing a REST API Server, on page 274, is a good candidate to run as a Linux container.

Wrapping Up

When it comes to distributing your application, Go supports many alternatives. Because Go applications don't require an interpreter or a runtime, you can distribute your application in binary form, and users can run it without installing or maintaining extra dependencies. You can also distribute it as source code so users can build it themselves according to their requirements.

In this chapter, you created a new package that enables your applications to send system notifications and supports different operating systems. You designed this package to use different implementations according to the target operating system by using Go build constraints. Then, you included the notification package in the Pomodoro application and used build tags to conditionally build it for different requirements. Finally, you explored several options for building and distributing your application in binary form and as source code. You used the power and flexibility of cross-compilation to build binaries for different platforms using a single-source system. You also created container images so users can run your application as Linux containers.

The Go toolchain provides a complete set of tools that allows you to develop automated ways to build your application in a consistent and repeatable way. With Go test tools, you can develop automated pipelines to test and build your applications.

You've used Go to build several command-line applications in this book. You started with a basic word counter, added new skills, and worked up to building a fully featured terminal user interface application persisting data into a database. You developed applications that deal with files and the file system, applications that read data from CSV files, and tools that launch and control external programs. You built a REST API server and a client tool to communicate with it, you used the Cobra framework to improve your tools and handle command-line arguments, and you connected to databases and built an entire terminal user experience. And you did it all while applying techniques to improve their performance, using interfaces and other Go features to develop flexible and maintainable code, and ensuring your tools are well-tested and functional.

You can now use the skills you acquired in this book to build other command-line applications. In addition, these skills provide a foundation for developing many other applications in Go, such as API servers and web applications. Go is an open source project backed by a growing and vibrant community. As you continue your journey in learning Go, you can ask for help in one of the many channels available on the official Get Help page.[11]

---

11. golang.org/help

Index

Thank you!

We hope you enjoyed this book and that you're already thinking about what you want to learn next. To help make that decision easier, we're offering you this gift.

Head over to https://pragprog.com and use coupon code BUYANOTHER2021 to save 30% on your next ebook. Void where prohibited or restricted. This offer does not apply to any edition of the *The Pragmatic Programmer* ebook.

And if you'd like to share your own expertise with the world, why not propose a writing idea to us? After all, many of our best authors started off as our readers, just like you. With a 50% royalty, world-class editorial services, and a name you trust, there's nothing to lose. Visit https://pragprog.com/become-an-author/ today to learn more and to get started.

We thank you for your continued support, and we hope to hear from you again soon!

The Pragmatic Bookshelf

Distributed Services with Go

This is the book for Gophers who want to learn how to build distributed systems. You know the basics of Go and are eager to put your knowledge to work. Build distributed services that are highly available, resilient, and scalable. This book is just what you need to apply Go to real-world situations. Level up your engineering skills today.

Travis Jeffery
(258 pages) ISBN: 9781680507607. $45.95
https://pragprog.com/book/tjgo

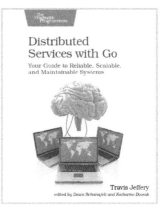

Build Websites with Hugo

Rediscover how fun web development can be with Hugo, the static site generator and web framework that lets you build content sites quickly, using the skills you already have. Design layouts with HTML and share common components across pages. Create Markdown templates that let you create new content quickly. Consume and generate JSON, enhance layouts with logic, and generate a site that works on any platform with no runtime dependencies or database. Hugo gives you everything you need to build your next content site and have fun doing it.

Brian P. Hogan
(154 pages) ISBN: 9781680507263. $26.95
https://pragprog.com/book/bhhugo

Small, Sharp Software Tools

The command-line interface is making a comeback.
That's because developers know that all the best features of your operating system are hidden behind a
user interface designed to help average people use the
computer. But you're not the average user, and the
CLI is the most efficient way to get work done fast.
Turn tedious chores into quick tasks: read and write
files, manage complex directory hierarchies, perform
network diagnostics, download files, work with APIs,
and combine individual programs to create your own
workflows. Put down that mouse, open the CLI, and
take control of your software development environment.

Brian P. Hogan
(326 pages) ISBN: 9781680502961. $38.95
https://pragprog.com/book/bhcldev

Exercises for Programmers

When you write software, you need to be at the top of
your game. Great programmers practice to keep their
skills sharp. Get sharp and stay sharp with more than
fifty practice exercises rooted in real-world scenarios.
If you're a new programmer, these challenges will help
you learn what you need to break into the field, and if
you're a seasoned pro, you can use these exercises to
learn that hot new language for your next gig.

Brian P. Hogan
(118 pages) ISBN: 9781680501223. $24
https://pragprog.com/book/bhwb

Concurrent Data Processing in Elixir

Learn different ways of writing concurrent code in Elixir and increase your application's performance, without sacrificing scalability or fault-tolerance. Most projects benefit from running background tasks and processing data concurrently, but the world of OTP and various libraries can be challenging. Which Supervisor and what strategy to use? What about GenServer? Maybe you need back-pressure, but is GenStage, Flow, or Broadway a better choice? You will learn everything you need to know to answer these questions, start building highly concurrent applications in no time, and write code that's not only fast, but also resilient to errors and easy to scale.

Svilen Gospodinov
(174 pages) ISBN: 9781680508192. $39.95
https://pragprog.com/book/sgdpelixir

Testing Elixir

Elixir offers new paradigms, and challenges you to test in unconventional ways. Start with ExUnit: almost everything you need to write tests covering all levels of detail, from unit to integration, but only if you know how to use it to the fullest—we'll show you how. Explore testing Elixir-specific challenges such as OTP-based modules, asynchronous code, Ecto-based applications, and Phoenix applications. Explore new tools like Mox for mocks and StreamData for property-based testing. Armed with this knowledge, you can create test suites that add value to your production cycle and guard you from regressions.

Andrea Leopardi and Jeffrey Matthias
(262 pages) ISBN: 9781680507829. $45.95
https://pragprog.com/book/lmelixir

Hands-on Rust

Rust is an exciting new programming language combining the power of C with memory safety, fearless concurrency, and productivity boosters—and what better way to learn than by making games. Each chapter in this book presents hands-on, practical projects ranging from "Hello, World" to building a full dungeon crawler game. With this book, you'll learn game development skills applicable to other engines, including Unity and Unreal.

Herbert Wolverson
(342 pages) ISBN: 9781680508161. $47.95
https://pragprog.com/book/hwrust

Learn to Program, Third Edition

It's easier to learn how to program a computer than it has ever been before. Now everyone can learn to write programs for themselves—no previous experience is necessary. Chris Pine takes a thorough, but lighthearted approach that teaches you the fundamentals of computer programming, with a minimum of fuss or bother. Whether you are interested in a new hobby or a new career, this book is your doorway into the world of programming.

Chris Pine
(230 pages) ISBN: 9781680508178. $45.95
https://pragprog.com/book/ltp3

Programming Kotlin

Programmers don't just use Kotlin, they love it. Even Google has adopted it as a first-class language for Android development. With Kotlin, you can intermix imperative, functional, and object-oriented styles of programming and benefit from the approach that's most suitable for the problem at hand. Learn to use the many features of this highly concise, fluent, elegant, and expressive statically typed language with easy-to-understand examples. Learn to write maintainable, high-performing JVM and Android applications, create DSLs, program asynchronously, and much more.

Venkat Subramaniam
(460 pages) ISBN: 9781680506358. $51.95
https://pragprog.com/book/vskotlin

Kotlin and Android Development featuring Jetpack

Start building native Android apps the modern way in Kotlin with Jetpack's expansive set of tools, libraries, and best practices. Learn how to create efficient, resilient views with Fragments and share data between the views with ViewModels. Use Room to persist valuable data quickly, and avoid NullPointerExceptions and Java's verbose expressions with Kotlin. You can even handle asynchronous web service calls elegantly with Kotlin coroutines. Achieve all of this and much more while building two full-featured apps, following detailed, step-by-step instructions.

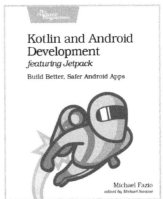

Michael Fazio
(444 pages) ISBN: 9781680508154. $49.95
https://pragprog.com/book/mfjetpack

The Pragmatic Bookshelf

The Pragmatic Bookshelf features books written by professional developers for professional developers. The titles continue the well-known Pragmatic Programmer style and continue to garner awards and rave reviews. As development gets more and more difficult, the Pragmatic Programmers will be there with more titles and products to help you stay on top of your game.

Visit Us Online

This Book's Home Page
https://pragprog.com/book/rggo
Source code from this book, errata, and other resources. Come give us feedback, too!

Keep Up to Date
https://pragprog.com
Join our announcement mailing list (low volume) or follow us on twitter @pragprog for new titles, sales, coupons, hot tips, and more.

New and Noteworthy
https://pragprog.com/news
Check out the latest pragmatic developments, new titles and other offerings.

Save on the ebook

Save on the ebook versions of this title. Owning the paper version of this book entitles you to purchase the electronic versions at a terrific discount.

PDFs are great for carrying around on your laptop—they are hyperlinked, have color, and are fully searchable. Most titles are also available for the iPhone and iPod touch, Amazon Kindle, and other popular e-book readers.

Send a copy of your receipt to support@pragprog.com and we'll provide you with a discount coupon.

Contact Us

Online Orders:	*https://pragprog.com/catalog*
Customer Service:	*support@pragprog.com*
International Rights:	*translations@pragprog.com*
Academic Use:	*academic@pragprog.com*
Write for Us:	*http://write-for-us.pragprog.com*
Or Call:	+1 800-699-7764